MW00617077

MIKE DENNY

The Shadow of a Single Man

By Delbert Reed

Above: Dr. Denny on the University of Alabama campus, circa 1940.

Cover: Dr. George H. "Mike" Denny, president of the University of Alabama, circa 1920. amd Denny Chimes, which was erected in his honor in 1929.

Copyright 2016©

ISBN 978-0-692-74012-5

Published by

300 Paul W. Bryant Drive
Tuscaloosa, AL 35487
(205) 348-4668 • bryantmuseum.com

To Peggie, who has patiently and lovingly stood with me for half a century now, and to the memory of Dr. George H. Denny, whose courage and dedication to the cause of education opened the door to a better way of life for the youth of Alabama during a difficult era.

All proceeds from the sale of this book, including author royalties, go to the Dr. George H. Denny Internship at the University of Alabama Paul W. Bryant Museum.

Foreword

Dr. Judy Bonner

Delbert Reed's arduous research and writing that spanned more than three years and culminated in *Mike Denny: The Shadow of a Single Man* confirms my belief that Dr. George Hutcheson "Mike" Denny is the most visionary leader the University of Alabama has ever had. His influence continues to be felt on our campus and in our state over a century later and this inspiring book is a fitting and long-overdue tribute to his dedicated efforts on behalf of the University and the citizens of Alabama.

During my tenure as president of the University, my refuge from the demands of a long day was to retreat to the front porch of the President's Mansion and watch the activities on the quad wind down and listen to the inspiring tolling of Denny Chimes—erected by students and alumni in 1929 in appreciation of Denny's loyalty to the University—as the day came to a close. I often thought about what the men who lived in that historic home before me would have seen from the front porch.

In January 1912, when Denny arrived in Tuscaloosa after serving for a decade as president of Washington and Lee University, his view from the Mansion would have been of the high gothic Victorian architecture of Manly Hall (1886), Clark Hall (1885) and Garland Hall (1888). Woods Hall (1868), which was used as a men's dormitory at that time, was directly behind these magnificent buildings. To the left of Manly were B. B. Comer Hall (1910), the Gorgas House (1829), Barnard Hall (1888 and now Oliver Barnard Hall) and Morgan Hall (1911). To the right of Garland were Tuomey Hall (1889) and Smith Hall (1910). There were no paved streets or sidewalks.

Denny's presidency (1912-1936) was marked by the phenomenal physical growth of the campus as we know it today. Even though his early years as president were challenged by the onslaught of World War I and later severely constrained financially by the Great Depression, President Denny somehow secured funding to construct 23 major buildings, 22 fraternity houses, 13 sorority houses and a football stadium and a bell tower that bear his name. The classical Greek revival architecture of the academic buildings that were erected during the Denny years and that now surround our picturesque quad (Doster, Reese Phifer, Graves, Carmichael, Bidgood, Little, Moore, Farrah, Nott and Lloyd as well as the Amelia Gayle Gorgas Library) make the University campus one of the most beautiful in America. Notably, nine of the buildings on our campus bear the names of long-serving deans (Doster, Bidgood, Moore, Farrah,

Gallalee, Lloyd, Barnwell, McLure and Harris) who stood alongside Denny during his twenty-five tenure at the University. Foster Auditorium and Carmichael Hall are named for former University presidents who were students at the University during Denny's early years on campus. Coleman Coliseum and Gordon D. Palmer Hall also bear the names of former Denny students who played significant roles in the development of the University.

This interesting, informative and inspiring book helps us understand the many obstacles that President Denny overcame without the benefit of the diverse pool of talented administrators and staff that are available to presidents today. Consequently, much of the operation of the University outside of teaching fell squarely on President Denny's shoulders. His wise financial management, his effective appeals for contributions from loyal alumni and the people of this great state, his ability to successfully lobby the legislature, the governor of the state of Alabama and the president of the United States enabled President Denny to be a transformational president despite the severe financial challenges facing our state and nation.

President Denny was personally in charge of student recruitment and University enrollment grew from 400 students in 1912 to almost 5,000 students in 1936 through his innovative efforts. He personally wrote every student graduating from high school in the state of Alabama, inviting them to attend the Capstone. When my brother and I went through our grandparents' home in the late 1990's after their remaining son passed away, we found the letter that President Denny had handwritten to our grandmother about her sons (our father and his twin brother) attending the University.

It was especially important to President Denny to insure that the power of an education was available to all young people. To facilitate attracting more young women to the Capstone, he established the women's campus that included the first dormitory for women. Named for Julia Tutwiler, who prevailed upon the board of trustees to admit women two decades earlier, Tutwiler Hall was built in 1914 next to the President's Mansion on the site that Rose Administration now occupies. Because of his hard work and dedication, the enrollment of young women increased substantially. A century after President Denny took specific actions to improve the campus academic environment and increase educational opportunities for women, I had the privilege of serving as the first woman president of the University as well as the first woman president of any university in the Southeastern Conference.

The greatest reward for working at a university is the opportunity to positively impact the lives of students. Unfortunately, most faculty and administrators never have the opportunity to see all that the students whose lives they touch accomplish during their lifetime. Delbert skillfully captures the legacy of President Denny by identifying a few of the students who could not have attended the University of Alabama without President Denny's personal interest and assistance and helps us realize some of what these students accomplished to improve the human condition for our state and for our nation. These chapters will make all who truly love the Capstone and the state of Alabama enormously proud.

It is important to remember and learn from the dedicated men and women who have come before us and left a lasting legacy at the institution we love. Just as clearly as the stately oak trees planted along University Boulevard during his presidency, Dr.

Denny's many contributions continue to cast a still-lengthening shadow over the place he fittingly called the Capstone.

Delbert has once again answered his alma mater's call with this important contribution to the history of one of the earliest public universities in America. With a B. S. in 1964 and an M. A. in 1988 from the University, Delbert's writing career spans more than a half a century. In addition to his work as an award-winning journalist, he is the author of four books (*Paul 'Bear' Bryant: What Made Him a Winner; When Winning Was Everything: Alabama Football Players in World War II; All of Us Fought the War: The University of Alabama and Its Men and Women in World War II,* and *Delbert Reed and Friends,* a collection of more than 150 of his best newspaper columns 1963-2002).

—Dr. Judy Bonner, 28th President
The University of Alabama

Dr. George H. "Mike" Denny was widely acclaimed as an educator.

Preface

The life of Dr. George Hutcheson Denny was one of unprecedented educational accomplishment; devout dedication to the uplifting of mankind; a sincere, inspirational kinship with the students entrusted to his care, and decades of courageous personal sacrifice in the exercise of his duty-bound mission.

Denny devoted his life to education—first to his own until age twenty-five then to others for the next half century, including more than thirty-five years as a college president. Forged in the mold of the men he most admired—Thomas Jefferson, General Robert E. Lee and his Presbyterian minister father, Denny learned their lessons, adopted their finest traits and emulated their devotion to God, country, truth and duty throughout his life.

Gifted with intelligence, imbued with a rural work ethic and inspired by poets and heroes to a high purpose, Denny eagerly grasped his opportunities in life. He stood first in his class at Hampden-Sydney College in 1892 and earned a doctorate at the University of Virginia in 1896 while serving as assistant headmaster at nearby Pantops Academy. He taught Latin and German at Hampden-Sydney 1896-1899 and Latin at Washington and Lee University 1899-1901 before his surprise election as president of the latter school in 1901 at only thirty-one years of age. Within ten years, Denny managed to triple student enrollment, add new buildings and improve older ones and place Washington and Lee's once-struggling finances on a sound footing. His work was widely acclaimed as Washington and Lee became one of the South's largest and most prestigious universities.

In answer to what he saw as a "call of duty," Denny accepted the presidency of the University of Alabama on January 1, 1912, with the missionary-like goal of bringing social, cultural and economic change to the poor, rural state he had toured in 1910 through education of the masses rather than only the privileged few. The University of Alabama had an enrollment of approximately 400 students, with only nine classroom and dormitory buildings and no sidewalks, curbs or paved streets, when Denny arrived on campus. He spent the next twenty-five years building a modern university to stand as "the capstone of public education in Alabama" before health issues forced him to retire on January 1, 1937. By then, there were almost 5,000 students on campus plus 6,490 more enrolled in extension courses. A total of 30,000 students passed through the University and sixteen new classroom and dormitory buildings, a football stadium, Denny Chimes, twenty-two fraternity houses and twelve sorority houses were added to the campus during Denny's tenure.

Denny was a master of both oral and written communication. Utilizing an innovative direct-mail campaign to reach rural youth isolated by distance as well social and economic barriers, Denny invited every high school graduate in Alabama and beyond to attend the University of Alabama, offering the opportunity of a college education and even arranging jobs for them if they needed financial aid. His letters reached into the red hills and backwoods of Alabama, calling young men and women from weathered tenant houses along rutted gravel roads to the University of Alabama, where he promised them a college education and a better way of life. Believing him, the students came, first by the score, soon by the hundreds and later by the thousands, and Denny knew each one by name.

Denny, who mysteriously acquired the nickname of "Mike" while president of Washington and Lee, challenged his students to seek and follow the truth and to serve beyond their chosen professions as leaders in civic, religious and governmental affairs. In the end, as he had promised, their lives were changed, and they in turn changed the lives of others, helping cast what became a long and ever-lengthening shadow of a single, idealistic man. Through thousands of men and women shaped by his inspiring words, works and life-long example of dedication to a demanding call of duty and service to others, Denny accomplished his mission of helping raise living standards for each generation to come not only in Alabama, but in the nation. And through those taught by those he taught, his work continues to reap rewards even today.

He united University of Alabama alumni through personal speaking appearances and the creation of an alumni newsletter. He used what he called "wise, tactful, aggressive agitation" to help win public support for tax-supported public schools. He personally hired football coaches who produced a combined record of 222-53-14, including five national championships, seven conference titles and six Rose Bowl appearances, as he directed the building of the Crimson Tide's winning gridiron tradition.

Following his retirement as president on January 1, 1937, Denny served as University chancellor until being recalled as president for almost a year again in November 1941 when his successor, Dr. Richard C. Foster, died from a sudden, rare illness. He stepped down again as he neared age seventy-two, but continued to serve as chancellor and close advisor to the board of trustees and future presidents and remained an alumni favorite until his death in April 1955 at age eighty-four.

Denny Chimes, the iconic bell tower built in 1929 as a tribute to his vision for and devotion to the University of Alabama, fittingly stands in his honor and in his spiritual image, a beacon lighting the way to enlightenment for those seeking the lessons of truth, duty and service he taught. With each tolling, the chimes still echo the living, lasting heartbeat he gave to the Capstone.

— **Delbert Reed**

Acknowledgements

Dr. Judy Bonner, President, University of Alabama, Tuscaloosa, Alabama, 2012-2015.

Dr. Lynda Gilbert, Vice President for Financial Affairs, University of Alabama, Tuscaloosa, Alabama

Ken Gaddy, Director, Paul W. Bryant Museum, University of Alabama, Tuscaloosa, Alabama.

Brad Green, Curator, Paul W. Bryant Museum, University of Alabama, Tuscaloosa, Alabama.

Associate Dean Mary Bess Paluzzi and staff members Tom Land, Kevin Ray, Marina Klaric, Gates Winters, Allyson Holliday and Lori Hill, Hoole Collections, University of Alabama Libraries, Tuscaloosa, Alabama.

Director Tom Camden and staff members Seth McCormick-Goodhart and Lisa McCown, Special Collections, James Graham Leyburn Library, Washington and Lee University, Lexington, Virginia.

William G. Bean Jr., Lexington, Virginia.

Dr. James F. Doster, Tuscaloosa, Alabama.

Camille Elebash, Tuscaloosa, Alabama.

George F. Hamner Sr., Tuscaloosa, Alabama.

Mrs. Troy Crawford, Mobile, Alabama.

Mary Pickens Skinner, Mobile, Alabama.

Photos courtesy of Hoole Special Collections and the University of Alabama yearbook *Corolla*.

Dr. Bonner photo courtesy of UA Strategic Communications.

Cover photo of Denny Chimes by Jeff Hanson.

Cover design by Laura Lineberry and Delbert Reed

Contents

Denny earned his doctoral degree from the University of Virginia in 1896.

Inspired by Poets and Patriots

"To seek the truth; to find the truth; to know the truth; to guard the truth; to desire the truth; to proclaim the truth—this is the prime condition of intellectual life and progress."

—Dr. George H. Denny

Dr. George Hutcheson Denny, acknowledged as one of the South's most progressive educators for more than half a century during his lifetime and for generations afterward, is a classic example of a man who became the product of his time and place in history. He was born in 1870 near Richmond, Virginia, where the scars of the Civil War were still visible but where the words and deeds of such Virginia heroes as George Washington, Thomas Jefferson, Patrick Henry, Robert E. Lee and Thomas J. "Stonewall" Jackson still inspired pride in heritage, selfless service to mankind and hope in the future of a young, fragmented and undeveloped nation.

Like the men he emulated throughout his life, Denny seems to have been destined to lead. As a youth, he was a gifted and eager student who learned his lessons well and answered the call to a life of purpose and service just as those he most admired had. He studied the words and works of Jefferson and Benjamin Franklin; the lifetime of devotion to duty and leadership of Lee; Jackson's religious faith, discipline and dedication to teaching; the devout life of toil, service and sacrifice of his father, and the inspiring words of ancient Greek poets and philosophers. He devoted his life as an educator to translating their words and ideals into action while advancing the cause for a better educated and a more civilized and democratic society.

Denny was born at Hanover Courthouse, a small, rural hamlet best known as the home of Patrick Henry, who gave voice to the American Revolution with his proclamation, "Give me liberty or give me death." Denny was the third of seven children of the Reverend George H. Denny, a Presbyterian minister and Confederate veteran of the Civil War. His mother was Charlotte Moore Denny, the first of his father's two wives.

"Mr. Denny grew up in the country amid the refining influences of a quiet Christian home. His father was a minister and his mother was a noble Christian woman of intellectual tastes who influenced her son greatly on his intellectual and moral side," an article in "Men of Mark in Virginia," a 1906 collection of biographies of the leading men of the state edited by Lyon G. Tyler, said of Denny, who was at the time president of Washington and Lee University. "From such a home, he entered a good Virginia college, where the old ideals of integrity and purity are still maintained by the faculty and the community. The efforts that had to be put forth by a country preacher in the South to send a boy to college may well be imagined, and young Mr. Denny rose to the situation and took advantage of the opportunities offered by his self-denying parents. Bravely, persistently, he met the difficulties of the struggle. Faithful attention to duty became his motto, and onward and upward he climbed until he secured an honored place among the teachers and professors of his state. In the making of President Denny's success, here are several potent factors: First, the home influence; second, contact with men in active life; third, early companionship; fourth, study at school and in private. He has let no grass grow under his feet. From his very boyhood he has led a life strenuous enough to please Mr. Roosevelt (President Theodore) himself. Patient industry, high ideals, unselfish service, plain living—these are the principal methods and habits which this very successful Virginian recommends to young men just starting out on the journey of life. Virginia needs men with these principles. Though the whole world elsewhere runs after gold, let the choisest manhood of Virginia take the motto "Plain Living and High Thinking" and the old state will ere long resume her place as 'mother of statesmen,'" the article added.

Denny received his early education in the public schools of Amelia County, Virginia, where his father served as minister of a church, and at age 17 entered Hampden-Sydney College, where he earned his bachelor's degree and stood first in his class in 1891 before earning a master's degree in 1892. Hampden-Sydney, a private, all-male liberal arts school, was founded in 1775 with Patrick Henry and James Madison among its first trustees. Denny secured work as a teacher and assistant master at Pantops Academy in Charlottesville in 1892 and began studies for his doctoral degree at the University of Virginia. Significantly, Denny also began a life-long love for the game of football while at Pantops, where he played guard on the school's team as he taught there for four years. After earning a doctor of philosophy degree at Virginia, Denny returned to Hampden-Sydney in 1896 as professor of Latin and German. He also coached the Hampden-Sydney football team in 1896, posting a 2-1 record with wins over Randolph-Macon and Roanoke and a loss to Virginia Tech.

Denny taught three years at Hampden-Sydney before being called to Washington and Lee University as professor of Latin in 1899. Two years later, at only thirty-one years of age and still hardly known in the educational field outside his small circle of faculty associates at Hampden-Sydney and Washington and Lee, Denny was elected president of the historic school endowed by Washington and once led by Lee. Denny studiously and tirelessly devoted himself to his new position, closely following the policies established by Lee during his tenure as president of the school, and achieved unprecedented success in leading the private, all-male school to national prominence over the next decade before resigning in December 1911 to become president of the University of Alabama. During his twelve-year tenure at Washington and Lee, Denny not only walked the same paths that Lee had walked, but he made a thorough study of Lee as a college president and adopted many of Lee's personal traits as a leader as well as his innovative ideas as a college administrator.

Lee, the son of Revolutionary War hero Henry "Light Horse Harry" Lee III, achieved national prominence during a thirty-two-year career in the U. S. Army and four years as one of the leading Confederate generals during the Civil War before serving as president of what was then Washington College from October 2, 1865, until his death on October 12, 1870. Lee said he accepted the presidency of Washington College because it provided him the opportunity "to train young men to do their duty in life" and to "accomplish something for the benefit of mankind and for the honor of God." Lee had previously served as superintendent of the U. S. Military Academy at West Point 1852-1855, an assignment which provided him with valuable previous experience as a college administrator. Denny's careful review of Lee's tenure at Washington and Lee provided him with a guideline for his own presidency and he wrote a seventeen-page speech on "General Lee as a College President" which he delivered first as president of Washington and Lee and on numerous other occasions throughout his life as he continued to honor his ideal of manhood.

"We hear much concerning the educational philosophy of Thomas Jefferson, though he was never directly in charge of academic work," Denny wrote in his speech. "We hear comparatively little of the educational policy and influence of Robert Edward Lee, though he was for five years the great head of an important institution of learning. There are two reasons to explain these facts. In the first place, Mr. Jefferson put into writing the views he entertained and the policies he advocated while General Lee did not except when occasion demanded. In the second place, the great military record of General Lee has so eclipsed every other phase of his career that few men, not even his own biographers, have undertaken to consider fully his masterful genius as a college president. I desire to emphasize the fact that General Lee was a man of wonderful executive ability. I do not offer in support of this statement his great record in planning and executing military campaigns nor do I purpose to discuss his notable service as head of the United States Military Academy at West Point. I maintain that as president of Washington College he exhibited executive ability and skill of the highest order.

"He came to Lexington as the executive head of this institution at a time when it had been literally blasted by the thunderbolts and charred by the fires of war. The college had reached the lowest point of depression it had ever known. It lay prostrate and bleeding. There were many an eye to pity, but as yet there had appeared no arm to save. The faculty numbered but four. The student body numbered not more than fifty and these were drawn from the region immediately contiguous to the college. The endowment was small even for those days and what remained was unproductive. There was left only grim courage and great-hearted hope. The institution was not only confronted with an empty treasury but in a time of financial distress, social disorder and political turbulence. But now a master pilot was at the helm. The college which General Lee had found practically bankrupt, disorganized and deserted, after less than five years sprang as if by touch of magic into national favor and recognition. It was the great executive who gave it organization, unity and a new career.

"…No college executive has ever given himself more completely or more methodically to his work. His clear, penetrating foresight made him aware of the magnitude of his undertaking, but his courage never failed him. General Lee was in constant and vital touch with everybody, no matter how humble, and with everything, no matter how minute. Nothing ever seemed to escape his notice. He had the genius of attending to details. He had the infinite capacity of taking pains.... Today he was visiting the lectures and recitations; tomorrow he was supervising the construction of buildings or planning improvements to the college campus. He was interested in the literary societies and in his time those organizations enjoyed a renaissance. He was a trusted friend of the Young Men's Christian Association (YMCA) and sought its purity and peace. But he was also busy shaping the larger academic policies of the college. He was constantly pleading and laboring for the restoration of the buildings and the library. He vigorously maintained that the college library ought to be the chief college laboratory, and true to his creed, he secured for it large gifts of books from every section.... He revised the scheme of instruction and established once and for all the high and exacting standards of work that have brought just renown to this school." Denny added that Lee, recognizing the practical needs of the post-war South and the nation, established at Washington College in quick succession the schools of law, engineering, commerce and journalism and added to the traditional studies of Latin, Greek, mathematics and philosophy the departments of English, modern languages, chemistry and natural philosophy. The schools of commerce and journalism were the first of their type at any college in America or the world, according to Washington and Lee University publications.

"...General Lee was the master spirit, the constructive workman, the executive genius of the institution over which he presided," Denny added. "It was he who sketched the comprehensive plan and wrought out its details. It was he who blazed the path for those who have followed and it was this work that in chaste and simple beauty will rest like a capital upon the solid, splendid shaft of his civic and international renown.... But General Lee was great as a college president not only on account of his executive genius, his influence and power over men and his consecration of purpose. He was a great college president chiefly on account of his fully orbed personal character and the unparalleled example he set for the guidance of young men.... He set before young men the example of simple habits, simple manners, simple needs, simple words, simple faith and simple duties. The discipline of responsibility and of service made him wondrously simple, and from him young men could imbibe a restful contempt for the non-essentials of life...."

In an effort to reconcile differences between the North and South, Lee also welcomed students from Union states to Washington College and encouraged a friendly campus atmosphere by asking all students to greet each other in every passing, a proud tradition that still exists today. A *Wikipedia* report also said that Lee "generally supported civil rights for all, as well as a system of free public schools for blacks," following the Civil War and was "a leader in the successful 1869-70 efforts to establish state-funded schools for blacks." Taking heed of Lee's actions, Denny included the need for educating the Southern Negro race in a speech entitled "Education in the South: Its Difficulties and its Needs," saying "No race can rise indefinitely above a lower race living on the same soil. The higher will inevitably be dragged down by ignorance, idleness and vice on the part of the lower. For this reason, if for no other, it is our duty to help the Negro.... It is surely better for the whites to have among them ten million thrifty, enlightened, law-abiding Negroes than ten million of the shiftless, ignorant, lawless kind.... Happily the day has come when this great problem is receiving a calmer and more faithful consideration. The minds of men are being swept clean of passion and resentment and the great heart of the people is anxiously waiting to welcome the day when every child of the nation, high or low, bond or free, shall be ushered out of the dark and forbidding valleys of ignorance into the threshold of humanity and light." As Lee had done at Washington College, Denny also welcomed students from northern states to the University of Alabama, although he once faced criticism when some thought he was using Alabama tax dollars to educate "foreigners" and "Yankees" sixty-five years after the end of the Civil War. A study revealed the opposite, however, as additional fees paid by out-of-state students actually helped educate students from Alabama during the Great Depression.

In answering a "higher calling" to the presidency of the University of Alabama, Denny saw the opportunity to combine Jefferson's theory of public education, Lee's insightful leadership as a university president and the example of dedicated, sacrificial service set by his minister father in leading the effort to build a statewide, tax-supported public educational system for all the children in the state of Alabama. Denny had studied Jefferson's 1785 proposal for a public educational system for Virginia as a doctoral student at the University of Virginia, where he formed many of his own ideas on public education based on his own life and time. Although Jefferson offered his plan from the perspective of an aristocrat, he recognized the value of basic education for masses. Denny, more than a century removed from Jefferson and not from an aristocratic family, had an even greater appreciation for the value and opportunity of education for all citizens. Jefferson proposed three years of primary education for all free males and the opportunity of education for only a select few beyond that. Denny's ideal system, presented soon after his arrival in Alabama in 1912, went much farther and included a statewide system of tax-supported schools from primary grades through college with the University of Alabama at its head, and he spent the next quarter century helping to develop that system.

Denny, considering his closeness in time and proximity to many of those who helped shape early American history, was obviously influenced by the educational theories and ideas expressed by those men. He was also influenced by the American Enlightenment movement and the American Philosophical Society. The American Enlightenment movement, which included such progressive thinkers as Madison, Franklin, John Adams, Jefferson and Alexander Hamilton, promoted such ideas as deism, liberalism, republicanism, conservatism, toleration and scientific progress and emphasized independence, free thinking and self-government. Many of the ideas of the American Enlightenment helped lead to the American Revolution and were later expressed in the Bill of Rights (first ten amendments to the U. S. Constitution). Those ideas include freedom of speech, freedom of religion, freedom of the press, the right to free assembly and the right to bear arms. The American Philosophical Society was founded by Franklin in 1743 to promote the exchange and advancement of knowledge through scholarly research, professional meetings, publications, libraries and community outreach. The society, which still exists today, also encourages the virtues of thrift, industry, humility, temperance, order, justice, moderation, volunteerism and philanthropy. Jefferson was elected to membership in the society in 1780 and served as president for 18 years starting in 1797. Other early members included Washington, Madison, Thomas Paine, the

Marquis de Lafayette, John Adams, Hamilton, John Marshall and Benjamin Rush.

Denny cited several members of the American Philosophical Society as he outlined the obligations of higher education in his inaugural address as president of Washington and Lee University on June 17, 1902. "These institutions are not merely laboratories for the investigation of chemical or physical properties. They have a higher mission and are expected to perform a more important function than that," Denny said. "They are training schools not merely for the making of scholars whose supreme thought is of a mathematical formula or a rule of syntax but also for the development of patriotic men who will lend a helping hand at this stirring period in the history of our country in the solution of the great problems of city, state and nation. These institutions must, therefore, teach the interdependence of learning and of life.... They must emphasize the fact that an intelligent citizen ought to be a great public blessing and that every man owes a duty to his neighbor, to the community in which he lives and to the commonwealth of which he is a member. They must recognize the fact that a democratic government founded upon an electorate without intelligence is as a house whose foundation is sand; that democracy is still on trial and has yet to establish its right to exist as the ultimate form of government; that education alone is able to save the masses from becoming the dupes of designing men and to give them the means of detecting a wrong and applying a remedy.

"Education, therefore, in a democracy where the people are sovereign, is not merely a question of philanthropy and expediency; it is also a question of life and death. The sovereign people must be educated or we must live under an ignorant sovereign. In our own country, for instance, great and fundamental questions concerning finances and trade, questions involving political expediency and moral right, are decided by the people as the court of final appeal. These questions are daily becoming more complicated and serious.... To whom has the nation a right to look for help and leadership in these matters? To whom has the nation always looked? Is it not true that the founders of states have likewise been the founders of colleges? Have we not ample testimony to support the view expressed by John Adams to the effect that 'our republic is indebted to her seminaries of learning for her liberty, independence, glory and prosperity?' Did not Washington, Jefferson and Franklin recognize this when they founded institutions to train young men for citizenship and public service? …We need not expect that the national life of the country will be stronger or nobler than its institutions of learning. It is evident, therefore, that these institutions are under obligation to exercise a proper influence upon the life of the state," Denny said.

"Washington's idea that a university is a place which should train not only the intellect, but the character, is the correct one," Denny added. "He recognized the fatal consequences of turning out upon the world the great host of college-trained men to constitute 'an aristocracy of knaves.' He recognized the fact that the 'dagger is not less a dagger because of its polished blade and its jeweled hilt;' that education without character is abnormal and abortive and could only be a curse to the public.... Who can doubt that Washington in endowing Liberty Hall Academy (which then became Washington College) was largely moved to that selection not merely from the conviction that national enlightenment and national morality are essential to the stability of a republic but also in large measure from his expressed belief that 'a sincere and fervent religious faith is the basis of moral conviction?' His was the belief that no one can so much as touch 'the hem of the garment that duty wears' without this foundation. 'Let us with caution,' said he, 'indulge the supposition that morality can be maintained without religion.' Such also was the view of the most illustrious executive (Lee) in the history of this university."

Jefferson's suggestions for a statewide, tax-supported educational system, first expressed in his "Notes on the State of Virginia" in 1785 and revised in 1817, clearly inspired Denny's interest in education as the means to a greater democratic, civilized society. Jefferson's earliest proposal suggested a system of public education "to diffuse knowledge more generally through the mass of the people," starting with three years of primary school and continuing, on a selective basis, through college. He proposed a statewide system of district primary schools in which all free males would be taught reading, writing and common arithmetic, to be supported by a tax on the people of the districts and that any schooling beyond that level be paid for by parents. "These (primary) schools to be under a visitor, who is annually to choose the boy of best genius in the school of those whose parents are too poor to give them further education and to send him forward to one of the grammar schools, of which twenty are proposed to be erected in different parts of the country, for teaching Greek, Latin, geography and the higher branches of numerical arithmetic. Of the boys thus sent in any one year, trial is to be made at the grammar schools every one or two years and the best genius of the whole selected and continued six years and the residue dismissed. By this means twenty of the best geniuses will be raked from the rubbish annually and be instructed at the public expense, so far as the grammar schools go. At the end of six years instruction, one half are to be discontinued (from among whom the grammar schools will probably be supplied with future masters), and the other half, who are to be chosen for the superiority of their parts and disposition, are to be sent and continued three years in the study of such sciences as they shall choose at William and Mary College.... The general objects of this law are to provide an education adapted to the years, to the capacity and to the condition of everyone and directed to their freedom and happiness.... By that part of our plan which prescribes the selection of the youths of genius from among the classes of the poor, we hope to avail the state of those talents which nature has sown as liberally among the poor as the rich, but which perish without use if not sought for and cultivated.

"But of all the views of this law, none is more important, none more legitimate, than that of rendering the people safe, as they are the ultimate guardians of their own liberty," Jefferson wrote. "For this purpose the reading in the first state, where they will receive their whole education, is proposed to be chiefly historical. History, by apprising them of the past, will enable them to judge the future; it will avail them of the experience of other times and other nations; it will qualify them as judges of the actions and designs of men; it will enable them to know ambition under every disguise it may assume; and knowing it, to defeat its views.... Every government degenerates when trusted to the rulers of the people alone. The people themselves therefore are its only safe depositories, and to render them safe their minds must be improved to a certain degree.... The influence over government must be shared among all the people. If every individual which composes their mass participates of the ultimate authority, the government will be safe; because the corrupting of the whole mass will exceed any private resources of wealth; and public ones cannot be provided but by levies on the people," Jefferson wrote.

Jefferson's 1817 revised system proposed three years of primary school (ages 6-8) education for all free males, intermediate schools (ages 9-16) for selected students who excelled in primary school and other students whose parents were able and willing to pay for it and a university for students (ages 17-19) who could afford it. He called for dividing Virginia into wards, or districts, with a primary school and tutor in each district supported by a tax on the people of the district. "The ultimate result of the whole scheme of education would be the teaching of all children of the state reading, writing and common arithmetic," Jefferson said. He added that the system would turn out each year some "students of superior genius, well taught in Greek, Latin, geography and European and American history and the higher branches of arithmetic." Jefferson designed and founded the University of Virginia in 1820, visualizing it as the head of Virginia's educational system, open to "any young, white male citizen of the commonwealth with the required ability and achievement as an earlier student." Jefferson wrote that the University of Virginia was to be founded "on the illimitable freedom of the human mind. For here we are not afraid to follow truth wherever it may lead or to tolerate any error so long as reason is left free to combat it." The University of Virginia opened in 1825, but the state of Virginia did not provide tax-supported public education for the masses until after the Civil War.

In an example of his personal devotion to education and truth, Jefferson once wrote, "I was bold in the pursuit of knowledge, never fearing to follow truth and reason to whatever results they led." Apparently inspired by Jefferson's words, Denny wrote an eleven-page speech entitled "Devotion to Truth" which he delivered to student assemblies at both Washington and Lee and the University of Alabama as he outlined the goals of higher education. "It will be our endeavor not to drive you in any direction, but merely to lead you in the ways of the truth with the simple faith that it will make you free," Denny told various classes during his career. "…The most cherished word in the vocabulary of education is truth," Denny said. "Our institutions of higher learning rightly pronounce this to be the very goal of their aspirations.... To seek the truth; to find the truth; to know the truth; to guard the truth; to desire the truth; to proclaim the truth—this is the prime condition of intellectual life and progress. To seek the truth for truth's own sake; to make this search for truth a vital principle; to allow it to animate and govern the operations of the mind and heart; and to remember that he who intentionally cheats himself will not scruple to mislead another—this should constitute the foundation principle of scholastic endeavor. Education will have missed the mark and we shall have fed only on its husks if it fails to affect the philosophy of our life and aspiration; if it fails to strengthen the moral purpose which sways our destiny or to lead us to a clearer conception of truth and duty," he said.

"No people can be both ignorant and free," Jefferson once said. Denny expanded that thought also, saying, "The untrained mind needs to be taught by the trained mind that individuality of thought and action is alone able to guarantee freedom; that a man can never be free until he thinks for himself, acts for himself and learns to make answer to his own conscience for his conduct; that such independence and individuality of character alone fit a man for the duties of life and their proper performance." In founding the University of Virginia, Jefferson took pains to separate it from any religious doctrine and symbolically placed the school's library at the center of the campus. Denny followed Jefferson's doctrine in this regard also. He rejected a bid for religious affiliation for Washington and Lee University while president there and planned the location of the University of Alabama's main library for the center of the campus while president there.

Denny's study of history provided him with examples of great orators whom he also emulated in scores of documented speeches from 1902 to 1946. In a speech praising the art of public speaking, Denny cited several influential men of history in describing "the moving power of the spoken word." "…Martin Luther used it when he desired to sway the opinions and actions of men. He did not undertake to stop when he had nailed his theses to the cathedral door, but thundered them from his pulpit. Such an influence Peter the Hermit found it to exert when he entered upon his immortal work. He did not undertake to merely issue a circular summoning men to join his crusade, but moved among them and through the power of speech set their hearts afire. Such an influence Patrick Henry found it to exert when he made his inspired utterance. He did not undertake to send out a printed program, but met the men of Virginia face to face and urged them to do their duty," Denny said in urging students to master the art of public speaking.

Denny read the works of the great poets and philosophers and was inspired and influenced by their words. He learned that education was the essential ingredient in a democratic society and to the social and cultural advancement of mankind. He heard the call of his father to a simple, frugal, disciplined life of service founded on a devout religious faith. He walked in the very footsteps of Henry as a boy at Hanover Courthouse, Jefferson as a student in Charlottesville and Lee and Jackson as a college president in Lexington. His father fought in Lee's Confederate Army of Virginia and his father-in-law with Jackson's "Stonewall Brigade" during the Civil War. Jackson had lived in Lexington and taught at Virginia Military Institute—whose campus adjoins that of Washington and Lee—prior to the Civil War, and Denny walked in his footsteps, too. Lee, his father and several other members of his family are buried beneath Lee Chapel on the Washington and Lee campus and Lee's gallant war horse Traveller is buried nearby. Jackson is buried in Stonewall Jackson Cemetery in the heart of Lexington and Denny rests nearby. The names of Lee, Washington and Jackson mark streets, buildings, chapels and monuments throughout Lexington, where their memory remains as much alive as the giant maples that shade the college campuses and decorate the quaint, historic town with a blaze of color in autumn.

Given his time and place in history, Denny had little choice but to live in the image of those in whose footsteps he walked. He studied, adopted, expanded, revised, refined, adapted and advanced the causes of the great men he emulated and eventually stepped from their giant shadows to cast his own. He was recognized and honored as a leader of men and a man of genius in his own right during a half century of service as an educator and friend to students, and his work on their behalf is remembered still. Fittingly, his name marks two streets near Washington and Lee University and Denny Chimes stands on the University of Alabama campus as a towering, beating-heart monument to his decades of leadership and service to the Capstone and to the entire state of Alabama.

Denny was elected president of Washington and Lee University at age 31.

2

Walking a Hallowed Path

"Show me the man you honor; I know by that symptom better than by any other what sort of man you yourself are. For you show me then what your ideal of manhood is, what manner of man you long to be and would thank the gods with your whole soul for being if you could."

—Dr. George H. Denny

There was widespread surprise when Dr. George H. Denny, a young, relatively unknown professor of Latin, was elected acting president of prestigious Washington and Lee University in June 1901, and no one was more surprised with the selection than Denny himself.

Recalling the occasion a quarter of a century later, Denny said he learned of his selection on returning to the campus from an annual boat race held in conjunction with commencement exercises. "The secretary of the board of trustees informed me that I had been elected acting president," Denny said. "Nothing could have been more unexpected. It surely had never occurred to me that such a thing was possible. I had no alternative other than to accept since the board had already adjourned. I was then thirty years old. Some months later this temporary action was made permanent." Denny served as president of the Lexington, Virginia, college through December 1911, when he resigned to become president of the University of Alabama. He recalled his decade as Washington and Lee president in a brief essay published in the school's 1926 *Alumni Directory and Service Record*, cautioning readers that the account was dictated from memory and "not designed to be historically waterproof."

"I do not claim for myself the achievements of my time. Many shared with me the burden and the heat of the day. They have my everlasting gratitude," Denny said in beginning his recollection of his acclaimed tenure as president of the historic school. "For more than a decade I devoted my best efforts in the up-building of an institution in whose origin, traditions and standards I profoundly believe. These years were in some respects difficult years; they were in all respects happy and fruitful years. The endowment of the university had been impaired; there was a floating debt; the material property required rehabilitation, and the student body needed to be enlarged. The period was, in reality, a critical period. It was infinitely more difficult to do any one of the things that had to be done in 1901 than it would be today. That was an era before 'drives' had gained popularity or high schools had sprung up everywhere or prosperity had inspired the giving habit and made it possible for the average man to go to college. Yet the thing was done. An accurate appraisal of comparative material assets will reveal the heartening progress made. And this progress was actual. No part of it consisted in merely placing an artificially higher valuation on existing property, as has been so frequently done in many institutions in recent years since real estate has practically doubled in money value.

"In 1901, there was not a square yard of concrete on campus. We waded through mud," Denny continued. "The entire system of walkways was built in the first decade of the twentieth century. The old college buildings had hitherto been heated by stoves. They were in poor physical condition and uncomfortable beyond words. They were renovated from top to bottom, on the inside and on the outside, in 1907. The library building—a gift from Andrew Carnegie—was erected. Engineering Hall was added through the generosity of William H. Reid, a man of rare personality from Chicago. A dormitory and dining hall were built. Newcomb Hall was modernized. The professors' houses were made comfortable; the power plant rebuilt; the athletic field enlarged and a grandstand provided. In 1901, professors' salaries were in a measure dependent upon student fees. They were at that time not only raised but put on a more definite basis. The School of Commerce was organized and an endowment of $100,000 raised to maintain it. This endowment is a memorial to William L. Wilson, who was my honored predecessor and a great man. The floating debt of the university was liquidated and the actual income-producing endowment increased by $250,000 over and above the large material assets that had been added...."

Denny added that when he became president of Washington and Lee a student could be admitted to the school "if he presented no more than three units in English, two in mathematics and one in history. There were approximately 200 students in the university. It seemed difficult to get them.... Scholarships had been offered for the asking. In 1911, twelve units were required, with fourteen as the standard for unconditional admission.... The growth of the student body to 630 represented for that time substantial progress. The quality of the student body was greatly improved. Phi Beta Kappa was organized during this period. For the first time, athletics were put on an efficient basis and the first triumph over Virginia in football was duly celebrated. The faculty of the institution was maintained on the high level of preceding years.... Finally, let me add that I cherish the friendships and associations of the years I spent in Lexington. I am loyal to these friendships. I value these associations. There is no finer civilization than the civilization of the valley of Virginia. I love every inch of that soil. The passing days serve merely to strengthen sacred loyalties. It is my good fortune to meet from time to time many of the boys of my period. Periodically I receive letters from them, particularly when good or ill fortune overtakes them. And here let me say to these boys again, as I have so frequently said to them before, that I am with them to the end, in the shadows as well as in the sunshine," he said.

Dr. John H. Latane, a former history professor at Washington and Lee (1902-1913) and Johns Hopkins University (1913-1932), offered a similar assessment of Denny's selection in recounting Denny's tenure at Washington and Lee after Denny left to become president of the University of Alabama. "When in the fall of 1901 the board of trustees of Washington and Lee University chose as president a young man barely turned thirty, of limited experience and completely unknown, many friends of the university had serious misgivings as to the wisdom of the election, and no one had the prophetic gift to foresee that the event marked the beginning of the most successful decade in the history of the college," Latane wrote. "This was not the type of man the public was expecting to see appointed. It was a radical departure from the precedent to place in the chair successively occupied by General Robert E. Lee, General G. W. Custis Lee and William Lyne Wilson a man of merely academic attainments and of whose existence the general public was hardly aware."

And Denny was in fact a complete unknown in comparison to his immediate predecessors. Robert E. Lee, who served as president from the time the school reopened in the fall of 1865 following the Civil War until his death in 1870, was one of the nation's best-known military leaders. Lee served thirty-two years in the United States Army after graduating second in the class of 1829 at the U. S. Military Academy, gaining national recognition for his service in the Mexican-American War and for his capture of abolitionist John Brown. He also served as superintendent of the U. S. Military Academy 1852-55, where he gained valuable administrative experience as a college president. Lee resigned from the U. S. Army in 1861 to lead the Army of Northern Virginia and eventually command the entire Confederate Army during the final months of the Civil War. His surrender to Union general U. S. Grant at Appomattox Courthouse, Virginia, on April 9, 1865, brought an end to the war. Lee rejected several lucrative business offers after the war to accept the presidency of what was then Washington College at a salary of only $1,500 per year. He reopened the school, which had been closed during the war, and slowly rebuilt it by welcoming students from all sections, including those from the northern states. He added courses in English, chemistry, engineering, commerce and journalism and established an honor system like that of the military academy, saying, "We have but one rule here and it is that every student be a gentleman." Following his death on October 12, 1870, at age sixty-three, Lee's name was added to the college, making it Washington and Lee College.

General Custis Lee, the oldest son of Robert E. Lee, succeeded his father as president in 1871 and served until poor health forced his resignation in 1897. Custis Lee had followed in his father's footsteps by finishing first in his class at the U. S. Military Academy in 1854 and also served in the U. S. Army until 1861, when he resigned to join the Confederate Army. Custis Lee's primary assignment during the Civil War was as aide-de-camp to Confederate president Jefferson Davis. He served as a professor at Virginia Military Institute in Lexington from 1865 to 1870. Wilson, who had served under Civil War generals Jeb Stuart and Turner Ashby and surrendered with Lee's troops at Appomattox, had served as president of West Virginia University, as a U. S. Representative 1883-1895 and as Postmaster General 1895-1897 before becoming president of Washington and Lee in 1897. He died in office on October 17, 1900. Denny, who joined the Washington and Lee faculty in July 1899, was selected as acting president by a 5-4 vote and a few months later was chosen president by an 8-5 margin. Little mention was made of the fact that Denny's father-in-law, Dr. Givens B. Strickler, was rector (president pro tempore) of the Washington and Lee board of trustees at the time except to say that Strickler abstained from voting in the election of the president. Strickler, a graduate of Washington College during Robert E. Lee's tenure as president, was a Presbyterian minister and served as a trustee of Washington and Lee from 1894 until his death in 1913.

"Never did a college board of trustees make a happier choice," Latane continued in his discussion of Denny's selection as president of Washington and Lee. "This young man was endowed by nature with a forceful personality, strong will, keen intellect and unusual sagacity in dealing with men and affairs—qualities which would have made him a marked leader in any field of public activity. He entered on the duties of the office with a deep sense of humility but with whole-souled devotion to the great task before him and quickly won the recognition he deserved. When he resigned the office in the fall of 1911 he had become one of the most influential and popular citizens of Virginia and one of the most widely known college presidents in the South. His service as president of the State Board of Charities and Corrections and as trustee of the Carnegie Foundation for the Advancement of Teaching, as well as his presidential office, brought him into contact with the great world of affairs, and with the passing of years his mental horizon continually widened. He developed into a public speaker of rare force and in private conversation his keen analytical power, his lucid statement of fact and his magnetic personality always commanded attention. Such is the man Washington and Lee has given in the full tide of his power to Alabama with reluctance but with a mother's parting blessing and pride," Latane added.

"Though a young man, Dr. Denny's popularity is attested by all who know him," wrote editor John A. McGilvray in announcing Denny's selection as Washington and Lee president in the January 1902 issue of *The Virginia School Journal*. "He is with the students on their athletic fields and takes a deep interest in all their undertakings. In fact, he has his mind thoroughly absorbed in his work and the good of those under his care. Though practically a stranger in Lexington, his views on all questions are listened to with keen attention. He is a profound thinker and well up on all the questions of the day. With the students he is a favorite."

Author Ollinger Crenshaw, in "General Lee's College: Rise and Growth of Washington and Lee," wrote that "the qualities of youth, energy, zeal, intelligence and unremitting attention to his duties which Dr. Denny revealed as acting president became increasingly evident in the decade of his leadership" as Washington and Lee president. "Endowed with a dignified bearing and striking profile, Dr. Denny received warm praise from the *Rockbridge County News,* which said, 'He is cordial, approachable and sympathetic and makes friends. His attractive personality and interest in the affairs of the students soon made him particularly popular among them here, and his abilities and character quickly earned for him the appreciation and esteem of his colleagues in the faculty and his fellow citizens in this community.'" Crenshaw added that although Denny was one of the youngest American college presidents, he "bore himself with an air of dignity which enabled him to walk alongside the graybeards of the trustees and faculty with no seeming inappropriateness.... The election of Dr. Denny brought to fore a young and vigorous individual who at once applied himself to his task with zeal and industry.... While attributing his election to 'a mere accident,' he attacked especially the twin problems that had baffled Wilson—finance and enrollment."

Crenshaw said that as president of Washington and Lee, Denny faced the "age-old problems of enrollments, sectarianism and finances and tackled each of these difficulties, solving some of them and assuaging others to the extent that at the close of his ten years at Washington and Lee he had built a more dynamic institution than college hill had seen since General Robert E. Lee's time." According to official Washington and Lee publications, the college was almost $61,000 in debt and enrollment stood at approximately 200 when Denny took office. The enrollment figure was half that of 1867-68, when more than 400 students were enrolled during General Lee's tenure. "Upon election as president in his own right in 1901, Dr. Denny addressed himself at once to that most important problem of placing his institution upon a sound financial basis and at the same time concentrated upon the enrollment," Crenshaw wrote. "The president achieved remarkable success in his handling of both these policies and they became his most important contributions to Washington and Lee."

Following his formal inauguration in June 1902, Denny immediately began to steadily increase enrollment and decrease the financial deficit. Enrollment increased to 308 in 1904, 335 in 1905, 375 in 1906 and to a school record 418 in 1907, prompting Denny to raise entrance requirements from six units to eleven as he worked toward the Carnegie Foundation standard of fourteen units. Enrollment continued to soar, however, reaching 480 in 1908 and 570 in 1909, forcing Denny to proclaim that the enrollment limit had been reached as overcrowded conditions existed in every department. Entrance requirements were increased to fourteen units in another effort to control enrollment, but Denny had set the wheels of progress in motion and growth continued. Enrollment reached 617 during the spring of 1911, prompting Denny to say that the number of students had overrun the faculty and plant to the point that enrollment must be checked in order to "afford the institution a breathing spell." Still, the enrollment reached 630 in the fall of 1911, Denny's final semester at the school.

During the same period, Denny had been active in extensive fund-raising efforts and had placed Washington and Lee on a sound financial footing. In his 1909 report to the trustees, Denny said, "At the beginning of my administration eight years ago, the valid investments amounted to $593,701.57. Moreover, there was a floating debt of $21,700. Today, the valid investments amount to $830,682.66 and the floating debt has been paid off." He also listed a dormitory valued at $28,986.66, Reid Hall at $36,611.25, a heating plant at $20,646.30, a library valued at $55,000 and other campus improvements valued at $20,000 for total of $161,244.21 in material growth of the university. Denny called the net gain of $419,925.30 during his tenure "an encouraging exhibit" and said that with continued conservatism and careful financial management, the results could be even better.

"The decade which brought so much in the way of financial improvement and even of a moderate prosperity was also one filled with activities of another sort," Crenshaw wrote of Denny's tenure. "Not only did many gifts come to Washington and Lee in those years, but legacies were either made or realized. Several new buildings were erected, the most important of which were Reid Hall (science) and the Carnegie Library shortly afterward. Enough has been said to establish President Denny's reputation as a financier and as one who attracted life to the campus. While these accomplishments, together with the successful Lee Centennial of 1907, constitute Dr. Denny's greatest contributions to Washington and Lee, steady efforts were made to improve educational standards in terms of admissions, to obtain from the Carnegie Foundation adequate provisions for retirement of professors, to maintain a faculty of training and eminence and to stimulate intellectual activity through the bringing to the campus of lecturers and commencement speakers. Another achievement of importance was the establishment in 1911 of the Gamma of Virginia chapter of the Phi Beta Kappa national scholastic honorary society," Crenshaw added.

Denny, while daily walking in the footsteps of General Robert E. Lee, also devoted a portion of his time to the study of Lee as president of Washington and Lee and wrote and spoke often on the heroic leader's impact on development of the institution. Denny also clearly emulated Lee in many ways throughout his career, both as a college president and as a leader of men. "General Lee's life after the war was not lived in the past tense of the subjunctive mood nor was he accustomed to express himself in the language of the unreal wish or of unfulfilled duties," Denny wrote. "He lived an active, aggressive, constructive life characterized by conspicuous determination and tireless energy, consecrated to a great ideal. It was on this campus that the great general, covered with the honors of many campaigns, great in victory and greater still in defeat, in simple devotion and unexampled dignity, wrote that splendid closing chapter of his career.

"…When General Lee accepted the presidency of this institution, it was not for fame or reward, not for place or rank," Denny added. "He was neither lured by ambition nor goaded by necessity. He acted in simple obedience to duty as he understood it. Other avenues offered larger returns and more inducements. But General Lee refused to take counsel of his personal ease or ambition, preferring to follow the path of duty, though it might also prove to be the path of sacrifice. He refused to hearken to the siren voice that has diverted so many men from the course of manly honor and consecrated purpose. But when there came to him in his modest cottage on the James a call to service as companion and guide of young men, he answered the summons and gave to the holy cause whose advocate he had decided to become a never-failing stream of devotion and of loyalty until his hair had whitened in the service. 'I have led the young men of the South to battle. I have seen many of them die on the field. I shall devote my remaining energy to training young men to do their duty in life. I pray that I may be spared to accomplish something for the benefit of mankind and for the honor of God,' General Lee said."

Denny gave the same speech, with penciled changes and additions, to a University of Alabama student assembly in January 1913, adding, "Such a life as that of General Lee cannot help but be an inspiration to the youth of our country. Indeed, it can be said of the great leader that he was a Caesar without Caesar's ambition, a Frederick without Frederick's tyranny, a Napoleon without Napoleon's selfishness and a Washington without Washington's reward." Any close review of Denny's tenure at Washington and Lee or at the University of Alabama will prove not only his admiration of the immortal general but numerous examples of similarities in character, countenance, attention to detail and devotion to duty. Denny, through studious attention to detail and a sense of duty that did not allow him to take a single day of vacation during his ten years as president of Washington and Lee, grew from what many considered an unlikely college president into one of the South's leading educators, and there is no doubt that much of that personal growth was rooted in his careful study of Lee.

"Inevitably, a strong president such as Dr. Denny accumulated enemies and critics," Crenshaw wrote. "The critics dwelt upon the rapid expansion of Washington and Lee through the admission of allegedly unqualified students, and on this point the Carnegie Foundation agreed with them, although in a private way. No doubt some—perhaps many—unqualified students were on the campus in those years, as they probably were to be found at Lexington and elsewhere both before and since that time.... Also, the stringent financial management of the ten successive years of prosperity evoked impatience and criticism, as Denny stated in his report for 1911. People objected to accumulated 'earnings' and complained of too much economy. Faculty members naturally had a different viewpoint from that of the president's office, and while full professors were paid well enough, they were overburdened with students.... On balance, however, President Denny's friends and admirers in town as well as among the faculty, students and alumni far outnumbered his critics and enemies. Dr. Denny's personal popularity derived from several factors. He wisely emulated General Lee in making it his business to know personally each student (and about his family). An apocryphal story grew up that he could identify a student by his step on the stairs. It is probable that he knew thousands of persons, and his hearty, direct, man-to-man manner was appreciated by the students, who knew where they stood with him. He encouraged them to attend to their studies and frequently wrote lengthy and forceful letters to parents analyzing their sons. A part of his success as an educator lay in his remarkable abilities as a letter writer, especially in his tireless recruitment of students.... Many parents received letters about their sons' academic and other problems, which while not always pleasant, indicated that the president of the university kept an eye on them. Rising enrollments, new buildings, cautious financial management, as good a faculty of full professors as any southern college could boast, a chapter of Phi Beta Kappa installed, devotion of students and alumni to their president and alma mater—these were the major achievements of the Denny years. Amidst these signs of material progress, President Denny often dwelt upon religion and Washington and Lee's priceless traditions as far exceeding its value in material possessions," Crenshaw said.

A 1998 Washington and Lee publication celebrating the 250th anniversary of the school's founding also offered a review of Denny's tenure as president, including his surprising election. "His election by the trustees had been far from unanimous. He was a Latin teacher, an expert on the subjunctive sequence, not an administrator; and he had only recently joined the faculty after receiving degrees from Hampden-Sydney College and the University of Virginia—two archrivals of W&L," the historical account said. "But Denny brought tremendous confidence, enthusiasm and energy to the job. The students loved President "Mike" Denny. He oversaw construction of Carnegie Library, Reid Hall, a dorm and a new heating plant. Most important for the future of W&L, he established the School of Commerce and delineated the philosophy that governed the relationship between professional training and liberal education at Washington and Lee for nearly a century.... Denny also resolved one old and sensitive issue. Backed by the alumni and the students, he faced down a coterie of trustees who wanted to attach the school officially to the Presbyterian church in a move that they hoped might prevent financial disaster. The sectarian debate, which had plagued the school since before the turn of the century, was settled. Washington and Lee had been and would be free of church control. For most of the twentieth century, the university would still offer a consciously Christian environment, but it would be neither secular nor sectarian.

"Perhaps Denny's most courageous action came in 1907," the publication continued. "He invited Charles Frances Adams Jr., a former Union general who had commanded African-American troops during the war and who was a distinguished historian and scion of the noted Massachusetts family of John and John Quincy Adams, to deliver the centennial address on the anniversary of Lee's birth. The speech, which received extensive national press coverage, was widely taken as a sign that the Civil War era had finally ended. The youthful Denny, whose focus was on the future, breathed fresh life into the university.... Denny, like later presidents, consciously built on Lee's legacy. He championed the speaking tradition (that students greet each other and which continues still), knew every student by name, and he was so popular that he was applauded each time he strode onto the athletic field. During his administration, students wrote the first student constitution, established the executive committee and crafted what was in essence the modern honor system, with its class elections, formal hearings, public trials and single sanctions." The article added that Denny encouraged fraternity life and that during his tenure the school began its "long love affair with big-time intercollegiate athletics."

Denny's development as an administrator and educational leader did not go unnoticed. He was in great demand as a speaker throughout the South, drawing praise for his insightful views on education, and his speeches included the 1907 University of Alabama commencement address, for which he drew wide praise. He also received honorary degrees from several colleges, including Furman in 1902, South Carolina in 1903, Washington College of Maryland in 1905 and Tulane in 1912. In recognition of his rise in national prominence, he was elected to the board of the Carnegie Foundation for the Advancement of Teaching in 1905, a position he held for more than forty years.

News spread in the late summer of 1911 that Denny was considering an offer from the University of Alabama, and Washington and Lee trustees met on September 8 to address the situation. The board immediately raised Denny's annual salary to $5,000 and offered to match any salary offer from Alabama. Trustee A. W. Gaines urged that "everything be done" to retain Denny, saying he feared a decline in students and in finances if Denny left. Petitions from the faculty, businessmen of the town and by the mayor and council of Lexington, all asking Denny to remain at Washington and Lee, were also presented at the meeting. "The disquieting news agitated the campus for several weeks while Dr. Denny weighed his decision," Crenshaw said. "It was scarcely surprising that other institutions should have become interested in the yet-young official who had built up Washington and Lee within a decade. He had wrought wonders at the old institution which had slumbered for many years prior to his election in 1901. No president in Washington and Lee's history had so completely won the admiration and affection of students and alumni as had President Denny."

Washington and Lee student leaders also adopted a series of resolutions urging Denny to remain in Lexington, saying that his "name had become interwoven with that of the institution," that his "strong hand was much needed in the guidance of the institution" and that his departure would "be a loss to the state of Virginia." The students also staged a mass rally in which they located Denny on the adjacent Virginia Military Institute campus, "where he had taken refuge from his own popularity," and escorted him to Lee Chapel. "One may easily picture the students, filled with emotion and cheering for 'Mike,' returning with their president to the chapel. With the college bell atop Washington Hall clanging, the extraordinary atmosphere suggested that of a football weekend. Nothing approaching it for drama has ever been recorded in the institution's modern history," a story in the student newspaper *Ring-tum Phi* said. Denny did not escape the pressure off campus, either. While in Richmond in early October to attend a meeting of the State Board of Charities and Corrections, of which he served as president at the time, "his room at the Richmond Hotel was in a constant state of siege. His friends telegraphed him, wrote to him, even pursued him into the country, whither he had gone on Sunday to find retirement," the *Rockbridge County News* reported.

The call from Alabama was not the first opportunity for change for Denny. He had previously rejected the presidency of "a large state school" thought to be Pennsylvania. Denny had special ties to Alabama, however. He had made a lasting impression on the University's trustees as commencement speaker in 1907 and had toured the state on an educational mission in 1910. He was also acquainted with Birmingham attorney Borden Burr, one of the University of Alabama's most influential boosters and a graduate of both Washington and Lee and Alabama. Burr played football at Alabama 1893-1894 while earning a bachelor's degree and played football and baseball at Washington and Lee 1896-1898 while earning a law degree there. Burr became a close friend, adviser and comrade-in-arms to Denny during Denny's tenure as president and chancellor of the University of Alabama. Burr served as president of the Alabama Alumni Association and as a sideline official at football games for decades and was shown in photographs with Denny at several Rose Bowl games.

Denny was heavily pressured to remain at Washington and Lee, but after more than a month of consideration and discussion, he accepted the University of Alabama offer, echoing Lee's words in answering "a call of duty to a greater cause." Denny was selected as a replacement for John Abercrombie, who abruptly resigned in July 1911 in a dispute with trustees at least partly stemming from his strict enforcement of academic eligibility standards for athletes. "Perhaps that feature of my administration which has occasioned the most dissatisfaction and criticism has been the policy pursued relative to intercollegiate athletics," Abercrombie said in recognizing criticism from alumni at the time of his resignation. "When I realized a few years ago that ineligible men were being paid money to register as students for the purpose of having them represent the institution on traveling athletic teams, and that at least one such man had been matriculated and graduated under an assumed name, I resolved that no such disgraceful imposition should occur again. Since that time the regulations as to scholarship and general eligibility have been firmly and effectively enforced, and as a result we have absolutely clean athletics at the University. As for myself, I do not consider the mere winning of athletic games to be the chief object of an institution of learning, and I am unwilling to subordinate thereto all scholastic standards and ethical principles." Abercrombie's comments seemed to confirm accusations made by Auburn athletic officials following a 6-6 tie between the two football teams in1907 that Alabama had used "ringers" in the game. Alabama made the same claim against Auburn and the dispute led to a break in football competition between the schools that did not resume until 1948. The Alabama football team had a respectable 50-25-7 overall record during Abercrombie's tenure as president, but that record included such embarrassing losses as 42-6, 54-4 and 30-0 to Sewanee; 78-0 to Vanderbilt; 36-0 to Georgia Tech and 30-0 to Georgia, prompting the alumni to call for changes as the sport grew more popular throughout the South. The University had also suspended collegiate basketball competition in 1906, disappointing students and alumni at a time when athletic programs were being recognized as a rallying point for alumni and a boost to campus spirit and student recruitment.

Abercrombie, who earned a law degree from the University of Alabama in 1888, was elected president of the University in 1902 after serving four years as state superintendent of education. He had previously served four years in the state senate and as a high school teacher, city schools superintendent and president of Ashland College in Clay County 1886-1887, Bowden (GA) College 1890-1891 and Anniston College for Girls 1897-1898. Although not a trained educator, Abercrombie was among the state's leading educational advocates and as state superintendent of education helped pass the state's first tax levies for education. Newspaper accounts said Abercrombie's failure to significantly increase enrollment at the University—partly blamed on the lack of success of the school's athletic teams—was a major factor in his losing favor with trustees and alumni. Abercrombie, along with former University Alumni Society president Hill Ferguson, had been influential in getting state funding for three new buildings—Comer Hall, Smith Hall and Morgan Hall—on campus near the end of his tenure. Following his resignation, Abercrombie continued to serve his state in many ways, including a term as Alabama's U. S. Congressman at large 1912-1916 and as state superintendent of education again 1920-27.

Denny (right) and a student assistant in his cluttered, primitive office at the University of Alabama, circa 1912.

3

Answering the Call of Duty

"As scholar, educator and public speaker and in attractiveness
of personality, Dr. Denny is second to no man in the South.
Virginia loses an able and useful man. Alabama gains one endowed
with a talent and administrative ability that will build up one
of the great universities of the country."

—Virginia Journal of Education

Surely no educator native to the state of Virginia could seek higher glory than to occupy the honored office of president formerly held by Robert E. Lee at a prestigious college endowed by George Washington. Surely one could not ask more than to be acclaimed by his peers as one of the leading educators in the South and recognized as the most influential citizen in the historical educational center of Lexington, Virginia.

But Dr. George H. Denny, who had reached that enviable position at the early age of forty-one, was not satisfied to bask in the light of his accomplishments or even to devote his life to educating the few gifted and wealthy boys who could afford to attend Washington and Lee University in 1911. In the same manner that his father was called to serve others as a Presbyterian minister and that Lee was called by a sense of duty to educate and lead young men following the Civil War, Denny was called to serve a greater cause on a new educational frontier. Although leaving Washington and Lee meant that Denny would no longer live in the home built for Lee in 1865 or walk daily in the footsteps of the immortal Virginia heroes Lee and Stonewall Jackson, he knew that education was the way to a more prosperous, civilized and democratic nation and he felt duty-bound to answer the call to educate the many rather than the few.

Denny's decision to leave Washington and Lee to become president of the University of Alabama on January 1, 1912, was not an easy one, even for a man of Denny's broad educational conviction. He sought advice from leading educators, family members and friends, many of whom urged him to reject the offer, and carefully studied the issue for more than six weeks before reaching a decision. Finally, on September 30, 1911, Denny wrote to Alabama governor Emmet O'Neal to accept the presidency of the University of Alabama. On the same date, he submitted his letter of resignation to Dr.

Givens B. Strickler, rector of Washington and Lee and his father-in-law. In each letter, Denny cited "the call of duty" as his reason for taking the Alabama position.

"Following the call of duty, I am now writing to accept the great opportunity and responsibility to which you have summoned me," Denny wrote to Governor O'Neal. "I appreciate the courtesy of the trustees in allowing me the ample opportunity to search my heart to try to find if this was indeed the task to which I should devote my life. I express to you, therefore, my decision to go to Alabama with an honest purpose and a large desire for usefulness, uninfluenced by any sort of ambition save to render service. It would be a task as impossible as it is unnecessary to describe to you the wrench that it costs me to leave Virginia, in whose service my life has been spent. I have been deeply touched by the appeals that have recently come to me from the trustees, alumni, members of the faculty and the student body of Washington and Lee. I have also appreciated the generous expressions of the public press and of leading citizens in every section of this commonwealth. Yet, in the face of it all, I am hearkening to your call. I feel that in taking this great step I shall have the sympathy and the cooperation of every patriotic man who is today helping to fashion the higher life of Alabama. The prevailing consideration that has moved me to accept the presidency of the University of Alabama proceeds from the conviction that there is a great opportunity to any man serving in that position to render constructive service to the entire system of public education in a progressive commonwealth rapidly growing in population and in power.

"It is not a mere question of transferring from one institution of learning to another institution of learning. If that were the sole question I should remain at my present post of duty," Denny continued. "To carry on the work consecrated by the benefaction of George Washington and by the service and memory of Robert E. Lee is a task amply adequate to satisfy the ambition of any man. Nor is it a question of salary. The trustees of Washington and Lee have habitually sought to deal with me in a spirit of utmost generosity. It is solely a question of service. The founders planned to make the University of Alabama the supreme intellectual achievement of your commonwealth. It is the duty, as it will be the pleasure, of the people of Alabama to understand the institution and to deal with it not as if they were doling out charity but as if they were increasing their noblest investment. No American commonwealth will, in the long run, grow greater than its moral and intellectual stature. If Alabama is to reap the richest reward of her remarkable industrial prosperity, there is supreme need of a truly great center of spiritual and intellectual power whose influence will reach out until it is felt among all classes and conditions of men. It is because I have faith in the integrity of the stock that is fashioning your civilization that I offer my best services in the great task of training your youth in the august serenity of ideas and ideals. It is because I have faith in the future of the University of Alabama that I am willing to leave my Virginia home and all the sacred associations of a lifetime to share in this work," Denny wrote.

"The University of Alabama only asks a fair opportunity to minister to the higher life of the people of the commonwealth," Denny continued in expressing his vision for the school. "It serves no selfish purpose. It recognizes that it exists not merely for those who administer and govern it, not merely for those who teach in it and not merely to gratify the pride of those who have graduated from it. It recognizes that it exists solely to serve humanity in high and helpful ways. It would seek to become a perpetual fountain to all who thirst for the lofty faith, the unquenchable hope and the super-abounding energy of the disciplined life. It would seek to train the rising generations in the mastering of all the great forces that sway the modern world. It would seek to reestablish the desire and capacity for creative activity, to enable men more fully to realize themselves and to guarantee the commonwealth that has nurtured it a leading position in the national life. It would strive to enrich every field of human endeavor and to fit young men and young women to perform a definite, specific task. But it would also strive to furnish to every young man and young woman whose life it touches such enlargement of spirit and such capacity for a wide and catholic view that the mere performance of a task will neither belittle nor crush them. It would aspire to send out into the world young men and young women who have learned to enlarge and to dignify whatever task they may be called upon to perform and who will be bigger than any task to which they shall ever put their hands; in short, young men and young women of sober discipline, of moral efficiency and of catholic vision. To the consummation of this task I would devoutly consecrate my life with an energizing faith in the essential rectitude of the cause and in its ultimate triumph. Appreciating fully what is involved in such a task and conscious of my own limitations, I pledge my best efforts to the up-building of the University of Alabama and to the advancement of every sound effort to promote the material, intellectual, social, moral and spiritual welfare of the commonwealth that created it," Denny concluded.

Denny's letter carried a tone similar to an essay he had written of General Lee years earlier in analyzing Lee's choice to become president of Washington College in 1865. "When General Lee accepted the presidency of this institution, it was not for fame or reward, not for place or rank. He was neither lured by ambition nor goaded by necessity. He acted in simple obedience to duty as he understood it," Denny wrote of Lee. "We speak of consecration. We speak of concentration. These terms faithfully describe the character of General Lee as college president. Consecration was not to him a penal servitude; it was freedom to realize a great purpose, an unselfish ideal. Nor was concentration, in his view, a waste heap for the sacrifice of physical, mental or moral energy; it was freedom to devote himself to essentials, to look at life with clear and steady eyes and to do a great, majestic work for the republic," Denny added in the essay, which he used as a speech many times during his career as president of both Washington and Lee and the University of Alabama.

In his letter of resignation from Washington and Lee, Denny cited the careful study he had given the matter before reaching a decision. "I have not acted hastily. I have proceeded with the utmost deliberation. It has been a most difficult question to decide. I have searched my heart to try to find if this was indeed the task for me," Denny wrote. "After giving to the whole matter the kind of consideration that I promised to give it, I have reached the conclusion that it is my duty to go to Alabama. I believe that I am uninfluenced in this decision by any sort of ambition save to render service. I am, therefore, transmitting through you to the trustees my resignation as president of Washington and Lee University, to take effect January 1, 1912, or at such other time as the trustees may, in their wisdom, choose to accept it.

"...The prevailing consideration that has served me to accept the presidency of the University of Alabama proceeds from the conviction that there is greater opportunity in

Alabama for constructive service to the entire system of public education than would be open to me at this time in Virginia, especially considering my position as executive head of an independent institution of learning," Denny continued. "In other words, I shall hope in my new field of service to find ampler opportunity to serve the general cause of education to which I have pledged my life. I shall hope to devote myself to every phase of education in a great commonwealth rapidly growing in population and in power. The background of it all is, of course, a great people and a great new era." Adding that salary was not a factor in his decision, Denny said, "It is solely a question of service, not measured in terms of a single institution but in terms of the whole, great problem. It would be an impossible task to describe the wrench and sorrow that this decision has cost me. I shall not attempt it....As I look back over these eventful years, I feel grateful that I have been permitted to share the high privilege of administering an institution that has been so greatly distinguished in its heritage of great names, great traditions and great memories; that has for so long a period illustrated a steadfast devotion to the highest ideals of conduct and achievement and that is today serving, without sham or pretense, the commonwealth and the nation with greater power and efficiency than at any other period of its remarkable history. I shall lay down my work at Washington and Lee with genuine regret," Denny continued. "I have put into this work a decade of sincere personal devotion and of willing and unremitting toil. It has been to me a happy service. The college has prospered in a remarkable degree.... Its growth has been far more rapid than anyone could reasonably have expected. I have my reward in the consciousness that I have attempted to do my duty in every phase of the work of the institution without fear and without favor, that I have sought to study the laws of its true growth and that I have devoted myself without reserve to its peace and prosperity.... It is a great sorrow to me to leave Virginia, in whose service my whole life has been spent. I shall cherish all the happy and sacred associations and friendships and loyalties of my life here. I am leaving all these things with my spirit unfretted by a single unhappy memory and with utmost affection for the history, the institutions, the traditions and the people of this commonwealth."

An editorial in the University of Alabama student newspaper *Crimson White* on October 10, 1911, commented on Denny's inspiring letter of acceptance, saying, "It gives his conception of the University of Alabama and its purposes. In this he makes evident a deep appreciation of the true aim and work of the school. To him, it appears as one of the great factors in the intellectual and moral advance of the state as a whole. All loyal citizens of the commonwealth should regard it as the crowning light amid those other beacons that point the way to a splendid and useful future. These words of Dr. Denny are not merely words by way of making known his acceptance," the editorial continued. "They are the results of a calm, impartial judgment and hold a deep significance to all those interested in the welfare of Alabama.... When a man with no thought of personal aggrandizement and only a high conception of duty and an abiding enthusiasm for a noble cause puts aside the press of personal desires and takes up a duty appealing to the finer, spiritual side of his nature, it may be looked forward to as a certainty that that duty, once entered upon, will be pursued with all possible vigor. Such a statement, when made in regard to a man of Dr. Denny's caliber, means that the cause fortunate enough to enlist his energies and his enthusiasm can attain to but one end—complete and overwhelming success."

An October 7, 1911, editorial in *The Tuscaloosa Times-Gazette* praised Denny's acceptance of the challenge facing him in Alabama, saying, "The easier period of his work in Virginia had come. He could sit quietly and easily in his honorable position as president of one of the great Southern universities and enjoy his rest, won by his own energetic labors. But he willingly resigns the place of ease and satisfaction to take on the more difficult work in Alabama. Dr. Denny knows full well of the differences of opinion which have centered about the control of the management of the University of Alabama. He is not and never has been identified with any faction of the University's friends or enemies. He only knows that it is a university which should properly head the educational system of a prosperous state rapidly growing in population and wealth, and he knows that the University has not fully occupied its appointed place in the educational life of the state. He comes, trained and efficient, from a place of comparative ease to undertake a place of difficulty.... It is inspiring to the whole educational system of the state to know that such a man is coming to Alabama to take up his part of the task before us. It is inspiring to know that such a scholar and such an administrator has come to Alabama to lead the way."

As prominent as Denny was as an educational leader in the South and as near-perfect as he proved to be as president of the University of Alabama, he was not the first or even the second choice of University trustees. Still, he did not let that fact deter him from accepting the office. Nor did he let the dozens of letters from influential friends, newspaper editorials or resolutions from faculty, student and civic organizations urging him to remain at Washington and Lee stand in his way. He saw the call to "the lower South" as a duty to make full use of his abilities in the service of others. He saw it as an opportunity to build a great public university accessible to all; to bring change to all the people of a state; to lead a state in educating its masses; to bring a better way of life to a disconnected, ragged, poor, struggling populace; to change a culture; to advance civilization and democracy; to make a greater difference in life's larger picture. To Denny, leaving the comfortable position of president of prestigious Washington and Lee University for the University of Alabama was in answer to a call to duty that perhaps few men could understand at the time, but the long-term results of Denny's leadership in education in Alabama and in the South and his inspiring example of service to mankind are not only easily visible but continue to bear fruit today.

Vanderbilt University Chancellor James H. Kirkland was the first choice of University of Alabama trustees following the resignation of Dr. John Abercrombie. Kirkland rejected the offer, however, as did Colonel William C. Gorgas, the commander of the Army Medical Corps who gained international fame fighting yellow fever, malaria and hookworm. A Tuscaloosa native and graduate of the University of the South and Bellevue Medical College, Gorgas was the son of former University of Alabama president Josiah Gorgas and long-time University librarian Amelia Gayle Gorgas. He was promoted to brigadier general in 1914 and named Surgeon General and promoted to major general in March 1915. He died in July 1920. Denny also rejected the University of Alabama position when it was first offered, just as he had rejected three previous offers from other colleges. The trustees returned to Denny a second time in early August 1911, however, and after what he described as a "wrenching" period of consideration, he accepted the position in the most important professional decision of his life. The decision proved to be the most important one in the first one hundred years of life for the University of Alabama as well.

Students at Washington and Lee knew Denny as "Mike," and they reluctantly accepted his decision to leave the private, all-male school for the greater good of others. The Washington and Lee weekly student newspaper *Ring-tum Phi* of October 10, 1911, spoke generously of Denny's decision even as it lamented his leaving. "Painful as it is to lose him, we cannot but feel that Dr. Denny's decision honors him," the student newspaper said. "He has placed the whole matter on the high ground of duty, and from his viewpoint there was but one thing to do. We find consolation in the fact that it was not just for a handful of silver that he left us; it was to him a clear call of duty which he could not ignore. And, after all, we have not altogether lost him as long as he and we have the best interests of the whole Southland at heart. Virginia is a missionary in the Southern educational field. As one editor puts it, 'Virginia, whatever loss that decision may entail, has yet the satisfaction of knowing that her younger sisters still look to the mother of states and statesmen for men of light and leading.'"

Several of the South's leading educators understood Denny's calling also, and in response to his requests for advice, many encouraged him to accept the University of Alabama offer. Denny's letter soliciting advice on the matter stated that he had been offered the University of Alabama presidency "at a salary of $6,500, a residence and certain perquisites such as electric lighting from the central plant," which he estimated to total more than $7,000. He added, however, that salary was not a consideration since Washington and Lee trustees had insisted on meeting the Alabama salary offer if he agreed to stay in Virginia. "The question of service, as I view the matter, is the most vital factor in the problem," Denny wrote to his friends. "There is no question that the patronage of this institution (Washington and Lee) in point of quality is superior to that of Alabama. There is no question that the traditions here are finer. There is no question that the institution itself has greater prestige, is better known, more respected and appeals more strongly to the affection and the imagination of the Southern people and of the nation. It draws its patronage from forty states. Viewing the question, therefore, merely in the light of transferring from one institution to the other, I would not consider it. On the other hand, I must remember that here I am in large degree serving merely an institution of learning. At Alabama I should be serving not merely a single institution but also a great state rapidly growing in power, in wealth and in population. There is an unusual opportunity for constructive work, attended, of course, with the usual perils and sufferings incident to such an opportunity. The background of it all is a great people and a great new era," Denny said in soliciting other viewpoints on the matter.

Henry S. Pritchett, president of the Carnegie Foundation for the Advancement of Teaching 1906-1930 and former president of the Massachusetts Institute of Technology 1900-1906, responded to Denny on September 5, 1911, saying, "As you very rightly say, the important question is which is the greater opportunity and which is the work best worth doing for a conscientious man interested in the progress of education? The Alabama situation is one in which I am much interested. I believe that affairs are ripe in Alabama for great progress in education in the next ten years. This can be brought about, of course, only by a development of the public school system, and the University must be the leader in that movement. The state is rich; it has been aroused to its shortcomings in education, and I believe there is the opportunity for the right man to go into the state of Alabama and do a tremendous work for education. To do this he must lead not only courageously but wisely. He must not go too far in advance of his people and his constituency, and yet he must have the courage not to give way when the question of reasonable standards is involved. I regard this place as one of the great opportunities in education today," Pritchett said, adding that the task would involve "hard work, tact, courage and patience. There are, in my judgement, few opportunities in America in education more arduous and yet more promising than this opening in Alabama," Pritchett added. "If you feel that you have the courage and the patience to tackle the job, it will offer you a larger opportunity than you will ever find in Virginia. To make a success of it, the man who goes to it must carry a high order of devotion as well as educational wisdom. My own feeling is that a man never arrives at any great or satisfactory conclusion by taking the smaller opportunity in place of the great one. It is better generally to put to sea and try the fortunes of the waves than to sit tied up to the bank."

University of South Carolina president Dr. Samuel Chiles Mitchell offered profound insight in his response to Denny's letter, saying, "In the University of Alabama you would exercise intense and creative force throughout the bounds of the state. You would go a long way toward *making* the state, and that is a task worthy of the ambitions of any man. Your activities would in no sense be confined to the campus. Perhaps your greatest work would be in the leadership of educational thought and construction. In this work you would overleap state lines and you would naturally quickly become the exponent of the entire lower South. Regarded in this way, your call to Alabama strikes me as a truly national concern.... I believe that you are singularly suited for the task in Alabama and I am perfectly confident that the whole state of Alabama would soon feel the effect of your presence. At the same time, I should grieve for Virginia to lose you."

Wealthy industrialist and philanthropist Andrew Carnegie, on whose foundation board Denny served, wrote, "It seems clear to me that the great influence in the South is to come through the state universities, and therefore in view of what your letter tells me and what I know of the Alabama situation, I should say the larger service could be rendered in the new place to which your call would seem to me to have the element of the providential, which to me is of very great importance in all aspects of true work."

Former Hampden-Sydney College president Richard McIlwaine, on whose faculty Denny had served in 1898, responded in a similar manner, writing, "It looks to me as if this is a call of providence, directing you to the place where, with your ability, activity and experience, you can do the most for the present and future generations. If this be so, then the way seems plain before you."

Edgar Gardner Murphy of Montgomery, Alabama, also urged Denny to take the new position, saying, "There is a real opportunity there—as great as there is in the United States—if a man of real culture will go there and stand for cultural ideals.... Our people are for education, and with a united, strong administration, will support the University; and I think they are ready for such work as you could do."

"You are up against a question which you alone can decide," University of Virginia president Edwin A. Alderman wrote to Denny in discussing the pros and cons of the issue. "I should advise you to go to Alabama. The place has difficulties, but so have all situations involving great opportunity.... We are not put here to achieve peace and quiet and contentment for ourselves.... Alabama is a great state with a great population. They appear to be determined to search the nation and to get the best at any cost. This is a very good sign of increasing breadth of understanding of university problems.... I believe they would trust and be instructed by you in the philosophy of true university development and would, when the light was turned on, rise to you and be very enthusiastic and helpful. I see here a great opportunity attended with the usual peril and sufferings of great opportunity. You seem to me to have the equipment for handling the situation and the background of it all is a great state and a great people and a great, new era. I sympathize with you in your crisis. I trust you will act wisely and chose the better path. Your going from Virginia would mean a most substantial loss to the educational force at work in the commonwealth," Alderman added.

Dr. H. B. Frissell, principal of Hampton Normal and Agricultural Institute, also encouraged Denny to take the Alabama post, saying, "I am much interested in Alabama. It has immense possibilities and needs leaders tremendously. While I dislike to think of your leaving the Old Dominion, I am inclined to the judgment that the cause of education in the South would be advanced by your taking control of the educational work of that young and growing state.... I feel that as head of the University of Alabama you could exert much power in the legislature and with the public officers, and that is very much needed. You have an excellent address and could do much to educate public officials. Their ignorance, as you know, is often pathetic.... But we have a chance in the South to make public institutions a great power for good, morally and religiously as well as intellectually."

Wallace Buttrick, secretary of The Rockefeller Fund of the General Educational Board, did not join the leading educators in supporting Denny in his "call" to Alabama. Responding to Denny's letter, Buttrick wrote, "Your review of the Alabama situation is so complete and exhaustive that I could hardly venture to add to it.... Personally, if I were well established in an institution of private foundation I should hesitate before accepting the presidency of a state university."

An editorial in the *Richmond Times-Dispatch* urging Denny to remain at Washington and Lee was typical of many throughout the state. Under the headline, "Stay Where You Are," the editorial said, "There is much difference between being president of a great institution removed from political influences and an institution which is dependent upon the favor of succeeding shoals of politicians who may be or may not be influenced by the true educational spirit...."

The News-Leader of Richmond called on Denny to remain in Virginia also. In a September 16, 1911, editorial under the headline "A Protest," the newspaper wrote, "Not only would Dr. Denny's acceptance of the call be a distinct blow to the institution he has done so much to build up, but a serious loss to the state. Apart from the high place he occupies and the vast influence he exerts as a leader in educational circles, Dr. Denny is a man of affairs whose impression is felt in all else that pertains to the elevation and advancement of healthy thought in Virginia. He stands today in the front rank of the molders of men who for years must control and determine, in the matter of living up to the best public and private ideals, the destinies of the commonwealth. No less than

Washington and Lee can Virginia spare Dr. Denny."

Attorney Vincent M. Miles of Fort Smith, Arkansas, wrote Denny a letter typical of dozens he received from Washington and Lee alumni urging him to reject the University of Alabama offer. "…After your nine years at Washington and Lee, you have made of that institution one that equals or surpasses to my mind anything of its kind in the South…. I cannot picture you lobbying and boot-licking a body of average legislators for money to add one more radiator to your heating plant, yet you know that before you have been at the head of such an institution two months you will want twice as much money as is being appropriated for it…. I am not the one to attempt to give any advice to you in the matter at all; this letter is intended to be only an earnest appeal from one of your alumni to stay with Washington and Lee."

Albert W. Gaines, a Washington and Lee trustee from Chattanooga, also asked Denny to stay in Virginia, writing, "I feel that you would be making a mistake to leave Virginia for Alabama. I note that you say 'The thing which most appeals to me in Alabama is the opportunity for constructive work in the field of general education in that state.' You will not be dealing with Virginians should you go to Alabama, and I think that the fact that you are not an Alabama man will militate against you in carrying to successful issue any work you may propose. I do not think that you will find the same congenial atmosphere that you have in Virginia; that you will not find it so pleasant a place to live, and especially in the summer, your family will probably have to go to Virginia to spend the heated term. I think, also, this being a state institution, it necessarily will be subject to the whims of politicians, and I feel that you will be making a mistake to give up a splendid position which you can have as long as you desire."

Virginia Governor William Hodges Mann appealed to Denny to remain in Virginia in a letter dated September 10, 1911, writing, "Now that it is known that you are considering the offer of the presidency of the University of Alabama, I think it is proper for me, having due regard for the interests of my state, to enter my protest against your leaving Washington and Lee, which in my judgment would be not only hurtful to that institution but a misfortune to the state at large…. I am not putting my protest on personal grounds but on the broader and I am sure more substantial and influential grounds of public interest and welfare. In my judgment your conduct of the great institution of which you are head has been successful and beneficial from every point of view. Your association with the students who have attended Washington and Lee during your administration has established personal relations with every one of them which must have impressed your character and ideals in such a way as to have influenced for good their future lives, and in this way you have done a work which cannot be weighed or estimated until the final accounting. I trust that the desire of your friends, of the council of Lexington, of the student body and now of your state will outweigh the call of any institution outside of Virginia and that you will long continue the work which has so signally resulted in the progress and advancement of a great university," Mann added.

Businessman, political activist and future Virginia governor (1914-1918) Henry C. Stuart also urged Denny to reject the Alabama offer. "If you will pardon me, I want to unite most earnestly with your many friends in Virginia in urging you to remain with us," Stuart wrote on September 19, 1911. "The higher educational interests of the state have been greatly promoted by your splendid administration of one of our universities, and many of us feel that you are even yet on the threshold of your career as a great educator.... Virginia is not in position to spare a man whose future usefulness may be measured by past achievements like yours.... I do not presume to speak with reference to your own interests. I am only voicing a sentiment of every Virginian who has watched your career and your splendid administration of the affairs of Washington and Lee University."

Denny received dozens of other unsolicited letters and resolutions urging him to remain at Washington and Lee, along with resolutions from the faculty, alumni, student body, Lexington town council and local civic organizations. A mass rally by students and townspeople also urged him to reject the Alabama offer. Washington and Lee alumni president Jonathan W. Davis wrote, "I have just heard that you have under consideration a proposition from the University of Alabama, and in my own right and as president of the alumni, I write to protest your acceptance of it. I think every alumnus of Washington and Lee keenly appreciates the extent and value of the work you have done and we cannot consent that you should lay it down."

In urging Denny to remain at Washington and Lee, the Lexington town council resolution read: "Whereas, the council recognizes in Dr. Denny one of the leading, if not the foremost, educators of the South, who by his wide learning, his broad and catholic views, his great executive ability, his untiring energy and his unswerving devotion to the high standard of duty he has raised for himself, has advanced Washington and Lee University to its proper and deserved position among the leading institutions of learning in the country; and whereas the town of Lexington has by the efforts of Dr. Denny greatly benefitted not only in the uplifting of its younger generation, who have enjoyed the great advantage of the high standard of instruction adopted by this institution, but in the advancement of the material prosperity of its people; and whereas the retirement of Dr. Denny from the presidency of Washington and Lee would be a great loss to that institution and to the town of Lexington, it is the earnest and sincere desire of the authorities and the people of Lexington that conditions may be such that he may retain his present connection with the University without entailing too great a personal sacrifice on himself."

Washington and Lee students gathered in Lee Memorial Chapel on September 26, 1911, to show their appreciation for Denny and to pass resolutions aimed at "holding him" as their president. The first resolution urged Denny to remain in his current position; the second said his resignation would cause a vacancy "well-nigh impossible" to fill, and the third cited numerous improvements at the school during Denny's tenure. "No man can deny that the improvement as shown by this record is almost exclusively due to him," the resolution said. "He has brought three students where there was but one; he has erected buildings on what fifteen years ago was a weed-grown hilltop. The present condition of the whole plant speaks of one man at its head whose energy and marvelous attention to detail has secured these results. Washington and Lee has prospered not only in material things, but its prestige and power has increased with every year also." Another resolution added that should Denny leave, the state of Virginia "would lose one of her most influential and valued leaders" and that the "empty space made by his departure would be felt in the hearts of every lover of this institution."

Responding to the student rally, Denny said, "Young gentlemen, I should be quite unfaithful to promptings of my heart if I failed to say that I appreciate the kindness and warmth of this demonstration today. I hoped it might pass away without undergoing the wrench and strain to stand here face to face with you. Of all the kind words that have come in the past six weeks, nothing has touched my soul more deeply than this demonstration today.... If I shall leave this institution it will not be merely to accept a call to the University of Alabama. If I go it will be to accept the presidency of the University plus other great responsibilities in serving the whole system of education in a rich and rapidly developing commonwealth. If I go it will be a great wrench and sorrow to me. I shall hope to have the sympathy of all in reaching my conclusion. I assure you that I shall not go until a sense of duty and deep conviction shall clearly say: 'Thou shalt go.'"

Washington and Lee professor H. D. Campbell urged Denny to remain at his post also, writing, "Your career at Washington and Lee has won for you an enviable position as a college executive along the lines to which you have given your untiring energy and masterful skill. You deserve to reap the fruit which has been growing and maturing during these ten years of vigorous cultivation under your supervision. The time has come when your versatile powers could be concentrated on advancing and maintaining Washington and Lee's educational standards and making the people of Virginia and the South recognize her as a wise and independent leader towards the highest ideals in education. This opportunity is yours, and it is within your grasp."

Denny, inspired by the life and words of Lee, had already made his choice, however. Bound by the call of duty, he submitted his resignation to Washington and Lee only five days after his unanimous election by the University of Alabama trustees on September 25, 1911. Alabama Governor O'Neal, himself an 1872 University of Alabama graduate, sent Denny a brief note on that date confirming the board's action, which also set his salary of $6,500 per year. "Permit me, speaking for myself and for the board as a whole, to say that we feel that in taking this action we have greatly promoted the interests of this institution, and we sincerely hope that you may see proper to accept our invitation."

News of Denny's resignation disappointed Washington and Lee supporters and others throughout Virginia. Dr. William F. Drewry, superintendent of Central State Hospital in Petersburg, expressed his feelings in an October 8, 1911, letter to Denny, saying, "It is useless for me to tell you that I am sorry indeed that you have concluded to leave Virginia and take up educational work in Alabama. Virginia is, as everybody knows, decidedly a loser and Alabama is preeminently a gainer. Not only will the educational interests of Virginia suffer by your going, but the organized charity work and various institutions that care for the afflicted, diseased, dependent and delinquent will miss the great influence you are exerting for the betterment of their conditions," Drewry said in reference to Denny's work as chairman of the Virginia State Board of Charities and Corrections 1908-1911 and as a member of the executive committee of the Cooperative Educational Commission of Virginia 1903-1912.

U. S. Senator Thomas S. Martin of Charlottesville also expressed his disappointment in Denny's decision in an October 12, 1911, letter, writing, "...That you could not see your way clear to remain with us here in Virginia gives me the deepest regret. While the ties of friendship which have existed between us so long will not be severed by your sojourn in Alabama, I feel that your going is a serious loss to me. I know your place at Washington and Lee cannot be filled as you have filled it. I do not know of a single man in Virginia whose leaving the state would be more keenly felt by so large a circle of friends. No college president or professor has ever in my day exerted a hundredth part of the wholesome influence on public affairs which you have exerted. As deeply as I regret your going and as great as the loss is to Virginia, I have not been able to answer the arguments which you gave for making the change...."

In announcing Denny's acceptance of the Alabama position, *Virginia Journal of Education* editor Joseph W. Everett wrote, "As scholar, educator and public speaker and in attractiveness of personality, Dr. Denny is second to no man in the South. Virginia loses an able and useful man. Alabama gains one endowed with a talent and administrative ability that will build up one of the great universities of the country. To the editor of this journal the loss is keenly felt because we were schoolmates and intimate friends."

Borden Burr, one of the University of Alabama's most active and influential alumni, wrote to Denny from an unusual viewpoint. In an October 3, 1911, letter, Burr said, "I have been awaiting the announcement of your decision in reference to accepting the presidency of the University with very much the same feeling that I had when Alabama and Washington and Lee met on the football field last Thanksgiving. Being an alumnus of both institutions has divided my affection, and your decision to accept the presidency of Alabama renders me torn between Alabama's gain and Washington and Lee's loss. I believe the pleasure of having you nearer and an opportunity to see you oftener will, in the course of time, cause the former to gain the ascendency." Burr became and remained a close friend, legal advisor and staunch ally of Denny's in the fight for adequate funding from the state legislature throughout Denny's tenure as University of Alabama president. Burr, also one of the school's leading athletic boosters, was chairman of the University's 1922 Million Dollar Campaign to raise funds for new buildings on campus.

University of Alabama trustee Daniel Pratt was prophetic when he wrote to Governor O'Neal on September 21, 1911, to inform him that the presidential nominating committee had selected Denny. "I believe that he is the man we are hunting," Pratt wrote. "And I further believe that the University will prosper greatly under his administration." H. O. Murfee, president of Marion Institute, made a similar prediction in an October 11, 1911, letter to Denny. Murfee wrote that "every patriotic Alabamian rejoices that you are coming to the state to lead our educational forces. No man has ever had, and no man will ever have, a warmer welcome and more enthusiastic and devoted support. In my opinion, the University of Alabama offers the largest opportunity for constructive work in America, and I believe that the man and the hour have met."

Louisiana State University president Thomas D. Boyd sent Denny a telegram expressing similar thoughts. "Hearty congratulations to you and to Alabama. You have been elected to the best position in the South and Alabama has secured the best man in the United States for the presidency of her University," the telegram read.

University of Alabama loyalists were anxious to meet their new president, and Denny traveled to Alabama on the weekend of November 17-19, 1911, where he was greeted at a banquet of three hundred alumni at Birmingham's Hotel Hillman on Friday evening, November 17. In addressing the group, Denny told of the difficulty of leaving his home state as he pledged his loyalty to his new assignment. "I cannot speak of the sorrow I feel in giving up the hallowed associations of a lifetime, but it is not necessary to be false to the old love to be true to the new, and I pledge you that I shall be true to the new," he said. "I have given up the sacred association of a most happy life in old Virginia to spend the rest of my life in Alabama. In coming here I can only say that I pledge my best efforts to do a man's work without fear or favor. I have lived there (Virginia) all my life and it was something stronger than new work that brought me here. I hope to accomplish something in Alabama."

Denny was kept doubly busy during his early months as president of the University. In addition to getting acquainted with faculty and students and taking on the administrative duties of his new position, he was in great demand as a speaker. Within days after arriving in Tuscaloosa and addressing the University student body, Denny was already scheduled to speak to a Montgomery alumni gathering in January and a Laymen's Missionary Conference in Chattanooga in February and give commencement speeches at Marion Institute, Bessemer High School, Alabama Girls Institute at Montevallo, Dallas Academy and Troy Normal College in May. He also returned to Lexington, Virginia, to speak at the May 7 inauguration of Dr. Henry Louis Smith as president of Washington and Lee University.

"You will believe me when I say that I am genuinely touched by this reception," Denny said in response to an emotional welcome from former students and old friends in Lexington. "There are some emotions that are very much deeper than the reaching power of a man's vocabulary. It is a gracious privilege to come back to the shadow of these beautiful hills and to greet again those with whom I was permitted to make those long forced marches in the wilderness through which a gracious and kindly hand has led us into the land of promise," Denny added. "Not one of us would forget the past even in the blaze of a more brilliant present.... To those of us who wrought here in that period there are grateful memories of friendships cemented, of service rendered and of progress made. Do you ask me whether it was worthwhile? Ask me rather, 'Is it worthwhile to live?' Ask me rather, 'Is it worthwhile to die?'"

Smith, who had previously served as president of Davidson College 1901-1912, served as president of Washington and Lee from May 1912 through 1928. When Smith announced his upcoming retirement in September 1928, Denny was asked to return as Washington and Lee president, and he all but accepted the position before deciding at the last minute to remain at Alabama. His decision to remain at the Capstone was celebrated by the construction and dedication of Denny Chimes as a student-led gesture of gratitude to him, and the bell tower remains an iconic symbol of his long and loyal service to the University today.

Denny labeled the University of Alabama the capstone of the state's educational system.

4

Capstone Vision Realized

*"The University of Alabama is the chief institution of learning
in the state, and, praise God, it shall be."*
> —Dr. George H. Denny

When Dr. George H. Denny became president of the University of Alabama on
January 1, 1912, he already had a clear vision of what the University could and should
become. He saw it as the head of a statewide school system offering tax-supported
public education to all children as a means of changing the economic, social and culture
climate in Alabama and thus improving the lives of the citizens of what was then a poor,
undeveloped, agrarian state still struggling to recover from the loss of many of its courageous men and boys and much of its wealth during the Civil War.

Inspired by the words and actions of such American educational and patriotic
leaders as immortal fellow Virginians Washington, Jefferson and Lee and seasoned by
more than two decades of study and experience as an educator and college president,
Denny had conceived what he considered an ideal statewide public educational system
and he was prepared to lead the way in developing that system in Alabama. Although
it would take almost two decades to fully realize, Denny was convinced of his vision's
possibilities as he set out on a long and difficult crusade to make the University of
Alabama the true crowning point—or capstone, as he soon acclaimed it—of a state
educational system leading to improved living conditions for the citizens of Alabama.

To Denny, the word "capstone" was not a mere catchword or marketing slogan. It
was a carefully selected, clear and concise definition of the position he felt the University
of Alabama should occupy in the state educational system. Although his first public
pronouncement of that single, perfect word to describe his vision for the University
came several months after his arrival, he—in his unique, eloquent and scholarly style—
explained that vision in the 1912 *Corolla*. Responding to a request to provide his "ideal"
for the University, Denny wrote:

"My desire would have it a place where scholarship, service and character are the
primary motives of both teacher and pupil; where fitness and quality energize their
hopes and inspire their ambitions; where courtesy and gentle manners sweeten the
routine of their official tasks and refine the intercourse of their private lives; where the
intellectual tone is sound and stimulating, the ethical ideal high and true, the moral

desire clean and elevating and the religious spirit devout and impelling. My desire would see it furnish to the commonwealth and to the nation young men and young women who will be fitted to perform with credit whatever tasks they shall undertake; who will enlarge and dignify their tasks; who will be bigger than any task they shall ever attempt; who will have such enlargement of spirit and such capacity for a wide and catholic view that no task, however humble or however exacting, shall either belittle them or crush them; who will carry with them to their various tasks such training as to equip them not merely to be squared to the exigencies of secular life, but also to become, ever more and more, real men and real women in the entire circumference of their possibilities and not simply along lines that will bring a larger money value when taken out into the market of professional and mercantile life. In brief, my desire would make the University of Alabama clearly and unmistakably a perpetual fountain to all who thirst for the lofty faith, the unquenchable hope and the super-abounding energy of the disciplined life."

Denny first used "capstone" publicly in describing the University on Saturday morning, September 14, 1912, as he addressed a student assembly that included his first freshman class among a record enrollment of more than 600. The term "capstone" was then used in an advertisement in every issue of the *Crimson White* for several years starting with the first fall of 1912 issue as it slowly became an affectionate and familiar nickname for the school. The advertisement, under the heading "University of Alabama, Capstone of the Public School System of Alabama," said the University offered study in "letters, science, engineering, education, law and medicine." The advertisement also promoted the University summer school and said that expenses were "exceedingly moderate."

The Tuscaloosa News, reporting on Denny's September 14, 1912, address, used the headline, "Denny Stirs Student Body," and called his speech to the Morgan Hall student assembly "a masterpiece that held the riveted attention of the faculty and students for nearly an hour. Dr. Denny outlined the vision that he entertained of a greater, more serviceable institution of higher learning. He said he wanted the college to be the capstone of higher training in this commonwealth," the story said. "It was not merely an institution to pour knowledge into the brains of young Alabamians that he desired. It was something more, something greater—something more fundamental. It was to meet the needs of the nation, which he said draws four-fifths of its leaders from the small body of college men which is only two percent of the male population. Dr. Denny did not care for a college whose aim should be, to each young man, to furnish money-making material. 'A thug can make money; a thief can make money,' Dr. Denny said. In following the ideals of a well-spent, individual college life, there were two things that college men should refrain from doing, Dr. Denny added. 'First, don't waste your time; second, don't waste your money.' He asked each student to make each hour of the day an hour of dutiful usefulness," the story added.

"It is to the alumni and to them especially that we are to look in making the University the chief institution of learning in this commonwealth," Denny said in a separate *Tuscaloosa News* story of the same date. "I find that even those who have been separated from their alma mater for many years still nurse warm sentiments for the college and stand ready to lend a hand for Alabama. The secondary schools of the state are also responding to the call for trained young men. The greater number of prepared students entering the University this fall speaks praise for the various high schools. There seems to be awakening a new spirit of cooperation between college and preparatory schools," Denny was quoted as saying.

Dr. James J. Doster, dean of the department of education, also used the term "capstone" on September 14, 1912, as he discussed the improved standards of education in the high schools throughout the state. "He (Doster) regards the educational system of Alabama as better articulated now than ever before and believes that the University as the capstone of the system is destined to a great future," *The Tuscaloosa News* story said. The fact that both Denny and Doster used "capstone" in describing the University on the same date and the fact that regular advertisements using the slogan "University of Alabama, Capstone of the Public School System of Alabama" began shortly afterward indicates that the term had been discussed and officially adopted as a scholarly, descriptive University nickname prior to September 14.

Denny was the genius behind the surge in University attendance, of course. He had reached out to the high schools through superintendents and principals and to the students themselves through a direct-mail recruiting effort that began in the spring of 1912 and grew to enormous proportions over the next decade. Meanwhile, Doster, as professor of secondary education and state school inspector, played a major role in the development of the state's high schools and became Denny's closest ally in the long fight for state and local funding for education. Both men traveled the state campaigning for tax-supported schools and Doster worked with local educators throughout the state to improve courses of study and standards of instruction. Together, the two men carried the banner in the development of the state public educational system atop which the University of Alabama truly became "the Capstone."

In addition to being used in the *Crimson White* advertisement each week, the term "capstone" was used again in the July 7, 1913, edition of *The Tuscaloosa News* as the newspaper reported on a special July 4 Independence Day celebration for University summer school students at Morgan Hall. "After a warm welcome to the summer school students, Dr. Denny took occasion to state clearly and emphatically the position of the University, the capstone of the state's educational system, on the question of coeducation," the story said. "He (Denny) said that here and there over the state the question is frequently raised as to whether the University wants young women students. In answer to the question, he said that most emphatically the University wants them."

"We have done everything that human ingenuity can do to let the young women of this commonwealth know that we welcome them to the University," Denny was quoted as saying. "Over my own signature I have stated that fact a thousand times. There is not a young woman graduate of a regular, four-year high school in the state of Alabama during the years of 1912 and 1913 who has not received an invitation to attend the University," he added in reference to the personally signed recruiting letters sent to all high school graduates in the state. "Moreover, the trustees have set aside still another University building to be used as a dormitory for women. The acts of the University officials show that the institution welcomes young women students, and I declare to you five hundred teachers here assembled that the University's doors are wide open to them," Denny added. Although he had come from an all-male school at Washington and Lee, Denny recognized the potential growth women students offered and their recruitment was among his highest priorities.

Although he more clearly defined his "capstone" ideal in a June 1912 essay in *The Tuscaloosa News* entitled "The University's Place in Industrial Education," Denny stopped just short of using the now-popular term "capstone." "It is the duty of a state university to serve the state in all high and helpful ways," Denny wrote in beginning his essay. "Standing at the head of the school system, it is charged with the duty of educational leadership. There is need not only to be constantly enriching the content of its curriculum, but also to be studying its wiser application to the needs of society. It must concern itself with all phases of the educational process, considered as one great whole existing to serve the needs of the state.... The University of Alabama is adjusting its work to meet the demands of a modern commonwealth," Denny continued. "It is keeping in mind the needs and the industries of the people of the state. It recognizes that there has been enormous progress in the industries and in the differentiation of vocation which has come with modern tools. It recognizes that in an industrial community of the present day there must be provided schools which shall give the theoretical and some of the practical foundation of vocational training.... It is the duty of a modern state university to assume the leadership in training its leaders of industry as well as the leaders in the other spheres of human activity.... We are therefore emphasizing the importance not merely of teaching ascertained facts, but also the obligation to teach young men the philosophy underlying these facts and the processes by which these facts are ascertained...."

"Capstone," defined in the dictionary as "the crowning point," was used in describing the University again on August 21, 1913, in a special third anniversary issue of *The Tuscaloosa News*. In a story discussing area educational progress in general, *The News* said, "As a capstone in the excellent preparatory school system that is detailed above, Tuscaloosa possesses the privilege of sending her youth to the state University at the minimum cost in money and inconvenience. Within the shadows of this famous institution the young men and women of Tuscaloosa are favored with the opportunity of securing an education second to none in the South and of mingling with associates that represent the society of culture and enlightenment."

Denny contributed a lengthy essay on the University to the August 21 edition of *The News* also, explaining his thoughts on the mission of the school and the support it should receive from the state as a whole. He did not use the term "capstone" in his essay, however. Instead he referred to the University as the "head and crown" of the state's public school system. "The University of Alabama is conscientiously meeting the demand for a sound type of educational leadership which is universally conceded to be the primary function of a modern state university," Denny wrote. "It is concerning itself with every phase of the educational process, considered as the great whole, existing to serve the needs of the state. It recognizes that it is the servant of all the people. It is training a fine group of young men and young women for the highest type of service. The work is going on in a scholarly, spiritual atmosphere devoted to the highest ideals of moral conduct and quickened by a devout religious tone. The University of Alabama is adjusting its work to meet the demands of a modern commonwealth," Denny wrote. "It recognizes that the apprentice system has disappeared and that the school today is called upon to do for the boy something like what his apprenticeship did for him a generation ago.... It is the duty of a modern state university to assume the leadership in training the leaders of industry as well as the leaders of other spheres of human activity.

"One of the most significant things looking to the future influence of the University of Alabama is the recent establishment of a separate and independent school of economics and political science," he continued. "That is the last great forward step that has been taken by the University in the service of the state. That step will contribute in a large way to the economic and civic life of this commonwealth. It will mean the raising up of a great body of trained men who will point the way to a solution of the many perplexing problems that are today and will be tomorrow demanding the attention of thoughtful men—problems relating to corporations and to transportation and to taxation and to scores of subjects that are intimately related to our economic and social life. The University of Alabama…has the fixed desire and purpose to send out young men who understand the value of an effective application of scientific methods and knowledge to governmental agencies.... It will furnish to the commonwealth men who believe that government, so far from being a sample of unintelligent patchwork, is a matter of orderly, expert investigation.

"The University of Alabama does not hesitate to stand on a platform that looks to an era of helpful cooperation with the individual citizen in his everyday tasks," Denny added. "It believes that knowledge should become more widely diffused and that the whole commonwealth should profit in a large and helpful way from the service that it can render. The importance of a policy demanding a systematic dissemination of knowledge in forms accessible to the people cannot be overestimated. When this policy has been carried out in a logical and definite way, the people of Alabama will be getting that kind of help from their University which will most surely be appreciated and in return for which they will desire to give a more liberal and adequate support. They will look to it, ever more and more, for their ideals of life and action." Denny added that the University should expect and receive the moral and financial support of the state in return for its service to the state. "The people of Alabama owe a debt of gratitude to their foremost seat of learning," he wrote. "This debt they should repay, not merely by expressions of sentimental pride in its fine history, but more especially by giving to the institution the kind of support that its service to the commonwealth entitles it to receive. They should support the acknowledged head and crown of their school system, not as if they were doling out charity, but as if they were increasing their noblest investment."

"Capstone" slowly became a popular nickname for the University, and within a few years was being used regularly in newspaper headlines and in a variety of other ways. By 1919, *The Crimson White* was using the heading of "Capstone Chuckle" to introduce amusing poetry to its readers while *The Tuscaloosa News and Times-Gazette* was regularly using "Capstone" to refer to the University. A September 25, 1919, *Tuscaloosa News and Times-Gazette* story even failed to refer to the University of Alabama at all, using "Capstone" three times in reference to the University instead as an indication of the popularity of the nickname. By the early 1920s the University cafeteria had become the "Capstone Cafeteria" and a five-member campus orchestra called the "Capstone Five" was playing nightly at a local tea room. There was also the "Capstone Literary Society" and the "Capstone Ice Cream Parlor," and a popular Tuscaloosa men's store even offered the college men a special hand-tailored spring suit called "The Capstone."

Just as the school's nickname gained popularity and wider recognition, so did the University's academic standing. In a 1923 message to University students, Denny wrote, "I wonder if all Alabama students realize the rich heritage they enjoy. Of course, they know that the University is the capstone of the state's educational system; that it is one of the oldest, most comprehensive and most historic seats of learning in the South; that it is the first-born child in the state's sisterhood of institutions of higher learning; that it has grown more rapidly than any institution of the lower South within the past decade; that its alumni have taken high rank in all the honorable walks of life, not merely in Alabama, but throughout the Union. But do we fully realize that the University is the only Alabama institution, and indeed one of the very few in the South, that has within a decade attained distinction by full recognition of its work by the Association of American Universities in the graduate schools of the country, by the establishment of a chapter of Phi Beta Kappa and by membership in the Carnegie Foundation. It does mean a great deal to most students, and it ought to mean a great deal to all students that their alma mater is recognized as a standard institution not only at home but also abroad."

Writing for the 1926 *Corolla*, Denny said, "The University of Alabama is the capstone of the public school system of Alabama. It is a part of the public school system and is maintained by the state.... No institution can present a finer record of service. No institution has grasped its opportunities with greater zeal. No institution is giving back to the commonwealth that established and is maintaining it a richer return. We look forward to the day when our beloved "Alabama" will be still more widely acclaimed for the service she has rendered and will continue to render in the high task to which her life is devoted."

Denny continued his work of recruiting students; teaching the lessons of character, duty, truth and service; hiring prominent and able faculty and staff; creating a campus culture of discipline, honor and service; constructing new dormitories and halls of learning, and speaking out for public support for education until he retired after a quarter of a century of service to the University of Alabama and the state. He had come to Alabama "to be of greater service to the cause of education" and to build a great university for the state of Alabama. It took him much of his 25-year career as University president to fully achieve his goals and lay the "capstone" atop the state's public educational system, but he had a clear vision of the final product from the start and began the task immediately after his arrival in Tuscaloosa.

University faculty members recognized Denny as creator and leader of the Capstone in October 1928 when he was recalled to the presidency of Washington and Lee University. A lengthy resolution by the University Faculty Council calling on Denny to remain as president of the University of Alabama said, "We believe it is fair to say that no man, no matter how wise or how strong or how experienced he might be, could possibly carry on nearly so well the great program you have in mind for making Alabama the finished 'Capstone of the State Educational System.'" Symbolically, one could easily say that the dedication of Denny Chimes in May 1929 marked the moment of attainment of most of Denny's goals as the University rode the crest of a wave of successes in building, academic, attendance and athletic achievement. With 3,200 students, a new football stadium named in Denny's honor, two recent Rose Bowl wins, eight new buildings in the last ten years, recognition by all academic standards agencies and new sorority and fraternity houses lining the streets, the University of Alabama had indeed become the "capstone of the public school system of Alabama," as Denny had labeled it almost two decades earlier.

Denny acknowledged the University's unprecedented achievements in his 1931 University centennial celebration address when he said, "During the last quarter of a century a new University has been developed out of the old. While clinging to the ancient ideals, it has cherished a new hope. It has adopted a new philosophy of education. It has related itself to the public school system of the state. It has taken its place at the head of that system.... As a result of this new hope and new philosophy, intelligent people now recognize that as the University goes, so go the public schools; that it is no mere accident that the strongest school systems are found in those states in which higher education is best developed; that in a sound educational body no member can say to any other member, 'I have no need of thee.' Such has been the rich fruitage of modern University effort and leadership. The University of Alabama has within a decade achieved the ideal of a university in a democracy. It has done this not merely by broadening the range of instruction and by opening its doors to all who are qualified to enter; it has done it by going out into the highways and making the entire state its campus through correspondence and extension courses. It has done it by the development of research and graduate work in the interest of the people of the state. It has taken its place as a university of the people, by the people and for the people, which is the proper role of a university in a democratic society," he added.

Denny did not go unnoticed for his extraordinary efforts in leading the University of Alabama to national prominence by any means. He received a number of personal honors during the 1920s and 1930s, as he had in earlier years. He was named to the National Advisory Commission to the Sesquicentennial Exhibition Association and named Alabama's Professional Leader of the Year in 1925; was elected president of the Association of ROTC Colleges in 1927; was named a member of the National Advisory Commission on Education in 1929; was elected president of the Association of Separated State Universities and selected to attend a White House Conference on Child Health and Protection in 1930; was elected to the national Phi Beta Kappa senate in 1931; was selected to speak nationwide on NBC Radio from New York on education in the South in 1933, and was chosen Tuscaloosa's first "Citizen of the Year" in 1934.

Denny immediately went about the business of promoting and building his ideal university as he addressed University alumni gathered in his honor in Birmingham on November 18, 1911. He called on the alumni to support his efforts to gain increased funding from the state, saying the University's greatest, most immediate need was money. "The state should be doing five times as much for the University as it is, not as doling out charity, but as increasing its greatest investment," he said in address repeated to a Montgomery alumni gathering on January 13, 1912. "The alumni must waken the public mind to realize what the state must do," he said. "This meeting should be the starting point for a movement for greater public support. It should be made plain to the people of Alabama that the University is not an end in itself, that it is not maintained for the benefit of its president, faculty or the gratification of the pride of its alumni. It is for the service of the state. I hear alumni talk of numbers and not the character of students, the size of buildings and not the nature of equipment. Much has been said concerning a great University. Frankly I do not believe we are ready for that term. Let's build first a great college. It will come sooner or later, but it has not yet come," Denny told the group. "The relative standing of this commonwealth in the sisterhood of American states will be determined, not by the census, nor by the size of its cities or its crops, but by the kind of men it shall turn out," Denny added in his Montgomery remarks. "There can be no doubt that there is need to adequately provide for the training of leaders to develop our forests and fields and mines, but there is even greater need to build up a majestic seat of learning that shall guarantee a sound type of personal culture, of social efficiency and of intellectual vigor," he added.

In his efforts to unite the University Alumni Society and spur its members to action soon after he took office, Denny organized it into districts and hired Thomas H. (Uncle Tom) Garner as alumni secretary in 1915. Garner, who had been managing editor of *The Tuscaloosa Gazette* (1893-1903) and *The Tuscaloosa Times-Gazette* (1903-1915), originated the Alabama Alumni News in 1917 and served as alumni secretary until his death in 1944. Garner was also widely known as founder of the popular University Glee Club in 1905 and served as director of the University Chorus and an instructor in music history from 1919-1942. An 1890 University law school graduate, Garner also served as choir director at First Baptist Church in Tuscaloosa from 1885-1942.

Fully aware that alumni discontent involving football had weighed heavily in the controversy that forced his predecessor from office, Denny did not overlook athletics in laying the foundation for the "capstone" of his vision in his November 17, 1911, remarks to University alumni in Birmingham. According to a *Crimson White* report of the speech, Denny mentioned his personal interest in football (He was a former player at Pantops Academy and coached for a brief season at Hampden-Sydney College.) and stressed the importance of physical training and its relationship to the development of the human mind and character before adding, "But like all other extracurricular activities, athletics must be kept within bounds. It is of importance in college life, of great importance, but it is a sideshow and not the main performance. College life must not be allowed to swallow up the college curriculum."

Improvements in athletic facilities were among the first actions taken by Denny, and by 1915 the University had new athletic fields for football, baseball, tennis and track and a new men's gymnasium for basketball, which was resumed as a competitive sport in 1913. There was a new football coach in 1915 and another new one in 1919, too, as Denny began the process of building an athletic program representative of the University he envisioned. Under his close watch (He attended all practices and games.) and guidance, Alabama athletics kept pace with the rest of the campus, evolving into the popular "Crimson Tide" and winning several championships by 1931, including three Rose Bowl appearances by the football team that brought national acclaim and money to build a modern football stadium in 1929 named in Denny's honor.

Academic standards had also been an issue of some controversy under former University president John Abercrombie, and Denny did not hesitate in addressing that subject as well. "The requirements for admission should be strong, but not unreasonable. Someone has said something of 1,000 students in the next four years. Get that idea out of your minds right now," Denny told the alumni. "There are not 1,000 prepared college students in all the colleges of Alabama combined at the present time. We should not be swept off our feet by false numerical standards. Forced to choose between a student body of 400 trained and prepared students and one of 1,000 men sent to college to gratify personal vanity, I should not hesitate to choose the former. We do not want numbers brought merely by winning teams, over-zealous solicitors or low standards. I have no idea of setting the woods afire. I shall merely try to do what I can with the tools at my disposal.... I pledge my best efforts to do a man's work without fear or favor," he added. From that moment forward, no one ever accused him of wavering in that promise as he labored on behalf of education in general and the University of Alabama in particular for a quarter of a century.

Denny began to instill his philosophy of scholarship, service and character in the students at the University of Alabama, as he had to the students of Washington and Lee University 1901-1911, soon after taking office. He stressed these crucial individual traits in welcome addresses to student assemblies at the start of each semester for many years, including his first speech to University of Alabama students on January 9, 1912. "Men can make money without education," Denny was quoted in *The Tuscaloosa Times-Gazette* of January 10 as saying. "They can also make money without purity, without character or animated faith. If education fails to affect one's philosophy of life or fails to affect the ideals of faith and duty, it can be counted a failure, but not if it does not stand for increased money making," he added. The newspaper report said Denny urged the students to think of the University as "a nursery of purpose—the fountain source of the desire for service—and to develop the finer traits of character, moral ideas and faithfulness."

Denny also introduced the idea of University extension classes as a part of his "capstone" plan during his first months on the job, and the extension division eventually grew to become an integral part of the school's overall educational system. The November 21, 1912, edition of *The Tuscaloosa News* reported on Denny's concept of "faculty extension lectures" to be offered throughout the state. "The idea is to have the University extend its usefulness to the people of the state beyond the mere instruction of the youth," the story said. "Through extension lectures delivered by members of the faculty wherever they are requested, the institution will offer its services to all the men and women of Alabama." The story said the idea, proposed by Denny in a faculty meeting, was patterned after similar programs in Virginia and South Carolina. "With the plans now being worked out by a committee, the University will be brought into closer touch with the lives of the people than it has ever before known," the story added. Although the extension program was slow in reaching its full potential, Denny reported in May 1923 that 850 students were enrolled in extension and correspondence courses. That number reached 1,410 two years later as the extension division continued to grow along with other University programs.

The Mobile Register, praising the growth in attendance and improvements at the University under Denny's leadership in a November 1914 editorial, said, "He (Denny) seeks to bring the University into intimate relations with the life of Alabama, and to be an aid in the moral, intellectual and material advancement of the people. With this plan *The Register* is in full sympathy and wishes for its success."

Responding to the statewide lobbying efforts of Denny, University professor of education Dr. James J. Doster and the Alabama Education Association, the state legislature passed a constitutional amendment in 1915 providing funds for the erection and repair of rural school houses; requiring compulsory attendance to a certain age; establishing county boards of education and permitting local taxation for the support of public schools, among other actions. "I doubt whether any Southern legislature in fifty years has done so much for education as did the Alabama legislature of 1915," Denny said of the unprecedented legislation. "Few, if any, American commonwealths can now claim a more progressive system of school laws than the Alabama system." Two years later, the legislature passed a constitutional amendment allowing an additional six-mill tax for the support of public schools, which Denny called "the most significant and far-reaching event in the history of Alabama within a half century." Denny and Doster also spoke to local groups in Tuscaloosa County in a public campaign for approval of a three-mill property tax for schools, which was approved in 1916. They were rapidly changing the state educational system atop which Denny saw the University. The Alabama legislature had passed a bill in 1907 providing funding for Alabama high schools, and Denny wasted no time in taking steps to help meet the growing demand for qualified high school teachers throughout the state. To meet the need for high school teachers, Denny hired Dr. James S. Thomas as professor of secondary education and reached out to the many unqualified teachers in the state, offering additional summer school classes to improve the standards of instruction. The state's Normal Schools, or teacher's colleges, at Troy, Jacksonville, Florence and Livingston, offered only two-year teaching certificates at the time. Summer school enrollment at Alabama in 1911 was 242, but with Denny's recruiting efforts, that number more than doubled to 517 in 1912 and grew steadily each year, reaching 782 in 1916, 1,250 in 1921 and 2,069 in 1922 as the need for qualified high school teachers increased.

In his first report to the trustees in May 1912, Denny said that only 398 resident students had completed the spring term after 452 had started in the fall. More than 500 students registered for the 1912 fall term as Denny began his ingenious recruiting campaign, and the numbers grew each year afterward, reaching 1,165 in 1918-1919 as enrollment surpassed the 1,000 mark for the first time. There were 1,216 students in 1919-20, 1,661 in 1920-21 and 2,134 in 1921-22. Classrooms and dormitories bulged as the numbers grew to 2,394 in 1924-25 and to 3,068 in 1927-28. Attendance hit 3,200 in 1929, 3,603 in 1930 and 4,073 in 1931 before finally slowing somewhat during the Great Depression. A total of 4,897 registered in the fall of 1936, Denny's final semester as president, as the effects of the Depression began to ease. From the mid-1920s on, the University was turning away hundreds of out-of-state applicants each year due to a shortage of classroom and dormitory space.

Response to Denny's direct-mail recruiting efforts had become overwhelming by the early 1920s. He was receiving—and answering—more 500 letters per month from prospective students from May through August each year. He had proven all his theories valid; the University was fully accepted as the capstone of the state educational system. But there was a downside to the unprecedented success, too: Funding for classrooms and dormitories could not keep pace with student growth, and Denny's calls for increased funding from the state brought little results, forcing him to deal with an on-going financial crisis for the last several years of his career.

Nine main buildings made up the University campus when Denny arrived as president in 1912. Those buildings included Woods Hall (1868), Clark Hall (1885), Manly Hall (1885), Garland Hall (1888), Tuomey Hall (1889), Barnard Hall (1899), Comer Hall (1910), Smith Hall (1910) and Morgan Hall (1911). The buildings housed the classrooms and male students while the fifty-five female students and faculty members lived in nearby houses, many of which still did not have electricity. Building funds were scarce in the early years, but Denny somehow found a way to add new buildings and facilities. His first priority, to aid in the recruitment of women students, was the addition of a much-needed women's dormitory (Tutwiler Hall) in 1914. His second priority was the upgrading of athletic facilities with the addition of a new men's gymnasium (Little Hall) and new athletic fields (Denny Field) in 1915. A men's dormitory (Gorgas Hall) was added in 1921 and Nott Hall was opened in 1922 to house the Medical School, which had been moved from Mobile in 1920. The Million Dollar Campaign of 1922 brought in pledges of approximately $950,000, providing funds for more buildings as the campus grew rapidly over the next decade. Construction after 1922 included the McLure Library (originally a post office, cafeteria and supply store, 1925); Carmichael Hall (originally the Amelia Gayle Gorgas Library, 1925); Lloyd Hall (chemistry, 1927); Farrah Hall (law school, 1927); Bidgood Hall (Commerce and Business Administration, 1928); Bibb Graves Hall (Education, 1929); Doster Hall (women's studies, 1929); Denny Stadium (football, 1929); Denny Chimes (monument to Denny, 1929); Barnwell Hall (women's gymnasium and pool, 1930); Reese Phifer Hall (originally the Student Union Building, 1930); Moore Hall (1935) and Hardaway Hall (engineering, 1936).

Denny's tireless efforts brought him widespread admiration throughout the South, and he was easily the most popular man in Alabama by the early 1920s. He was named the state's outstanding professional leader and elected to the state "Hall of Fame" in 1925 and named to Who's Who in America in 1926 in addition to receiving widespread encouragement to run for governor, a temptation he seriously considered but eventually rejected.

Former University of Alabama history professor James B. Sellers praised Denny's accomplishments in "*The History of the University of Alabama*" (University of Alabama Press, 1953). "He had done more than fashion a university and set it on the road to greatness," Sellers said in discussing Denny's tenure as president of the University of Alabama. "He had lifted the eyes of all who worked with him to a vision of what the institution could and must become. His three-fold concept of the task of the University has remained valid: 'the adjustment of man to life as it is, the creative advancement of human knowledge and direct and immediate service to the people of the state of Alabama.' He believed that 'the things of the mind and the things of the spirit' are the very life of the University and should never be forgotten," Sellers wrote. Writing of Denny's retirement as University president, Sellers said, "Friends of the University tried in vain to express their great admiration and gratitude for President Denny's contributions to the University. Some spoke again and again of the wizardry with which he made one dollar do the work of five. Monuments of his administrative skill were everywhere before their eyes—a great University plant, building by building erected with funds saved by his careful management and wonderful foresight. Others spoke of his creation of a great institution of learning, a university in truth as well as name, a university in which a competent faculty held scholastic standards high. Others cited the increase in on-campus enrollment from 533 in 1912 to 4,897, one-third of whom were women, in 1936. He had lifted the schools of law and medicine and engineering and education to full professional stature and he had launched the School of Commerce and Business Administration, the School of Home Economics, the School of Chemistry and the Graduate School. Some spoke of his encouragement of student activities, his encouragement of athletics and his friendly concern for women and their needs. The alumni remembered his warning that the goal of one thousand students should not be too quickly expected, but smiled when they recalled that enrollment of women alone had long since passed that mark. By any test the growth of the University during his administration had been phenomenal, and the rise of its reputation had kept pace. The University was now truly the Capstone of Education in Alabama."

Denny (left) with U. S. Representative and University of Alabama alumnus William B. Bankhead.

5

Wise, Tactful, Aggressive Agitation

"Let us teach our people the fundamental truth that no man is free who cannot read and write; that no tyranny is so great or so dangerous as the tyranny of ignorance, inefficiency and poverty."
                                        —Dr. George H. Denny

Dr. George H. Denny was selected as president of the University of Alabama with the hope that he could transform the small, floundering state university into "a great university," just as he had done at historically rich Washington and Lee University during the previous decade.

Denny arrived in Alabama with an even broader goal in mind, however. He fully recognized that the obligation and opportunity of a state university was far greater than that of a private, all-male institution like Washington and Lee, and perhaps even greater than the concept of a "great university" held by the trustees and alumni of the University of Alabama. Denny came to Alabama determined to build a statewide, universal educational system emanating from the University downward to the high schools and even to the most remote one and two-room rural schools in the state. Through a public educational system accessible to every boy and girl in the state, Denny hoped to cultivate a more civilized and prosperous populace capable of developing the state's natural resources, improving daily business practices, making more efficient use of its farmlands and advancing the cause of democracy through more ethical, efficient and effective government. Denny called his idealistic plan for widespread social, cultural and economic change—first envisioned while president of Washington and Lee University, fully conceived in his early years at the University of Alabama and encompassing far broader goals than those of an ordinary college president—"commonwealth building."

Denny was not simply espousing scholarly, grandiose ideas in proposing such lofty goals for the University. He was completely sincere and totally confident in his mission and his methods. He knew from his own experience the rewards and possibilities that education offered and he had concluded that his duty in life was to lead the effort to revitalize the stagnant economy of the state of Alabama through the education of its citizens. He knew the difficult task he faced in an agrarian state whose widely scattered and doggedly independent population consisted mainly of poor farm families far more concerned with such critical matters of livelihood as summer droughts, boll weevils, leaky roofs, cattle ticks, under-fed and poorly clothed children, clean drinking water and the hope found in late-summer revival meetings than algebra, chemistry and Latin. He also knew that those farmers, even if they failed to realize it, could eventually benefit, directly or indirectly, from the universal educational system he championed. Denny had developed a prominent university in Virginia; he came to Alabama with the vision of helping guide the destiny of an entire state through a university capable of reaching and affecting the lives of every citizen. His unprecedented, fully documented success in that endeavor is easily proven more than a century later, as is the success and service of the many flagbearers who carried his message of leadership and service forward in business, industry, government, educational and civic life.

Denny knew the task that lay ahead in his mission to bring dramatic change to a state still mired in the aftermath of the Civil War. He had spoken of it at educational conferences throughout the South. "To say that education is the supreme question of civilization, whether viewed from the standpoint of the individual, the community, the state or the nation is only to express the conviction of a great multitude of men whose keen foresight, sober patriotism and sympathetic service have most contributed to the growth and prosperity of our common country," Denny said. "Education of all the people is the foremost task of our statesmanship and the most worthy object of our philanthropy. Many have expressed the conviction that universal education should be the primary policy and immediate duty of our Southern section. But, unhappily, this is not enough," he said. "It remains to make this conviction the common and universal expression of our civic patriotism and civic aspiration. How are we to convince all our people, or even the great majority of them, that every human life without a single exception is a plan of God and has its place in the divine economy? How are we to convince all our people, or even the great majority of them, that it is a social and moral wrong to make education a thing apart from the condition and participation of the great mass of men? How are we to make them understand that universal education is from every rational consideration the fundamental need of our civilization and the bulwark of our liberty?"

Denny pointed out the obstacles confronting the advocates of universal education, listing social tradition and social prejudice; a poor, scattered, heterogeneous population; a regional spirit of ultra-individualism, and a prejudice on the part of some "as to the wisdom of including the negro race in any scheme proposed." Denny also pointed to the argument by some against general taxes for education, saying that the lack of such taxes "doomed hundreds of thousands of Southern children to the tyranny of ignorance, weakness and poverty on the pretext that the individual rather than society is responsible for education of the masses. Local taxation for local needs is a fundamental doctrine in democratic government and local taxation for education— the greatest of all needs—is a fundamental duty in a democratic society," he added. In answering his own question as to how to convince the majority of the people to support education, Denny said, "The facts must be studied and frankly stated by educational experts. In other words, we need an educational campaign conducted by specialists who have devoted their lives to the problems and who can speak words of wisdom and authority.... These skilled experts can present the facts of the situation as no other class of men and upon them devolves the duty of arousing the masses to the privilege and opportunity of meeting the issue and solving the problems. Universal education permeating every phase of our industrial life is the first great step in the remaking of our Southern country," he continued. "We hear much concerning preparedness. The kind of preparedness that is most needed in the South is intellectual discipline that will fit our youth for industrial leadership and for intelligent farming.... Our greatest asset, therefore, in commonwealth building is the schoolhouse. The school is the great agency which democracy has set up to train men for productive and efficient citizenship. Property has no value of itself; it is merely the creature of education.

"Our institutions of higher learning, so long set apart in their Olympic isolation, need to seize their opportunity at this crisis," Denny continued. "It cannot be denied that these institutions are only in their infancy as engines of popular enlightenment. Our great need, then, is wise, tactful, aggressive agitation by trained specialists who know the truth and are not afraid to speak it. The teacher as well as the statesman must point the way to this great Southern people, a nobly patriotic and self-sacrificing people willing to pay taxes without limit for the freedom and happiness of their fellow men if the path of duty is made plain to them. Let us as educators devote our lives, if need be, to this issue. Let us teach our people the fundamental truth that no man is free who cannot read and write; that no tyranny is so great or so dangerous as the tyranny of ignorance, inefficiency and poverty. And when people know the facts, we shall have their sympathy. When they know their duty, they will do it without fear and without faltering though it means sacrifice and even death."

Denny added that the development of any public school system depended on self-imposed taxes to build and equip schools and hire competent teachers. "It requires money to erect buildings. It requires money to command the services of competent men.... Our people need to know the value of education, even on the farm. They need to appreciate the fact that the farmer who understands chemistry, who is able to analyze the forces of nature, to mix brains with the soil, is to be the farmer of the future. They need to learn that it is no longer a disputed fact that the material progress of a people, to say nothing of their political and social prestige, is in direct proportion to the quality and quantity of its education. Teach this important lesson and we shall hear less of our poverty and incompetency. We shall no longer be saying that we are too poor to educate our youth. The fact is, we are too poor to neglect it."

Because of his success and rise to prominence as president of Washington and Lee University, Denny arrived on the campus of the University of Alabama amid a tide of high expectations. "His arrival has been anticipated with highest hopes by the students and faculty of Alabama," a story in the December 12, 1911, issue of the *Crimson White* said. "They believe that with him comes a new era of progress, prosperity and greatness. Then the University will slough off once and for all the narrow limitations that have held it in the position of a college. It will become a university in fact as in name. As a convincing basis for this belief they need only point to the prodigies performed at Washington and Lee University under the leadership of Dr. Denny. There he began with much less promising material than is afforded at Alabama and wrought out a modern university. This change, too, implied more than merely material expansion. It was marked by a great intellectual advance in the work of the college and graduation from it now bears a deeper value and significance than before."

A January 9, 1912, *Crimson White* story announced that Denny had arrived on the Tuscaloosa campus and taken up his work "without ceremony or fanfare" at his own request. During his first days on the job, the story said, Denny met with Dr. W. H. Saffold, who had been acting president from September 1 through December 31, 1911, and former president John Abercrombie and briefly greeted faculty members. The story added that Denny also traveled to Birmingham with trustee Henry B. Foster to meet with Governor O'Neal before settling down to begin a thorough, critical review of all University operations. "Since his acceptance of the position (of president), all those interested in the University have looked forward to the coming of the great Virginia educator as an event marking an era of advancement hitherto unknown in the school," the *Crimson White* story said. "Alabamians believe in Dr. Denny and are expecting great things of him—not a wild bound into greatness but a steady, thorough growth under a sane, wise rule. The new president has done great things at Washington and Lee and will do greater things at Alabama."

The same issue of the student newspaper announced a January 19 student banquet at the McLester Hotel to allow the students to meet the new president and to "draw closer the ties that bind the students and the three distinct departments (academic, engineering and law) in a get-together spirit." A later *Crimson White* report on the student banquet said Denny proved to be "a very amiable and interesting talker" and that his time was currently "occupied in becoming thoroughly acquainted with the situation." Denny was quoted as having told the students that "The University presents many varied propositions demanding great thought and attention. There is nothing to be said now except that we have problems which will be solved." The banquet, reportedly attended by approximately 150 students, followed a January 5 "smoker" at which Denny was greeted by "scores" of Tuscaloosa citizens who welcomed him to the city, according to a *Tuscaloosa News* report.

In his first formal address to the student body on Tuesday, January 9, 1912, Denny delivered what *The Tuscaloosa News* called "an inspiring appeal for thorough work and high standards." Denny told the students that "The soundest plea for college training is not an increase in a man's earning capacity. If that's what brought you to the University you would be better off at home, for money can be made without character or education. College training is not true if it fails to affect the philosophy of your life and give you a clearer conception of truth and character." The brief report on the address added that Denny "seemed to strike a keynote of enthusiasm" and that students and faculty were "eager to praise Denny and the principles which he outlined." The speech was the first of many touching on character, responsibility and service that Denny delivered during his twenty-five-year tenure as president of the University.

The University of Alabama floundered under the nine-year leadership of Abercrombie from 1902-1911. Campus enrollment hovered near the 400 mark, even after the state legislature passed bills in 1907 supporting the development of high schools and providing funding for the construction of Comer, Smith and Morgan Halls at the University in anticipation of a brighter future. Leadership, unity and direction were lacking, however. The primary challenges in Tuscaloosa were similar to those Denny had faced at Washington and Lee a decade earlier: low student enrollment and financial insecurity. At the University of Alabama, there were the added burdens of a fragmented and disillusioned alumni and a disorganized and mediocre athletic program with outstanding debts. Denny also faced in Alabama in 1912 a scattered and struggling farm populace still unconvinced of the value of education beyond grade school and wary of the burden of taxes to pay for it. And most challenging of all, he found in Alabama an unfriendly state legislature with which he pleaded for adequate and equitable funding for the University with minimal success throughout his career. Yet the confident, scholarly, forty-one-year-old Denny set his course without fear. He had obviously been fully informed of the problems confronting the University of Alabama before accepting the presidency of the institution, and he arrived in Tuscaloosa with a proven plan and the determination to solve many of those problems. During the spring of 1912, he scrutinized every University expense to ensure financial stability; launched an extensive and innovative recruiting program to bring in more students; organized University alumni into districts to which he traveled to generate legislative and student recruiting support, and began a search for new, key faculty members.

Some alumni equated greater numbers of students with the definition of a great university, a premise with which Denny disagreed. He did, however, consider increased enrollment vital to the growth of the University and he immediately set out to recruit more students. Increasing student enrollment proved to be an easier task for Denny at Alabama than it had been at Washington and Lee, where he adopted an idea from faculty member Addison Hogue and wrote to high schools seniors in a successful recruiting effort. Denny used the same approach at Alabama, sending printed but personally signed letters to every high school senior in the state beginning in the spring of 1912 urging them to attend the University of Alabama and offering his personal assistance in the effort. After getting a list of names from the high schools, Denny sent separate letters to male and female seniors outlining the opportunities available to them at the University. Denny did not express concerns over enrollment numbers at the May 1912 board of trustees meeting, and with good reason. His spring recruiting letters were already bringing results and eventually produced a record enrollment of more than 500 on-campus students—almost half of whom were freshmen—in September. A *Tuscaloosa News* report said fall registration included 249 new students (freshmen) and that sixty-two of the state's sixty-seven counties were represented in the overall number. With only 127 high schools and no mandatory attendance requirements in the state in 1912, responses to Denny's letters were minimal at the start, but they grew steadily as the number of high schools increased and within a decade the responses to Denny's annual recruiting letters numbered more than a thousand a year. Campus enrollment also increased steadily from 1912 onward, reaching 4,896 during Denny's last semester as president in the fall of 1936. Enrollment could easily have been far greater, however; the University rejected from 350 to 850 out-of-state students per year due to campus overcrowding during the decade beginning in 1930.

Denny had also utilized on-campus employment for students at Washington and Lee, and he offered similar assistance at Alabama to help students hurdle the financial barrier that would otherwise have kept many away. Denny soon established a formal self-help bureau—his version of today's college work-study program—that employed scores of students in various campus jobs that allowed them to work their way through school. "There have been in past years intimations from uninformed sources that the University of Alabama is largely patronized by the sons and daughters of well-to-do people," Denny told the trustees in June 1915 in discussing the success of his "self-help" program. "Never was there a more erroneous impression. The student body of the University of Alabama is typically representative of the population of the state. The institution is patronized by all classes and conditions of men. It is a pure democracy. There are gathered here the sons and daughters of farmers, mechanics, lawyers, clergymen, laborers, bookkeepers, blacksmiths, clerks, carpenters, engineers, paperhangers, physicians, seamstresses, bankers, merchants and men and women engaged in scores of others occupations. It is estimated that more than one half of the student body of the University is wholly or partially self-supporting. Including the summer school, it is estimated that more than three fourths of the students who attend the University belong to this worthy class," he added. He said the students were employed in such jobs as janitors; power plant, laundry and cafeteria workers; clerical assistants, and groundskeepers. "The fine thing is that the young men accept every opportunity. Our only problem is to supply positions to all who are seeking work," Denny added. Room, board and fees for the thirty-six-week regular session were $168 for male students in 1912 while women students paid $15 more. By 1918-1919, fees had increased $9 per year for men and $20 per year for women. Fees for off-campus students were $24 per year in 1912-1913 and $33 per year in 1918-1919.

University enrollment figures from the early 1900s included students enrolled at the Medical School in Mobile. Those figures include record marks of 573 in 1907-1908 and 591 in 1908-1909. Tuscaloosa enrollment for the years 1908-1911 remained near the 400 mark each year, however, and Denny reported to the trustees in May 1912 that only 398 on-campus students had completed the spring semester following a reported fall 1911 enrollment of 453. A high dropout rate at the time was normal because many of the students entering college were poorly prepared, and Denny told the trustees matter-of-factly that some students had been eliminated due to poor grades. "It is not to be expected that each student allowed to matriculate will be filled by preparation or by tenacity of purpose to do the work that is required of a high-grade college," he said. "It is best for the individual and the for the college that the unprepared and the indolent student shall, after a fair period of probation, be eliminated from the institution by fixed and wisely administered regulations such as now obtain at the University of Alabama." The comments were Denny's first and final warning that he would not compromise the academic standards of the University to maintain enrollment numbers. Denny also raised entrance requirements regularly over the next few years as the University acted to meet and maintain the highest national entrance and graduation standards.

There were few fully qualified high school teachers in the state in 1912 and Denny saw an immediate need and opportunity to recruit and further train the teachers in the public school system. "It is undoubtedly the duty of the University to furnish the great mass of men and women who are to teach in the high schools of Alabama," he told University trustees. "It is essential that these teachers shall have an opportunity to secure standard college training. This training should include the work offered in the School of

Education at the University of Alabama. Such an opportunity is available to them in no other college in Alabama." Denny wrote to the state's high school teachers in the spring of 1912 also, personally inviting them to attend summer school to work toward a degree that promised higher pay. That effort paid a double dividend for the University, of course, as it increased summer school enrollment and prepared more teachers to better prepare more high school graduates who might also attend the University. Records show that summer school enrollment had remained below 300 during the years 1908-1911, but Denny's recruiting letters brought 517 students to campus in the summer of 1912, more than doubling the enrollment of 1911. Summer enrollment, made up almost exclusively of high school teachers, increased steadily each year afterward, reaching 562 in 1913, 633 in 1914, 735 in 1915, 782 in 1916 and 790 in 1917 before a slight drop to 695 in 1918 due to World War I. Summer enrollment reached 1,250 in 1921, surpassing the 1,000 mark for the first time.

Only fifty-five women students were enrolled at the University in the spring of 1912 and any possible increase in enrollment was hampered by the absence of adequate women's housing, prompting Denny to immediately push for construction of a modern women's dormitory. Governor O'Neal, keeping a promise made during the hiring of Denny to support the new president, released $40,000 in previously appropriated University building funds and the first phase of Tutwiler Hall, the first modern women's dormitory on campus, was completed in 1915. Located on the site now occupied by the Rose Administration Building, Tutwiler was immediately filled to its capacity of fifty-four students. "This action has been universally acclaimed," Denny told the trustees after completion of the dormitory. "It is obvious that in taking this great forward step the authorities of the University are performing a long-deferred duty and correcting an essential injustice to the women of the commonwealth." A 1914 *Crimson White* editorial praised the addition of women's dormitory, saying, "Now our co-eds are to have a beautiful home, designed in colonial architecture, having all modern conveniences, including reception parlors, ample dining rooms, kitchen, matrons' apartments, steam heat and electric lights. Besides, the site is so desirable that they will be suitably segregated from the (men's) barracks and will at the same time be within convenient distance from lecture rooms."

Men and women students were routinely kept at a distance except during classes during the early 1900s, although a December 1913 *Crimson White* story did mention that women students had been allowed to join the men for Thanksgiving dinner in the Woods Hall cafeteria in their second joint dining experience of the year. Prior to the construction of Tutwiler Hall, women students lived in a campus house known as "The Ranch" or boarded in private homes nearby. The number of women students jumped from eighty in 1915 to 214 in 1920 following the completion of a fifty-room addition to Tutwiler Hall and reached almost 500 in 1926 after the addition of a second Tutwiler wing and the completion of the first three sorority houses on campus. To further support the increasing number of women students, Denny selected Mrs. Frederick Losey as the school's first dean of women in 1914. Lousea Keys, who had previously taught at Alabama College in Montevallo, joined the University faculty in 1917 as head of the new department of domestic science and arts as additional courses for women were added. A department of music was organized in 1917 also, with Robert Lawrence as the first professor of music.

Within two years after his arrival in Tuscaloosa, Denny's problem relating to student numbers shifted from too few to too many. He announced in January 1914 that more than 600 students had enrolled for the spring semester and that all campus housing was filled to "uncomfortable and inconvenient" limits. Enrollment continued to grow, however, reaching more than 633 in the summer of 1914, 745 in the fall of 1914, 735 in the summer of 1915 and 774 during the regular 1915-1916 session. Denny, of course, did not claim credit for the rapid growth. Reporting to the trustees in May 1916, Denny instead attributed the increase in University enrollment to the growth of the high school system and "the high quality of service" offered by the University. He also told the trustees that the University had "reached its limit in numerical growth pending the time when there shall be a larger income available for the employment of a larger teaching staff."

In addition to organizing University alumni into districts and touring the state speaking to the various groups to gain their support, Denny hired popular Tuscaloosa newspaper editor and music director Thomas H. "Uncle Tom" Garner as alumni secretary in 1915 and an alumni newsletter was begun in 1917 to help maintain communications between the campus and alumni. Garner, who had led the University Glee Club since 1906, served as alumni secretary until 1944.

Fully aware of student and alumni interest in football and other competitive sports, Denny also began a complete overhaul of the school's athletic program, including restoring competitive basketball in 1913 and the construction of new athletic facilities in all sports. By the summer of 1915, football, baseball and track had been moved from what is now the Quad to what became Denny Field behind the President's Mansion and a new, $40,000 gymnasium (Little Hall) had been constructed. Under Denny's close supervision, the athletic program, which had been in debt on his arrival, was profitable by May 1913. Thomas Kelley, a proven coach who had played for Amos Alonzo Stagg at the University of Chicago, was hired as head football coach in 1915 and posted a 17-7-1 record in three seasons as Denny, who had played football and even coached for a season, gave his personal attention to the sport that would eventually win national acclaim for the school. During his tenure as president Denny hired four football coaches who produced a combined won-lost record of 222-53-14, claimed five national and eight conference championships and posted a 5-2-1 bowl record from 1915-1946. Denny recognized the value of a successful football program in uniting the alumni and attracting students and received a great deal of credit—and some criticism—for his hands-on supervision of the program.

Denny took several actions to build campus spirit during his early months as president, including the establishment of an honor system similar to that established by General Lee at Washington and Lee; the development of a student government association; creation of a Phi Beta Kappa chapter to encourage academic achievement; installation of campus sidewalks, curbs and graded streets, and the organization of a student band with physics professor Dr. Gustav Wittig as director. The 15-member band made its debut at the first home football game in 1914. One of Denny's last hires as president of the University came in 1935, when he chose high school band director Carlton K. Butler as University band director. Butler, later awarded the honorary rank of colonel by University ROTC leaders, led the Million Dollar Band until his retirement in 1969. Denny took another significant step in early 1912 when he revealed a plan to move fraternities from off-campus locations to the campus, with the University providing the property and low-interest loans to build the modern fraternity houses on what would soon become "Fraternity Row." Denny said bringing the fraternities to the campus would allow the students greater involvement in campus life and provide additional student housing. Phi Gamma Delta opened the first fraternity house on campus on February 21, 1914, and Sigma Alpha Epsilon was second when it opened in September 1914. Sorority Row developed several years later in the same manner, with the first three sorority houses opening in 1924.

Denny also took a personal hand in the general appearance of the University by supervising the planting of trees and shrubbery, construction of sidewalks and curbs, grading of streets, campus design and especially in the choice of architectural style of buildings constructed during his tenure. Morgan, Comer and Smith Halls, constructed of Missouri yellow brick in the Beaux-Arts architectural style, were the newest buildings on campus when Denny arrived, having been built between 1907 and 1911. The thirty-nine permanent buildings constructed during the Denny era were of the Georgian architectural style, patterned after the President's Mansion.

Denny made significant changes and additions to the faculty soon after his arrival, creating a new, revitalized academic environment. New faculty members who joined Denny's team during his first two years included Albert J. Farrah; Dr. George J. Davis; Dr. James S. Thomas; Dr. John Gallalee; Lee Bidgood and Shaler Houser. Farrah, a Virginia native educated at Cornell and Michigan, came to the University in 1912 from the University of Florida, where he had served as dean of the law school. Farrah was first named assistant dean of the law school and became dean of the school the following year when former dean W. B. Oliver was elected to the U. S. Senate. Bidgood held an A. M. degree from University of Virginia and was later named the first dean of the School of Commerce and Business Administration. Thomas, a graduate of Milligan College, joined the University faculty in 1912 as professor of secondary education and later became director of extension services. Houser, a University of Alabama graduate, joined the University in 1912 as professor of engineering and treasurer, bursar and registrar. Davis, a graduate of Cornell University, was hired in 1913 as professor of chemical engineering and dean of the College of Engineering. Gallalee, another University of Virginia graduate, was hired in 1913 as professor of mechanical engineering and ended a forty-year career at the University by serving as president 1948-53. Dr. Jack Montgomery, who like Denny held a doctoral degree from the University of Virginia, had also joined the faculty in September 1911 as a chemistry professor.

The new faculty members joined a staff that included Dr. James J. Doster, professor of secondary education and dean of education who had joined the University faculty in 1907; Dr. Charles Barnwell, dean of the University faculty, dean of the School of Arts & Sciences and English professor; Dr. Stewart Lloyd, dean of the School of Chemistry, Metallurgy and Ceramics and professor of chemistry and metallurgy, and others comprising a faculty of only twenty-nine members when Denny arrived. Others who joined the faculty and staff during Denny's tenure as president and rose to prominence included Fred Maxwell; Martha Parham; Mary Burke; Hudson Strode; Dr. Walter B.

Jones; Ralph E. Adams; Gordon D. Palmer; Dr. John McLure; Jeff Coleman; Dr. James S. McLester; Agnes Ellen Harris; Dr. Albert B. Moore; Clarence Cason; William F. "Billy" Adams, and football coaches Wallace Wade and Frank Thomas. McLester, a University of Virginia Medical School graduate, joined the faculty in 1925 as a professor of medicine and later became head of the University Medical School faculty. He played a key role in Denny's November 1928 decision to remain at the University rather than return to his former position as president of Washington and Lee University. Denny had apparently made up his mind to accept the Washington and Lee offer, but changed his mind after McLester warned him that the change might endanger his fragile health. Many of these pioneer educators—builders of the modern University alongside Denny—are remembered on campus today as buildings bearing their names stand in their honor. Those key faculty members made up Denny's closest associates and friends, and in addition to recommending that campus buildings be named in their honor, Denny remembered them in a February 22, 1936, address to alumni in Montgomery when he said, "God being my witness, I shall never forget those who have wrought with me in the stirring events of the quarter century now drawing to a close."

Denny took his self-imposed mission of "wise, tactful, aggressive agitation" for the cause of education seriously. He began a long and difficult task of educating the citizens of Alabama on the value of education immediately after his arrival by accepting every possible speaking engagement tendered. Without radio or television and little in the way of newspaper coverage in 1912, personal appearances obviously provided the main means of communication. Denny traveled the state like an elixir drummer, promoting education as a cure for the ills of poverty and ignorance and the way to independence and better government. He spoke at civic club luncheons, high school graduations, hardware conventions, YMCA meetings, educational and religious gatherings, student assemblies and any other place he was invited, often speaking as many as six times a week, as he once noted in a letter to a friend. He urged development of the state's natural resources, the state docks in Mobile, the mineral-rich Muscle Shoals area and river navigation, but always included his exhortation that "our greatest natural resource is the neglected child." His dreams of better living conditions were an easy sell to young farm boys and girls who believed his statement that "Ignorance is lack of opportunity for education," but it was far more difficult to convince legislators and taxpayers to provide that opportunity.

Although Denny attempted to make it so, education was not the major concern of most Alabamians during his early years in the state. He competed for newspaper headlines with typhoid and flu epidemics, World War I, the women's suffrage movement, the arrival of electricity, mine disasters, cotton prices, prohibition, train robberies, lynchings, moonshine raids, rabid dogs, automobile accidents and politics. And although Denny had told University alumni in November 1911 that athletics were "important but not the main attraction," news of victories by Alabama's "Thin Red Line" or "Crimson Tide" regularly attracted more attention in newspapers than Denny's frequent calls for more taxes to build schools in which to educate the leaders needed to build a better society, state and democracy. It was surely far from true, but a review of newspaper reports of the era gives the impression that Denny stood alone in his fight to build a "great" University. Denny's impassioned pleas for additional funding, made in annual reports to trustees during commencement weekend each year, were often lost in newspaper reports focusing on the number of graduates rather than the issues raised by Denny, and if any newspaper editorial took issue with legislature's failure to equitably and adequately fund the University, it has thus far escaped discovery. Denny, frustrated but undeterred, simply continued to appeal to the legislature to "do its duty."

Few if any leaders outside the field spoke out for improved schools of any kind; supporters did not march to Montgomery to echo Denny's calls for equitable and adequate funding for the University, and no one called for the impeachment of Governor Charles Henderson when he vetoed a special $10,000 legislative appropriation in 1915 that would have secured a $40,000 grant for the University from the Peabody Foundation. Henderson, a Troy banker and cotton buyer with many other business interests, was a founder and a trustee of Troy Normal School (now Troy University) and later also a trustee of Alabama Polytechnic Institute (now Auburn University). During the same 1915 legislative session, Marshall County senator John A. Lusk, a member of the finance and taxation committee, called the University of Alabama "Auburn's greatest enemy" as he spoke out against appropriations for the University when Tuscaloosa senator James C. Brown originally offered a bill appropriating $170,000 to the University for housing for women students and the upgrading of the medical and law schools. The appropriation was cut to $10,000 in the House before Henderson, saying the state could not afford the expenditure, vetoed the bill and deprived the University of the much-needed $40,000 Peabody Foundation grant.

Governor O'Neal, speaking at a University of Alabama alumni banquet on June 3, 1914, called for changes to the state constitution to aid education. A June 3, 1914, *Tuscaloosa News* story quoted O'Neal as saying that the constitution "hampered the state in making many progressive moves which are necessary for the advancement of the people." The story added that O'Neal, an 1873 University of Alabama graduate, "called attention to the fact that under the present constitution there could be no inheritance tax, no income tax, no local taxation for schools…and that with certain changes in the constitution there could be provided regular income for the University and other institutions…." The 1915 state legislature, responding to the ex-governor's call, passed a comprehensive constitutional amendment aiding public education in the state. The amendment, approved by voters in November 1916 and effective October 1, 1917, provided for the creation of a state illiteracy commission; allowed local school taxes where approved by voters; offered a special state appropriation to counties that levied local taxes; established a compulsory attendance law requiring children ages 8-16 to attend school 80 days per year until completion of the eighth grade; provided a special fund for rural schools, and made women eligible for election to boards of education.

"I doubt whether any Southern legislature in fifty years has done as much for education as did the Alabama legislature of 1915," Denny said in an address to the Educational Association of Virginia in November 1917. A 1919 U. S. Bureau of Education report on education in Alabama also praised the 1915 legislation. "The machinery was now provided for supporting a system of free public schools— machinery which from the birth of the state the framers of constitutional provisions seemed loath to see pass to the hands of the people…. If now the people will clearly see a public responsibility in the provision of schools and will wisely put ample public money in them as an investment paying large dividends the state may soon take educational rank suited to its great material advantages," the report said. Although there is no mention of Denny's direct involvement in the writing and passage of the 1915 amendment, it is evident that he was influential in the content and passage of the law since he had been a leading and outspoken advocate of such action since his arrival in the state more than three years earlier.

Denny, often praised as a financial genius during his tenure as University president, expressed his initial frustration with University finances in his first report to the trustees in May 1912 when he pointed out that the University was receiving only $35,000 per year in actual annual state appropriations, including $5,000 for the medical school and $5,000 for summer school. An additional state payment of $36,000 per year was in fact interest due the University "in settlement of old claims," Denny said. "No stretch of the imagination could in justice transform this interest charge into an appropriation. It is a sacred debt, just as sacred as the landed debt of the commonwealth." Saying that on his arrival at the University, there had been "a decided feeling of depression concerning the condition of the University treasury," Denny told the trustees that he had made it his first duty to study the financial situation of the institution and had meanwhile insisted on "the most rigid economy in every direction as the one remedy to the then existing condition of affairs." Setting the fiscal policy for his entire tenure, Denny added that he had "personally investigated and approved every expenditure and not a single dollar has gone out of the treasury without the most painstaking and critical examination of the purposes for which it was to be used. The results of this policy are made manifest in the treasurer's report," Denny continued. "It will, I am sure, be deeply gratifying to the trustees to note that in spite of all the unusual demands that have been made on the treasury, the actual financial condition of the University is better than anyone could have hoped," he added, pointing to a balance of $25,627.46 in the maintenance fund when a balance of $9,804 had been anticipated.

Telling trustees that much of his time from January through May had been spent in "careful and critical study of the cardinal problems and needs of the University," Denny listed several concerns, including physical, financial, organizational and course offerings. He focused mainly on financial matters, however, saying that "the legislature has perhaps given too little study to the real needs of the University of Alabama. It is giving to the state University little, if anything, more than is being appropriated annually to the agricultural and mechanical college (Auburn), which, in addition to the state appropriation, enjoys a large and increasing annuity from the federal government." Denny also offered a long list of University needs during his 1912 report to trustees, including a school of commerce or business administration; a women's dormitory; a men's gymnasium; a men's dormitory; a library building; increased funding to provide a larger teaching force to meet the needs of increased enrollment; a campus hospital; proper furnishings for existing dormitories; the upgrade of the law school from a two-year course of study to three years, and additional funding to maintain buildings and grounds.

The Montgomery Advertiser followed Denny's first report to University trustees with an enthusiastic editorial offering praise for his efforts after only six months on the job. "Greater, richer and more powerful as an influence for good than at any time in the past is the University of Alabama, whose annual commencement exercises have just come to a brilliant close," the editorial began. "*The Advertiser* is gratified beyond measure at the splendid spirit of harmony which now exists in the University organization. There is no friction among the faculty or board of trustees. The alumni are at peace with the makers of the University. President Denny, an educator of force and character, is withal a diplomat and a splendid executive. There is no doubt that he is the central personality about which the University organization revolves. He has worked energetically all of this year endeavoring to strengthen this already powerful institution. He wants the summer school to make the greatest record of its history this year. He wants more co-eds—by the hundreds if he can get them. He wants more young men students, and he is getting them. *The Advertiser* is gratified particularly with the moderate recommendations of the president concerning the finances of the institution. His ideas along this line appeared so conservative and practical to the trustees that the board adopted his budget without change." And in even more flattering and perhaps somewhat premature praise, the editorial added, "The University is rapidly working itself into the forefront of Southern educational institutions. It is turning out men and women fit to enter the professional and industrial world and make a living. The *Advertiser* is happy over the present conditions of the University and but echoes the sentiments of every true Alabamian when it wishes for our institution the brightest future possible."

The *Birmingham Age-Herald* took note of the record summer and fall enrollments of 1912, and in late September, after Denny had proclaimed the University of Alabama "the capstone of the public educational system in Alabama," applauded Denny's early success. "The University, in entering upon its new era of progress, has made its leadership strongly felt," the editorial began. "Dr. Denny, the president, is evidently the right man in the right place. He believes in thoroughness in university achievement. He is making the University of Alabama attractive to aspiring youth and it may be safely predicted that this time next year the registrar's books will show an enrollment of not less than 1,000." The prediction was overly optimistic, however; enrollment did not reach the 1,000 mark until September 1918, when 1,165 students registered for the fall semester.

The 1913 *Corolla* was the first of three dedicated to Denny (The others were 1936 and 1956.) and read as follows: "Words of dedication need not be written. The Corolla for 1913 is only one of the scores of tasks and labors whose successful completion by the students of the University of Alabama has been materially aided by the inspiration drawn from the force, the vigor and the power for good exemplified in the life and arts of President George H. Denny." The 1912 *Corolla*, published only a few months after his arrival in Tuscaloosa, had also praised Denny, saying that as an educator he "exhibits a many-sidedness that makes him particularly fitted for a college presidency. He is a keen observer of human nature and his understanding of college life and college affairs makes him an appreciative sympathizer and a kindly adviser of all students with whom he comes in contact. His evident sincerity, his earnestness of purpose and his simple, direct methods have already won the admiration and respect of all students of the University. Alabama is indeed to be congratulated in obtaining for her executive head a man so capable of placing her among our leading institutions of education, where she of a right belongs."

By May 1914, Denny had fully analyzed state funding of higher education and found that the University was receiving only fifty-seven percent of the average funding per student for twenty state institutions shown in a study conducted by the University of Kentucky. The average per-student income for the twenty schools was $317 while the University received only $180 per student excluding summer school and only $115 per student including summer school. "I find that there is almost a total lack of correct information in certain quarters concerning the whole question of state aid to the University and the per capita cost of maintenance," Denny said. "I have therefore given this matter exhaustive investigation. I find that the amount of money unconditionally appropriated to the University under fixed statue is materially smaller than is the case in any other tax-supported university in the nation. I likewise find that the per capita cost based on the amount of aid received from the state is strikingly lower than in any similar institution in the country…. It is, however, to be hoped that the legislature will unhesitatingly determine to give to the institution standing at the head of the public school system of the state at least a reasonable annuity. The University has already for a long period suffered from its position of isolation at the bottom round of the ladder in the matter of state support…. It is the duty of the state to change this unsatisfactory situation."

Denny also presented figures showing that under the 1907 legislation granting the University of Alabama $35,000 per year in total funding Auburn received an appropriation of $40,000 from the state and another $27,500 from a federal grant. He also showed figures representing total income from all sources from each school for 1912-1913, with Alabama receiving $152,527 and Auburn $186,487. "There is a general impression that the federal grants are made directly to the agricultural college," Denny continued. "That is far from the fact. They are made to the states, and the disposition or distribution of these funds has been left to the state. It is therefore legally and ethically true that a federal grant is nothing more or less than a fund appropriated by the state. I have taken pains to discuss these matters somewhat in detail in order to make clear to the trustees the simple, outstanding fact that the University is not receiving state aid in any such way as its importance and its needs imperatively demand. I have the utmost confidence that if the facts are clearly shown, the legislature will be disposed to remedy a situation that ought in justice to be remedied without further delay." After presenting the need for additional state funding, Denny told the trustees that the financial status of the University, "in spite of the very inadequate support it is receiving from the legislature, has been steadily improving in view of the rigid economy practiced. It is, however, exceedingly important that the trustees shall squarely face the outstanding fact that largely increased appropriations from the state treasury are imperatively demanded if the University is to do its full duty and to keep in line with the universities of other states. We are charged with presenting to the legislature all the facts that relate to the institution—its needs, its plans and its ever-increasing responsibilities. I desire that this matter shall be fully considered by the trustees at this meeting. It is by far the most important question that can at this time engage our attention," he added.

Denny testified at a legislative committee hearing in March 1915 that he had accepted the presidency of the University of Alabama on the condition and promise that Governor O'Neal would release appropriations to the University made by the

1911 legislature. The University received warrants—the equivalent of IOUs—for the funds in 1914 after lending the state $27,500 from its endowment fund to meet interest payments, prompting the legislative committee to question the timing of the transactions. A *Tuscaloosa News* report on the hearing said Denny was asked why the University got one hundred percent of its appropriation while other institutions got only fifty percent. "Dr. Denny asked Representative Joseph Green of Dallas County if he thought it discriminatory if the institutions which got only fifty percent (Auburn and Montevallo) got at the same time more actual money than the institution which got one hundred percent (Alabama). Representative Green answered 'no,'" the *News* report said.

In addressing the legislative hearing, Denny said, "There can be in my opinion no possible justification for the historic and habitual parsimony that has been shown in the matter of supporting our most important seat of learning. The University of Alabama has been reduced in large degree to the necessity of living on the income derived from a modest endowment, from student fees, from rental of rooms and from the constitutional provision made by the state to pay the old land grant debt.... No human being can deny that we have practiced the most rigid economy. It is simply impossible to administer the institution on a more economical basis. I submit that it is not an economy to allow valuable property to depreciate owing to the lack of a modest fund for upkeep. I submit that it is not an economy to be carrying less than half the insurance protection than is imperatively needed. I submit that it is not an economy to be overcrowding classrooms when fundamental educational efficiency demands smaller groups instead of larger groups. I submit that it is not an economy to be conducting a two-year law school when the national standard demands a three-year course. It is true that we have reduced the per capita cost of instruction to a startling minimum, yet there is a limit to all things, and I am here to say that we have reached that limit. Four years ago, when the student body was only half its present size, the legislature deliberately decided that the so-called conditional appropriations should be voted. By what rule of reason should these essential appropriations be denied the institution at this time when it is serving two students for every one that was being served at the time the appropriation was made?" Denny asked.

Denny's pleas for equal funding fell on deaf ears, however. A report of state funding for education in 1918, published in the February 6, 1919, *Crimson White*, showed a total expenditure of $3,385,385.95, with $2,527,847.69 going to public grade schools; $171,000 to county high schools; $117,280 to Auburn; $81,345 to the Alabama School for Deaf and Blind; $71,000 to the University of Alabama; $54,932 to Alabama College, and $55,987 to the Boys Industrial School as the major recipients. The state, for whatever reasons during Henderson's tenure as governor, did not redeem the 1914 warrants issued to the University, and the 1919 legislature eventually repealed the 1911 act granting the appropriations, making the warrants worthless and costing the University $150,000, according to a Denny report to the board of trustees. The same 1919 legislature, at the urging of new governor Thomas E. Kilby, approved new University appropriations totaling approximately $210,000 for 1919-1922, however, as it more than doubled state funding for education at all levels over the next four years. University of Alabama appropriations included $115,000 in building funds, $40,000 for the Medical School, $12,500 for the extension division and additional maintenance funds. Kilby, in a letter to Denny following his election, had thanked Denny for an assessment of the state's educational needs and said the information would form the basis of his 1919 educational reform proposal, indicating at least one political victory for Denny.

"While these sums are entirely inadequate in view of the depreciated dollar and the increased burden resting on the institution by virtue of the growing number of students, we feel a sense of gratitude that the legislature found a way to give even partial relief in a critical financial situation," Denny said of the 1919 appropriations. "While the $115,000 for building purposes is a very small sum, it will enable us to build one structure of reasonable size. There is an overwhelming demand for new buildings, including a library, a social-religious building, a chemistry building, a law building, an educational building, additional dormitories and an administration building. These and other buildings are greatly needed, but perhaps the most pressing demand is to give some sort of relief in the chemistry department and to provide permanent quarters for the preclinical courses in medicine," Denny added in recognition of the fact that the Medical School was being moved from Mobile to Tuscaloosa in 1920 after being downgraded from Class A to Class B by the Council on Medical Education. There was indeed great need for new buildings. There were only nine main buildings on campus when Denny arrived in 1912 and only two—a men's gymnasium and a women's dormitory—had been added during his first seven years in office due to lack of funding, even as enrollment had more than tripled. Although it appeared that little could be done with the $115,000 appropriated by the legislature, it provided the kindling for an astounding building boom that added eleven major buildings, a new football stadium and numerous fraternity and sorority houses to the campus over the next decade.

The initial funding for the extension division proved significant also, as Denny had predicted in citing the need for an extension division in his 1915 report to University trustees. "The University lacks the means to perform so obvious a duty as to engage effectively in any single phase of extension work, which constitutes a large and so important a part in a modern university program," Denny told the trustees. "This great field of service, by means of which an institution projects its educational focus beyond the campus, is carried on in state universities through various agencies. Through the aid of the General Education Board, the department of secondary education, cooperating with the state department of education, has done a monumental work in developing and strengthening the public high schools. Yet the legislature has done nothing to provide an opportunity to organize the extramural service that it is eager to render. We shall not desist until we have been permitted to satisfy every community needing help to enrich its life if such help can be found in these halls." Denny added that "The great task of helping to conserve the public health, of bettering social and economic conditions, building up a sound school system, of suggesting modern methods in taxation and in municipal procedure, of establishing correspondence study, of giving lectures in various communities, of providing extension teaching, of conducting community conferences and institutes, of stimulating debate in the high schools, of making surveys and investigations on subjects of community and state importance and of reaching out into an infinite number of other avenues of human service is a task that challenges our fundamental efficiency as a state university. The state cannot afford to deny to us the opportunity to serve the people in every high and helpful way. The trustees have already put on record the fact that they are not unconscious of the duty and the responsibility of the University to do for Alabama in this great field what is being done by the state universities of other progressive states. It is simply and solely a question of finances. The legislature alone can remedy the situation." With Dr. James Thomas as its director and only minimal funding, the extension division began operation in September 1920 with 186 student enrollees but quickly grew to 501 in 1921, 850 in 1922 and to 1,261 in 1923. Enrollment in extension courses reached 2,129 in 1925, 3,085 in 1929, 4,102 in 1934 and 6,490 in 1936.

The additional funding also allowed the University to establish the School of Commerce and Business Administration and extend the law school course to three years to comply with national standards, as Denny had long requested. His wish list was far from fulfilled, however. In reporting record enrollments of 845 for the summer of 1919 and 1,216 for the spring 1920 session, Denny told the trustees in May 1920 that the numbers brought "a sobering sense of responsibility and a note of warning." He said enrollment figures showed that the University was "carrying a load out of proportion to its financial strength. The state has not provided the means necessary to meet the situation. The per capita cost is far too low to guarantee the best results. The teaching force is too small and the salary scale is inadequate," he added, pointing out that the average teaching salary at the University of Alabama was $2,800 compared to $3,600 at the University of Mississippi. He added, however, that the financial status of the University had been steadily improving "in spite of the very inadequate support it is receiving from the legislature."

World War I had a temporary negative impact on the University, as it did for much of the nation and world. In addition to losing students to the war effort, Denny answered the call of duty himself when he left the University in March 1918 to serve as director of the Cotton Seed Industry in the U. S. Food Administration for approximately eight months. He resigned from his government post soon after the November 11 Armistice and returned to the University on December 1. The 1918 Crimson Tide football season was cancelled because the University was under military control from October 1 until mid-November and most male students were involved in military training and not granted time for practice. In April 1920, members of the Tuscaloosa American Legion planted oak trees along University Avenue from one side of campus to the other in honor of Tuscaloosa County men killed in World War I. At time they were planted, each tree had a marker dedicating the tree to an individual soldier. Many of the trees remain almost a century later.

Despite the tireless efforts of Denny and other state educational leaders, there had been little overall social, economic or cultural change in Alabama by 1920, due mainly to the lack of funding for education. As pointed out in "Alabama: The History of a Deep South State" (University of Alabama Press 1994), the state still spent only fifty-four percent of the national per-pupil average on education in 1920 and state funding for higher education per capita was less than any state except Arkansas. The book also noted that in 1918 the Alabama educational system ranked fourth from last in one national survey and that during the 1920s seventy-eight percent of the state's population still lived on small family farms, "mired in the world of their grandfathers—a world of sharecropping, one-mule farms, slavish reliance on cotton and ruinous economic cycles." According to the National Bureau of Economic Research, Alabama ranked forty-fifth among the forty-sixth states in per capita expenditures for education, forty-sixth in literacy and forty-sixth in per capita income in 1920. There was a ray of hope on the horizon, however. University of Alabama enrollment had quadrupled during Denny's first eight years, indicating an increased interest in education. In one of the most important steps, sixty of the state's sixty-seven counties had approved a local three-mill property tax for public schools by April 1919, and Denny had actively campaigned for approval of the tax, as he had earlier for the constitutional amendment that allowed the vote. Denny made speeches at three locations in Tuscaloosa County, where the tax was approved by a 667-262 vote on May 15, 1919. He also had letters printed for University students to send home to their parents urging approval of the taxes in their home counties. And in a major sign that Denny's voice was finally being heard, the 1919 state legislature had doubled funding for education at all levels.

Little physical change come to the University of Alabama campus during Denny's first ten years as president due to a lack of funding. Only two new buildings had been added, and older campus buildings had not been modernized. A memo from a professor to Denny dated February 10, 1922, complained of classroom conditions in Clark Hall. "The two small stoves that are present in this room are not in any way enough to provide sufficient heat. In my opinion it will take four stoves, each of which will have to be twice the capacity of the present ones. I also find that provision has been made for electric lights, but there are no bulbs. On dark days, it is almost impossible for the men to do any drawing in this room," the memo said, indicating the basic needs still existing at the time.

There was clearly a clash of cultures during Denny's years as president of the University of Alabama. As a liberal, Denny reached out to educate all the youth of the state, including men and women, rich or poor, in his effort to build a major liberal arts university and to help bring social, economic and cultural change to the state. Opponents pushed in the opposite direction of course, almost at every step. Denny brought fraternities onto the campus; others wanted them banned entirely. Denny supported women's rights to education, voting and holding public office; Alabama U. S. Representative Tom Heflin opposed the idea, saying the movement was supported only "by old maids, unhappy married women, cranks and faddists." Denny allowed dances on campus; local ministers spoke out against them. Denny campaigned for local property taxes to support public schools; many wealthy landowners opposed the taxes. Denny sought equal per capita funding for each institution of higher learning in the state; the state legislature consistently rejected the idea. As an apparent example of the determination of some to keep political power in the hands of the few, the Alabama legislature voted in February 1920 to reject the 19th amendment to the U. S. Constitution, which eventually gave women the right to vote in all states when Tennessee became the thirty-sixth state to ratify the amendment on August 18, 1920. The Alabama legislature finally ratified the amendment as a formality in September 1953, thirty-three years after it had become law.

Although Denny's star had soared among University of Alabama loyalists and those interested in education, the progress he sought came slowly and in small, grudging steps and the battles took a toll on his health. Starting with his tenure at Washington and Lee, Denny worked for two decades without a vacation, even as his workload increased year by year, and by the spring of 1920, he had reached a state of exhaustion that forced him to consider immediate retirement. Nearing what he felt was total collapse, Denny wrote to Carnegie Foundation president Henry Pritchett on May 8 to request an application for the retirement benefits provided by the foundation.

"I am writing you regarding a matter that I have been for some months delaying. Whenever I have been on the point of doing it, I have found myself shrinking from taking the step. I refer to the condition of my health and the apparent imminent necessity of seeking retirement from active service," Denny began. "For the past five years I have been losing flesh and strength. For two or three years I have been resorting to medicinal remedies. The heart is the primary cause of my trouble. During recent months I have experienced growing nervousness. I have found it increasingly difficult to do my work with any degree of physical comfort or mental satisfaction. I am willing to remain at my post, to attempt to stick it out to the end if that is the only alternative, but I have decided to let you know the conditions under which I am attempting to do my work. It is, of course, possible that my health may improve. It is possible that I may in a measure, regain my health; but frankly, I do not expect to be entirely well again. Apparently the doctors give little hope…. I realize that I am hardly beyond middle age. I was born in 1870. I realize that I ought to have some years of active service ahead. I attribute my trouble largely to the fact that I started quite early in life—perhaps too early—in executive work, and under difficult conditions. I have been burning the candle at both ends since I became a college president nineteen years ago. The simple fact is I have for years worked beyond my strength and the physical machinery is now breaking under the load…. I am quite conscious that in suggesting such a step at my age I should be certain that I am not in any way moved by any consideration other than my health. The one thought that moves me is that at the rate at which I have been losing ground recently I cannot hope much longer to do my work at all efficiently. Of course, if I should by any chance regain my health, I should be more than glad, for financial reasons as well as for more important reasons, to get into harness again if the way should be open."

University trustees urged Denny to take an immediate leave of absence of up to six months to regain his health rather than retire and his brother-in-law, Atlanta physician Dr. C. W. Strickler, urged him to take a rest of at least two months. Denny mentioned his health issues in a letter to Auburn president Spright Dowell in August 1920, saying he was considering a leave of absence in an attempt to recuperate, but he continued to work through the rest of the year before finally going to Atlanta during the 1920-21 Christmas break for a thorough physical examination by Strickler, coupled with a few weeks of rest. A *Tuscaloosa News* report on January 5, 1921, said Mrs. Denny had returned to Tuscaloosa with "the most cheering news" regarding Dr. Denny's health. "No organic trouble of any consequence whatever was discovered. It is simply a case of overwork, and every assurance is given that a period of rest in bed for a few weeks, and then an outing of a few weeks more will set everything right," the report said. "It is a well-known fact that not in twenty years, if ever since his entry into public life, has Dr. Denny taken a single day off. There is a limit to all things."

Dr. John Gallalee wrote to Mrs. Denny on January 13, 1921, to express his concern for Dr. Denny, saying "I have never met anyone who, in my judgment, has to as great a degree as Dr. Denny the many-sided qualities and abilities to solve Alabama's problems to the benefit of the state and of the University. The University needs him, but his friends want him well."

Trustee Henry B. Foster wrote Denny on January 19, 1921, saying that he was "delighted to know that there is nothing serious in your condition. I have felt for years that your continuous hard work would sooner or later break you down and that you would be compelled to take a rest. I wish to assure you that we (the trustees) have such a deep appreciation of the wonderful work you have done at the University that we are unwilling that your career shall be cut short on account of over work. Our warm personal regard for you requires that we demand you take such time as necessary to fully restore your former health and strength," Foster added.

Dowell, responding to a February Denny letter mentioning his possible retirement, wrote, "Your confidential letter comes as a distinct shock to me. I knew, of course, that you had been unwell for some two or three years and that you had spent several weeks in the hospital, but I was all the while confident that your extraordinary vigor, your exemplary habits and your indomitable will would bring you through safely. It is nothing short of a tragedy that a state should have overworked so distinguished and invaluable a leader that at the very prime and flower of manhood he should have to put in for repairs…. It is pathetic to the nth degree that such a heavy toll should be exacted of you personally…. Your proposed retirement comes with appalling force."

Strickler consulted with Johns Hopkins University Hospital regarding Denny's health in February 1921, and possible prostate surgery was discussed but not acted upon. Strickler, in letters to Denny, discussed several health issues, including muscle strains, proper diet, a possible ulcer, dental problems, anxiety over his health and general physical and mental exhaustion. "The one thing I want to insist upon is that you forget about yourself, do what we tell you to do and keep happy. Until I give you something to worry about, just forget that you have ever been sick," Strickler wrote in addition to sending prescriptions for several medications.

Weighted down by both health issues and University funding problems, Denny confided to friend in an "absolutely confidential" letter in May 1921 that he was tiring of the daily trials. "I confess that sometimes I crave…retirement far away from 'the maddening crowd's ignoble strife.' Of course, I am writing under a feeling of depression. Perhaps I am unduly depressed. But as Harry Ayers said in his editorial in the *Star* last Sunday, one cannot help feeling that in the absence of adequate financial support, our entire people ought to be willing to give undivided moral support. The bright side of the picture is that the press and the intelligent, unbiased public undoubtedly have rallied overwhelmingly to the University in the recent controversy." The controversy involved a proposal by then-Governor Thomas Kilby for increased property taxes to aid higher education. Denny, of course, campaigned for support of the proposal, which failed. In another indication of his frustration, Denny wrote close friend Borden Burr shortly afterward to say, "…It is difficult ever to make the right progress if our leaders are not willing to listen to expert suggestions."

Denny continued to fret over his health, however, and continued to consider retirement. In October 1922, he wrote to University of Virginia president Edwin Alderman seeking recommendations for a possible successor. "You ought not to be thinking, if I may be dogmatic, of getting out entirely," Alderman began his response. "You are too young. You are ten years my junior, if I recall correctly your age. I know your sensations, however; I have them about once a month…. You are most wise and far-seeing, however, in the matter of thinking about the succession, or certainly the relief."

University trustees, aware of Denny's continued leaning toward retirement, suggested in late 1922 that Denny take an extended vacation. Trustee J. K. Dixon, in writing Denny on October 23, said he had polled the trustees and they had all agreed that Denny should take a vacation of approximately six months "or longer if you want it." Dixon added that trustee Daniel Pratt had written, "I believe that we should really insist on his (Denny) taking a vacation and making it an absolute rest from anything that would tend to worry or annoy him. He is too valuable a man, not only to the University but to the state at large, to allow him to work himself to death if we can keep him from it." Dixon suggested that Denny make any necessary arrangements or suggestions for a prolonged vacation and added that the trustees would readily approve any plan "with the confidence that you will come back to us renewed in health and strength." Denny did not take the immediate action suggested, however.

Denny had another complete physical examination in December 1922, with results similar to those of two years earlier. Dr. James S. McLester, in providing Denny with a written summary of the examination, cited fatigue as his most important health issue. "It is evident that you have experienced years of hard work and close attention to detail. While you take pleasure in your work, the weight of it has nevertheless told upon your nervous system. I am satisfied that there is a nerve weariness which could perhaps be called 'psychasthenia' and that it forms today the basis of your discomfort…. The state of your nervous system is such that little sources of irritation can give you great discomfort and even unhappiness," McLester wrote. After recommending actions for several minor issues, including diet, McLester added, "The above suggested treatment will, I believe, be of little avail unless we go to the bottom of things and give you a long rest with diversion. My feeling is that a leave of absence of several months—six months or even a year—would be advisable. You should go where you will find pleasure and entertainment without serious responsibility. A trip to Europe would be fine. I know this seems radical, but I believe such radical measures are necessary to counteract the effects upon you of twenty-five years of hard, continuous mental labor."

University Medical School Dean Dr. Clyde Brooks wrote Denny in July 1923 to offer his advice on the matter. "…A few vacations each year (about four of two weeks each) would ease the situation. Activity; rest; activity; rest…that is the law of life. After each heartbeat there is a period of rest. It is God's law. You might as well cooperate and get ready to take that vacation. It is the only safe, logical, economical, intelligent thing to do, so I am going to expect you to do it…. It is entirely within your hands to attain a happy degree of physical health and well-being," Brooks said. Denny pushed forward, however, buoyed by the University building program and the successes of the Crimson Tide football team. His health problems persisted as well, however. and Denny told University trustees in May 1927 that he hoped his health would allow him to complete twenty years of service (at the end of 1931) before retirement. In a surprising development in October 1928, Denny seemed prepared to return to Washington and Lee University as president until Dr. McLester advised him that taking on a new task could seriously jeopardize his health. Denny cited McLester's advice in his letter rejecting the Washington and Lee offer soon afterward.

Trustees, alumni and students convinced Denny to remain on the job past his scheduled 1931 retirement, but he mentioned his failing health often over the next few years as he spoke of his impending retirement. In a letter to University trustees dated October 12, 1934, Denny said, "I greatly regret to have to tell you that my health within recent months is not at all what it has been and I am under the necessity of asking many indulgences in the performance of my daily tasks." Another letter, dated later in the month, said, "I have been very unwell during recent months and I find that my responsibilities constitute a growing burden from which I really desire to get some kind of relief. Instead of getting relief, however, it seems to me that the burdens become greater and greater all the time." By December, he was too weak to attend the January 1, 1935, Rose Bowl game in which Alabama defeated Stanford 29-13 to claim its fourth national championship.

Denny urged University trustees to relieve him of his duties in May 1935, but the board, avoiding the inevitable, again delayed action, hoping he would reconsider. Citing exhaustion, Denny finally wrote the trustees in December of 1935, just after his sixty-fifth birthday, to set a firm retirement date of December 31, 1936. When recalled at age seventy-one in 1941 following the sudden death of University president Richard C. Foster, Denny bravely served as president again for ten months, saying, "My strength is not what it once was, but such strength as I have I am glad to give to the cause of the thing that I hold most dear."

Denny waged a constant campaign to raise funds for the University of Alabama.

6

Building a Greater University

"I have thought at times he would kill himself with work, worry and lack of support from the state. Mike likes to see to it himself. I have seen him working for three hours trying to bamboozle a student into staying at the University."

—Dr. Clyde Brooks

Only Mike Denny, who had envisioned the University of Alabama as it should be even before arriving on campus, could have predicted its phenomenal growth in student enrollment and national prominence during the 1920s. He knew from the hundreds of letters from high school seniors each year that the youth of Alabama wanted a college education and he was fully prepared with an extensive building plan to accommodate those students. The seeds of success had been planted; Denny needed only money to move forward with his "Greater University" plan. And as he had done each year since 1912, he continued to call on University trustees, alumni and state legislators for increased financial support throughout the 1920s in an effort to secure that support.

Denny's campus building plan of 1920, presented to the trustees and surely scoffed at as beyond reality by many, included fifteen new buildings with a total estimated cost of three million dollars. The University had managed to construct only two buildings—Tutwiler Hall (women's dormitory, 1914) and Little Hall (men's gymnasium, 1915) during the previous eight years and Denny had only the $115,000 state appropriation of 1919 with which to begin his ambitious undertaking. Somehow, however, with Denny's leadership and usual financial wizardry that made "one dollar do the work of five," the successful "Million Dollar Campaign" of 1922 and an additional $250,000 from the state in 1927, the University managed to construct eleven of those buildings, update two others, provide financing for several fraternities and sororities and more than double its endowment fund over the next decade while adding several new departments and schools of instruction and upgrading academic standards in all areas.

Desperate for building funds and with no additional funding from the state in sight, the University launched a "Million Dollar Campaign" on October 3, 1922, to solicit funds from the school's 6,000 alumni to be used for the construction of new buildings. The drive was patterned after a similar University of Georgia drive that raised

$1.1 million in a month in 1921. The University of Alabama goal was to solicit a pledge of $305 each from University alumni and additional pledges from current students. Alumni pledges were to be paid at the rate of $61 per year for five years while student pledges were to be paid over ten years. Birmingham alumnus Borden Burr was named chairman of the drive and he and Denny toured the state speaking to alumni gatherings in dozens of towns in Alabama and even in New York City during the two-month fundraising campaign. Although no exact final campaign total was publicized, newspaper reports declaring the drive a success indicated that pledges of approximately $957,000 were eventually received. Birmingham and Tuscaloosa had the largest quotas, with $350,000 and $90,000 respectively. Tuscaloosa, with an anonymous donation of $50,000, raised $140,000 in pledges in only three days to far exceed its goal while Birmingham reported $295,000 in pledges on November 25. "It was a splendid and inspiring demonstration of the loyalty of the alumni and friends of the University," Denny said of the drive in his annual report to University trustees in May 1923. "However, the normal period over which the subscriptions are payable is five years. Unfortunately, this means that no large amount of money will be available for any single year and that we must wait for a considerable period to reap the full benefits of the campaign."

A September 27, 1922, *Tuscaloosa News* editorial described the University's financial plight as it called for local support of the drive. "Alabama sounds the call to you, its sons and daughters, in this critical hour of its existence! In the past your University has not failed to give the advantages of an education to any man or woman who came to its doors, and it is proud of this record. But unless expansion is made, your University will be forced into the humiliating position of saying to the state, 'I am helpless. I can do no more. I can carry no farther the work it is my task to do.' All of you know how its attendance has increased four-fold in the past ten years, how no money has been available for the construction of new buildings, how the present buildings are crowded beyond capacity. You know also that the state treasury has not the money for new buildings. In the past the University, considering the large number of departments and branches of instruction, has received proportionately less from the state than any other agency. It is futile to hope for adequate appropriations in the future. And this is the critical hour! Either your University will expand and carry into the future the proud tradition of the past or it will see itself sink backward into the humiliating position of being a follower where it has always led. One million dollars must be had at once to decide the issue. Men and women of the University, when state or nation has called, you have answered, loyally and courageously, unselfishly, with brilliant valor. Men and women of the University, for the first time in its history, Alabama calls!"

Boosted first by the $115,000 state appropriation then the Million Dollar Campaign, Denny immediately launched an extensive campus expansion program that more than doubled classroom space over the next decade. Construction during the 1920s included Gorgas Hall (men's dormitory, 1921), an addition to Tutwiler Hall (women's dormitory, 1921), Nott Hall (medical school, 1922), McLure Library (initially a post office, cafeteria and supply store, 1925), Carmichael Hall (initially Amelia Gayle Gorgas Library, 1925), Farrah Hall (law, 1927), Lloyd Hall (chemistry, 1927), basement addition to Smith Hall (1927), Bidgood Hall (commerce, 1928), Doster Hall (home economics and art, 1929), Graves Hall (education, 1929), Barnwell Hall (women's gymnasium, 1930) and the Alabama Student Union, (now Reese Phifer Hall, 1930). Law school dean Albert J. Farrah raised $42,000 to help build the law building during a 1927 summer campaign in which he personally called on most of the state's law school alumni for contributions. The building was named in his honor for his efforts.

With the help of federal funds from the Works Progress Administration, three more new buildings (Moore Hall, Hardaway Hall and the Bureau of Mines) were constructed during 1935-36, giving the University fourteen of the fifteen major buildings Denny had asked for in 1920 with only $365,000 in total financial assistance from the state. WPA funds also helped build a 6,000-seat East sideline addition to Denny Stadium in 1936.

The Alabama football program gained the national prominence long coveted by avid alumni during the 1920s also as Crimson Tide teams posted an overall record of 82-21-6 from 1920 through 1930. Alabama claimed four Southern Conference championships and three national championships during the period and went unbeaten in three Rose Bowl games. The first two Rose Bowl appearances generated a profit of approximately $75,000, which was used to construct the first 12,000-seat phase of Denny Stadium in 1929. Denny Chimes was also built in 1929 as a gesture of gratitude to Denny for his decision to remain at the University rather than return to Washington and Lee University as president. The major building campaign of the 1930s, including Fraternity Row and Sorority Row, dramatically changed the campus and gave it many of the landmarks of today. By the end of the decade known as the "Roaring Twenties," the University of Alabama had risen to a level of national academic and athletic prominence far exceeding the hopes and expectations of everyone in the state except Denny, who envisioned, inspired and directed the growth.

Student enrollment, as Denny had predicted, kept pace with University expansion. As additional dormitory and classroom space became available, new students quickly filled them. Regular session enrollment grew from 1,216 in the spring of 1920 to 3,891 in the spring of 1930 while summer school enrollment jumped from 845 in 1919 to 2,109 in 1930. Extension division enrollment grew from 186 in 1920, its first year, to 3,085 in 1930 and reached 6,490 in 1936. Many of those enrolled in extension classes were able to hear lectures over radio station WAPI, which was jointly owned by the University of Alabama, Auburn and Alabama College. As the decade of the 1920s ended, Denny could not have been happier. He finally proudly proclaimed the University of Alabama a "great" university and the true capstone of the state's public educational system. The University's rapid expansion soon made it the second-largest University in the South, according to a 1933 U. S. Office of Education publication. The publication listed the University of Tennessee first with an enrollment of 5,174 compared to 4,650 for Alabama. Other universities listed included Kentucky (4,058), Louisiana State (3,832), North Carolina (2,825), Tulane (2,760), Florida (2,242), Auburn (1,721), Vanderbilt (1,338), Mississippi (1,069), Mississippi State (852) and Alabama College (793).

University of Alabama out-of-state student enrollment grew from only three in 1920 to more than 1,200 by the early 1930s, due mainly to the widespread publicity of the football team. More than 350 out-of-state students were turned away in 1930 and more than 850 were rejected two years later as the school's national reputation grew. A University study, prompted by questions from the trustees, showed that out-of-state fees of $60 per year per student added greatly to the University's financial success during the Depression.

Although distracted by his continuing health issues and even the tragic death of his second-oldest daughter in January 1927, Denny did not relent in his "wise, tactful, aggressive agitation" for support for education during the 1920s. In 1921, Denny told the trustees that additional funding was needed to relieve overcrowded classes and overworked instructors. "The state must be prepared to make largely increased appropriations if we are to maintain the University on an adequate basis," he said. "Other Southern states are rapidly developing their universities. Alabama must not be content to lag. The youth of the state must pay the price if its manhood fails. The University has blazed the way to all that is best in our civilization. The proper support of the University as the outstanding agency in this section in training leaders of thought and of industry, in developing our resources, both human and material, and in establishing educational standards is a matter of supreme importance to our civilization…. It deserves well of the commonwealth." A year later, he told the trustees, "The vital problem now confronting the University is the problem of finances. The future depends on the manner in which this problem is solved. It is a critical matter. We have reached the limit of numerical growth pending the time when larger financial resources are available. The state must now say definitely whether it will meet the situation. We are merely the agents of the state. We can do no more than the state is willing and ready to have us do. We are already endeavoring to make one dollar do the work of three. We have reached the ultimate limit in this matter. It is now a question of calling a halt or else enlarging our resources…. Private benefaction must be invoked. We appeal to the people of Alabama to rally to our support." It was those comments that gave rise to the Million Dollar Campaign later in the year.

Even as student enrollment increased dramatically after World War I, the University of Alabama continued to receive inequitable funding from the state legislature. A state auditor's report showed that the University received $278,000 from the state for the year ending September 30, 1921, compared to $352,780 for Auburn. Auburn received $318,280 from the state the following year compared to $263,000 for Alabama, and for the four-year period ending September 1922, Auburn received $1,030,620 in state funding compared to $783,000 for the University of Alabama.

As Governor Thomas Kilby explored tax options to support progressive reforms prior to the 1923 legislative session, Denny campaigned strongly but unsuccessfully for an additional millage tax for higher education. He wrote to Kilby and newspaper editors in the state to plead his case, saying, "All forward-looking citizens deplore the miserly support that has been given our state colleges." He went farther than simply asking for more money, however; he also issued a passionate plea for strict controls on the use of that money to end duplication of courses at the state's three four-year colleges. "I refer to the responsibility of requiring a sane and economical use of the money made available," Denny said. "Wise regulation of the use of money devoted to higher education means that a million dollars will go further than two million under a system of useless duplication of institutional effort…. If the law-making power fails to do its plain duty in this matter, there will be an ever-increasing duplication of work resulting in wanton waste of the taxpayers' money. There will be an ever-increasing spirit of institutional antagonism. There will be a lamentable lack of institutional unity and efficiency which will delay indefinitely the building of a comprehensive, modern system of higher education.

"A reasonable regard for the rights of the taxpayer demands that the law-making power shall require the institutions of higher learning to subordinate their own individual ambition to the larger good of the state…. The question is: Who shall decide what is the sane and right thing to do? Only the disinterested expert is qualified to render that service. Four years ago we summoned a body of experts to show us the way. We have on record their findings. Shall we refuse to accept the findings of our own experts in this matter? Are we to ask the taxpayers to meet the useless expense involved in a refusal on the part of their representatives to meet courageously this issue? If we refuse to meet it, chaos will result. Money will be wasted. The partisan spirit will flourish ever more and more. Inefficiency in the whole field of higher education will be the certain fruit of our folly. Our institutions of higher learning need money and must have it. But in giving it to them, we owe it to them and to the taxpayers to demand in advance of embarking on any program involving largely increased expenditures that disinterested, expert advice shall be respected by them in formulating the curricula they adopt. That is the only way to guarantee economy and efficiency. Let us, therefore, get together and arrange a wise, progressive, statesmanlike program within which all can work with a sense of conviction and enthusiasm—a program that will be approved by the non-partisan expert and which will guarantee real relief from the present congestion rather than leave us at the end with the problem unresolved, the congestion unrelieved and the costly and unnecessary duplication and waste infinitely more acute than it is today. We need money and yet more money. But we also need wisdom and yet more wisdom. Finally, we need courage and yet more courage," Denny poetically added. Kilby responded to Denny's letter by writing, "It is a splendid presentation of the subject and will be of great benefit to me in the preparation of my message."

As part of his overall University expansion plan, Denny wrote to Sidney J. Bowie, chairman of the Alabama Education Commission, in 1922 suggesting "the establishment in Birmingham of a technical school of junior college rank, under University of Alabama control, for young men of meager means who are unable to go off to college but who crave an opportunity to specialize in those branches of engineering which the district needs and which the University is exclusively authorized to develop. Fifty years hence, logically and inevitably, the University is going to be a real factor in Birmingham. Foreseeing men of 1922 will desire to visualize the possibilities of the future…."

Denny did not relent in his annual call for additional financial support, even as new buildings were under construction in 1924. His focus, as always, was on the future. His report to University trustees in May included an introductory oration on the state's responsibility to provide the opportunity of higher education to the rural youth of the state. "There is unmistakable evidence on the part of Alabama parents of a determination to make every sacrifice in the matter of educating their children," Denny began. "Apparently no sacrifice has been or is too great…. They correctly believe that the richest legacy they can leave their children is a sound college education if they can afford it. In voting the millage tax for local county and district schools some years ago, this spirit was manifest. The public schools are crowded. The colleges are overflowing.

The one unifying demand in Alabama other than good roads is the demand for education, overshadowing all differences of politics, religion or prosperity. Parents will not indefinitely tolerate the inability of institutions to provide instruction adequate to meet the needs of all high school graduates who can satisfy the requirements of these institutions. They will repudiate any policy that denies to large numbers of worthy students admission to college." Adding that University of Alabama student enrollment included approximately 2,200 during the regular session and almost 3,000 more in summer school and extension courses, Denny said. "No intelligent man will claim that the state has remotely met this situation. These students come from our own homes. It is interesting to note that there are this year from the farms of Alabama more students at the University of Alabama than at any institution in the South north of Texas, if available statistics are trustworthy. Will anyone say that these boys and girls from our rural homes should be denied admission? Are we ready to turn them away on the ground that the state is unable or unwilling to provide facilities adequate for the instruction, for the housing and for the service of all who desire to fit themselves for useful service? The foremost task of Alabama is to meet this situation.

"A democracy owes its youth the fullest measure of opportunity by which they may profit," Denny continued. "Their gain is the state's gain in terms of leadership in a life of increasing complexity. The University has no passion for numbers as such. It does, however, welcome the opportunity for ever-expanding usefulness to the state which its increased responsibilities bring. For nearly a century it has touched young lives and enriched them to the eternal good of the state. It is now faced with the challenge to perform on a larger scale this same great task. Will the state whose servant the University is deny it the privilege of accepting this challenge? No American commonwealth has ever had a finer or more appealing or more vital opportunity than that which now presents itself to Alabama. For the sake of our future prosperity and for the sake of civilization itself, we cannot afford to turn a deaf ear to this supreme call…. Recently, financial campaigns have been staged for the benefit of the tax-supported institutions of higher learning. The necessity for that kind of thing reveals the pathetic lack of appreciation of the real problem. It reveals also a vital need in the matter of arousing the responsible leadership of the state to the seriousness of the situation. Why cannot Alabama support its state-controlled colleges in accordance with the recognized methods used in the rank and file of other American states? What is needed is a keener and more statesman-like educational conscience and a sounder conviction regarding the social, economic and spiritual value of liberality in solving our educational problem. These things will inevitably be forthcoming sooner or later. When that day comes, there will be a renaissance of education in Alabama and a new era of civic pride and economic power."

Denny added that "Every effort has been made to keep the University's face to the future and to add to her force and effectiveness in each of the three great domains of services, in teaching, in research and in direct service to the state through extension. In spite of every handicap we have made progress in building, equipment and teaching forces. It is my judgment that we have used aright every dollar that has come into our hands. The pity is that more dollars have not been available. I doubt if it is known that we are carrying a heavier load than any state university south of Washington with the single exception of the University of Texas. It is a tremendous responsibility. It is also a tremendous opportunity. The University will become precisely what the state is willing to make it. Conversely, the state will, in its larger intellectual, social, economic and spiritual life, become largely what the University is enabled to make it. There is no escape from this fact. What is our ideal? What kind of civilization do we desire to build? Shall we be 'penny wise and pound foolish?' That is the great, outstanding question of the hour."

A year later, Denny seemed almost resolved to defeat as he provided a brief, routine report to the trustees citing construction progress and the continued increase in women students. "The perpetual problem confronting the University is the problem of finance," he added. "For thirteen years we have been hammering on this problem. Sometimes I wonder if hammering does any good. Yet I have the consciousness of duty done in keeping our financial need in the foreground. If we are to do our full duty, the state must be prepared to make largely increased maintenance appropriations in addition to providing greatly enlarged material equipment."

In sounding a similar call in May 1926, Denny said, "It is the foremost task of our civilization to educate the youth of the commonwealth. Those of us who do our day's work on the campus are merely the servants of the people. We can do no more than carry into execution the mandate of those who have called us to the task. The ultimate responsibility rests upon the people themselves. I wish that the people of Alabama understood more fully our problems, our responsibilities, our hopes and our financial burdens. Our desire is to render service. We are forward-looking in spite of our handicaps. We believe that our days of greatest usefulness are yet to come. Complex and varied as is our task, we have, after all, only one primary purpose. That purpose is the advancement of our commonwealth."

The Denny family, the University family and the entire Tuscaloosa community was saddened in January 1927 by the tragic death of Denny's daughter Charlotte. A 1923 University graduate, Charlotte was in her second year as music supervisor for the public schools of Jackson, Mississippi, when her clothing caught fire as she warmed herself by an open fire on January 14 as temperatures hovered in the teens in Jackson. Although early news reports said her chances for recovery were good, Charlotte died on January 26, adding heartbreak to Denny's list of depressing problems.

Although Denny's annual reports to the trustees rarely made the newspapers, he continued to speak out each year in his efforts to educate the public and spur the legislature, which met only once every four years, to action. "State universities are a social product," he told the trustees in his May 1927 report. "They are as deeply rooted as is the government itself. They are as essential to society as commerce or industry. Higher education is the hope and aspiration of the people. All who are capable of profiting from higher education should be given an opportunity to get it. Supporting higher education through taxation is infinitely more important from the viewpoint of the poor man than from the viewpoint of the rich man, who can go to college wherever he pleases. State universities cannot exist apart from that which creates them, yet they also set the intellectual standards of our civilization. They constitute the most vital agencies of human progress. They furnish our leadership. The most advanced states long ago grasped the idea that prosperity is directly related to education. It is now almost axiomatic that a state's financial and economic status can be measured by its provision for higher education. Do we really want to see Alabama prosper? The way is clear. The chief victim of the stringent financial situation of an institution of learning is not the overworked and underpaid professor but the boy or girl who has to work under such a handicap."

Denny also recalled being recently asked what he considered his most outstanding achievements during his first fifteen years as president of the University of Alabama. "I gave it then and I give it now," he told the trustees. "My conviction is that the financial administration of the University has been the outstanding achievement of these years. Only those who understand what it means to make one dollar do the work of five can understand what is here implied. And no one outside of the board of trustees, the faculty and the administrative offices of the University can understand what it has meant to build up the endowed fund of the institution in the face of crying needs to which it had for years in large part been improperly diverted. Not a dollar of the principal has been thus diverted for fifteen years. Do not misinterpret this statement. I am claiming no credit for myself. Far from it. I am simply thanking the trustees and the faculty for permitting me, without interference, to share in this fundamental service." Even under dire financial constraints from the start, Denny somehow managed to increase the University's endowment fund from approximately $475,000 in 1912 to $954,337.12 in 1920, $2,181,227 in 1930 and to $4,538,843 in September 1936.

"Higher education in Alabama now faces a great opportunity if the situation is met in the right way," Denny continued in his 1927 report. "There is no doubt that the University is now known internationally. For the time being it is the most widely known institution in the South. Its great achievements in football on the Pacific Coast have given to it publicity that nothing else has done in all its history. The legislature alone can determine whether this favorable publicity shall be capitalized. It would be a tragedy if the state should fail us in this crisis. No institution of learning can safely allow its chief claim to fame to rest on athletic achievement. Alabama ought to rise to this great opportunity. It may never come again. The best investment Alabama can make is in its schools of all grades. However, there can be no sound system of schools without a strong and well-nourished head. No state has developed an efficient system of common schools in the absence of a sound and well-supported system of higher education. High schools and normal schools are, of course, essential and should be adequately manned. But where are we to get the teachers who teach in these high schools and normal schools? Where are we to get soundly trained manufacturers, publicists, lawyers, real estate men, engineers, bankers, industrialists, transportation chiefs, farmers and doctors? How many of the more remote rural communities of Alabama now have physicians under forty years of age? When the older doctors are gone, how are they to be replaced? These are searching questions. Someone recently asked me whether the farmers of Alabama are interested in the University. My answer was, 'Apparently so, since there is in the regular session a larger number of boys and girls from Alabama farms on our campus than at any other institution in the world.' What is the meaning of this great fact? Could there be any greater evidence that we are offering the thing that the farmer wants his children to have?"

Denny, obviously growing tired of "hammering" trustees and legislators with the same message year after year, also made reference to his on-going health issues in May 1927, saying, "Perhaps I may be allowed in this connection to express the hope that my physical strength will permit me to carry on until the second century of our corporate life shall have been ushered in four years hence, and that you will then permit me to surrender to other hands the great trust with which you honored me fifteen years ago and in which I have found so many satisfactions. Twenty years of service would mark the longest administration in the history of the University," he added in setting May 1931 as a target date for retirement. Trustees, alumni and students began an immediate and constant campaign that kept Denny on the job until he completed twenty-five years as University president on December 31, 1936.

There was good news from Montgomery in late 1927 when the state legislature authorized unprecedented appropriations for all levels of education. "The legislature of 1927, under the leadership of Governor Bibb Graves, did more for education than any other legislature in the history of Alabama," Denny told University trustees in May 1928. "It was an epoch-making achievement. Every phase of education has felt the beneficent touch of the now famous House Bill 318. The University, under that bill, is receiving by direct appropriation approximately one-third of a million dollars annually in addition to its former appropriation." The bill also included $250,000 per year for three years, or $750,000 total, for new buildings, just as Denny had requested. "For this action we should feel profoundly grateful," Denny said. "The result is that the University is today, for the first time within recent years, doing its work approximately as it ought to be done. With the resources now available, there is no reason why the University of Alabama should not rank with the very best institutions of the country, North or South, East or West, as a teaching institution. That is our confident hope and well-founded expectation.

"Our legislature has, after many lean and trying years, placed in our hands for administration a comparatively generous sum of money," Denny continued. "Of course, we should be grateful, and we are grateful. But we should be more than grateful. We should feel a sobering sense of responsibility to use this money wisely, economically and cautiously. The legislature of 1931 will hold us to a strict accounting. We must be ready to render an account of our stewardship. I am glad this is true. My own training and my own sympathies are rigidly in line with economical procedure. Extravagance is positively distasteful to me. We should hold constantly in mind the fact that colleges are operated on somebody else's money and that the other man's money ought to be conserved by us as trustees with even more sacred care than our own," he added. Denny made good use of the University's initial $250,000 appropriation by combining it with income from the 1922 Million Dollar Campaign to construct Doster Hall and Bibb Graves Hall in 1929 and Barnwell Hall and the Alabama Student Union in 1930. Other 1927 appropriations enabled the University to grant pay increases to faculty and staff. Trustees boosted Denny's salary to $12,000 per year while deans got $5,000, professors $4,500, associate professors $3,600, assistant professors $3,000 and instructors $2,400 per year.

The 1927 legislature also appropriated $200,000 per year to the state board of education for the promotion and improvement of teacher training, including $100,000 for the training of high school teachers. State Superintendent of Education R. E. Tidwell, in administering the funds for training high school teachers, said the University of Alabama should get a larger share of the funds and offered the results of a study to support his plan. "Heretofore, Alabama has not kept pace with the more progressive of her sister states in developing the teacher training curricula required for the preparation of superintendents, supervisors, principals and research specialists, all of which fall largely in the graduate field of professional education," Tidwell said. "The University of Alabama has for years endeavored in some measure to offer such training within the limited means at its disposal. Obviously it would appear to be logical for the state to develop this service at that institution." Tidwell pointed out that of the 889 public high school teachers in the state holding degrees from state-supported colleges, 157 were from Alabama College, 220 from Auburn and 512 from the University of Alabama. He added that of the state's 3,376 public school teachers who had taken summer-school classes, 471 had attended Alabama College, 835 had attended Auburn and 2,070 had attended Alabama. Tidwell also pointed out that recent state appropriations had given Alabama College $300 per student enrolled compared to $255 per student at Auburn and $183 per student at Alabama. In an effort to equalize funding on a "services rendered basis," Tidwell provided $70,000 to the University, $20,000 to Auburn and $10,000 to Alabama College from his office's first $100,000 appropriation for the training of high school teachers.

Public focus suddenly shifted from the good news of unprecedented state aid and University growth in October 1928 to the shocking news that Denny had been elected president of Washington and Lee University and had all but accepted the position. The news created bedlam in Tuscaloosa as Denny traveled to Lexington for a week to investigate the opportunity. Students, faculty, alumni and townspeople in both Tuscaloosa and Lexington rallied in support of Denny as the schools vied for his services. University alumni and faculty presented resolutions at the October 20 trustees' meeting urging Denny to remain in Tuscaloosa, as did numerous business and civic organizations in Tuscaloosa, Birmingham and Montgomery.

The University Council presented a lengthy resolution recounting Denny's many accomplishments and asking him to remain as president of the University. "Alabama has grown under your wise guidance and stimulating leadership to be one of the outstanding educational institutions of the South, and to it our people are naturally looking for ethical, intellectual, professional and commercial leadership," the resolution said. "In addition to these more material accomplishments, we would emphasize our appreciation of your foresightedness in building a campus which already is a fitting home for the state university and is destined eventually to be one of the most attractive in the South. We recognize also that one of the outstanding features of your administration has been your rare and sympathetic understanding of student life and its problems. No boy or girl, no matter how humble, has escaped your fatherly oversight. We are assured that the people of this state look upon you as the man who, especially fitted by force of ideas, character, strength of will and administrative ability, naturally occupies the chief place in the educational system of the state. There are those among us who have been close to the people in every section of the state for many years and we are all convinced that the citizens of this state in every walk of life regard the possibility of your resignation as a calamity from which the state and the University would not recover for years to come. Great as these accomplishments have been, we feel, Dr. Denny, that your work here is not yet done. If you looked upon the situation as challenging seventeen years ago, then the situation today must carry a challenge many times as great. Your experience here and your own intimate knowledge of local details, as well as your personal relationships with the men of influence in the educational organizations of the United States, makes you more than ten times as strong as you were seventeen years ago…. Above all, that power which springs from the intangible thing called "University spirit," of which the love and devotion of your faculty and of your student body are but expressions, must be fostered in the light of the University's illustrious history and for the sake of its greater future. No one but Mike is equal to this greatest of all tasks and no one can possibly take his place in this crisis…. We believe it is fair to say that no man, no matter how wise or how strong or how experienced he might be, could possibly carry on nearly so well the great program you have in mind for making Alabama the finished 'capstone of the state's educational system.' We hope you will share our feeling that it seems your duty to stay. We pledge you individually and collectively our united and loyal support and our purpose to help you in every way we can."

University trustees adopted a similar resolution, saying, "We appreciate most deeply the magnitude of the burden our president has carried, at times almost alone, and we desire publicly to pay highest tribute to his unremitting labor, his self-sacrificing devotion, his remarkable idealism, his unblemished integrity. We agree most heartily with the expressions of opinion from many quarters that he has richly earned a much-needed rest and we renew our previous urgent demand that he take several months for complete relaxation, feeling confident that the administration of the University can safely be entrusted to the organization he has developed and that his program and his policies will be ably and conscientiously carried forward by the trusted executives and faculty until his return. We appreciate fully the inclination any man must feel to return to the scene of his early labors in his native state, but we also feel deeply that Dr. Denny's life is inextricably entwined with the life of the University of Alabama. This state claims him and we feel certain its people fully appreciate him…."

In response to the many resolutions, Denny said he appreciated the expressions of support and the thousands of letters and telegrams he had received from "everyone connected with the University." In telling the board that he planned to make a visit to Washington and Lee prior to making a final decision, Denny said he did not want to decide the matter from the point of view of his feelings and that he would keep in mind the interests of the University and the state of Alabama. "As I mentioned some years ago, I have expected to retire as president of the University with our centennial celebration (1931) and since the call came from Washington and Lee I have decided to consider it," he said, adding that his emotions at the time were "too deep for clear thinking and far too deep for any adequate utterances."

University of Alabama students honored Denny with
a bronze bust in 1932 and Denny Chimes in 1929.

7

A Beating-Heart Tribute

"Everywhere on our campus we are reminded of your vision,
of your faith, of your industry and of your sacrifice."
—Alpha Mu Rho Honor Society

Denny Chimes, the most recognizable and cherished icon on the University of Alabama campus, was built in 1929 as a tribute to "Mike" Denny by grateful students and alumni after the near loss of Denny to Washington and Lee University at the pinnacle of his popularity and triumph at the University. Denny, after sixteen years as president of the University, had decided to return to his former position before appreciative students rallied in protest to help persuade him to remain at the Capstone. Denny Chimes stands as a reminder of Denny's loyalty to the University as well as a reminder of the loyalty of his many students to Denny.

Jerry Britchley, writing in the student newspaper *Crimson White*, first suggested a set of chimes for the campus on September 20, 1928, as a replacement for the old-fashioned factory whistle that had called students to class for years. Less than three months later Britchley was leading a student drive to raise money to build Denny Chimes, although his idea might never have gained momentum if not for Dr. Denny's surprising interest in leaving the University to return to his former position as president of Washington and Lee University.

Acting on an encouraging letter of response from Denny, the Washington and Lee board of trustees elected him president on October 11, 1928, creating a storm of reaction among University of Alabama students, who rallied in protest of his impending departure when news of the unexpected action spread. Capstone students gathered in protest, calling Denny from his office with chants of "We want Mike! We want Mike!" as they urged him not to leave. Faculty members, trustees, local civic organizations and University alumni from around the state rushed to show support for Denny as he spent an emotional month considering his future.

Denny was deluged with mail from every old friend and dignitary in Virginia urging him to return to his home state and to Washington and Lee, the private college he had led to prominence during ten years as president before coming to the University of Alabama in 1912. It seemed clear to all concerned in both states that he was intent on returning to Washington and Lee unless he had a change of mind. And there is no doubt that Denny, weary from overwork and having taken no vacation in a quarter of a century, missed the historic Virginia campus where ghosts of the immortal Robert E. Lee and Stonewall Jackson still walked and the spirit of the courageous Freedom Hall Volunteers stirred the blazing autumn leaves. He said as much to old friends there, and his secretive letter citing his willingness to consider the position was taken as a virtual acceptance of the position by Washington and Lee trustees, who immediately and unanimously selected him as president.

"All of our trustees are delighted that we now have the big end of our troubles solved. I sincerely hope that nothing will intervene to prevent your coming," wrote Washington and Lee trustee George W. St. Clair at 5:40 p.m. on October 11, just after the trustees had adjourned the meeting in which they elected Denny to the presidency. "I hope to have the pleasure of seeing you in person soon to tell you in person of my gratification of your decision," St. Clair added, along with the statement that Denny's salary would be $7,500 per year plus the historic home built for Robert E. Lee as his residence rent-free. "It all seems too good to be true," trustee Harrington Waddell wrote to Denny on the same day. "God bless you and old Washington and Lee," he added.

Frank Moore, a Lexington attorney and long-time Denny friend, wrote, "My dear Dr. Denny: How delighted I was to hear yesterday the good news of your reelection as president of Washington and Lee. It has indeed put a thrill over the entire community and I sincerely trust that you can see your way clear to accept the call and come back, take the helm of our alma mater and guide her in the future as you have so ably done in the past. Come, Doctor, come; we need you so badly." Another Denny friend wrote to offer congratulations, saying, "I assume that the trustees would not have made a public announcement unless they had some assurance from you that you would accept, or at least give the matter very careful consideration. It will be a great delight to me personally to see you and Mrs. Denny back in Virginia."

Virginia newspapers immediately announced the action of Washington and Lee's trustees, who had in fact taken the action with the full assumption that Denny would accept the position. The news caught the entire state of Alabama by surprise, creating panicked responses among University students, faculty and alumni. University students, led by student body president Lewis Smith, called Denny from his office to the Mound on October 13 to ask him to stay. University faculty members gathered on October 16 to approve a resolution asking Denny to reconsider what seemed clearly his decision to leave. Dr. George Lang suggested a response greater than a simple resolution—one "that would indicate our sense of the grave danger that confronts us. It is a simple thing to know what Dr. Denny is going to do. He has told the students and has said privately many times that his own attitude would be determined very largely by the revelation to him of what would be the greatest field of service. If Washington and Lee has this, he as much as told us that he is going there. We know that Dr. Denny has had to move every inch of ground through the greatest opposition," Lang said. "He has had to face opposition on the part of even those who have benefited by the products of his vision. There is something now of weariness in Dr. Denny. He is a little bit tired of fighting for every inch of ground…. If Dr. Denny does stay here, it will be knowing that he has got to fight. Then let him know he has a faculty that will fight with him to the last ditch…. We must let him know how much we feel the responsibility that rests on us and our willingness to stay with him in all the struggles that are before him."

Dr. James J. Doster, Denny's closest friend and associate through all his years at the University, said, "I know personally the weight of the burden he has been carrying during these seventeen years. I have been with him in some terrible, nerve-wracking struggles. He has put forth efforts that an ordinary man could not make. Dr. Denny is simply weary; he is tired. The outlook in the state is not encouraging…. He is being attacked now below the belt by influences he can't reach. They are bound to affect him. The leading papers in the state are not sparing him in the least. Now that this opportunity has come, he would be other than human not to feel that he ought to respond to the call from his native state."

"The state cannot afford to lose Dr. Denny," said Graduate School Dean Albert B. Moore. "He is respected by people throughout Alabama as a great educational leader. We have just gone through one of the greatest crises in Alabama educational history. Dr. Denny was the outstanding character in the struggle. The great things for education that were done could not have been done without Dr. Denny. We should make it known to Dr. Denny that we stand ready to uphold his hands in the fight that must go on."

Mathematics professor Dr. William Ott, a Washington and Lee graduate during Denny's tenure as president there, voiced his respect for Denny as he recalled receiving a letter from the University president inviting him to join the University faculty. "I did not need to come down to look things over. I knew that if that man, who had drunk so deeply of the fountain of culture, was at the helm, I wanted to be here," Ott said. "For the sake of his own peace of mind, we could not wish him any better place than Washington and Lee. I can't think of anything better than to get back there away from taxpayers, legislatures, corporations, coeducation and all those terrible things, but I certainly shall personally plead with him not to leave us because I do not know what would happen to us if he did."

Dr. Clyde Brooks, Dean of the University Medical School and one of Denny's personal physicians, said: "I have thought at times he would kill himself with work, worry and lack of support from the state. How easily we could take off some of his burden. Mike likes to see to it himself. How often we see him working at what seems to be a detail. I have seen him working for three hours trying to bamboozle a student into staying at the University. We can do that."

The University's Alpha Chapter of Alpha Mu Rho Honor Society sent Denny a laudatory letter congratulating him on his selection by Washington and Lee, but at the same time begged him to remain at the University. "It is at such times as this that we are permitted to assure our friends of loyalty and affection and esteem. May we be allowed to say to you that never at any time have we inadequately recognized that the marvelous growth of our university is due to your labors. Everywhere on our campus we are reminded of your vision, of your faith, of your industry and of your sacrifice. Your qualities of personal character have not failed to impress us, and no less visible to us than the buildings which you have erected for our material use has been your unfailing and persistent appeal to moral and spiritual excellence. If wisdom is the highest quality of intellect and is made manifest in the vision of the true ideal of life and in the practical tact which enables one to see the means and find the way that leads to this ideal, you have been wise; if justice is the high quality in the sphere of feeling, your rightheartedness has made itself felt in every contact with the student body of Alabama. If temperance is the ideal quality in the sphere of desire, we have found you unfailingly temperate. Ever sober-minded, you have met opposition with dignity, opportunity with quiet and unostentatious labor; you have been a Carlyean aristocrat and a morally responsible democrat; if you have erred, it has been on the side of generosity; if you have been zealous it has been for the University of Alabama, not for self.

"If courage is the high ideal of will, you have been brave in a degree known better to your students than to others. There is a courage which is active, which shows itself in brave deeds of love and in bold witnessing for truth; not few but many are the students of the Capstone who have felt your bold touch of affection. There is also a passive courage, a fortitude which shows itself in patient endurance of hardship and pain and suffering in duty's cause. We have not been blind to the courage which you have shown in sacrifice for our sake and for the sake of the University of Alabama. We remind you of these classic virtues that you may know by what measure we have measured you. You have not been found wanting in the balance of our judgment.... When student life and the college age are exposed to so many and to such contradictory judgments that we stand in danger of having any and all standards of excellence thrown into hopeless obscurity, the students of the University of Alabama have learned by precept and example that there *are* standards and fine issues to life, not least by the instruction of your example.

"We turn to ask you not to leave us. Sixteen years ago you came to our campus because here you saw the greatest opportunity for service. You announced at the mass meeting of students on Monday that by the standard of opportunity for service you would decide whether or not to remain at Alabama. We accept that challenge. The plans for building up a "greater Alabama" have not yet been carried to fulfillment; there is much yet to be done.... We think also of your leadership throughout the state at a time when with enlarged vision and renewed energy the people of Alabama are eager to bring their state to a just position of achievement in agriculture, industry and education. To these interests you have contributed without reserve of physical energy or of will and wisdom. To leave us at this time would mean chaos and confusion to those who have learned to trust your counsel and to be guided by your integrity. The task before you is no easy one. It does not invite to ease, but only weaklings court ease; it does not invite to popularity, but 'popularity is the privilege of mediocrities;' it will make enemies for you, but 'enemies are the interest one draws on greatness;' it will take your life, but 'what does it profit a man to gain the whole world and lose his own soul?' We challenge you, therefore, to a service for the state of Alabama and for the University of Alabama and for all high interests in Alabama at this critical time," the letter, signed by president Percy Fountain and secretary Marian Shirer, concluded.

Denny had received offers of other positions before, but none as tempting as this one. And from every indication, he had decided to return to Washington and Lee after almost seventeen years in Alabama, where he had been met by appreciative followers and often-unappreciative governmental leaders. Virginia was his home; it offered the familiar majesty of the Blue Ridge Mountains and the peaceful beauty of the Shenandoah Valley. Washington and Lee offered the inspiring memories of Lee and Jackson and old, admiring friends who needed him. In Alabama he had been held back from his goals by an often hostile, politics-driven legislature. At privately funded Washington and Lee, he would not be forced to beg for every dollar. His closest University of Alabama friends—Doster and Moore—felt certain that he was leaving. He might well have gone, too, except for the surprising, last-minute intervention of Dr. James McLester, head of the University Medical School faculty and one of Denny's personal physicians. McLester, a Tuscaloosa native acting out of concern for Denny's physical welfare, advised Denny that the move to Washington and Lee might be detrimental to his health, causing Denny to abruptly reconsider his leaning toward Washington and Lee. McLester's evaluation, whether totally sincere or a ploy designed to play on what had become Denny's constant health concerns, seems to have had a major impact on Denny's decision to remain at the University.

On October 24, 1928, Denny wrote to St. Clair indicating a change of attitude toward the Washington and Lee offer based solely on McLester's advice. "If you could know just what I have been going through with during the past ten days, with an entire state on my back, you would understand why I have not written you sooner," Denny wrote. "…Recognizing as I do that my letter to you of October 5 expressing to you in sincere, plain terms what I had already substantially said to Paul Penick and to Harry Waddell regarding my willingness to go back to the dear friends at Lexington, if in their best judgment I could, better than anyone else now available, help you solve the special problems now confronting the institution, undoubtedly led the board to the action taken on October 11 and that in the absence of such a letter no such action would have been taken, I feel that in advance of translating that "willingness" into concrete action I should, in justice to all concerned, carefully weigh and frankly set forth two factors, one of which has entered since I wrote the letter of October 5.

"The new and really vital factor is the voice of my physician, one of the most eminent in the entire country, who advises me that a great new task involving the strenuous kind of effort through which I have been passing for years would be ill-timed and positively dangerous," Denny wrote. "This is a tremendous surprise to me, as I have during the past year felt quite my old self again. That this view is deliberately held by Dr. McLester is evidenced by the fact that, without my having even consulted him or asked his opinion, he made a special trip from Birmingham a few days ago to urge me not to risk my health by undertaking new work which would necessarily involve far greater strain than the reorganized work here would involve. This view of Dr. McLester was transmitted to our board by the head of our School of Medicine with the result that the board, on last Saturday, ordered for me an indefinite period of complete rest. The second factor, which, of course, I did have in mind when I wrote you on October 5, was the attitude of the friends in Lexington. While I have every reason to conclude from the letters and telegrams which I have received that my election has been generally, if not universally, acclaimed, I have at the same time gotten the distinct impression that many of these friends are expecting the impossible. Even at my best, I am not a magician. Under present conditions, I cannot expect to give to Washington and Lee the vigorous leadership of a young man, physically fit and fired with the enthusiasm of one who would be 'winning his spurs.'

"Frankly, I find myself in an embarrassing situation," Denny continued. "The overwhelming Alabama protest would in itself be sufficiently embarrassing. But I was perhaps vain enough to anticipate that phase of the problem when I wrote you on October 5, and I believe I have been strong enough and can still be strong enough to resist that factor in the situation. But the new factor which I have frankly presented is too serious to ignore. If I would succeed, I must have vigor. Otherwise a breakdown is inevitable. I must know what I am doing if I am to be fair to all concerned. Of course, you know that finances do not figure in the matter at all. I have positively refused to allow the Alabama trustees to increase my salary under any conditions. It is solely a question of what is my duty in the light of the new factor involved in the problem." Denny added that "following the action of the 1927 legislature, the trustees have so enlarged the administrative staff that I am now comparatively at liberty to get freedom from many details. Yet, even with this relief for the past year, the board is demanding a period of indefinite rest for me. You see my situation. I want to go over the whole matter with you promptly," Denny concluded. The letter included a hand-written and signed postscript by Dr. McLester stating that the letter "accurately expresses my orders."

Denny returned to Lexington for a week around the first of November to visit with Washington and Lee trustees and faculty members and review the school's financial status. "There was jubilation among the students, to whom Denny had become a legend," a local report of his visit said. "He was greeted at the railroad station by nearly a thousand students accompanied by a band, with several hundred sympathetic townspeople on hand. He rode triumphantly up the hill in an antique tallyho, festooned with blue and white and drawn by fifty freshmen, through fireworks and cheering students aligned on each side of the street." The report said Denny also addressed a student assembly at Lee Chapel and attended a football game between Washington and Lee and the University of Virginia in Charlottesville while considering his future.

Soon after returning to Tuscaloosa, Denny announced on Friday, November 9, that he had decided to reject the Washington and Lee offer. "After careful study of the problem, I have decided it is my duty to remain in Alabama," Denny said. He added that he had notified Washington and Lee authorities of his decision two days earlier. "The past three or four weeks have been trying weeks for me," Denny added. "The overwhelming outpouring of fine sentiment both at Alabama and Washington and Lee has greatly moved me. I am profoundly grateful. I have also been touched by the demonstrations of loyalty on the part of the people of Alabama. Such demonstrations have made me feel that these seventeen years of service have been rewarded far more generously than they deserve." A month later, Denny told six hundred guests at an annual loyalty dinner gathering in Birmingham, "I found that the roots of my life had been sunk more deeply here than I realized in seventeen years and that I had not the physical strength to pull them up. No people anywhere, not even in my native Virginia, are more courtly and kindlier than here in Alabama, I have come to realize, and with all this in mind, my decision was made to remain here."

"I say it is a great day for Alabama" Alabama Governor Bibb Graves said on learning of Denny's decision to remain in Alabama. "Dr. Denny has heard the call of duty. In his hands at this time he holds the opportunities for leadership in the building of a state's citizenship, in the education of the youth and in the development of ideals of the true southland."

Former governor Kilby wrote Denny on November 10 to say that he was "delighted beyond my power of expression" that Denny had chosen to remain at the University. "I feel you have acted with wisdom. Your work at the University has been so remarkably successful that it would be a pity for it to be interrupted at this time. I do earnestly hope that your fondest hopes for the future of the institution may be fully realized and that in carrying out your plans you may enjoy good health and great happiness," Kilby said. Kilby explained that he had purposely not written Denny earlier for fear of influencing his decision. "I was so anxious that your decision in this matter should be the one that would bring the most happiness and satisfaction to you in the years to come and so anxious that your personal judgment should prevail that I did not wish to place the weight of a feather in the way of its absolutely free exercise. For that reason and that alone I did not write you, earnestly hoping all the while that your decision would be favorable to your remaining with us."

University trustee Gessner McCorvey of Mobile wrote Denny to say that "I do not know where in the world the board of trustees could have turned to find a worthy successor. To use a slang expression, anyone whom we might have selected, had you decided to leave us, would certainly have rattled around in your boots."

The *Mobile Register* praised Dr. Denny's decision in a November 11 editorial, saying, "From one end of Alabama to the other there will be rejoicing over the announcement that education in this state is not to lose the services of Dr. George H. Denny, president of the University.... No man has taken a more conspicuous part in bringing about the present situation in Alabama than has Dr. Denny as head of the University. He has been a tower of strength in the cause. During the seventeen years of his administration at Tuscaloosa he has not only been the chief motivating power in raising it to a position of national prominence and recognition, but he has evidenced a passionate and continuing interest in the advancement of the public school system and has had much to do with molding the sentiment of the state in favor of providing the requisite public funds for school expansion. That he has elected to remain and to carry on in Alabama is evidence of the depth and sincerity of his devotion to the cause he has championed and fought for through so many years. His decision gives new hope and new enthusiasm to every friend of education in Alabama."

"Whatever reason or reasons may have constrained Dr. George H. Denny to stay in president's harness at the University of Alabama rather than return to Washington and Lee at the earnest solicitation of that university really makes no great matter in view of the fact that he has made his decision," a *Birmingham News* editorial said. "It may be that the emotional side of his nature leaned toward Washington and Lee yearningly, but the reasoning side—the dominantly progressive note in his nature which senses more constructive work ahead for him here—directed him to carry on for the good of Alabama and for the youth of Alabama. Yet these are synonymous terms. Whoever serves Alabama's youth serves the commonwealth. And when that particular section of this state's youth enrolled at the Capstone turned out one day, practically to a man, and shouted itself hoarse for 'Mike' Denny to stay on his job, it may be that the whole weight of President Denny's nature didn't really lean so much toward that first educational love of his situate at Lexington, Virginia, as toward those eager youth surrounding him. Indeed, it is that human touch in 'Mike' Denny's system—that fluid, affectionate nature of his that draws the young toward him and draws him to the young—which, expressed almost daily between the University head and the sons and daughters of this institution, has conspired to make him cleave to his present engagement."

The 1929 *Corolla* called Denny's decision to remain at the University "the greatest service he has yet performed," and added, "It is true that by his great ability and splendid judgment as to the needs of our state, he has in a brief period developed a small arts and science college with a handful of students, a few buildings (and those inadequately equipped), of low academic standards and slight recognition in the educational world outside of Alabama into a university equal to any in the South. But his very success has made it imperative that his guiding hand shall still further direct the destiny of the University. A great institution calls for a great executive. The work yet to be done is difficult and complex and Dr. Denny, by declining the flattering offer extended to him by another institution, has brought conviction to the minds of the friends of the University that this work will be well done."

Denny's decision to remain at the University, announced on November 9 after a month of pressure from all sides, quickly inspired further discussion of the chimes, but this time as a tribute to Denny's loyalty, and in a December 6, 1928, *Crimson White* editorial, Robert Kosower offered the name "Denny Chimes" and suggested that the monument be "situated opposite the Denny Mansion" as he discussed the void to be filled by the chimes. "Again and again it has been said by students, faculty members and rival schools that something is lacking in the student spirit of the University of Alabama....Although it was at times generally admitted that something was lacking—some great spiritual influence—which might serve to bind the student body into a closer unit, no great constructive work has been undertaken which can be said to have materially remedied this situation," Kosower wrote. "Can it be that so splendid an institution, with its beautiful campus, still lacks a nucleus, a central kernel, to serve as the beating heart of the University? Fortunate indeed is that institute which inspires and unites. Such a unit has been suggested. Well-laid plans have been formulated to erect a campanile. It is the opinion of many that a huge chime tower would be one of the greatest spiritual assets of the University. Ultimately situated opposite the Denny Mansion, it would be in the center of the campus. Aside from its great utilitarian aspect, which will make it invaluable, its worth as an inspirational factor in the daily life of the students may be said to be prodigious. The quaint sound of chimes seems to be the fitting summons to classes and is obviously superior to the present raucous whistle. There can be no doubt that harmonious peals of a set of chimes are more in keeping with the beauty of the campus than the harsh hoot of our factory whistle.

"It would probably be impossible to find a single person on the campus who is opposed to the campanile. But we need more than the mere desire," Kosower added. "The funds with which to erect the tower—a prime requisite—must be secured if the Denny Chimes are to be erected. The alumni and interested people of the state have intimated that they will support the project if the students themselves show the initiative and the desire to raise the initial funds. Plans are at present under way to raise money by contributions from the students. If the scheme is to succeed, every student must show the alumni that he earnestly desires its success. Contributions, though they may be small, are more desired if they come from everyone. A united student body cannot fail to succeed in this undertaking," Kosower, a student from New York, added.

A front-page story in the same *Crimson White* issue announced that Britchley, a senior from New York, had been chosen as chairman of the Denny Chimes fund drive with student body president Lewis Smith, Hugh Dowling and Clemson Duckworth as other members of the executive committee. The story added that each student was expected to contribute one dollar to the drive in an effort to raise $3,000 toward the overall cost of the chimes and tower. That amount was raised within ten days, and alumni, faculty and others soon joined the campaign, giving the project an additional boost. A newspaper report said any shortfall in public donations would be made up from funds received from the University's 1922 Million Dollar Campaign and the project was soon under way.

The chimes tower was designed by Miller and Martin Architects in Birmingham. Skinner Maxwell Construction Company of Tuscaloosa entered the low bid on the project at $25,319 and construction began in March 1929. Cost of the chimes, purchased from J. C. Deagan Inc. of Chicago, was $12,000, including installation. Built of oversized "Old Virginia" brick and Alabama limestone with cream-tinted mortar, the chimes tower is eighteen feet square at the base and one hundred eighteen feet tall above the terrace of forty by forty feet. With the base added, the final cost of the tower was $28,500, making a total cost of just over $40,000 after the chimes were installed.

Formal dedication of the chimes was held at 5 p.m. on Monday, May 27, 1929. The ceremony, which included brief remarks by Governor Bibb Graves and Dr. Denny, was broadcast over WAPI Radio. One-hour musical concerts played by the chimes were also broadcast on WAPI on Sunday morning, Sunday evening and Monday evening following the dedication ceremony. Motion picture photographs of Denny Chimes including Dr. Denny and several University students, taken by Paramount Newsreel Services, were also shown at the Bama Theater in Tuscaloosa on Monday and Tuesday. Graduation exercises were held Tuesday morning, May 28.

"I desire to express here and now my grateful appreciation of the honor done me in the installation of the chimes through the generosity of the student body, alumni and friends who have made this action possible," Denny said at the dedication. "The chimes will supply a long-felt need. They will be useful in many ways. In addition, they will add to the life of the campus something that will contribute in the finest way to the things of the spirit. Undoubtedly the time has come when a larger emphasis may well be put on the imponderable, the aesthetic and the artistic factors that ought to enter more largely into our daily life. Such things will contribute immeasurably toward the best development of our student body. I express the hope that the chimes may stimulate mightily our desire for and interest in the fine arts," Denny added.

"Jerome Britchley gazed upon the assemblage and the ceremony with great pride and satisfaction," said a *Crimson White* report on the dedication of Denny Chimes. "It was he, the chairman of the student committee, who raised the money for the chimes, and it is well known that Britchley was the main factor in this movement." Britchley is listed among University alumni records as being a 1930 graduate from New York City. He earned Phi Beta Kappa honors at the University and was a member of Jasons, Omicron Delta Kappa, Junior Faculty, ROTC Officers Club, Pre-Law Club, Glee Club and Excelsior and served on the staff of the *Crimson White*, *Rammer Jammer* and *Corolla*.

Denny Chimes, symbolic of Denny's dedication to the University he led from stagnation to national prominence, remains the beacon of hope and achievement to students, alumni and visitors today. The dedication marker made it clear that the monument was a show of affection from the appreciative students, each of whom he knew by name and each of whom benefited directly from his service to the state and to the University. The inscription on the marker read: "Erected by students and friends in honor, not of Dr. Denny, A.M., Ph.D., L.L.D., D.C.L., but of Mike, constant friend, benevolent counselor."

Britchley's suggestion for what became Denny Chimes had been offered without fanfare, and might well have slipped by unnoticed had the dramatic and perfectly timed Washington and Lee situation not developed. The near loss of Denny came at an opportune time, however, and the end result of Britchley's idea far exceeded his highest hopes. And Kosower's editorial calling for a "great spiritual influence" to give the campus a "beating heart" could not have foretold the eventual and lasting effect of the chimes more appropriately. Britchley, in proposing a set of chimes in a September 20, 1928, *Crimson White* editorial, had simply hoped to secure support to replace what he called "the raucous, screeching factory whistle" then being used to call students to class. "It is deplorable that this campus should not have a set of chimes in place of the steam whistle," Britchley wrote. "Upon as beautiful a campus as we have, it seems lamentable that the pervading, natural quietness and serenity should be impaired by as prosaic a signal as a factory whistle. It has neither the mournful tone of a riverboat nor the deepness of a calliope." Britchley suggested that a set of chimes, "situated atop Clark Hall, would lend a more pleasant aspect to the campus." He added that "in some manner the present factory whistle must be abolished and replaced with a more melodious means of class summoning—a signal which is more in keeping with this beautiful campus than the harsh whistle." Britchley suggested that alumni and students contribute to the cost of the proposed chimes and asked for input from students and faculty on the matter, saying, "This cause, as far as I know, has never before been put before the public."

A similar proposal had in fact been made in *The Tuscaloosa News* almost exactly six years earlier, on September 24, 1922, during the University's Million Dollar Campaign. The story suggested a set of chimes and an amphitheater as possible additions to the campus during its building campaign and said the idea offered "an unusual opportunity to some Tuscaloosa capitalist or philanthropist to contribute a memorial befitting a great university that would stand as a lasting memory to his or her name." The story suggested that "a set of chimes, placed in a handsome stone tower, to be used in calling the students through the years to come to their classes, vesper services and other purposes, would add greatly to the general atmosphere of culture of the University and would become a distinct feature of University life." Tuscaloosa Judge A. S. Van de Graaff had also suggested a "tower in honor of the men who went from Alabama and helped to win the World War" in 1919, but the idea never gained wide support.

Denny Chimes has been updated through the years, starting during World War II when the brass chimes were removed, melted and used in the war effort. An electronic system that sounded like chimes was installed in 1945 and modernized in 1966. The chimes were fully restored in 1986, when 25 new bronze bells were installed following a fund-raising drive. The chimes ring every quarter hour and chime on the hour, reminding students of the time as they hurry to class. The University alma mater plays each night at 10 p.m., signaling a reverential end to the day and leaving students with lasting memories of the chimes and the nostalgic mood of the campus. Other music is played on special occasions. An additional feature was added at Denny Chimes in 1947 when the tradition of having permanent football captains place their handprints and footprints in a "Walk of Fame" at the base of the chimes as part of annual A-Day activities began. All-America halfback Harry Gilmer and All-Southeastern Conference center John Wozniak were the first players honored in the Walk of Fame.

No one closely connected to the University could argue even today that the dreams of Britchley, Kosower and the author of the editorial in *The Tuscaloosa News* have not been fully realized. And surely no one today could imagine a more fitting tribute to Denny and his service to the University and to the state of Alabama. Denny Chimes does indeed provide the University campus with a "beating heart," just as Denny did as its president.

Denny Chimes was not the first University landmark named in Denny's honor. New athletic fields for football, baseball, tennis and track were built in 1915 just south and east of the President's Mansion and the football field was named Denny Field in his honor on October 14, 1920. It had previously been known as University Field. When a new 12,000-seat football stadium was built in 1929, it was named George Hutcheson Denny Stadium and the old Denny Field sign removed from what became a practice field. Denny Stadium, originally built for approximately $150,000 using proceeds from two Rose Bowl games, has undergone numerous additions through the years to reach its current capacity of 101,821. It became Bryant-Denny Stadium in 1975 when the Alabama legislature amended the stadium name to include that of long-time Crimson Tide head football coach Paul "Bear" Bryant.

Among Denny's personal files archived at Washington and Lee University is a letter dated January 8, 1948, from John Little Jr. of Louisville, Kentucky. The writer said he had heard Denny address a graduating class at Washington and Lee many years before and even recalled a passage from the speech as he had recently driven through Tuscaloosa and the University of Alabama. "I have seen the mighty university over whose campus the chimes in your memory still ring. From the base of those chimes, in the drenching rain, I picked up the enclosed leaf which I thought you might like to have with a word of appreciation from a friend you have never heard of. God willing, some day we may meet. We never know the future nor how God will use our lives." The small oak leaf— fully intact more than 68 years later—was still clipped to the letter in 2013.

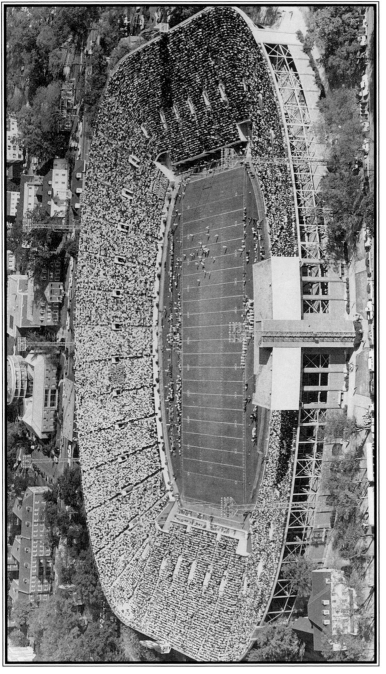

Bryant-Denny Stadium on the University of Alabama campus is shown here circa 1966 as Dr. George H. Denny first envisioned it in the 1920s. The first phase of the stadium was completed in 1929 and the stadium named Denny Stadium in honor of the beloved Capstone president. Paul "Bear" Bryant's name was added to the stadium in 1975 in recognition of his contributions to the University as a player, assistant coach and head coach of Crimson Tide.

8

Triumph and Trial

"Education is one thing on which no people has ever spent too much; the more they spend the richer they become."

—Dr. George H. Denny

The University of Alabama had become the state's shining symbol of educational growth and cultural advancement by September of 1929 and Denny himself was by far the state's most popular and best-known citizen. Record numbers of students filled new classrooms at the University and in the public schools throughout the state. Cheers for Denny's recent decision to remain as president of the University still echoed across the rapidly expanding campus and beyond. Denny Stadium had been built with proceeds from two Rose Bowl games; new buildings dedicated to women's studies (Doster Hall) and the training of teachers (Graves Hall) were open; Music from Denny Chimes—the new, towering Capstone beacon of hope and triumph—filled the air amid the rustling leaves of autumn.

"No American college has made greater progress in recent years. The entire state ought to feel a sense pride in view of what has been accomplished," Denny had proudly proclaimed of the University in his annual report to the trustees in May of 1929. And although Denny himself was never content with the rate of progress in education, even he must have enjoyed a brief moment of satisfaction as the new school year began in September. He had achieved—in spite of constant wrangling over funding—much of his original vision of a system of universal education in the state with the University at its head. In doing so, he stood alone as its triumphant champion, praised and admired by all for the hope of a better life he had brought to thousands in the state. If ever Dr. George H. Denny looked at his work and said "Well done," that was surely the time. And if ever he enjoyed a moment of true happiness, it had to come on October 6, 1929, when his beloved Crimson Tide football team claimed a 22-7 homecoming win over the University of Mississippi as the new 12,000-seat Denny Stadium was dedicated in his honor. He could now see and hear the rewards of his many years of labor—a new, thriving University—in every direction from the balcony of the President's Mansion.

Still, Denny did not see his work as finished. "Of course, those of us who are intimately associated with the daily routine of the institution realize that many needs still have to be met," he had told the trustees in May as he listed a women's gymnasium, a student union building and new library among his next priorities. And with $500,000 still due from the 1927 construction appropriation from the state, Denny was confident of the school's future and pleased with his 1928 decision to remain at the University rather than return to Washington and Lee. At long last, Denny's vision and long crusade for the University and for tax-supported public education for the state's masses was coming to fruition. Denny said the main problem confronting the University in 1929 was the development of the School of Medicine. "If our rural sections are to have adequate medical care, it is essential to organize in Alabama a four-year medical school. There is no other sure way. Many of the young men who attend out-of-state medical schools never return. The time is ripe for action. The leading doctors of Alabama are fostering the movement of looking into a four-year school, but in the final analysis, it is a matter of money," he said.

Denny's hour of triumph was fleeting, however. On Tuesday, October 29, almost exactly five months from the date of the dedication of Denny Chimes, the fortunes of Denny, the University of Alabama, the state of Alabama, the nation and the entire world were reversed. The New York stock market crash on that date brought a sudden, disastrous end to a care-free decade of wealth and excess known as the Roaring Twenties and led to a prolonged financial crisis known as the Great Depression. The ensuing worldwide financial collapse crippled the daily functions of business and industry and eventually that of government and education throughout the country for much of a decade. As the effects of the Depression spread, the focus in Alabama was more on the mere survival of state agencies than on the idealized state educational system Denny had worked for almost two decades to build. And although Denny never took a step backward in the fight, the Depression gave rise to a tumultuous period of financial struggle and discontent for the University that lasted through the remainder of his tenure.

The stock market crash had a devastating domino effect. Cotton prices fell. Banks failed and factories closed. Unemployment skyrocketed. Millionaires facing financial ruin leapt to their deaths from New York skyscrapers. Tax revenues dwindled. Fewer students could afford to attend college, even at a time when room, board and tuition cost only $250 a year. The state of Alabama was soon unable to make good on its promised appropriations to public schools and colleges. Self-preservation dominated every conscience thought as fear and distrust spread to all corners of the country. Although the full impact of the Depression was not immediately felt, it slowly forced cutbacks in payments to all state agencies, making competition for state funding even more heated than ever. In time, Denny was forced to slash University faculty and staff salaries twice as he struggled to maintain full staffing and keep the University open. Worst of all, Denny's once-hailed financial management policies were called into question as legislators challenged his funding requests. Denny, of course, was an easy, highly visible target. He had placed the University, with its many new, towering buildings and throngs of students, in the spotlight by achieving national recognition at what the public perceived as taxpayer expense. And, of course, to most, Denny *was* the University. Adding grist to the grumblings was the fact that the University continued to add new buildings and break enrollment records year after year, even in the most difficult of times of limited funding from the state.

Denny's first major distraction came from an unexpected direction and made larger and far more dramatic headlines than his annual reports of record enrollment, new buildings and need for more money. The distraction involved the school's football program, around which University alumni and much of the state had rallied in near-fanatical fashion in recent years due to the team's unprecedented success. What most football fans saw as devastating news came on April 1, 1930, when head football coach Wallace Wade, who had led the Crimson Tide to two Rose Bowl appearances and the school's first two national championships during the previous seven seasons, announced that he was leaving the University at the end of the year to become head coach at Duke University. Alabama's trips to Rose Bowl games following perfect seasons in 1925 and 1926 had played a large role in the University's rise to national prominence, of course. Denny, who had hired Wade in December 1922 and who had a more than passing interest in the football program, naturally shared much of the glory of those years because he had personally selected Wade and because he had been a staunch supporter of the teams. Widespread publicity for Crimson Tide teams led by such star players as Pooley Hubert, Johnny Mack Brown and Hoyt "Wu" Winslett had helped legitimize Southern football and national coverage of Alabama's 20-19 victory over Washington on January 1, 1926, and 7-7 tie with Stanford on January 1, 1927, had helped attract students and student-athletes from out of state, thus contributing to the growth of the school and enhancing its overall image.

Wade's teams of 1927 (5-4-1), 1928 (6-3) and 1929 (6-3) did not live up to his (or Denny's) standards, however. Still, Wade's surprise announcement that he would be leaving when his contract expired came as a shock to Crimson Tide fans. Reports of Wade's action were accompanied by widespread rumors that he had resigned because of criticism of his teams' lackluster performance the last three seasons. Others said he was leaving in a dispute over pay. Wade, a man of high principle and few words, gave no hint of a dispute as he rejected Denny's offer of a new contract and moved on to Duke. Remarks by former University faculty athletic committee chairman Dr. James S. Thomas, published in the *Miami News* on October 24, 1964, confirmed the rumor most Alabama fans repeated through the years. Thomas said Wade had "left Alabama because he and Dr. Denny were incompatible, not because of more money as was said at the time. As faculty chairman of athletics, I spent my time keeping them apart and pacified. Each wanted to run things his way," Thomas said.

Wade closed his career at Alabama by guiding the Crimson Tide to another 10-0 season capped by a 24-0 Rose Bowl victory over Washington State. The win was led by All-America stars Fred Sington (tackle) and John Henry "Flash" Suther (halfback) and gave the school its third national championship in eight years. As the coach who first led Alabama to national acclaim, Wade remains one of the Crimson Tide's most honored and respected athletic heroes. By leaving as he did amid rumors of discord with Denny, Wade cast perhaps a symbolic stone of disapproval toward the University president's hands-on—if not dominating—management style. New, even more disruptive brushfires of discontent were on the horizon, however, and Denny was kept busy stamping them out during the remaining years of his tenure as president.

Seemingly unflustered by Wade's recent announcement and with his eye always on the future, Denny confidently praised the University's continued progress in his

May 1930 report to the trustees as he announced the completion of Barnwell Hall (women's gymnasium), the near-completion of the Student Union Building (now Reese Phifer Hall) and a record enrollment of 3,603 students in the semester just ended. "The University of Alabama has now reached a position in which, with anything like adequate support, it can say with confidence to the state that its youth can be trained in an institution willing to measure itself not by mediocrity, but by the best educational standards of the nation," Denny boasted. While emphasizing that the University had "not wasted a single dollar" during the past year, Denny reminded the trustees—and thus the state—that there was still a need for money and work to be done as the school neared its centennial year. "Let us renew our vows. Let us resolve to build a greater institution," Denny said. "Let us ask ourselves this question: Does the state of Alabama want, in this new day, a mediocre, routine-minded, per capita-cost-ridden educational factory for quantity productive purposes or does it want a distinguished university? Alabama can have whichever it chooses. Let it not be forgotten at such a time as this that the University is the state's most important instrument of securing its own future, and that the obligation of the state shall be envisioned, not alone in terms of any temporary financial stringency, but also in terms of the commonwealth which the Alabama of tomorrow must become. A university of quality and distinction is the best investment by the state of today for the state of tomorrow," he added in his usual scholarly tone.

The next stumbling block—one of the most frustrating of Denny's administration because it came as a result of success rather than failure—came during a homecoming gathering of the trustees in October 1930 and involved questions regarding the large number of out-of-state students attending the University. The criticism, whether from legislators, local citizens, University trustees or all the above, charged that the University was educating "foreigners" at the expense of Alabama taxpayers. Some of the complaints might have been legitimate considering economic conditions; others were likely based on ethnic or regional prejudice. Either way, it was more than evident that out-of-state student enrollment had increased dramatically over the last decade and as a result Denny was handed a new, distasteful and distracting public issue with which to deal.

Responding to questions from the trustees, Denny reported that University enrollment was at 4,073 students, with 1,806 of those from out of state. There had been a steady rise in out-of-state students over the past decade with a phenomenal snowball effect. The 1920 Corolla listed only three out-of-state students among the 128 seniors. Two of those three were from Columbus, Mississippi, and the other one, significantly, was from Brooklyn, New York. By contrast, the 430-member freshman class of 1930 included 171 out-of-state students, with 67 of those from the greater New York City area. The 1931 freshman class of 419 students included 206 from out of state, including seventy-nine from New York. The freshman class of 1932 included 432 students, with 219—more than half—from out of state and sixty-seven of those from the general New York City area as the influx of "foreigners" continued. By 1934, there were four Jewish fraternities, two Jewish sororities and one Italian fraternity on campus, and the University was turning away up to 800 out-of-state applicants each year. In effect, Tuscaloosa was being overrun with "Yankees," and people were raising eyebrows about it.

"They flooded the place; I'd say there was a justifiable complaint," former University history professor Dr. James F. Doster said in 2013 of the "invasion" of out-of-state students, many of whom were Jews and Italians. Doster, the son of long-time University dean of education Dr. James J. Doster, was a student at the University 1928-34 and had lived on or near the campus all his life. He said he noticed a significant cultural change on campus and heard the talk off campus. "There was talk about them (the out-of-state students) around town, but only as people usually talk about new and different people and events," Doster, at age 101, said. "It was part of a complex situation. Dr. Denny needed every dollar he could get. The Jews weren't welcomed in the usual fraternities, but otherwise I really think they were treated better here (Tuscaloosa) than they were back in their home states," Doster added. Doster added that he thought many of the out-of-state students had come to the University of Alabama because of the widespread publicity of the Alabama football team playing in the Rose Bowl after the 1925, 1926 and 1930 seasons.

Camille Maxwell Elebash, a 1946 University of Alabama graduate and former journalism instructor at the Capstone, recalled hearing her father, long-time University faculty member Fred Maxwell, talk about the large number of Jews and "Yankees" on campus during the 1920s and 1930s. "I think they (the University) did it to get the out-of-state fees. Any money was helpful during the Depression," she said. And the income from the out-of-state students was certainly significant. One financial report showed that the University received $110,773.41 in out-of-state fees during the year ending May 1936 as part of a total income of $706,663.80 from student fees, tuition and room and board for the year. "A lot of the students from out of state were Jews from New York and New Jersey and they had to be noticed around town. I'm sure people referred to them as "Yankees," and "Yankee" was a dirty word back then," Elebash said in 2014. The "Yankees" label was a carryover from the Civil War era, when Confederate "Rebels" faced Union troops, or "Yankees," on the battlefield from 1861-1865. The war proved especially costly to the South as federal troops destroyed factories and cotton crops, took food, valuables and livestock from individuals and burned public buildings and mansions as they plundered the region in the last days of the war.

The bitterest memory of all for citizens of Alabama was the April 4, 1865, Union raid on Tuscaloosa in which Federal troops led by Brigadier General John T. Croxton burned the University of Alabama along with stores, factories and many other structures in the city, killing one University cadet and wounding another in a brief skirmish in the process. Many people in Tuscaloosa still remembered that raid decades later and most others had heard the horrors of the raid repeated time and again. To those citizens, the ashes of that destruction had not yet cooled even in the 1920s and 1930s. Former U. S. Representative Carl Elliott, who served as president of the Student Government Association as he earned a law degree from the University 1930-1936, recalled the mixed emotions that he and other in-state students of the era held in his memoir, *The Cost of Courage.* "Federal troops, after being slightly delayed by cadets from the University, burned all but four of the college's buildings despite pleas from the town's leading citizens. It is memories like that that make resentment die hard," Elliott wrote.

Hardly any Southern family had been untouched by the war or the bitter Reconstruction period and carpetbaggers that followed, and a genuine hatred for "Yankees" was handed down for several generations. The University had sent seven generals, twenty-five colonels, twenty-one majors, one hundred twenty-five captains and two hundred ninety-four privates to the Confederate Army, and many of those were from the Tuscaloosa area. To families of these men, many of whom were killed or wounded, the war was not so long ago that they had forgotten the defeat, destruction and ensuing poverty the South had endured. If anyone had forgotten, *The Tuscaloosa News* reminded them on January 27, 1929, when it ran a front-page feature story recalling the 1865 raid in which University cadet captain Ben Eddins was fatally wounded and another cadet injured as the young students made a brief stand against the invading Union troops. Several citizens recounted their memories of the raid in the story, which was headlined "Local Residents Vividly Recall Yankees Coming to Tuscaloosa." Whether by design or by strange coincidence, the story came in the midst of the controversy over the high number out-of-state students and could not have helped ease any real or imagined tensions. Other news reports of the era might well have influenced public concerns, if not prejudices, over the "foreigners" as well.

Notorious big-city Italian and Jewish gangsters like Al Capone, George "Bugsy" Moran, Meyer Lansky, Carlo Gambino, Frank Costello, Lucky Luciano, Charlie Fischetti and Frank Nitti became widely known through news reports, including the headlines of February 14, 1929, that told of the St. Valentine's Day massacre in Chicago in which seven members of Moran's gang were executed by rival gang members. Whether caused by ethnic bias or a general distrust for "Yankees," there were surely feelings of resentment for the out-of-state students in the early 1930s, and if local newspapers—or anyone else—stood with Denny on the issue, they escaped discovery. *The Anniston Star*, in 1935, finally spoke out in defense of Denny and the University's enrollment of large numbers of out-of-state students, but the support came well after the controversy had quieted and seemed too little and far too late.

Prompted by the questions from University trustees in October 1930, Denny said the University had begun a detailed study of the situation and asked that any judgment or action to change admission policies or increase out-of-state fees be delayed until the study was completed. "I cannot resist the feeling that friends of education in general and of this institution in particular would not approve any action based on mere guesswork or on mere ex parte opinion rather than on a mature and exhaustive and unprejudiced weighing of the facts at issue. My one concern is that whatever is done shall be done only after careful and exhaustive study," Denny said. He added that the University had raised out-of-state fees by fifty percent, from $45 to $60 per semester, in 1928, and that testimony from faculty members "has been that the better average preparation of the out-of-state student admitted has meant a perceptible quickening of scholastic standards, resulting in an advantage of Alabama students that cannot be measured in dollars and cents."

The University, reacting to questions and criticism, conducted two studies related to the escalating number of out-of-state students. One study, led by executive secretary Ralph E. Adams, reviewed school admission and transfer standards with the finding that the standards of the Association of Colleges and Secondary Schools of the Southern States were being "carefully administered in all divisions of the University." The February 1931 report noted that the University had rejected more than 800 out-of-state applicants during the past year, including 300 applicants for medical school, and that approximately half the rejected applicants were "Jewish boys from the area of which New York may be considered the center. There is little doubt in my mind that we have in the past five years shown a greater degree of liberality in admitting out-of-state Jewish boys than has been the case with other state universities of this region. And we have done it in the face of a rather persistent criticism from many alumni and citizens of Alabama," Adams wrote in his report.

Adams added that "other state universities of the South, though not so acutely, are likewise confronted with a somewhat similar problem" and concluded that the "unusual increase here apparently had its beginning in the unprecedented nationwide publicity given to the University in 1925 and 1926. At any rate, we know that four or five years ago, following two trips to the Pacific coast in successive years by the football team, largely increased numbers of out-of-state students sought admission to the University," he added. Although Adams did not list them at the time, other contributing factors probably included the Crimson Tide's 9-7 win over Pennsylvania in Philadelphia in November 1922; transfer of the medical school to the main campus in 1920; limited admission of Jews in many Eastern colleges, and perhaps most of all, Denny's long-standing admonition that each returning student bring two new students each year.

Rose Bowl appearances also helped Crimson Tide football recruiting, of course, as out-of-state athletes came to Alabama because of the widespread publicity. An unusually large number of the players came from Arkansas, where Pine Bluff pool hall operator Jimmy Harland helped the Alabama cause. Harland became an Alabama fan during the Crimson Tide's early Rose Bowl days and steered a large number of players to his adopted team. Those players included such stars as Don Hutson, Charlie Marr, Paul "Bear" Bryant, J. B. "Ears" Whitworth and brothers Herschel, Norman and Russell Mosley from Arkansas and Billy Cadenhead from Greenville, Mississippi. Bryant, of course, served as head football coach at Alabama for twenty-five seasons (1958-1982), posting a record of 232-46-9 while winning six national championships and thirteen conference titles.

Another out-of-state student who came to Alabama because of the football team was Tom Griffin, who said he came to Tuscaloosa from Chicago in 1935 with friend Bill Berk because they wanted to attend a college with a good football team. Griffin graduated in 1939 and was commissioned a lieutenant in the Army through ROTC. He became a navigator in the Army Air Forces during World War II and earned life-long fame when he guided one of the sixteen B-25 bombers used in the dramatic "Doolittle Raid" on Tokyo on April 18, 1942, as the U. S. struck back at the Japanese after their December 7, 1941, surprise bombing attack on Pearl Harbor, Hawaii. Griffin was among a number of former University of Alabama students featured in the book *All of Us Fought the War* and honored by the University in 2012 for their service in World War II.

Adams, noting that an additional study of the policies relating to out-of-state students was under way, wrote, "Meantime, we have already taken steps to go behind the scholastic records of out-of-state students with a view to getting information concerning them other than the information ordinarily given in high school transcripts. These matters, of course, relate to the enforcement of entrance requirements, perhaps not directly, but nonetheless certainly as indicating that our problem for the future is to pursue with increased vigor the policy of restricting admissions. Of course, I do not wish to be understood as opposed to the policy of admitting out-of-state students. Moreover, I am convinced that the presence of the out-of-state student has exercised a liberalizing influence on the campus which has meant a great deal to our Alabama students."

"A few of our citizens, judging from their statements, have assumed that the presence of these out-of-state students is resulting in a net financial loss to the University and therefore, in the last analysis, to the state," Denny said in choosing Lee Bidgood, dean of the School of Commerce and Business Administration, to chair a committee to determine the actual financial effect of out-of-state students on the University budget. The extensive study covered 1929-30 and included building maintenance, equipment, utilities, instruction, etc. The results, which found a balance of $58,196.45 in favor of the University, were no doubt shocking to critics and perhaps equally surprising to Capstone officials. Bidgood's report showed that the University had collected $187,341.97 in tuition and fees from out-of-state students during 1929-30 against actual costs of $129,145.52. The report pointed out that approximately $60,000 of the total came from out-of-state fees alone. A similar study of the 1930-31 year found a balance of more than $82,000 in favor of the University. "This study shows conclusively that the University has profited from the presence of the out-of-state students," Bidgood wrote in his report on the first study. "The net financial gain to the University treasury, of course, is only a fraction of the economic gain to the state at large due to the presence of the students, who undoubtedly contribute greatly to the economic strength of this section and thus ultimately to the taxpaying ability of citizens in this section," Bidgood wisely added in his report.

Even after the Bidgood report, Denny had to muster allies from all sides to defeat a 1932 bill supported by Governor Benjamin M. Miller that would have allowed the state legislature to set fees for out-of-state students for all institutions of higher learning in the state. The bill was clearly aimed at limiting out-of-state enrollment at the University of Alabama, whether prompted by ethnic or regional bias or jealousy from cross-state rival Auburn, with which the University competed for students and funds. With the statehouse controlled by Auburn-leaning farm interests, Denny knew he had to fight, and fight he did.

Citing figures from the latest Brookings Report, Denny reported that the University had an enrollment of 4,073 students during 1930-31, with 1,806 of those from out of state. Auburn, meanwhile, had an enrollment of 2,006, of which only 275 were listed as out-of-state students. "It therefore follows, whether intentionally or otherwise, that this legislation in its practical effect is against the University of Alabama alone," he said in an emphatic statement against the action. "The legislature should not undertake by statutes…to handle matters of internal finances and administrative management of an educational institution. Such matters should be left to the management and discretion of the board of trustees and its executive officers. They alone are in a position from year to year, from month to month and sometimes from day to day to determine what charges should be made and what charges should not be made. They alone have expert and actual experience in dealing with these matters," Denny said.

Denny said that some advocates of the proposed legislation had "reached the conclusion that the University is using appropriations to educate out-of-state students at the expense of state students. As a matter of fact, the University is educating state students from funds acquired from out-of-state students. Is it proposed to cut off this out-of-state revenue and at the same time reduce state appropriations, thus reducing the size, efficiency and influence of the University to the status that obtained a quarter of a century ago?" he asked the legislators. And calling attention to possible ethnic bias, Denny added that "a great deal of unfair information has been distributed to the effect that an undue percentage of the out-of-state students are 'Eastside Jews.' Exaggerated statements are being constantly made on this point." Ironically, two of the "Eastside Jews" whose mere presence helped create the controversy were New York City natives Jerome (Jerry) Britchley and Robert Kosower, the two *Crimson White* writers who had led the drive to build Denny Chimes just two years earlier.

"Recognizing the advantage of having a cosmopolitan student body, Dr. Denny encouraged the out-of-state students to come to the University," a 1939 *Crimson White* editorial said in praise of Denny and the growth of the University. "The wisdom of this plan was soon proven. Each year the number of students increased, and last year a new high was reached when over 5,400 persons from all over the country enrolled at the University. They are the ones who upon their graduation will carry the cherished ideals and traditions of Alabama to every state in the union."

Although Denny reported an enrollment of 4,073 in May 1931, he was again forced to defend University needs as state funding to education faced severe cuts because of the Depression. "There has developed in the minds of some good citizens an impression that higher education has been given preferred consideration. This impression is not justified by the facts," Denny said in his annual public address to the trustees. He added that total appropriations to higher education in the state represented only a "small percentage of the sum total of the expenditures on education in Alabama…and even if the institutions of higher learning were penalized in drastic fashion, the net results to the public schools in the matter of lengthening terms or of increasing the pay of teachers would scarcely touch the hem of the garment of the real financial problem involved in promoting the interests of the public schools." He justified continued funding for higher education by saying, "Not only is the public school system dependent on the development of higher education, but every interest of Alabama—intellectual, spiritual and material, is at stake. I wish the state at large understood fully the entire problem, especially the building problem concerning which there has been widespread misinformation," Denny said.

Denny pointed out that of the $750,000 appropriated in 1927 for construction at the University, only $250,000 had been made available in cash. "Warrants for an additional $250,000 were issued, but still remain unpaid," he said. Denny added that from the beginning of his administration in 1912, funds paid specifically by the state for University of Alabama campus construction amounted to only $365,000. That total included the $250,000 in 1927 plus $115,000 in 1915. "Meantime, the student body has increased more than ten-fold," he said.

Denny said the University had sought subscriptions from private individuals in many instances, as in the case of Farrah Hall (law building), but that the lack of state funding "has stood in the way of proper development of the libraries and laboratories. It has made impossible the expansion of the School of Medicine. It has impeded research.

It has retarded the growth of the Graduate School. It has prevented the essential enlargement of the faculty in keeping with the growth of the student body. Classrooms are sorely needed. Important departments like music, art, sociology, geology and botany need development. A dormitory for women, an adequate library building and a laboratory for biology must be erected. The power plant needs enlargement. Dormitories for men should be constructed. Such a situation cannot be permitted to continue without serious injustice to every interest involved. Educational standardizing agencies have definite requirements that must be met and ought to be met. The University owes it to the state and the state owes it to the University to meet every requirement squarely. Anything short of this is unfair and impossible," he said.

Denny told the trustees that the University needed an increase in its current expense budget of "at least fifty percent," saying, "If we are to do our work effectively and in accordance with modern requirements, larger revenues and greater stabilization of financial policies are essential. The present low per-capita cost makes impossible the doing of the job as it ought to be done." He pointed to Auburn as he asked for research funding, saying, "Agricultural research work is being fostered by the state and federal governments with ever-increasing liberality. Yet we have found it difficult to secure resources essential to the development of research in the fields for which the University is responsible. The future will ultimately depend upon what happens in the laboratories of men." A treasurer's report submitted with Denny's written report to the trustees in 1931 did not strongly bolster his request for an increase in funding, however. The report showed an income of $1,004,107.20 for the past year against expenses of $534,825.32, leaving a balance of $469,281.88 on hand. Meanwhile, the University's endowment fund had increased to $2,623,371.05, an increase of $270,000 over the previous year. Instead of receiving praise, Denny's sound management of University funds only opened the door for more resistance to his requests for increased funding.

Urging action from University of Alabama alumni and graduates in his 1931 commencement remarks, Denny said, "This is our centennial year. Will the people of Alabama celebrate this great event by clothing the institution with renewed power or by allowing it to slip backward? This is the supreme question to be answered. Mere verbal eulogy without substantial action would be as sounding brass. The University is the state's greatest intellectual asset. The fathers who founded it pledged the good faith of the state to its liberal support…. If the state is able to establish new agencies and give them such financial support as to acclaim them as of first rank in comparison with similar agencies of the most progressive commonwealths, how can it justify inadequate support to its first-born spiritual child? The opportunity is ours. The goal will not be reached in a quadrennial or even in a decade. The rate of progress, however, will be determined in large measure by the unity of purpose, the devotion to correct ideals and the unselfish cooperation of the friends of the institution wherever they may be. I make appeal again for such unity and devotion and cooperation," he added. Denny, as always, was calling for moral and monetary support, and his sermon surely inspired his Capstone audience. It did not carry over to the legislative level, however. His campaign for increased funding went unheeded as the state's financial crisis grew worse and the Depression touched more and more of the population.

The University of Alabama, through what Denny called "heroic efforts," managed somehow to continue its upward spiral over the next year also. Reporting to the trustees in May 1932, Denny reported a thirteen percent increase in student enrollment for the year just ended, saying, "The teaching staff and the physical equipment of the University are heavily taxed in our effort to care for the rapidly growing student body." Enrollment for the year included 4,639 resident students, 2,356 in summer school, 3,122 in extension courses and 107 in medical school.

"It will be surprising perhaps to many that the University has continued to grow so rapidly in these times of financial stress," Denny said in his annual address to the trustees. "While it is undoubtedly true that many students who would otherwise be in college are unable to attend, it is also true that unemployment in industry is resulting in bringing into college a vast number of young people who in more prosperous periods would not have continued their training beyond high school. Intelligent youth is observant. The fact that the educated person is being given preferred consideration in the matter of employment makes a great appeal to them. The result is that parents are making tremendous sacrifices to keep their children in college in preparation for the better days to come rather than have them at home. This is one of the bright spots on the horizon looking to the future. We shall have better trained leadership in the next generation. That means in itself an improved economic status for the entire region.... It is now almost axiomatic that a state's financial and economic status can be measured in terms of higher education. Knowledge is power. Education is one thing on which people have never spent too much; the more they spend the richer they become," he added.

Denny said the University had been placed in an "impossible situation" due to the "acute financial situation of the state" which had allowed only sixteen percent of the University appropriations for 1931-32 to be paid by the state treasurer. "Apparently, education has, in this all-important particular, fared relatively worse than any other single agency of the state. Through heroic efforts, we have been able to operate in the face of many handicaps," Denny said. "The time has now come when there must be relief. There is a limit to our ability to carry the burden.... It is true that Alabama has a large debt, funded and unfunded. It is true that this debt must be paid. Since, however, it is also true that the educated citizen is our chief resource, financial and intellectual, we do need to drive home the fact that if we are ever to liquidate our debt, we must refuse to strike down the chief resource by which it can be paid."

Based on an August 11, 1932, letter from Bidgood to Denny, an increase in student tuition rates was considered that summer to help offset the lack of adequate state funding. "Pursuing the line of thought expressed in our recent conversations and exchange of letters, I should like to call your attention to the case of a student who has been enrolled in the University, taking Commerce, this summer," Bidgood began. "The young man is named Troy Crawford. He is a country boy from Lamar County.... When he registered for his course this summer, I thought his situation an impossible one, and confidently expected that he would soon quit. But he is still here, made a grade of A on his accounting course, and says that he is going to stick to it until he graduates. The day he registered he told me that he had arrived with ninety cents in his pocket. He had no expectations of receiving any money whatever from home. He got Mr. Adams to defer his University fees with the understanding that they would be paid gradually during the summer on the installment plan. He got a job on Mr. (Perry B.) Hughes' campus gang (grounds and maintenance crew) through the student self-help bureau and has been mowing grass, chopping weeds and the like for three or four hours a day since he came. He told me last Saturday that he was applying all his earnings to the payment of his fees and expected to have them discharged by the end of the summer." Bidgood wrote that Crawford was living with an uncle in Northport and they were eating potatoes that Crawford grew in Lamar County and brought to Tuscaloosa when he came to school. "The thing that is worrying Troy now is that the uncle is thinking of going back to the country on account of lack of work in Northport. Troy is trying to get a sweeping job, or some similar place, and stay on anyhow.

"The point about Troy Crawford is that his case is exactly similar to about two hundred Alabama boys in the School of Commerce," Bidgood continued. "Troy's ninety cents and potato patch make a little more dramatic story, but the conditions are essentially alike. Any attempt to finance the University of Alabama by a further increase in fees will absolutely close the door of hope to Troy Crawford and the others like him. It means those ambitious, capable and hopeful fellows would be permanently cut off from a university education. These are the young people whom Thomas Jefferson saw in his day when he demanded equality of opportunity and sought it through the medium of state-supported higher education. These are the young people whom the Constitutional Convention of Alabama, meeting at Huntsville more than a century ago, had in mind when they provided for the establishment of a state university. These are the ones for whom democracy has provided a door of opportunity for the exercise of their talents in the state-supported colleges of the land for these past three or four generations, and they are the ones to whom Alabama looks with hope for the progress of her people during the coming generation. It seems to me that those who are responsible for the financial problems of Alabama at the present time might well consider Troy Crawford of Lamar County and the many hundreds of others like him," Bidgood concluded.

Crawford worked at a number of jobs on campus and earned a degree in business in 1935, according to University records. His surviving widow Sarah said in June 2015 that he still owed fees when he graduated and did not receive his diploma until a few months later, when he made his final payment after finding work with the Tennessee Valley Authority in Knoxville, Tennessee. Mrs. Crawford said her husband often told the story of how he hitched a ride on a milk truck from Lamar County to Tuscaloosa and "went straight to Dr. Denny and caught him by the coattail and asked him for a job and got one. He said he waited on tables and mowed grass with the grounds crew to work his way through school," she added. Crawford worked for the TVA and at Hercules Powder Plant before serving in the Coast Guard during World War II. He worked at Brookley Field in Mobile after the war and later started and ran his own business. He died January 29, 2004. Mrs. Crawford is a 1952 University of Alabama graduate and former teacher.

Further proof that the state's school systems were in dire financial need came in November of 1932 when a news report announced that funds for the new fiscal year were being distributed and that "public school teachers, many of whom have not had a payday in months," would receive some relief. The state comptroller's office said that $437,967 of a $608,492 distribution to the state department of education would be used for teacher salaries. At the same time, the University of Alabama and Auburn received $72,016.63 each while Alabama College received $48,608.50 and the state teachers colleges received $7,059 each.

Another indication that the University was under attack came in a November 1932 letter to Denny from trustee Daniel Pratt, who wrote, "…I don't see how you have put up with a lot of things which have confronted you recently. The majority of the legislature seemed determined to kill all higher education in Alabama and especially the University. Since you have been at the head of the University, I believe firmly that you have done more for Alabama than all the present members of the legislature and senate combined. While I voted for (Governor) Miller, it was solely on account of his campaign pledges which I believed he would attempt, at best, to carry out. Never again for me. I have had good and plenty of Miller (an 1889 University of Alabama law school graduate) and all his ideas. I am certain that the trustees will in every way possible sustain everything which you have done during the trying period through which you have passed."

Pratt also wrote to Judge Henry B. Foster, chairman of the board of trustees executive committee, asking him to draft a resolution "endorsing Dr. Denny's work in trying to persuade the legislature to treat the University fairly instead of trying to kill it as they seem determined to do." Pratt, saying that he did not blame Denny for being "sore and disgusted" over the University's treatment by the legislature, asked Foster to "make the resolution good and strong…. The main thing is to make it absolutely plain and clear to anyone reading the resolution that the trustees are backing Dr. Denny to the limit and that the people of Alabama should be doing the same thing." If such a resolution was passed, no report of it was found in this work. And it is certain that there was no immediate change in appropriations to the University.

There was a plea of desperation in Denny's report to the trustees in May of 1933 as he recounted the financial stress caused by a thirty percent cut in state funds in 1932 followed by an additional forty-five percent cut. "That makes a total cut of seventy-five percent," Denny said. "Yet comparatively few people in Alabama know anything about what has transpired in regard to the budget reductions. That kind of news has not traveled with great speed. Every effort is being made to bring about rigid reductions in the various University expenditures. These additional reductions are being made effective as rapidly as a reasonable regard for the morale of the teaching staff would justify," he said, acknowledging the fact that overall budget adjustments included salary cuts for faculty and staff. Denny's previous salary had already been cut to $7,700 at this point, and it soon fell to $4,491.69 for the next two years. The 1934 pay was half his salary of $9,166.70 for the year ending April 30, 1930, and was the result of his across-the-board salary cuts, although lower paid faculty and staff faced cuts of smaller percentages. Denny also reported that "severe fiscal conditions" had caused the withdrawal of a large number of students, leaving only 4,650 students enrolled in May 1933. The Tuscaloosa News, acknowledging the University's plight, spoke out on Denny's behalf in a May 21 editorial, saying, "The University is ending a year in which it has proved itself through the ordeal by fire. Never before, except during that disorganized Reconstruction period, has the institution met greater obstacles with the fortitude, wisdom and determination exemplified by President Denny and his associates in coping with the financial emergency that has faced them for the last eighteen months."

"The University is in critical need of operating funds in view of the unprecedented reduction of its revenues," Denny added in his address to the trustees. "In the course of great business depression, we test our intelligence and inventory our convictions. Nothing is so costly as ignorance. Ignorant people possess few of the blessings of life. That commonwealth which has courageous and visionary leaders who dare in crises to foster education, including education for leadership, will be the commonwealth that will make history. Alabama is on trial. Our people have yet to decide that they really regard higher education as an asset rather than a liability." Ominously, he added that he had seen evidence of "an unfriendly attitude from unexpected sources toward higher education in Alabama" during the past year, including some in the state legislature, where there had been talk of cutting higher education appropriations and an effort to drive out of Alabama the out-of-state student. "Here again, the unfriendly attitude is to be traced in large degree to a mistaken conception," Denny said.

"Three years ago it was being proclaimed here and there by people who neither knew the facts nor sought to ascertain them that Alabama was using the resources of the state to educate 'foreigners,'" Denny said in addressing one of the unfriendly attitudes. "There followed an exhaustive, scientific and detailed study of the entire problem by an able commission, and it was clearly demonstrated that instead of educating 'foreigners' at Alabama's expense, these 'foreigners' were in fact substantially helping to educate Alabama students. The simple and undisputed fact is that without the help derived from this source the University would now be in a most unhappy situation." Denny said further that he was concerned with what he saw as "an effort being made at the state level to minimize or obscure the real facts concerning the drastic reductions already made in appropriations to higher education and the tomb-like silence regarding the amazingly low per capita costs at the University. The per capita cost of instruction at the University of Alabama, even prior to the radical economies of 1932-1933 the lowest in any state university in the country, is now far below any figure that can be justified."

A *Tuscaloosa News* editorial on May 23, 1933, said Denny's challenge to University trustees and alumni had brought about "a fusion of minds and perceptions which welded a more united alumni than any the University has seen in recent years. Many pleaded ignorance of the facts which the executive so clearly depicted. All offered steadfast assurance that the future will find them not wanting in zealous loyalty to the institution and also to the future welfare of their state. In this time of crisis the Alabama alumni have seen the vision and shown the spirit that will not countenance defeat," the editorial concluded. Another *Tuscaloosa News* editorial on June 4, 1933, reminded readers of Denny's recent statement that the state of Alabama had imposed greater penalties on higher education than any other state and called on the alumni to lend its financial support. "That is a situation that cannot be allowed to continue, for we are primarily dependent on the university, Auburn and Montevallo to furnish our leadership and on the teacher colleges to turn out a higher grade of instructors for the boys and girls who enter the primary and secondary schools.... If the state will not support higher education as it should be supported, then the alumni should endow these institutions in such a way as will allow them to fulfill their higher missions.... Dr. Denny has done a great job at the University. He has managed to pay his teachers when other schools of the state were in default. But he has not had the support to which he is entitled by the alumni of Alabama, nor has Auburn or Montevallo. The average graduate seems to feel that he owes nothing to his alma mater after he secures his sheepskin other than to support its football team and to rally around the college banner on festal occasions…. Every college graduate should become a student of the theory and practice of education, and if this were done the interests of our schools would be seen as a whole and their welfare would be promoted not only financially but scholastically as well."

Denny reported a five percent drop in enrollment a year later as only 4,433 students completed the spring semester of 1934, but he added that "the solvency of the institution has been maintained in spite of all handicaps." He added, however, that the University "cannot continue to exist on the severe reductions in appropriations made in 1932 if higher education is to do its duty. There is constantly recurring evidence that a considerable portion of our population does not fully realize the essential value of higher education in our civilization. Many people have little conception of the relationship of the colleges to science, to industry, to social welfare," he said. "There is perhaps a growing recognition of the functions of these colleges in training teachers, and perhaps in other restricted fields. Yet it is a fact that there is an overwhelming need of a finer and more comprehensive appreciation of the fact that higher education is essential not to a mere segment…but to the entire circumference of our possibilities as an enlightened commonwealth."

Denny was unable to continue his aggressive building program during the lean years, of course. After the opening of the Student Union Building and Barnwell Hall in 1930, there were no new buildings until Little Hall (men's dormitory) in 1935 and Hardaway Hall (engineering school) in 1936. There was a silver lining behind the dark clouds of 1934, however. Because of the continued success of the football team, which capped a perfect 10-0 season in 1934 with a 29-13 Rose Bowl win over Stanford to claim conference and national championships, there was money to expand Denny Stadium to 29,000 seats in the coming months as Denny's vision for the Capstone continued to materialize.

Dr. Denny, then University of Alabama chancellor,
at a University dinner, circa 1944.

9

Crisis and Controversy

"His achievements in the face of baffling obstacles are unsurpassed in the history of education in this country and will be a brilliant chapter not only in the annals of the University of Alabama but of the South."
—University of Alabama Board of Trustees

There was new-found hope in Alabama and across the nation as the year 1935 began. Denny had skillfully steered the University of Alabama through five turbulent years of financial hardship; the Crimson Tide football team had captured national headlines again with a glorious January 1, 1935, Rose Bowl victory; President Franklin D. Roosevelt's New Deal programs were putting people back to work and helping send young men and women to college, and University enrollment for the spring semester was 4,717 compared to 4,033 a year earlier. There were good reasons to believe that better times lay just ahead.

Any feeling of cautious optimism that Denny might have enjoyed at the time was merely a moment of fleeting calm before the next storm, however. Less than one hundred days later, University of Alabama fortunes turned upside down when the *Birmingham Post* reported that Denny had resigned following criticism of University financial policies by a state legislator. The legislator—Senator Shelby Fletcher of Madison—threatened to cut funding to the University rather than increase it as Denny asked and an ensuing "row" over the matter had been the last straw for Denny, according to the stunning report.

"Denny Quits as President of University," said the front-page headline in the *Birmingham Post* of Wednesday, April 3, 1935. And if that news wasn't shocking enough, additional subheads said, "Action Comes as Climax to Legislative Row on Endowment," "Dissension on Campus" and "Faculty Members Ask Probe of Living Conditions after Pay Cuts." The news story came out of Montgomery, where Denny and members of the executive committee of the University board of trustees had appeared the day before to discuss future budget needs with the legislative recess committee on finance and taxation. Fletcher, Senator James Simpson of Jefferson County and Representative Clint Harrison of Marengo County made up the committee, which controlled funding for state agencies.

On the eve of the April 2 committee hearing, Denny had told an informal gathering of trustees that the University was in desperate need of more state funds, saying, "It cannot be too strongly emphasized that the University cannot continue longer on its emergency budget. This budget must undergo a radical revision. The very life of the University as a university is at stake." At the same meeting, he told the trustees in confidence that due to health issues and his age, he would like to retire as soon as a suitable replacement could be found. In response to Denny's comments about the University's funding needs, the trustees adopted a resolution calling on state legislators to restore full funding to the University, saying that such funding had been restored in most other states. Somehow, the "confidential" status of Denny's pending retirement was leaked to the media along with the resolution, resulting in the "Denny Quits" headline.

An aroused, spontaneous crowd of approximately 4,000 students, faculty and townspeople greeted Denny on his return to the University on Wednesday afternoon, according an April 4 *Tuscaloosa News* story headlined "Denny Spikes Resignation Story; Students Rally to Display Faith." Denny assured the crowd of supporters that his resignation, whenever submitted, would "be effective only after my successor has actually been installed. I have never for a moment thought of any summary action. I have always made it clear that my resignation, whenever it was submitted, was to be effective only after my successor had actually been installed…. I have every desire to serve the highest and best interests of the institution which we all love and which I have striven to serve in high and useful ways." Denny also told the students that even when he retired, he planned to continue an "intimate association" with the institution, the community and the state. "I love the University of Alabama. For nearly a quarter of a century I have sought to serve it with devotion. Whatever the future may hold in store for me, I shall always stand ready to serve it," he said. In a brief formal statement issued to the media refuting much of the *Post* story, Denny said, "…For several years I have discussed with the trustees the whole problem of lightening my load. It is true that I have felt the burden and strain of it. It is not only proper but also clearly my duty to add that my wish to be relieved of heavy burdens has no connection whatever with any hearings before the legislative committees. Equally untrue is the statement that there has been a word of complaint to me regarding the reduction of faculty salaries."

An April 5 story in *The Tuscaloosa News* also reported that the American Association of College Professors had not received a request to investigate living conditions or reduced salaries of professors at the University and said that faculty members interviewed "expressed strong resentment of the insinuation and declared that they had not heard the slightest intimation of faculty dissension." At the same time, the University of Alabama Chapter of the American Association of College Professors adopted a resolution denying any faculty dissension and voicing full confidence in Dr. Denny and his policies. "The statement to the effect that certain members of the faculty had asked the American Association of University Professors to investigate the financial conditions of the University with a view to having salary cuts restored is entirely without foundation and convey an utterly false impression of the attitude of the faculty towards the administration. The national headquarters of the association, in reply to a telegram of inquiry, states that no request for an investigation at the University of Alabama has been received," the resolution began. The resolution voiced support of the building of the endowment fund; recognized that salary cuts were "necessary and unavoidable;" expressed support for Denny's "business-like management of the University's finances, especially during these last critical years when the University has been the only institution of higher learning in the state that has been able to meet all obligations promptly;" assured Denny of the faculty's "very high esteem and regard for him as a man and administrator;" expressed confidence in his judgment, and urged him to "remain with us as long as his physical condition will permit."

University Graduate School Dean Albert Moore, one of Denny's most loyal friends, sent Denny a long, emotional personal letter dated April 7 in which he recalled the rally of support that welcomed Denny on his return to the Capstone on April 3, praised the University president for his many achievements and gently urged him to reconsider his pending retirement. "What a beautiful tribute of affection, loyalty and confidence has been paid you in this, probably your last magnificent fight on behalf of the University of Alabama!" Moore wrote. "Those of us who have been close to you and who understand your marvelous achievements against odds that would have broken the morale of any but the stoutest of hearts are profoundly gratified. The outpouring of faith and affection from the faculty, the student body and the people of Tuscaloosa was a beautiful spectacle. No doubt our sentiment is shared largely by the fine people all over Alabama. Rarely, indeed, has one stirred the imagination and gripped the hearts of his people with bonds of faith and high esteem as you have done. It will all be recorded in Alabama history as the achievement of a great personality, a great mind and a heart full of courage and unflinching devotion to duty.... You have achieved immortal recognition and honor in Alabama. No conspiracy of disparagement among the selfish and spiritually dwarfed, no efforts of disreputable and craven journalists can compromise you in your exalted position or detract from the glory of your accomplishments.

"One hazards nothing in saying that in years to come those in Alabama who would serve intelligently and faithfully will find in your career the most inspiring example. Your great work, recognized even by partisan opponents, will gain added luster as the years go by and people are enabled to see it in truer perspective. When the true history of education in Alabama during this generation is written, it will be developed around leadership. The University of Alabama will continue to have its trials, but it will surmount all obstacles. You have laid its foundations securely and infused into it the spirit and ideals that will make it continue to grow and to broaden its influence and service. It will ever be a resplendent monument to the power of your personality and ideals and the wisdom of your leadership. Surely the tender emotions and the confidence and loyalty manifested on all sides have tempted you to toil on to the end. When I reflect on your problem, my emotions impel me in one direction, my judgment in another. Whatever your final decision may be, and you have a right to make it, your devoted faculty will labor faithfully with you to the last minute of your administration. None of them would want you to deal unjustly with yourself, but if you should decide, after due consideration for the welfare of yourself and your family, to postpone indefinitely your resignation, all would feel supremely gratified," Moore added.

Other faculty members sent personal notes of support to Denny as well. Associate Professor of Education H. C. Pannell wrote, "Since the *Birmingham Post* attack I have wanted to renew my pledge of loyalty and to express my admiration of your courage and untiring efforts on behalf of the institution which you have served with unsurpassed zeal and devotion. While I appreciate the fact that you are tired, it is my sincere belief that the institution cannot afford to lose your guiding hand at this time. You have given yourself so unselfishly in the past to the institution that it seems almost a selfish wish that we cherish when we ask you to carry on even at the risk of your own health. However, I hope very much that your physical condition may permit you to do so," Pannell added in his April 22 note.

The unsubstantiated report of faculty complaints about prolonged salary cuts apparently had an impact on Denny and the trustees, who restored at least a portion of the previous forty-five percent reduction on May 1. Dr. Ott wrote to Denny on May 8 acknowledging with "surprise and appreciation" the pay increase. "…I never had the slightest doubt that you would take this step at the earliest possible moment. I happen to know that some of the younger men have been sorely pressed of late. To them this increase means a great deal, albeit there has never been a word of complaint of their former status," Ott said.

Fletcher, an 1892 University graduate, ignited the firestorm of controversy when he criticized Denny's management of University funds after learning that the school's endowment fund had grown from $2,623,371.05 in 1931 to $4,734,256.67 in 1935 even as faculty salaries were slashed by almost fifty percent and Denny continued to plead for additional funding from the state. Fletcher said bluntly that "if the University has been able to increase its endowment by $3 million during the lean years, it is getting too large an appropriation from the state." Protesting the use of student fees to increase the endowment rather than using the money for operation and maintenance expenses, Fletcher responded to the University's funding request by saying that instead of restoring full funding from its fifty percent of appropriation level, he might well suggest an additional fifty percent cut. That comment, according to the *Post* report, set off the reported row between Denny and the committee. Fletcher's comments, coupled with reports of faculty unrest, painted a picture of a wealthy, perhaps mismanaged University instead of one in dire need of increased funding and likely cast Denny and the University in an unfavorable light in the eyes of the state's citizens, who faced a proposed sales tax to support education in the midst of the Depression. Denny, of course, was forced to defend his request, and he did so strongly, saying the additional funds were needed for new buildings, repairs, classroom equipment and library needs. It is unlikely that Denny would have engaged in a common "row" as the *Post* story indicated, but it is certain that he would have stood his ground in any debate over the funding issue. And it is certain that Denny traveled fully armed with facts, figures, logic and passion when he spoke of the needs of the University; and no one knew those needs better than Denny.

In what *The Tuscaloosa News* called "a sharp difference of opinion" with Fletcher, Denny pointed out that for several years the state had paid only $250,000 of an appropriated amount of $500,000 per year to the University, thus funding it at the lowest per-capita level of any college in the country. He also explained that the increase in endowment funds was brought about partly by the purchase of unsecured state warrants. Denny had shrewdly bought the warrants at fifty percent of face value during a period when the state could not redeem them and held them until their value was fully restored, thus doubling the University's investment. Fletcher's committee, after hearing requests for increased funding from all the state's colleges and universities, did not recommend any increased funding for higher education. Based on financial statements, state funding to the University during the Depression era included $230,698 in 1929, $198,323 in 1930, $269,135 in 1931, $69,965 in 1931, $266,000 in 1932, $247,000 in 1933, $242,000 in 1934 and $127,000 in 1935. The significant increase in University endowment funds during the same period, although applauded by many as financial wizardry by Denny, did in fact leave Denny and the University open to criticism. University trustees stood firmly behind Denny and his management of University funds, of course. They issued a lengthy, detailed statement explaining all University fiscal actions and needs and invited a review of the matter "by an impartial, expert group of specialists in educational administration—men of national standing in the field—to render authoritative judgment regarding the adequacy of the total income of the institution from whatever source derived to meet its total educational responsibility."

A *Tuscaloosa News* editorial on April 4 criticized the April 3 *Post* story, saying it had taken "half-truths and twisted them into sensationalism…in an effort to harass and if possible destroy one of the most successful and valuable public servants in the history of the state of Alabama…. The nastiest dig of all has been the attempt to make it appear that there is a near revolt brewing among the members of the faculty over salaries, for it is doubtful if there is a more loyal group in America than that which teaches in the classrooms at the University every day. No more 'loyal to their chief' crowd ever drew a breath. It is true that they are badly underpaid in some instances but it is also true that they have shouldered their hardships with a smile in the knowledge that half a loaf was better than none and that if the day came when 'Mike' could restore those pay cuts he would do so…. That Dr. Denny has wanted and needed relief from some of the terrific load which he bears has been known for several years, but to seize on that well-known fact to make it appear that he has resigned in a childish huff because he does not see eye-to-eye with the legislative committee is ridiculous to all who know the fighting qualities of the South's greatest educator. Marked success makes a shining mark of any man who achieves it. George H. Denny has achieved it to such an outstanding degree that many have seen fit to use him that they might draw themselves to the public eye for a moment and those who care not who or what they destroy aim their darts of poison at him. This is a jealous world and the price of success is great. It carries with it many an unfair sting, but neither jealousy, envy, political chicanery nor 'yellow journalism' can… prevail against success, integrity, fair play and truth. 'Mike' has not resigned and our prediction is that when he does leave that institution which he loves as a part of himself it will be when they carry him from the campus on the last mortal journey," the editorial concluded.

The *Montgomery Advertised* joined in the widespread support of Denny, saying in an April 5 editorial that "While there are some jealousies among educational leaders because of the wonderful growth of the University under Dr. Denny's executive direction, the average Alabamian believes that Dr. Denny has accomplished a herculean task in his 23-year connection with the University. And when you take Alabama alumni, they are unanimous in expressing love and affection for Dr. Denny. They know intimately of his work…. Today the University is equipped to compete with the best universities in the land. That does not mean that there is no need for more facilities at the University…. Dr. Denny's ears must be burning constantly now because people all over Alabama are saying fine things about him and his work. There will be no resignation if Dr. Denny harkens to the trustees or to University men and women generally and to the average citizen as well."

Other newspapers spoke out on Denny's behalf as well. The *Selma Times-Journal*, in a brief but emphatic editorial, said: "The trustees should give Dr. Denny a long leave of absence to build himself up. The state can ill afford to lose the labors and influence and wise guidance of such a man. If comparisons are in order, it is more important to keep Dr. Denny at the University than the football team, and we know of no way of giving greater emphasis to the point than that."

"Every thoughtful person who is interested in the cause of higher education in Alabama will be pleased to learn that there is no immediate danger of the resignation of Dr. George H. Denny as president of the state university, and his statement that he has no intention of leaving the school until his successor is named will be applauded," *The Anniston Star* wrote on April 7. "This attitude, in spite of the treatment he recently received from the recess committee on finance and taxation, is in keeping with the character of the man and his well-known love for the institution to which he has brought such remarkable growth during the last twenty-three years. The proposal of the recess committee to reduce the appropriation to the University because Dr. Denny has been able so efficiently to manage the affairs of the institution during the critical period of the Depression as to increase the endowment is little less than astounding. It is probably the first time in history that efficiency has seemed to call for a penalty, and instead of criticizing the University president for his able management it would seem that the members of the committee would have been inspired to hold up his record as an example to be emulated.

"But to those who are familiar with the attitude of the chairman of the recess committee toward the University, the short-sighted policy that has been proposed comes as no great surprise, because for some unexplained reason Shelby Fletcher has held a grudge against the Capstone and its president for several years. It was not believed, however, that he would undertake to impede the progress of the institution out of spite, as it seems, because he himself is an able businessman and is generally credited with breadth of vision. Nevertheless, having been credited with gubernatorial aspirations, he is now being given credit for an attempt to array the common schools against the schools of higher learning, although *The Anniston Star* is loath to believe him capable of such a demagogic gesture. As a matter of fact, if all the money that is given by the state to the University were diverted to the common schools, it would not enable them to operate but a few hours longer. It is contended that Alabama has more than twice as many students per full time professor as any other Southern state university and that too many graduate students are employed as teachers. This, we think, is a valid criticism, but it does not justify the penalization of the University because Dr. Denny has shown the foresight to build up the University's endowment, which was an act of business acumen in light of the experience of other state universities that have had their appropriations cut because they were not operated to suit the fancy of some politicians that were temporarily clothed with power. For the greater the endowment the greater is the prestige of any college."

In another editorial during the same week, The *Star* wrote, "Alabama has in the person of Dr. George H. Denny one of the greatest educational executives in the United States and it is sincerely to be hoped that he will be so supported by the legislature that he can be persuaded to remain at the University for at least two more years, thus rounding out a quarter of a century of progress that will forever remain as a memorial to his ability and his loyalty to his adopted state. It is because the prestige of Alabama has been enhanced under the Denny administration that so many out-of-state students have come to the Capstone in recent years; and yet Dr. Denny is criticized because of this accretion, although without it some of the colleges at the University would not have been maintained. It is surprising, too, that any thoughtful person would want to stop these young men and women from coming into Alabama, where many of them remain as citizens, as it is time that we began to get back some of the millions in populations and money the South has lost to other sections since the War Between the States. Especially do we need more educated citizens, as every such immigrant adds to the riches of the commonwealth. It is time, too, that we begin so to strengthen our own state university that it will no longer be necessary for Alabama parents to send their boys and girls out of the state to get that technical knowledge that is enabling so many trained men and women from other states to capture the highly paid positions in Alabama industries. This cannot be done, however, if the University is to be made the tool of political prejudice and thereby robbed of the funds it so drastically needs for its larger development in the realm of scholarship," the editorial added.

Despite universal pleas to reconsider his retirement plans, Denny had already quietly made up his mind to step down. The decades-long battle for fair and adequate state funding; the Depression-era financial stress; misinformed criticism of his shrewd fiscal management policies; biased questions regarding the large number of out-of-state students, and the weight of thirty-three years of hands-on toil as a college president had stooped his shoulders and finally weakened his spirit at age 64. While voicing a sincere concern for higher education in the state, Denny asked again that he be relieved of his responsibilities as president at the annual spring meeting of the University board of trustees on May 27, 1935.

"For more than a third of a century, first at Washington and Lee and now at Alabama, I have been wrestling with the ever-increasing strain of executive work. That is a long term of service for a college president; only one or two presidents of American state universities have served for so long a period," Denny said in reiterating his plans for retirement. "For several years it has been clear to me that I should seek to lighten my load. From time to time I have discussed the situation with friends intimately related to the entire problem. I feel now that in justice to myself and to the University, I should without further delay request the trustees to relieve me of my official responsibilities as soon as my successor can be installed. I shall not attempt to give expression to the multitude of emotions that spring up in my heart as I contemplate the step I am now proposing to take. Yet I do ask the privilege of saying that I have for all these years attempted to give to the University of Alabama the best service my strength has justified. While no one realizes more fully than I the imperfections of that service, I am entirely willing to subject its integrity and its devotion to the scrutiny of Him whose eye is in every place. This is, I am sure, the fitting time to record a clear expression of my gratitude and appreciation in full view of the unfailing loyalty and cooperation of thousands of people, including trustees, faculty, alumni and friends scattered here and there throughout the country. My single regret is that I have not been able to do more than I have to accomplish the great objectives that governed my purpose when I agreed, in the fullness of my physical strength, to give the best years of my life to this work in which, in spite of all its cares and anxieties and handicaps, I have found so many compensating factors," he added.

Borden Burr, representing the University of Alabama Alumni Association, presented a resolution asking Denny "to remain as our leader" and asking that the trustees "use every effort to induce him to continue his splendid services, giving him such assistance as he requests and as may be needed for the purpose of lightening the heavy load he is carrying." The trustees agreed in a similar resolution, saying, "We are firmly convinced that the solution of the difficult problems confronting us during the years immediately ahead require his wisdom, courage and experience as never before in the history of the University and that any change in presidency at this time would precipitate a crisis which might be disastrous to the institution we all love."

Denny reported a spring 1935 enrollment of 4,717 students compared to 4,433 a year earlier, then addressed the usual budget problems, saying "We cannot go on as we have been going during these Depression years. We are pleading for relief. The real issue that we need to settle just now is imperative. It relates itself to this fundamental question: Shall we have a modern state university? The answer to that question cannot be longer evaded. The friends of the University ought not to deceive themselves in this situation. The real solution to our particular problem can come only by intelligent and resolute action. There is but one test. It is the per capita test. Can we expect our University to do its work and to maintain its standing with a relative per capita support that unduly handicaps its process? No informed citizen can fail to feel a sense of grave concern regarding the support of higher education in Alabama. It is not merely a matter of the Depression. There are other factors involved," Denny continued. "One of these factors is a certain lack of conviction regarding the importance of our colleges. Perhaps there is need of reinterpreting the objectives of college training—not merely the more obvious and immediate objectives, but more especially those remote and little understood objectives by means of which it is molding the future of our commonwealth…. Nothing is so costly as ignorance. Men pay for the things they do not have far more dearly than for the things they do have. An undisciplined nation possesses few of the blessings and comforts of life. On the other hand, nations which have courageous and forward-looking leaders who dare in crises to foster education, including especially education for leadership, are the nations destined to make history and are in fact making history. Alabama is on trial. Our people have yet to decide once and for all that they really regard higher education as an asset rather than a liability.

"We have had during recent years the evidence of an unsympathetic attitude toward higher education in Alabama, and from unexpected sources," Denny continued. "Naturally such an attitude finds here, as elsewhere, more frequent expression in periods of economic distress. Nothing has caused me greater concern than to find in this group of critics some of our own graduates—men who in their youth enjoyed the intellectual offerings of this University and who apparently now fail to interpret correctly its social importance and its spiritual significance. It is difficult to grasp the meaning of such a situation," Denny added, citing inequitable funding from the legislature and "the persistent misinterpretation of the significance of the presence of the out-of-state student, both as an economic and as an educational factor in the life of the University" as two examples of the unsympathetic attitudes toward the University.

The inequitable funding from the legislature was nothing new in 1935, of course. In 1927, the legislature's appropriations to the three four-year colleges for 1933-34 included $304,420 to Alabama College, $833,636 to Auburn and $640,556 to Alabama. Those amounts were cut by thirty percent by the 1932 legislature, but through the state budget act the schools actually received less than half the reduced appropriations. Actual funds received by the schools for 1933-34 included $243,817 by Alabama, $341,267 by Auburn and $113,049.44 by Alabama College, according to figures cited by Denny. At the same time, the University had an enrollment of 4,883 compared to 1,892 at Auburn and 864 at Alabama College. Later figures showed that Alabama College received state funding of $222.27 per student for 1934-35 compared to $148.64 for Auburn and $72.32 for Alabama. The numbers were similar for 1937-38, when Alabama College received $258.57 per student compared to $122.23 for Auburn and $66.91 for Alabama. Denny complained loudly of the inequitable funding problem throughout his tenure as president, but received no relief from a legislature controlled by agricultural interests which seemed determined to limit the University's growth. His only advantage had come from out-of-state students, and the legislature had even attempted to control that avenue of income. His run-in with Fletcher, who represented a district dominated by large farm operations in the Tennessee River Valley of North Alabama, had been the proverbial straw that broke his will to continue the fight.

University trustees, seemingly attempting to bolster his dampened spirits and persuade him to delay his retirement, passed a resolution at the May 27 meeting praising Denny for his "brilliant leadership" throughout the Depression-era financial crisis. "We record again our gratitude for his self-sacrificing and statesman-like conduct of the affairs of the University and our pride in its remarkable progress under his masterful guidance; that in our judgment, his achievements in the face of baffling obstacles are unsurpassed in the history of education in this country and will be a brilliant chapter not only in the annals of the University of Alabama but of the South; that in no time during his distinguished career have his wisdom and accomplishments shone more brightly than during this period of economic depression when they have been put to the acid test; and finally, that the progress of events have beyond question proven the sagacity of his judgment and the soundness of his policies. We earnestly urge that he remain as president of the University of Alabama as long as he feels able to do so," the resolution concluded.

In pledging Denny their "militant, unfaltering and united support," the trustees also appointed a committee headed by executive committee chairman Henry B. Foster to arrange "for such relief as President Denny may be willing to accept" in the daily operation of the University and to proceed, when requested by Dr. Denny, to search for and nominate his successor. The committee was instructed to "spare no effort and to take as much time as may be needed" in its search for a new president, "keeping in mind at all times the sacred obligation imposed upon the trustees to maintain the management of the University free from any influence except those of recognized educational standards of the highest order and of the sound public opinion of the state."

Denny, in response, told the trustees that the "major consideration underlying my thought of release from grinding responsibility has been the fear of overtaxing my strength. Indeed, this has been a matter of some concern to me for several years. Even under normal conditions, it is necessary that I exercise constant care. The situation, however, is that so far as higher education is concerned, conditions in Alabama are quite abnormal. That means that constituted as I am, there is constant temptation to overtax my physical and nervous energy. I find it difficult to shirk obvious duties and responsibilities. I have had the feeling that under the circumstances the time may be approaching when I should find myself in the position of doing both the University and myself an injustice. Indeed, the present abnormal situation would be, as I view it, a tax on the strength of any conscientious college president, even though he were in the full flower of physical vigor," he added.

Denny discussed the inequities in appropriations to state colleges, special interest groups, politics in education, recent criticism of the University's endowment fund and the uncertain future of higher education in the state as some of the "abnormal" problems with which he was faced, leaving no doubt that those frustrating factors had added to the usual daily strain of office and perhaps played a deciding role in his decision to retire. "Our appropriations have at no time been in keeping with our load. Limited to Alabama students only, the University carries a load as heavy as the other two major institutions combined. Yet its appropriations have never reflected the disparity," Denny said. Calling the situation a time of crisis, Denny said, "For surely it is a crisis when it is seriously proposed not only to destroy established procedures, but to destroy them for a single purpose, namely, to accomplish through group pressure an unfair division of public funds as between our institutions of higher learning.

"And now a personal word in conclusion," he added. "For the modest part that I have been privileged to play in the significant achievements of the University in the quarter century now drawing to a close I am superlatively grateful. My life has been given to it, and gladly given. My text has been, 'This one thing I do.' To that text I have religiously adhered. I am loyal to the history and the traditions of this place. I love every inch of its soil. I have faith in its mission and in its destiny. Periodically it has been beset with trials but it has hitherto never failed to emerge with the light of morning on its face. It has actually risen from dust and ashes. Its past is both a pledge and a guarantee of its future, which in spite of the handicaps of the moment, will reflect ever more and more the best ideals of this commonwealth. The destiny of this first-born spiritual child of Alabama is largely in your keeping. It is a sacred trust. I have the utmost faith in your purpose to administer that trust with courage and devotion."

Despite his frustrating experience in April, Denny wasted little time in returning to the political battlefront. He joined trustees Foster and R. E. Steiner Jr. on a return trip to Montgomery to seek help from Governor Bibb Graves. Graves, an 1893 University graduate and a member of the school's first football team, had begun his second term as governor a few months earlier and had been governor in 1927 when the legislature passed a major educational reform package that included new taxes and a $750,000 construction appropriation for the University, although only $250,000 of the appropriation was actually paid due to the Depression. Bibb Graves Hall, which houses the School of Education on the University campus, was named for Graves when it opened in 1929. University alumni also occupied sixteen seats in the state senate and 30 in the house in 1935, offering faint hope of a political compromise that would help the University. The trip proved fruitless, however. Although Graves met with Fletcher's committee, Fletcher introduced an appropriations bill on April 30 funding the state's higher education institutions for the next four years at the same level they had received in 1933-34. Instead of receiving the $550,000 per year for the next four years as Denny requested, the University received $243,817 while Auburn received $341,267 and Alabama College $113,049. Enrollment figures for 1933-34 showed Alabama with 4,433 students, Auburn with 1,510 and Alabama College with 757.

The resignation of Alabama College president Dr. Oliver C. Carmichael two weeks later to become dean of the graduate school at Vanderbilt University drew statewide attention from Denny, at least briefly, as state newspapers pointed to Carmichael's loss as another byproduct of inadequate funding for higher education. "…Who can blame a college president for resigning to take a position where he will not have to worry and fret about what a legislature is liable to do in regard to the financial end of the college machinery?" a *Greensboro Watchman* editorial asked. "Such a president is in constant dread of not being able to raise sufficient money to carry on the school as it should be. And so we do not blame Dr. Carmichael for accepting the position at Vanderbilt, where he will be able to let George (Denny) do the worrying."

"The opinion of Alabama newspapers is unanimous that the state is to suffer a great loss when Dr. O. C. Carmichael leaves Alabama College to go to Vanderbilt, but maybe the loss will not be without its compensations," the editor of the *Talladega Daily Home* wrote. "All feel that the financial trials which have weighed heavily on Alabama school heads as well as the rank and file of teachers in recent years had something to do with Dr. Carmichael's decision to leave, and this should bring home to the state the peril of pauperizing education in dollars and cents…. Schools should certainly have enough money to do the best work of which they are capable and give teachers sufficient pay for a decent living."

The Anniston Star called Carmichael's departure "an argument in favor of the unification of the educational system in Alabama and the focus of our educational leaders from the role of beggars for funds every time the legislature is called into session. It is a vicious circle in which we exist here in this good state. We are poor because we are uneducated, and we are uneducated because we are poor. But we are not so poor that we cannot give our children a better break than that which they have enjoyed. We have penalized the University of Alabama because its president, one of the ablest business men Alabama has ever known, was able during the Depression to keep his school out of the red and to make provision for its future financial stability."

A June 10, 1935, *Crimson White* story described Denny as a "white-haired old man" who spoke "in quivering tones" as he was greeted by "a tremendous and prolonged acclamation of applause which brought every person at the banquet to his feet" at an alumni gathering during spring commencement activities. "The University is at a crisis. There is a group of people in the state—a minority I hope—who would keep appropriations down to such a point that the University could not operate; who would cut out our out-of-state students and who would cut out our endowment," Denny was quoted as saying. He added that when he was invited to take the presidency of the University, he had been assured that the state would provide the University with the financial support necessary to build a great state university. "Trusting in these words, I set out for distant shores," Denny said, "but the University has never received the whole-hearted support of the state of which I had been assured." While he said that he had faith in the integrity of the state and in enlightened public opinion, Denny called on the alumni—as he had on his arrival in the state in November 1911—to "marshal this opinion in favor of the great work that is being undertaken at the University. I love the University. I have given my life to it. Someday I hope to write its history. I am fatalist enough and old enough to be resigned to my fate, whatever it may be. But I hope that I shall never be so old or so fatalistic that I will not fight in any battle affecting the University. I will not stand on the sideline, but will enter the thick of the fight and enjoy it," he added in showing a bit of his old spirit.

Denny had every reason to point to the lack of financial support. He had been forced to operate the University of Alabama in crisis mode throughout his tenure due to inadequate and inequitable funding from the fickle, farm-interest-controlled legislature. His constant pleas for additional funds often fell on deaf ears. Sample figures show clearly that the University ranked third—and last—in per capita funding among the state's three four-year colleges. Auburn and Alabama College were favored in funding throughout Denny's career, much to his displeasure. Examples of funding, even as late as 1932 and 1935, published by the University of North Carolina and found with Denny's hand-written notations in the margins, illustrate the disparity in state appropriations to the three schools. The report, based on a survey of thirty-two state universities, showed that state universities outside Alabama received an average of $241 per student from their respective state legislatures for 1935-36. In Alabama, the largest per capita appropriation went to Alabama College, which received $268 per student for 1935-36. Auburn received $153 per student while the University of Alabama received only $72. The appropriations meant little, however, as only 28.58 percent of the amount was actually paid, with Alabama College receiving $77 per student, Auburn $44 and the University of Alabama only $21 per student. Denny had scribbled in the margin of the study figures showing that the University of Alabama actually received only 8.7 percent of the national average amount appropriated to state universities. The University of Alabama had 4,896 students in 1935-36 while Auburn had 2,348 and Alabama College 822. Similar appropriation disparities existed throughout Denny's career, and the fact that the University made great strides in all areas due to his keen financial skills and frugal management methods did little to salve his wounds of discontent over the matter as he surely imagined all that might have been accomplished with adequate funding.

Former state senator Coma Garrett Jr. of Clarke County wrote state senator Harry C. Glover in August 1935 to urge more equitable treatment of the University of Alabama in Montgomery. "I notice from the papers that the House committee has given Auburn a $263,000 increase over the appropriation made to that institution in 1932. I also notice that no increase was given to the University," Garrett wrote. "I do not think this is treating the University fairly. It is true that the University has made a success under the able leadership of Dr. Denny and his co-workers, but as you know, the University needs funds as badly as Auburn. I am not fighting Auburn. We need Auburn as we do the University, but I do believe in fair play. I have been told that Senator Bonner is going to lead the fight for the University. Won't you please promise to stand by Bonner and see that the University is given a fair deal?"

The outpouring of moral support for Denny, a record enrollment of 4,896 in September and the distraction of a football season that ended in a disappointing 14-6 loss to Vanderbilt brought a relative sense of calm to the Capstone during the waning months of 1935. Talk of Denny's resignation quietly disappeared from the headlines until November 9, when trustees gathering prior to Alabama's 33-0 homecoming win over Clemson passed a resolution asking him to give up his plans for retirement. University alumni, meeting at a luncheon on the same date, passed a similar resolution asking Denny to remain as president and urging the trustees to stop their search for his successor.

Citing their "appreciation and hearty approbation of the brilliant leadership of President George H. Denny during the quarter century of his service nearly completed" and repeating their comments of May, the trustees stated that "we are firmly convinced that the solution of the difficult problems confronting us during the years immediately ahead require his wisdom, courage and experience as never before in the history of the University, and…that we earnestly insist that Dr. Denny remain as president of the University of Alabama, and to this end we request the executive committee to urge Dr. Denny to remain as president of the University and to discontinue all efforts to select his successor." Congressman Archie H. Carmichael, a member of the board of trustees, told the alumni association luncheon that "the board wants to put an end to talk all over Alabama that Dr. Denny is going to resign."

Denny, in addressing the alumni gathering, said, "I will not attempt to paint the picture of problems now confronting the University. Many already know those problems, which are difficult, complex and perplexing. At no period since I have been at the University have these problems been more difficult, complex and perplexing. I appreciate the opportunity of having served these many years. The best years of my life I have given the University of Alabama. When I came here I took as my motto the phrase, 'This one thing I do.' Now I feel that I can say with a change of tense, 'This one thing I have attempted to do.' I cherish the memories and associations of these years and I wish to express personally and officially my appreciation to those loyal sons, high and low, rich and poor, who have served with me. May their service be henceforth laid up as a cross of honor. May God in His infinite wisdom direct the destiny of this great old place," he added with a tone of finality.

Education in Alabama was dealt another financial setback on December 5 when the 1935 Tucker Act making education an essential function of state government was ruled unconstitutional by the state attorney general. State senator Hayes Tucker of Tuscaloosa had authored the bill, which had declared education to be an essential function of state government in an attempt to prevent educational funds from being apportioned in the event of budget cuts. State comptroller Charles Lee immediately announced that the ruling meant that he would have to revise the entire state budget to conform to the Fletcher Budget Act. Within days Lee announced that the budget revision required a $4.7 million cut to conform to estimated revenue, leaving education, health and other "non-essential" agencies with severe appropriation cuts. The crushing result, announced by Lee on December 17, left the University with an appropriation of only $104,107 rather than the previous $229,000. The cutback in funding also forced State Superintendent of Education J. A. Keller to announce that public schools would be able to operate only five and a half months before closing for the year.

Denny had lost yet another battle in his lonely crusade for public education in general and for the University of Alabama in particular. If he needed a defining reason to go forward with his planned retirement, he clearly had it. He was now sixty-five years old, in poor health and weary of politics and disappointment. On December 23, he sent a letter to the presidential search committee directing it to "prosecute its search without delay to insure a successor as soon as possible" and setting "the end of 1936" as his firm retirement date.

Denny enjoys his pipe in a rare moment of relaxation.

10

Frustrating Finish

"I love the University. I have given my life to it. I am fatalist and old enough to be resigned to my fate, whatever it may be. But I hope that I shall never so old or so fatalistic that I will not fight in any battle affecting the University. I will not stand on the sidelines, but will enter the thick of the fight and enjoy it."

—Dr. George H. Denny

Public discussion of Denny's pending retirement fell silent during the winter of 1935-36 as University trustees kept quiet his December 23, 1935, letter setting his definite retirement date of December 31, 1936. Thinking that no news was good news, many students and alumni still held out hope that Denny would change his mind and continue as president of the University.

Such an event as the retirement of the University of Alabama president, who also happened to be the state's best-known and most popular citizen, was not news that could be kept secret, however. The University Alumni Association, acting with the two-fold purpose of honoring Denny for his twenty-five years of service and attempting to persuade him to further delay his retirement, hosted a silver anniversary banquet for him on February 22, 1936, in Montgomery. A February 14 *Crimson White* announcement of the banquet under the headline "The Significance of the Banquet" left no doubt that the banquet was designed to sway Denny as much as to honor him.

"The silver anniversary banquet for Dr. Denny should attract the attention of not only all University alumni but also that of every man and woman in this state who desires the continuance and support of higher education," the story began. "…If any other man were to be appointed to take over the reins of the University administration now, it would spell disaster for the Capstone. Any other man not possessing equal portions of business sense and academic learning would fail in his attempt to manage the University with the appropriations now received by it. Dr. Denny has nursed the University of Alabama through its infant years. If in later years his guidance proves to be the vaulting pole that places the University on the high level that she should properly maintain, then this testimonial anniversary banquet shall have been significant."

Denny left little doubt that his decision was final, however, as he used the banquet as a platform to deliver an eloquent and emotional farewell address in which he recalled his vision for the school and the triumphs and defeats during his quarter century of service to the University. "I shall not attempt to put into formal words my gratitude to and appreciation of those who have made possible the events of this, to me, deeply moving hour. Indeed, there are no words, formal or informal, that are adequate to express the emotions that spring up in my heart as I face this great gathering," Denny said as he addressed the alumni gathering.

"On January 1, 1912, I came to Alabama over the unanimous protests of the best friends of my younger days and with a single objective. To that objective I have subsequently devoted every conscious hour. 'This one thing I do,' has been the daily text and the daily guide of all these years," Denny continued. "I would have you believe that the University has meant to me not something to profit by, but something to love and to serve. As the state's first-born spiritual child dedicated by the founders to every high and helpful end, I have conceived its mission in terms of service. This child of destiny is, I am persuaded, Alabama's supreme asset and supreme hope in the struggle forward to a happier and better-ordered life.

"I have conceived my own mission as president of the University in terms of stewardship to the people of this commonwealth. That conception I have sought to clothe with majesty and power. And now, as the shadows lengthen, I ask the privilege of saying in the presence of this great company of friends to whom I acknowledge myself debtor, that I have without any shadow of turning, attempted, under every circumstance however trying, to keep the faith. And there have been, in truth, trying circumstances all along the way. The saving factor in the record is that there has been in the foreground, everywhere and all the time, on the part of trustees, of faculty, of alumni and of successive student bodies the unquenchable spirit of service and of sacrifice. Largely because of that spirit the University of today has emerged with the light of morning on her face and immortal hope in her heart. As I look back over the years, I wonder how it all has happened. For my own part, I wonder if I could again summon either the courage or the energy to attempt what has been attempted. And here let me add that it has been by no means a triumphal procession. There have been defeats as well as victories, and really—I am convinced—more defeats than victories. Yet I have found and still find comfort in the fact that, after all, it is not so much what we actually accomplish in this world but rather what we attempt together that makes us brothers and friends.

"I am aware that many of you think that I have attempted to travel faster than my physical strength has justified," Denny continued. "Perhaps that is true. Perhaps I have gone too far on the theory that it is better 'to waste health like a spendthrift rather than hoard it like a miser' when so much needed to be done. Perhaps I have taken things too seriously. Perhaps I have undertaken too much. Perhaps I should have lightened the burden, even when it refused to be lightened. The simple truth is that no one can do the kind of work he ought to do if he does it merely with his mind. He must put his whole soul and his whole self into it, particularly when he is dealing day by day with the issues of human destiny. And so I made my choice. As a result of that choice I can testify that after frankly reckoning all the liabilities resulting therefrom, the fact remains that the greatest satisfaction and the greatest reward of all these years have come, not from the investiture and the trappings of high office which are sure to vanish like a shadow, but from daily association with vital and picturesque youth, all the way from their scholarly enthusiasms in the classroom to their victorious shouting on the fields of sport. I am superlatively happy to say that it is in that association with a vast army of young men and women numbering some thirty thousand human souls and scattered throughout the world that I have found and now find all the compensation that I covet."

Denny concluded his remarks by adding, "I shall never forget those who have wrought with me in the stirring events of the quarter century now drawing to a close. Happy days to all of you who love the University and are striving to keep her commandments. Happy days to all of you who give unstinted credit to a faithful foster mother for nurturing in your youth those ideals of manhood which now in your prime have flowered into your richest and most enduring possession. I pledge you one and all that in whatsoever fashion memory shall bring back in future years this day to my mind, it will say to me, 'That was a great moment!'"

"No man has left his imprint upon Southern education more indelibly than has Dr. Denny," a *Montgomery Advertiser* editorial said following the banquet. "No other is as rich in educational experience. No other has given more of what he had. Everyone may not have agreed with him, but all will agree that what the University has been for the last quarter of its life, what it is today and what it may be in the future has been determined in large measure by him. Further than that, his influence is reflected down to the lowest primary grade in Alabama."

A February 24 *Mobile Register* editorial said, "The grateful throng gathered in Montgomery two days ago was eloquent and sufficient proof of the esteem which is held for Dr. Denny by thousands of Alabamians—his friends and alumni, self-made men and college men, old and young alike. They were there to do a great man honor.... That greatness has been recognized time and again by men who are admirably qualified to do so. Mr. Claude G. Bowers, a man who knows and understands the South, is given to no practice of idle and meaningless flattery. In the spring of 1931, Mr. Bowers said, 'You have here perhaps the greatest man the South has produced in the last two decades. I refer to George Hutcheson Denny.' Although he is a native of Virginia, the state of Alabama calls Dr. George H. Denny her own, and this state does well to push her claim for him. It will be, perhaps, a long time before Alabama is able to call another such man as one of her leaders."

If anyone continued to hold out hope that Denny would remain as president, those hopes were dashed during his annual report to the trustees three months later when he publicly and emphatically announced that his mind was unchanged from a year ago and reiterated that he "must be relieved of the responsibility of this position." It was at that moment that the stark reality of the inevitable set in for University students and faculty, thousands of alumni and other loyal Denny supporters. The man who had shaped the course of the University for all time and who had personally influenced thousands of students would in fact step down, and he asked to be relieved of his executive duties by July 1.

Although he reported a record graduating class of 500, a record campus enrollment of 4,896 students for the 1936 spring semester along with 4,597 others taking extension classes and an enrollment of 2,287 in summer school in 1935, Denny was far from satisfied with the University's overall circumstances. "It is a fact that the University has now been operating on an emergency budget for a period of approximately six years," Denny told the board. "It has been difficult to impress this fact on the public mind. The salaries paid, the number of teachers employed in proportion to the student load, and the equipment provided have been and are drastically inadequate. The present situation unhappily calls for further sacrifice. There is apparently nothing to do except to continue for the time being the present Depression budget. While I greatly deplore this fact, I see no other alternative. I stress again the obvious fact that it is not an economy to attempt the impossible. Unfortunately, there are all too many people in Alabama who do not understand just what has been done here in the face of odds, and all too many people who have surprisingly little knowledge of the facts in spite of every possible effort to present them. One is tempted at times to wonder whether there is any widespread interest in conservative and economical institutional management," he added, showing continued disappointment not only with the lack of adequate state funding but also for the lack of public support for such funding.

In a review of his twenty-five years of service, Denny also presented a brief "survey of progress made in broadening University services and in advancing academic standards" since he assumed the role of president on January 1, 1912. "A great deal has been said and written regarding the remarkable growth of the University of Alabama during the past quarter of a century," he said. "Naturally much of this comment has related to the material development of the institution and to the size of the student body. These are the aspects of college growth that are easily grasped by casual observation. The advancement of standards in academic and professional fields is less readily discerned. The University, as a matter of fact, has shown even greater relative progress in the development of its essential functions as an educational institution of high rank—including its steadily advancing standards—than it has shown in its increased enrollment and enlarged physical plant." Denny noted that the faculty of 1936 included one hundred twelve teachers with Ph.D. degrees and almost one hundred more with advanced degrees as he cited membership in or recognition by such organizations as the Southern Association of Colleges and Secondary Schools; Southern University Conference; Association of American Universities; National Association of State Universities; Carnegie Foundation for the Advancement of Teaching; Council on Medical Education of the American Medical Association; Association of American Medical Colleges; Association of American Law Schools; American Association of Collegiate Schools of Business; American Association of University Women; New York State Education Department; National University Extension Association, and such national honorary scholastic fraternities as Phi Beta Kappa, Beta Gamma Sigma, Gamma Sigma Epsilon, Phi Delta Kappa, Tau Delta Pi, Phi Beta Sigma and Alpha Lambda Delta.

Denny also pointed out the growth of the University libraries, saying, "It is believed that no institution in the country with like financial support can show greater accomplishment in this direction. A quarter of a century ago some twenty thousand volumes constituted the University library. Today there are more than one hundred fifty thousand volumes in the library in addition to a large collection of government documents. Strong, well-stocked departmental libraries have been developed in the schools of laws, medicine, commerce, education, chemistry and engineering as contrasted with practically no separate departmental libraries twenty-five years ago." He also cited improved scholastic standards; increased enrollment of women students and the organization of the School of Home Economics in 1929; the School of Mines; an extension division that reached every county of the state, and organization of the graduate school in 1924 as major developments in the school's growth.

"That the University is giving thorough and standard training in all of its divisions is attested by the nationwide recognition which it enjoys and the phenomenal success of its graduates who have gone into professional study elsewhere," Denny said. "Increased enrollment and an enlarged physical plant have come to the University, it is true; but there has also come, from every side, recognition of and respect for its standards as one of the foremost educational institutions not merely of the South, but of the entire country. Surely the people of Alabama will be happy to acclaim their University for the place it occupies in the educational world. They will be glad to know their University and appreciate it for its intellectual stature even more than for its large student registration, its modern buildings and its outstanding successes on the fields of sport."

Denny concluded his report to the board by adding, "For the opportunity of serving the University of Alabama for nearly a quarter of a century, I express again profound gratitude. During this long and eventful period there has been unbroken harmony in every relationship I have sustained to the board of trustees, the faculty, the alumni and successive student bodies. I shall always cherish the deepest sense of loyalty to and appreciation of all who have generously wrought with me through these years. Finally, I greatly desire to make clear once more the fact that, just as far as my health may permit, I stand ready to respond to any call that the University may make on my remaining energy. Of one thing I am certain: I shall miss my daily routine far more than it will miss me."

Later in the day, Denny spoke to a record crowd of 500 at the annual alumni banquet, where he was introduced by trustee and executive committee member Hill Ferguson. "We have spent the entire day trying to get Dr. Denny to agree to continue as president without success," Ferguson said, adding that the board would meet again on June 2 to "resume the discussion." *The Tuscaloosa News* reported that Denny delivered "a brief address which in some quarters is interpreted to be his farewell to the alumni as executive head at the Capstone."

"I shall make no speech tonight. My emotions are too deeply stirred for me to get away with it," Denny told the overflow crowd. "A day like this deeply affects one whose roots go down so far into the ground. Every interest I have is here in Alabama, whether it be material or spiritual. I have given my best and I know that I need rest and freedom from responsibility. I am deeply grateful as I think of the University one quarter of a century ago and today. I have never for one moment regretted that I came here in my vigor and prime and have given these years to Alabama. To me this is the most beautiful spot on earth."

Denny did not refer to his pending retirement during commencement remarks the following day, choosing instead to focus on the graduates in a brief but inspiring message. "And now, my dear friends, you have reached the end of another chapter in the book of life," he said as he faced his twenty-fifth and final graduating class as University president. "This is a significant day for all of you. It is a day of memories. It is a day of hope. It is a day of anticipation. We acclaim you as you face the great and uncertain future. We have faith in you. We count on you. These diplomas which we hand you today are not merely certificates of sound training and of high purpose; they are pledges of good faith. They summon you to the first-line trenches where life's real battles are fought and won. They are designed to clothe you with power to do your part in a work-a-day world. We bid you carry your share of the load. The University expects you to do your part; to keep up with the great procession or ahead of it. Some of you will lead in that procession. The rest of you will surely strive to keep step according to the talents committed to you. It would be little less than a tragedy to take away from this spot, whose great traditions and great ideals are in your keeping, any impression that you have yet attained. The summation of achievement lies ahead of you.

"...We expect great things of the great class of 1936," Denny continued. "We expect you, with simple faith and devotion, to make living a great adventure. For it is in this way that you will make life significant and happy. The path leading to the ultimate goal is not an easy path. The only sure way to that goal is through service, and if need be, through sacrifice. A group of five hundred young men and women going out into this immense world would seem, in comparison, a relatively small group. Yet history furnishes many instances of groups smaller than this group which, moved by great faith and great desire, have wrought far-reaching changes, material and social and spiritual. It is not a matter of mere numbers or of mere chance or of mere circumstance. It is a matter of purpose. It is a matter of spirit. It is a matter of power."

The record 498 graduates in the University of Alabama class of 1936 included Denny's youngest daughter Margaret, who had earned Phi Beta Kappa honors. Her three older siblings, Frances (1920), Charlotte (1923) and George H. Jr. (law, 1929), had already graduated from the University.

Although there had been fair warning from Denny, his public request for a retirement date of July 1 shocked and saddened University loyalists. Within days, Denny's desk was piled high with telegrams and letters from friends and former students expressing praise for his long and tireless service and disappointment at his pending loss. Some letters were as long as five pages. Most were short, emotional notes.

"Yesterday's newspapers told Alabamians of perhaps the greatest calamity that has befallen the state in ages. It was the announcement of your resignation.... The state needs you, and certainly the University will be a ship without a rudder in the loss of your services," one letter said.

"A quarter of a century ago, Mr. Daniel Pratt asked me to recommend a president for the University of Alabama. I have never regretted that recommendation. I place you in the class of Kipling's proconsuls—'They that dig foundations deep, fit for realms to rise upon,'—with this exception: you have both laid the foundation and reared the superstructures.... May the glow in your western horizon be not simply the light of a setting sun but also light from the gates that are ajar," wrote Bruce McGehee, pastor of the Methodist Episcopal Church South in Troy, Alabama.

"I know that you get very tired and that the way seems long," another letter said. "Perhaps the mountains of Virginia woo you. Perhaps you long for a rest. I wonder if, however, there is any rest for you and men of your stamp. The pioneer can never rest. He sails 'beyond the sunset,' as Tennyson has it in his Ulysses. I am thinking of the friendships you have made in your public career. I count the conquests that you have affected in your active life. Best of all I see an endless line of youth to whom you have been a teacher, counselor and friend."

Birmingham native and 1920 University graduate Joseph R. Smith wrote on November 21, 1936, to say, "I would like to express my personal appreciation for having the opportunity to attend the University, if for no other reason than it offered an opportunity for contact and association with you. It is for this reason that I want to join with your thousands of friends in extending to you the sincere gratitude that I feel for your continued association with the institution which you have so largely built and which in common with most worthwhile things represents very largely the shadow of a single individual."

Similar notes followed:

"It is a sad day for the University and for the state. It will be absolutely impossible to find a man who can fill your place at the University and in the hearts of the alumni."

"You have already accomplished more than a dozen men in a lifetime. No one man was ever more universally loved than you are among the alumni and student body of the University of Alabama."

"Your presence has been a definite inspiration to the many thousands of students who have attended Alabama during your term of office, and I am certain that they all realize it has been your leadership which has put the University on its present high standard. Your successor will have to be a mighty good man to fill the place of Mike Denny."

"To the many thousands of us who love the University and you, your resignation comes as a distinct shock—the loss of one near and dear to us."

"I will watch the press eagerly, hoping it will bring the good news that you will reconsider your resignation."

"One ray of hope to me is that I understand you have agreed to remain as advisor of the University in the years to come."

"I know you had a hard time, but you have done a glorious work and I hope you have gotten and will continue to derive great satisfaction for the wonderful years you have headed our University."

"Please stay with us. We need you and love you."

"You have done a thousand times more for that great institution than should be expected of any one man."

"There is no man, living or dead, whose services have meant more to the state of Alabama than those of Dr. Denny."

"To those of us who know and love you, your place cannot be filled."

"I did not go back to the University yesterday. The fact that you had tendered your resignation took from me all desire to go back. It could not have been a gala occasion for me. I want you to know, however, regardless of what it means to the University, that personally I feel that it is asking too much of you to further endanger your health."

"To those of us who have been fortunate enough to attend the University during the past twenty five years, it can never be the same without you."

Attorney Leon McCord of Montogmery wrote, "I have never amounted to much in life, but have all along been able to measure men fairly accurately. Moreover, I've hated sham and hypocrisy. Guess I've been guilty of playing to the galleries with the best of them, but all the way I have loved men who were big and clean and worked. All this is written that I might say this: You are my kind of man. You speak my language and you travel my way. I regard you as one of the big men of this country and I wish to God that we had more like you."

"I wonder if you could not be interested to become a candidate for governor," wrote Dr. David T. McCall of Mobile. "At this time your qualities and qualifications are in demand to relieve the deplorable exigency—financially, educationally and morally. There is now a crying need for a man of your business acumen and constructed leadership as governor of Alabama. I know of no man in the state who could approach your fitness for the position. I can't reconcile losing you from the state's government and welfare."

The Anniston Star praised Denny as "the greatest educational executive Alabama thus far has known" in a May 24 editorial as it cited the lack of state funding as the probable cause of his resignation. "If the resignation of Dr. George H. Denny as president of the state university fails to rivet the attention of the people of the commonwealth on the equally deplorable fiscal affairs of our institutions of higher learning, the sources whence must stem the future leadership of Alabama, it will have failed to impress one of the most fundamental lessons inherent in the existing crisis," the editorial said. "Dr. Denny is one of the most astute financiers in Alabama. He has been able to administer the affairs of the University on a basis of about half the current expense and instruction cost per student that obtains at the two other institutions of higher learning, according to the Brookings Institution report. But he has undermined his health in the effort to stay within his budget and it is doubtful if he would have tendered his resignation at this time had he not been penalized by the present administration because of his excellent business management. There is not another institution in the country of comparable size that has been dealt with so penuriously by the legislature as has the University of Alabama. When Dr. Denny came to Alabama about twenty-five years ago, he found at the University four classroom buildings, three dormitories and one fraternity house. The enrollment was then only 400, including 55 girls. Today there are 4,800 men and 1,000 girl students, 16 major buildings, 22 fraternity houses, 12 sorority houses, a football stadium, a swimming pool and Denny Chimes as a memorial to the man who has wrought this great transformation. But Dr. Denny is more than a mere business executive. He is a scholar of wide recognition, thoroughly schooled in the humanities and capable of imparting his knowledge to all who come in contact with his dynamic personality. He is a contributor to the Encyclopedia Britannica, a member of the Carnegie Foundation board and has succeeded in gaining recognition for the institution which he heads by practically every standardizing agency in the country. Dr. Denny's influence has been by no means confined to the University campus. His personality has been projected into every phase of the state's cultural, social and economic life and it is reassuring to know that he will continue to make his home among a people whom he has served with such marked distinction and by whom he is loved and admired," the editorial added.

Newspaper headlines of June 8 announced the good news that Denny had agreed to remain in office through the end of the year, as he had originally planned. Judge

Henry B. Foster, president of the board of trustees, made the announcement following a meeting in which Denny was authorized to set up a temporary administrative council consisting of four deans and two other executives to assist him with his daily duties. Denny confirmed the arrangement on June 10, saying, "It is, I believe, quite generally understood that for some months I have sought relief from the burden and the responsibility of a large executive task. A year ago the matter was fully considered and I yielded to the judgment of a multitude of friends. And now, a year later, I frankly confess that, in view of the debt I owe to the people of Alabama in general and to the University in particular, I am constrained to yield again to the appeal that the trustees be allowed additional time for the selection of my successor. This I do gladly and without the slightest feeling that I am, in spite of my health, being asked to do more than my plain duty. Meantime, the trustees are making provision for the lightening of my load."

Judge Foster, saying his committee would press forward in its search for a new president, recalled the guidelines previously established for the hiring of Denny's successor and said, "The more we have studied the problem, the more we have become convinced that those qualifications which would enable the new president to serve most efficiently this particular state and this particular university were of paramount importance. This naturally has narrowed the field of possible candidates very materially. At the same time, we have been impressed with the repeated expressions from alumni and citizens in all walks of life in Alabama and from the public press in all parts of the state that every effort should be made to keep Dr. Denny as long as possible."

Denny's December 23, 1935, letter providing a retirement date of December 31, 1936, had finally set the search committee in motion. After conferring with Denny, the committee reluctantly began its search by setting guidelines for the position. The committee said the new president "shall have had such experience as would help him to understand Southern people and Southern problems; that he shall have demonstrated ability for wise and successful administration of an educational institution, preferably, but not necessarily, a tax-supported institution; that he shall be a man possessed of such character, personality, intellect, training and experience as will enable him to establish effective leadership in the public life of this state and to continue to hold the support of its best citizenship and that he shall be a progressive educator as well as an efficient administrator." Judge Foster reported that the committee—made up of Foster, Ferguson and Daniel Pratt—had "looked at over one hundred possibilities, written hundreds of letters and traveled thousands of miles" in its search. Foster said the committee had held out hope that Denny "might eventually be persuaded to continue in the presidency" until his letter informed the group that his mind was firmly made up to retire at the end of 1936. "Inquiries have been made of practically every educator of note in the country," Foster reported to the trustees. "Literally hundreds of letters have been written; members have traveled extensively and consulted with educators whose advice was valued and we have conferred with several men who seemed especially worthy of consideration."

One of those men was Richard Clarke Foster, a prominent Tuscaloosa attorney and a 1914 University of Alabama graduate. The May 26 issue of *The Tuscaloosa News* had reported that Foster, "who has been mentioned for several months as a possible successor to Dr. Denny," had met with some members of the board of trustees for more than an hour the day before, leading to speculation that he was a leading candidate for the president's post. Foster was a member of one of the area's pioneer families and a relative of Judge Henry B. Foster, who not only served as chairman of the search committee but as president of the board of trustees and chairman of the powerful executive committee.

The search committee might well have interviewed other candidates following the June 10 meeting, but when the trustees met in a special session on October 10 to select a new president, the only nominee submitted for approval was Richard C. Foster. Minutes of the meeting said the resolution to elect Foster as president was "discussed at length by trustees J. Kelly Dixon, Gesssner McCorvey, Robert Steiner Jr., Archibald Carmichael, Hill Ferguson, Governor Bibb Graves (ex officio) and Dr. J. A. Keller (state superintendent of education, ex officio). In these discussions, all of the speakers expressed unreservedly their very high estimate of Mr. Foster's high character, fine ability, excellent scholarship, broad learning, unusual culture and refined background. The one and only question raised by anyone had reference to Mr. Foster's inexperience as an educational administrator," minutes of the meeting reported. Following the discussion, Foster was elected to succeed Denny by a 7-4 vote, with Graves, Keller, Steiner and Dixon casting the nay votes. A second vote made the selection unanimous in a show of support for Foster.

Prior to nominating Richard Foster, Judge Foster told the trustees that "It goes without saying that this committee has at all times been greatly influenced by the opinions of President Denny, with whom it has had numerous conferences. The committee has also been deeply impressed by a letter received a year ago from the Honorable Newton D. Baker, a member of the board of trustees of several leading educational institutions, including Johns Hopkins University and Washington and Lee University. This letter is so pertinent to our problem that we believe time should be taken by the board to consider it carefully."

Baker's letter, in response to a request for advice by the committee, spelled out several specific preferred qualities, all of which seemingly pointed to Foster as the obvious choice. "The absolutely indispensable characteristic of a successful university or college president is character," Baker said. "This does not necessarily mean, but certainly does not exclude, deep religious conviction. No college or university president is worth considering unless his character is such, and is known to be such, that when he walks across the campus, the students will spontaneously wish they could be like him. A president ought to be a good executive so that the fiscal affairs of the university will be prudently managed and he should have a tactful but firm way of dealing with both faculty and students. His sympathies with the departments of knowledge in which he is not himself a specialist ought to be keen if the esprit de corps of the faculty is to be maintained. So far as the University of Alabama is concerned, I think they ought to select a man not younger than thirty-five and not older than forty-five. It would be better if he were a Southern man, and of course, he should have the sort of platform presence and social experience which would make the friends of the University proud of his representation of it. These qualifications are difficult to find in any one man. I am not at all sure that the board should limit its view to persons who are at present college or university teachers or executives. Every now and then a man from the outside who has been a cultured and scholarly lawyer or doctor or businessman makes an ideal university president," Baker added, offering Stanley King at Amherst and John S. Bryan at William and Mary as examples. "If your board could find in Birmingham or elsewhere in Alabama a lawyer of about forty, of known scholarship, who was willing to begin a new career by devoting himself with enthusiasm to the University, your faculty might at the outset be disposed to criticize you, but the result would, I feel sure, vindicate the wisdom of your choice," Baker concluded.

"For president, with full authority and responsibility, beginning January 1, 1937, we nominate Richard Clarke Foster, a native of this state, a graduate of the University of Alabama with a degree of A.B. in 1914 and a graduate of the Harvard University School of Law with the LL.B. degree in 1917," Judge Foster said. "Mr. Foster's appointment has been earnestly urged by many of the University's most loyal alumni and friends, men prominent in the professional and civil life of the state and by many members of the faculty of this University. In particular, last May, when the deans understood that Mr. Foster was being nominated for president, they sent to him resolutions pledging their cordial and hearty cooperation and their undivided loyalty" Judge Foster added.

Judge Foster offered other details regarding Richard Foster, including the fact that he was forty-one years old and "therefore in the full vigor of his young manhood, with energy and strength to meet the most exacting demands of the office." He also noted that the nominee was familiar with the traditions of the University and was descended from several ancestors who had been associated with the University since its beginning. Pointing out that Richard Foster's paternal grandfather, John Collier Foster, had entered the University as a member of its first class in 1831 and that his maternal great grandfather, Thomas Jefferson Burke; his maternal grandfather, Richard Henry Clarke, and his father, John Manly Foster, had all graduated from the University, Judge Foster said "the traditions and the welfare of the University of Alabama are bred in his blood and bone." It was also noted that Richard Foster was a vestryman of Christ Church of Tuscaloosa and a veteran of World War I, during which he served as a captain in the field artillery. John Manly Foster earned a law degree from the University in 1883 and served in the state legislature 1890-91 and 1903-1907 in addition to practicing law in Tuscaloosa until his death at age sixty-seven.

The executive committee also submitted a letter from Dr. Denny endorsing Richard Foster as the nominee for the president. "After a careful review of the data gathered by the committee, I have no hesitation in stating that I have reached the same conclusion as that reached by the committee, namely that, all things considered, the nomination of Mr. Richard Clarke Foster for president is the best which can be made from the long list submitted recently to the trustees," Denny wrote. "Mr. Foster is a man of charming personality, of the very highest character and of outstanding ability. He is in the physical prime of mature young manhood. He has had the best education available in this country. His degrees, with honors, in arts and sciences from the University of Alabama first and then in law from Harvard are the full equivalent of the best type of the Ph.D. degree. Mr. Foster's intimate relationship to and association with the University has given him thorough knowledge of its finances, its organization and its educational policies. It means something, too, that three generations of his family have been graduates of the University of Alabama and have taken a prominent part in the public affairs of his native state. From time to time I have consulted with Mr. Foster on University matters of importance. He has fine judgment and rare insight. Mr. Foster is a scholar of proven capacity; he has high educational ideals; and a man of his culture and training and tastes will speedily master technical details, especially with the unanimous support of the deans of the various divisions of the University. No one can doubt that with this expert cooperation, the educational programs of the University will move forward in uninterrupted fashion. It is my conviction that Mr. Foster measures quite as fully up to the requirements of the situation as any available college president within my acquaintance and, in some important particulars, I rank him higher than any man available for the position," Denny added.

The resolution approving Richard Foster's nomination as president beginning January 1, 1937, also set his pay at the same rate as Denny's current pay ($7,700) and conferred upon him an honorary LL.D. degree. The resolution also elected Denny as chancellor and set his salary at $300 per month. Richard Foster's election as president of the University came just weeks after his wife Lida died on September 21 following an extended illness. It was also revealed that Dr. Foster had turned down the offer of the position in May, likely because the office required a great deal of travel and he wanted to stay near his wife. After taking office, Dr. Foster moved into the President's Mansion with his eleven-year-old daughter, who was also named Lida.

State newspapers strongly endorsed Foster's selection as president, even as unusual as the choice might have seemed. Most editorials dealing with the issue cited Foster's ancestors and their role in leadership and service to the state and his knowledge of the University and its traditions among his major qualifications.

"Alabamians have every reason to feel confidence in the selection the University of Alabama's trustees have made in the choice of a successor to Dr. George H. Denny," wrote *The Mobile Register*. "Alabama's new president, Richard C. Foster, is eminently suited to the post he has been asked, and has agreed, to fill. In the narrower academic circles there may have been some eyebrow-raising at the selection of a man who until Saturday had no honorary academic degrees and who has been best known in this state, not as an educator, but as a distinguished attorney. More discriminating Alabamians, however, cannot have been slow to recognize that technical training is all that Mr. Foster lacks and that deficiency, if it is one, can and will be quickly overcome…. He has enjoyed an unusual success as an attorney and as a leader of cultural and civic affairs in Tuscaloosa and has demonstrated that he is a man of genuine scholarship. More than that, he has displayed a character that contains all the elements that a university president ought to have. Mobilians, incidentally, should take a special pride in Dr. Foster's appointment, since he was named for his maternal grandfather, Richard H. Clarke, one of the best known and most respected men in local history…. The University has been one of his abiding interests, and he assumes the presidency not as an outsider but as one immensely capable of fulfilling the exacting tasks of his new office. The trustees have chosen well," the editorial concluded.

"The trustees of the University of Alabama have made a happy and wise selection of a successor to the able and widely beloved 'Mike' Denny," *The Huntsville Times* said. "In turning to look for one who would step into his shoes, they had to get a young man of sane and balanced judgment, of administrative ability, of wide cultural background, of financial judgment, of proven executive experience, of tact and of organizing force. This was a large order, but it seems that Richard Foster fills the bill admirably. He is steeped in the traditions, not only of the state of Alabama, but of the University of Alabama. By reason of his location at Tuscaloosa, he is familiar in a large way with the problems of the University and can step to the helm without the difficulties that would face a president drawn from another state."

"The selection of Richard Foster as president of the University of Alabama brings to the job a man who has had no direct connections with college life and university education since his own college days. To some persons that will seem like putting an inexperienced man in an important job," *The Birmingham News* said. "The choice, however, is recognition of the fact that universities have come to days when being a trained educator is not a sine qua non for a university presidency. The work of the large university has so broadened out that a wide variety of talents is needed in the president's office. There is need for a social vision much wider than the classroom. There is need for a business executive and a personable leader. Whether it be for good or bad, the scholar who loves exclusively his books is out of place today in a college position that calls for constant and exacting contacts with a busy world of men. President-elect Foster brings to his new responsibility the enthusiasm and energies of comparative youth, a rich endowment of useful knowledge gained in varied law and business life and a broad viewpoint of a college's place in society. He comes also with a love for the University—a love generated as a boy when he played beneath the shadows of its great oaks and the Gothic beauty of its quadrangle; a love intensified by his own undergraduate life there and the knowledge that his grandfather was one of the earliest graduates of the school. This loyalty, guided by intelligence and experience, will not be the least of his assets in his new honor. These characteristics Mr. Foster brings to a position in which he has the best wishes of all Alabamians who rejoice that it was not found necessary to go outside the state for a man to fill this position. Alabama, it appears, is developing its own educational leaders. Heartening also to the state is the knowledge that Dr. Denny will not sever completely his long and honored and successful connections. He remains as chancellor, a position created for him as he leaves the most active and confining office of president. While his new duties were not announced, it is assumed that they will permit the fullest use of that wisdom and experience which are the fruit of his twenty-five years of loyal labors. With President Foster as its active head and with Chancellor Denny as its Nestor, the University of Alabama should go to new heights of social usefulness and leadership," the editorial added.

The Mobile Press said the selection of Foster "is probably regarded in many quarters as daring…. The choice of the board of trustees is unquestionably unconventional. It would also seem to be wise…. There is every reason to suppose that the University has found a worthy successor to the tireless Dr. George H. Denny. In a very short time Dr. Foster will be able to familiarize himself with the more technical aspects of university administration. That special knowledge is all that he lacks. In every other way, Dr. Foster would appear to be ideally suited to the post which the conscientious board of trustees has seen fit to offer him. It ought to be a matter of deep pride to Alabama that the board of trustees was courageous enough not only to select a native Alabamian, but to select one of Dr. Foster's background. Instead of putting narrow academic requirements before all other qualifications, the board found a man whose brain and heart make him altogether fitted for a position of great honor and great trust. The board has done well."

"The new president of the University, Richard C. Foster, is an ideal selection in many respects," wrote *The Opelika Daily News.* "In ability, temperament and love for the institution he now heads, President Foster could hardly be excelled.... Dr. George Denny, who has done so much for the University, is to be retained as chancellor. His service is to be mainly in an advisory capacity. So this is a combination that would be hard to beat—youth and age, vigor and balance, ambition and experience. The University is fortunate."

The Tuscaloosa News also praised Foster's selection, saying, "The University of Alabama has had its trials and tribulations; it has had its defeats as well as its triumphs. But it has been a fortunate institution, and never more fortunate than in the choice of Richard Clarke Foster as its new president. We do not presume to congratulate Mr. Foster on his selection for that position—a position of dignity and responsibility which any man might covet. But we do congratulate the University and we do congratulate the state as a whole. Indeed, all of us should feel fortunate. We can think of no harder task than that thrust upon the University trustees in the selection of a successor to Dr. George H. Denny. He made it a well-nigh impossible task to find a man capable of carrying on his work. But one has been found and viewed from every angle. No more admirable choice could have been made. Mr. Foster has all the qualifications. He has the scholarship, the mental capacity, the courage, the executive ability and the knowledge of his fellow man necessary to carry on such an exacting work. But above all, he has character. It is this character which has made him, in spite of his relative youth, one of the most beloved men ever reared in this community. No matter what his background, Mr. Foster would be an apt choice."

The Birmingham Age-Herald joined in the praise of Foster's selection, saying that he "has the admiration and respect of all who know him, for he is modest, sincere and thoroughly honest. He has served Tuscaloosa in several public capacities and it is safe to say that hardly a man in the community is more genuinely regarded. Dick Foster did not seek the job that is now his. If anything, it was forced upon him against his will. But now that he has accepted that large responsibility he pledges to give his entire self to its fulfillment. We know Dick Foster to be always a gentleman in the finest sense of the word. We know him to be intellectually honest. We know him to be frank in his dealings with others. We know him to be a man of unimpeachable integrity. We know him to be a man of high purpose, with a full sense of his public obligations and privileges. We believe that the new president will command the trust and respect of the faculty. He will gladly listen to its counsels. His time and sympathy will always be for the University, and the student body will soon know him as a friend. The new president has a glorious future for himself and under his guidance the University can become an even greater source of wisdom and of strength. This newspaper, knowing Mr. Foster and having faith in him, commends him to the people of Alabama."

The *Crimson White* voiced the opinion of the students regarding the University's change of command with mixed emotions. "Last Saturday, the board of trustees selected Richard Clarke Foster to succeed Dr. George H. Denny as president of this University.

For the last two years we have known that the board was considering such a step, but nevertheless, the news is a shock to most of us. To picture in our minds this University without Dr. Denny as president is impossible at the present time. We must have time to think and reason before we will be able to get a clear perspective of the change that will be made," an October 16 editorial began. "For twenty-five years 'Mike' Denny has not been just a part of the University but to most of us he has symbolized the University itself. Since early childhood we have heard the names of Dr. Denny and the University always linked. Whether it has been a raise in scholastic standards, the construction of a beautiful building or a victory in the Rose Bowl, he has always been the guiding spirit behind it all. When most great men die they are honored with monuments of stone to commemorate their works, but our president has had the joy of seeing monuments to his greatness spring up around him as he went about his daily labors—massive buildings in which the youth of this and other states are taught to be finer men and women. Could any man have done a nobler work?

"Perhaps we are wrong to feel sad. No matter what happens, Dr. Denny will never leave us in spirit. For the present he will remain as chancellor and give us and our new president the benefit of his counsel. We must and will rejoice because he has been relieved of a task which had become a very heavy burden. That task will be turned over to Richard Clarke Foster. Dr. Foster, because of his background, his modesty, his character and his intelligence, has been proclaimed by all who know him as the best man available for the position…. No man could command such unbounded respect and confidence from those who know him without being a remarkable character. He is a graduate of the University, has lived in Tuscaloosa and has been high in the counsels of the heads of this school for some time. It would be foolish to say, 'Welcome, Dr. Foster,' or even, 'Welcome home, Dr. Foster,' but we do say, 'We are glad that you will be with us, Dr. Foster, and we are looking forward to the development of the same spirit of respect and love on the part of the student body toward you that past generations of students have felt toward Dr. Denny," the *Crimson White* editorial, likely written by editor Frank Davidson, added.

The Alabama Journal wrote that Foster was not widely known outside University alumni circles and that he was without previous experience in education, but added that those factors "may not prove the handicap that has been feared because of the board's action in promoting Dr. George H. Denny to the newly created position of chancellor. This no doubt means that the retiring president will continue to be a powerful factor in the institution's affairs in an advisory capacity. This is perhaps what the people of the state are most eager to see," the *Journal* continued. "The prospect of losing the invaluable services of Dr. Denny has been viewed with concern ever since the great educational leader first began to make suggestions that his impaired health was going to make it necessary for him to retire. If a plan has been worked out whereby the onerous burdens of the office of president can be gradually shifted to younger shoulders and the institution at the same time continue to have the benefit of Dr. Denny's wise counsel, it would appear that there is no need for fear of any losses to the enormous prestige the University has attained. Naturally the people of Alabama recognize that the advancing years of Dr. Denny and his gradual retirement from active service mark the ending of an unprecedented era of growth in the University's life and the beginning of a new era which it is hoped may be on a scale commensurate with the past. Alabama has no honor too great to be accorded Dr. Denny in appreciation for what he has done at the University. This great institution has not only become great in numbers and fame, but it has steadily enhanced through the years its position as the capstone of the educational system of the state. In his first statement upon notification of the board's action, Mr. Foster declared that he expected to 'lean heavily' upon the chancellor. That should be convincing to the friends of Dr. Denny that the new executive is to pursue closely the line of policy that has brought the University to such outstanding position under Dr. Denny's administration. For Dr. Denny, the universal wish is that the relief from active duties may prolong his life and that he may be spared for many years to give the University and the state the benefit of his advice and gifts for the promotion of education and Alabama's well-being."

Denny was not overlooked by *The Montgomery Advertiser* in the wake of the announcement of Foster's selection as president-elect. "After a long and distinguished career as president of the University of Alabama, Dr. George H. Denny can at last have his way and retire from active service," the newspaper said. "The board of trustees has bestowed upon him the title of chancellor and put another man in his place as president and active administrator. Hereafter, 'Mike' will have nothing to do except what pleases him. Whenever anybody on the campus wants advice he will be glad to give it. But mostly he will be preoccupied with the athletic interests of the University. He is especially interested in football and will now be able to give all of his time during the appointed season to following that game. At other times he can live in his summer home. At all times he can smoke his pipe and be at peace, knowing that the burdens of the University will rest upon younger and stouter shoulders. 'Mike' can rest upon his laurels. He has brought the University from a lowly place to a place of eminence. That is honor enough. It is all that he asks. What he does not ask is the good will of all the friends of the University everywhere. This is not necessary for him to ask; it will be given freely. 'Mike' goes into old age honorably and beautifully."

Although he did not officially take office until January 1, 1937, Foster quickly became involved in official University activities. He made his first official speech as president-elect on October 28 when he addressed an assembly of University women students. In remarks similar in tone those Denny might have used, Foster told the students, "When you have been out (of college) as long as I have, you will realize that this (the college experience) has been one of life's great epochs." He urged the students to get the most out of college life, saying, "It is possible to go through any university and miss ninety-nine and forty-four-one-hundredths of the opportunities there. Whether you realize it or not, the years you are spending here will mold your lives and your characters. I hope each and every one of you has a high opinion of yourself—not conceit, but such a fine opinion as will enable you to say, 'I am too fine to be lazy, too fine to do mean or cruel things and too fine to do anything which my parents have taught me I should not do,'" Foster added. Foster's next public appearance came on November 17, when he was called on to welcome approximately 500 members of the Alabama Baptist Convention to Tuscaloosa because Dr. Denny was confined at home due to illness. Reading a statement from Denny, Foster called on the congregation to consider the religious needs of the students on the University campus and for the efforts being made to meet those needs. Denny's message also praised the conduct of the students and said the University "strives to teach the young men and women not merely to open their eyes in the presence of nature but more important than that, to close them in the presence of God."

There was no ceremony or fanfare as Foster officially assumed the office of University president on January 1, 1937. In fact, Foster and his daughter were in Washington, D. C., where he was attending a conference of the American Association of University Presidents. Denny, meanwhile, was in Lexington, Virginia, where he had been resting for several weeks. *The Tuscaloosa News* had reported on December 31 that Foster had spent the last two months familiarizing himself with his new responsibilities and had addressed "a number of alumni and public gatherings, pledging his utmost efforts to carry on the magnificent work done by Dr. Denny at the Capstone during the last quarter of a century." Denny, meanwhile, was quoted in an *Associated Press* story from Lexington as saying, "I feel happy in turning over to Dr. Foster the reins of the presidency. He is a brilliant scholar and I know the school will continue its progress under his leadership." Denny also said he was recovering from a bout of grippe, but that he hoped to return to Tuscaloosa within a few days. "As long as I live, I hope to remain there," he was quoted as saying.

Chancellor Denny, University president Richard C. Foster and
University alumnus Johnny Mack Brown (left to right) circa 1937.

11

A Working Chancellor

"What the University has been for the last quarter of its life, what it is today and what it may be in the future has been determined in large measure by him. Further than that, his influence is reflected down to the lowest primary grade in Alabama."

—The Montgomery Advertiser

If anyone doubted the wisdom of the University of Alabama trustees in selecting Tuscaloosa attorney Richard C. Foster—a relative of the chairman of the search committee—as president, that doubt was erased as the new president settled into his new position. Foster, with Denny as his close mentor, soon proved to be all the search committee promised and more.

First and foremost, Foster was wise enough to heed the advice of Denny, who took his newly created position of chancellor and advisor to the new president seriously. Denny, meanwhile, was wise enough—and tired enough—to allow Foster to step fully into his new role. The Denny-Foster combination probably worked far better than the trustees might have hoped, if for no other reason than the fact that each man placed the interests of the University above his personal feelings. If anyone had thought Denny considered the title of chancellor—which came with no job description—an honorary one, he would have been mistaken. University trustees had shown similar wisdom in hiring Denny as president twenty-five years earlier, even though he had been their third choice. Denny was a man of ideals and passion answering a higher calling to build an educational system and a university. Foster was an attorney, a man of character dedicated to details and pledged to staying the course that Denny had set. And Denny was still around to offer sage advice, having moved into a small apartment in Smith Hall, as Foster, his daughter and a housekeeper moved into the President's Mansion.

Denny enjoyed the early years in his role as chancellor. "His" students were still around to bring him the youthful enthusiasm he enjoyed; his many friends fawned over him. Foster was a loyal friend and follower. He strolled under the oaks, watched football practice and games and basked in the glory of his many accomplishments, including the many new buildings composing the beautiful campus he had helped build. Denny split his time between Tuscaloosa and his home in Lexington, Virginia, where he went frequently to rest and spend time with his wife and other family members. He was at last getting the much-needed rest he deserved.

Foster, with complete support from faculty, students, trustees, Denny and the community, quickly—and by necessity—stepped into his role as president. Following a Denny tradition, Foster addressed the student body in a January 1937 issue of the *Crimson White*. "Twenty-five years ago, in January 1912, our beloved Dr. Denny came to the University as its president. I was a freshman then," Foster wrote. "I recall that the whole student body gathered in Morgan Auditorium and there Dr. Denny addressed us. To address all the students of the University of today in that manner is scarcely possible, therefore I am glad to have the opportunity to greet you through the *C-W* in its first issue of the new year....We of this generation are most fortunate in the benefits we have inherited from those who have dreamed and worked before us. A fine physical plant, an excellent faculty and a scholarly atmosphere are ours as a result of the foresight and sacrifice and devotion of Dr. Denny and his associates and their predecessors.... Happily, Dr. Denny is to remain with us as our chancellor to give us the benefit of his wisdom and experience," Foster added.

And Denny did fully and freely share his wisdom with Foster. It is clear from correspondence between the two that Denny took his role as chancellor seriously and that Foster not only accepted but regularly sought Denny's input. In addition to their campus discussions, they corresponded regularly when Denny was in Lexington, touching on every possible subject as Foster adapted to the academic world. In one early letter to Foster, Denny advised him to "stress industry, attention to detail, common sense and business judgment" in the hiring of a new employee. In an early letter to Denny, Foster asked his advice on such subjects as a commencement speaker, politics and pending state and national legislation that might affect the University.

With Denny present as chancellor, Foster presented his first president's report to the trustees on May 24, 1937, following Denny's established pattern. He reported that campus enrollment for the spring semester had been 4,897, with another 6,490 enrolled in correspondence courses and an attendance of 2,333 in the previous summer school session. The numbers were in sharp contrast to those of a quarter of a century earlier, when Denny reported only 398 students on campus at the end of the spring session and just over a hundred more enrolled in medical school courses in Mobile.

"The past few years have witnessed a grim fight by the University to hold fast to its high standards and to maintain financial solvency, successful under the brilliant leadership of Dr. George H. Denny and achieved by him and this board through ingenuity, foresight, courage and the practice of rigid economy. The solvency was maintained, emergencies were heroically met. The faculty and staff cheerfully accepted increased duties, and in like manner, severe reductions in their compensation," Foster said in a review of recent difficult years. "The University carried on its thorough and standard work, continued to grow, and met as best it could many new demands on it. All true friends of the University and of Alabama must glory in the accomplishment of a well-nigh impossible task," he said. Foster added that in order for the University to recover from its lingering financial problems it should receive "a larger percentage, if not all, of the state's appropriations" rather than the reduced amounts of recent years.

Foster praised Denny for his material accomplishments then added, "The intangible results are perhaps even greater. Thousands of young men and women from Alabama and from the nation have felt his influence. For them he had genuine sympathy and affection and wise counsel. From him they learned nobility of character, the beauty and strength of religious faith. The path of duty was the way to glory no less so for Dr. Denny than for the 'Great Duke.' Along that way he found more—the way to the hearts of his boys and girls, where his memory is enshrined and will endure in admiration and affection such as come to only the truly deserving." Foster also expressed appreciation for the advice, aid and encouragement received from Denny during his first five months in the office of University president.

Trustees promptly lifted the spirits of Foster and the entire faculty and staff at the meeting by approving the restoration of salaries to the pre-Depression level, then passed a resolution at the meeting honoring Denny for his long tenure as president of the University. The resolution said:

"Whereas, since the last meeting of this board of trustees, Dr. George Hutcheson Denny has, at his own insistence, retired as president of our state university although he has agreed to continue serving this great institution in the capacity of chancellor; and,

"Whereas the service of Dr. Denny in assuming the office of president of this university when it was nothing more than a small college with a few hundred students and hardly known beyond the confines of Alabama and developing it into a great university with approximately five thousand students in regular attendance and which is now known throughout the world as one of the greatest institutions of higher education in America is a feat which is probably unparalleled in the educational history of this or any other country; and,

"Whereas the exemplary Christian life led by Dr. Denny has had an influence for good on the lives of countless young Alabamians, which is almost impossible for our people to as yet fully appreciate, to say nothing of the high standards of scholarship which have been maintained and the material developments at the University which have taken place under his able leadership; and,

"Whereas his executive ability has been of such a high order and his business judgment and foresight have been so superb that through the period of our greatest depression when many institutions of learning closed their doors or piled up debts which they were unable to pay, he at all times maintained the University of Alabama in a thoroughly solvent condition, meeting all obligations as they fell due; and,

"Whereas, the members of this board, who through their association with Dr. Denny are better informed than any other group as to the greatness of the work done by Dr. Denny not only for this university but for Alabama and the South, now desire to place in the permanent records of this board a proper appreciation of the debt of gratitude which we and our people owe to this distinguished scholar, educator and Christian gentleman:

"Now, therefore, be it resolved by the board of trustees of the University of Alabama in meeting assembled, that this board does hereby express to Dr. George Hutcheson Denny, our retiring president, the deep sense of gratitude which each member of this board and which every informed man and woman in the state of Alabama feels toward Dr. Denny for the magnificent service which he has rendered to us during the past quarter of a century; that we do also express to Dr. Denny, through these resolutions, our admiration for him not only as a great university president, executive and scholar, but as a man who represents and typifies all that is best in our civilization; that we further especially convey to him our great appreciation, which is shared in by all fathers and mothers of Alabama who are advised in the premises, of the exemplary Christian life which he has led and the influence of such a well-spent life upon the young men and young women of this state who have had the good fortune to come under his influence; and that we do further hereby express to Dr. Denny the sincere wish and hope of each member of this board that now as the heavier burdens of managing the affairs of this institution and directing its destinies have been transferred to younger shoulders, he will be able to obtain some of the rest which he has so well earned and that he be spared to us and to the people of Alabama for many years to come in order that we and the other authorities of the University may have the benefit and guidance of his wise counsel and advice."

Foster wrote Denny in October 1937 to ask his advice regarding the matter of requiring freshmen to wear "rat" caps. "We have been through that experience, and unless freshmen over age twenty are exempted, trouble is ahead," Denny responded. "Older men refused to come to the University (and a few who actually came left) because they had to wear rat caps…. Colleges can get away with some procedures that do not work at universities," Denny added in voicing his disapproval of the idea.

Although Denny and Foster maintained regular contact by mail, Denny did not attend the May trustee meetings of 1938 and 1939 due to health problems. Foster reported continued increases in enrollment in 1938, with 5,210 students registered for the spring semester and another 7,753 taking correspondence courses. In 1939, he reported 5,409 students on campus and 8,032 taking correspondence courses. Each year, more than 2,200 were also enrolled in summer school. Foster outlined what he saw as the University's primary responsibilities in 1938, listing conservation of knowledge, teaching and the advancement of learning, saying, "Within these fields we must recognize our obligation to meet the demands which society makes upon us. We must be the center of culture and learning in our state."

Denny, meanwhile, was dealing with health issues and the difficulty of adjusting to retirement. "I am trying to build myself up, but it is slow work," Denny wrote in a nostalgic letter to Dr. James Doster in January 1938. "I rarely leave my suburban estate. I have no real interest here. Nearly all of my old friends are gathered in God's acre. The remaining few, of course, have, like myself in a quarter of a century, established new interests. There is little in common. Alabama is my home."

Denny wrote Foster several letters in May and June of 1938. In one note he offered advice on the football schedule, suggesting "games that might make the most money" and the wisdom of also keeping "breathing spells" in the schedule. In another letter Denny had listed the University of Alabama graduates in the state senate, saying, "This seems to give Alabama alumni practically a majority in the senate. This is the best showing in many years. Dean Farrah should write to 'his boys.' It is a fine group. I congratulate them and you. Those whom you do not know should be cultivated."

In obvious response to questions from Foster, Denny wrote on June 27 to offer his thoughts on proposed new dormitories and other building projects. "For all self-liquidating projects, I think we should borrow," Denny said. "The University's permanent funds (endowment and reserves) are its chief source of strength. Draw on them beyond annual income from them and the institution is weakened rather than strengthened. Meantime, please tell Houser that I favor nursing his reserves in order to be ready when the next gong sounds. These reserves are our best friends—better than the Dixons or the Rockefellers or the Carnegies. They are, in the very truth, really the University, and I am proud of the fact that instead of presiding over the institution 'straight-jacketed,' you have begun with a financial outlay that must have enormously eased the burden. I know that some have not appreciated the rigidity of the policy, but without rigidity, there can be no real policy," Denny added. He sent a brief note to Foster a few days later suggesting that Foster consider further expansion of Denny Stadium among plans for the future.

On September 8, 1938, Denny wrote to Foster saying that he would soon leave Lexington for Tuscaloosa, where he would spend some time before joining Foster and the football team on its trip to Los Angeles for a September 24 game against Southern Cal. "I shall enjoy the California trip, provided our boys win," Denny wrote. "Naturally I want to go, but on the other hand, I get so deeply concerned over games that I always fear that I may worry both coaches and players," he added in accepting Foster's invitation to attend the game. Alabama won the game, its first of the season, 19-7, and went on to a 7-1-1 season record.

In an October 18, 1938, letter discussing plans to meet Foster in Washington, D.C., to lobby for Works Progress Administration (WPA) funds for a new library and other projects, Denny wrote, "I am ready to go to Washington Sunday if needed. Secretary (of Interior Harold) Ickes will hardly reach Washington before next week and he is the only one I could possibly influence. I hope you will remain in Washington until everything is definitely settled. There is a suspicion that the president has told Ickes to put on the brakes in order to save money for war or defense preparations. We should stay on the job continually now until our fate is settled. Tell WPA that we haven't had a single loan approved and that every other college in Alabama has." Denny urged Foster to contact University of Alabama graduate and Florida senator Claude Pepper in addition to asking the "vigorous cooperation" of the Alabama delegation. "Let me know if you want me to depart Sunday. The powers that be say that I can travel by the end of this week. I have had a fearful time with a deep, dangerous cold," Denny added. Published reports said that Denny and Foster met with President Franklin Roosevelt, and after Denny reminded him that the University of Alabama had been destroyed by federal troops during the Civil War, the University received WPA funds to help construct the Amelia Gayle Gorgas Library, Foster Auditorium and additional student housing.

Denny spent less and less time in Tuscaloosa as age and health issues restricted his travel. Letters continued to flow back and forth, however. On February 1, 1939, Denny responded to a Foster letter regarding the new Bureau of Mines division. "I understand the situation you confront," Denny said. "It is enough to worry you. In the beginning I doubted too sudden expansion. I am perhaps too conservative. It seemed to me that we should start modestly and test thoroughly every detail of procedure, especially the man selected to head the bureau. He is undoubtedly a problem. He is very unpopular on campus and in addition is now making enemies for us in Montgomery. Apparently he lacks common sense. Yet I can see little to be done directly for the time being. The damage has already been done. Any direct action now would lead to a row. However, we can keep in close touch with our alumni in the Senate and in the House with a view to softening the blow and explaining our utter innocence of any meddling. After all, our chief and perhaps only hope is in keeping our alumni loyal, interested, helpful and wide awake." Denny added a postscript, saying, "Now is the time to plan for next year's enrollment. The admissions and withdrawals at mid-year were disappointing."

The usual crisis regarding state funding arose in late February, prompting Foster to write to Denny for additional advice after the governor's budget failed to include an increase in funding for higher education. "I think it is important that in some way you should directly contact our legislative alumni. It cannot be done effectively by anyone else," Denny responded. "I assume that in presenting the budget, the governor was acting on existing facts. It would be tragedy otherwise. He must expect to correct present injustices. I hope you will insist on separating our appropriations into campus, teaching, extension and research categories…. We need money. As I have previously said to you, I think the budget is far too heavily burdened with salaries and wages. I shudder to think of the rapidly growing process of straight jacketing. I strongly believe in retaining permanently only the obvious fraction of really first-class men and allowing the others to go whenever they have better offers," Denny added in discussing salaries for instructors. "I am convinced that our first duty is to the University's maintenance of a conservative budget and to the top-notch men (rarely over twenty percent of newcomers). Mediocrity ought not be paid to stay," Denny added with emphasis.

In response to a Foster report that he had received complaints that some deans were not teaching, Denny suggested that Foster "have each and every dean file a teaching schedule for everyone, including the deans," with the president. "I realize the pressure you have to endure from department heads in the matter of increasing their staffs and the salaries of their teams, but it is the irony of the situation when some of those same men who are saying that too many men are brought into departments other than their own while their own departments, without their knowledge, are being criticized by the very men whom they have criticized. The only thing, I imagine, that one can do is to remind these men that the legislature has not appropriated a single dollar to the University since 1935 while the state board of education has actually cut the School of Education. In spite of all this, the expenditures of the University have been mounting. Maybe they will understand this and let up in their demands and comments. The best friend you will ever have as college president is not the fellow who flatters you for yielding to his demands and who criticizes your predecessors for being stingy; the best friend is a sound budget and a generous balance for all emergencies and a growing endowment," Denny wrote. He added the warning of additional future budget problems as well, citing increased maintenance costs due to a $2 million increase in building. "Then, too, sooner or later the entire New York group (students) will disappear," Denny added, noting that the loss of a large number of out-of-state students would create further financial problems. He also suggested that "every effort be made to recruit more female students to raise enrollment in view of the loss of some men to military service."

Letters continued to flow steadily back and forth as Foster sought Denny's input on every issue and Denny responded freely with wise advice. The placement of a government-sponsored aviation school on campus; the purchase of eighty acres of property known as Baker's Field (where the University Law School is now located) for $95,000; the filling of faculty positions and other personnel matters; Denny's "thirst" for campus news and bouts with the flu; state politics; the possible effects of the war on the school; football, and the possible effects of "the Missouri decision in the event some qualified Negro should apply for admission" were among the topics discussed in writing by the two friends as they jointly tried to deal with the daily problems confronting the growing campus.

Meanwhile, Foster was winning support from all corners. He was recognized as a leader in the Southeastern Conference and among regional and national educators. And he had quickly earned the respect of University faculty and students. The 1939 *Corolla* carried the usual photograph of the president with a brief story headlined "President Foster Wins Student Acclaim." The story—somewhat of a report card—said, "The position of president of the University of Alabama has seemingly agreed with Dr. Richard Clarke Foster since he took over supervision of the Capstone in January of 1937. He has grown in prestige and esteem with each new day at his work and the University, which he guides, has likewise expanded and won new laurels and recognition. Jovial 'Dick' Foster has completely won the respect and affection of the student body and faculty through his convincing display of those qualities that mark a man as both a wise and far-seeing leader and a sincere and friendly counselor. From president of the freshman class in the fall of 1911 at the University of Alabama to the executive chair of that same institution in 1937 is the story of the life and progress of Richard Foster during the last quarter century. This progress and development on his part and the recognition of it by the board of trustees are logical results of his character, intellect, industry, disposition and personality and of the training and experience enjoyed by him in college, in the army, in the practice of his profession and of the way in which he has conducted himself in his daily life. But intimates knew the caliber and potentialities of Alabama's president long before he became widely known either in legal or educational circles. The *Corolla* of 1914, his graduation year, carried a prediction that he would someday be recognized as a man of ability and merit. It is evident today just how good that early prophecy was. Alabama has enjoyed a splendid growth under the leadership of Dr. Foster. Interest in scholarship and achievement has widened and deepened. The student body is the largest in the history of the University. The physical plant has been enlarged, courses of study have been added and additions have been made to the faculty. No finer tribute could be paid to the Capstone's president, Richard Clarke Foster, than to say that he is continuing the noble work of building a great and fine university," the *Corolla* added.

In an August 1939 letter discussing pending legislation, Denny wrote Foster, "Don't forget to check on the official appropriations bill, both before and after engrossment and signing by the governor. I saved an error of $10,000 annually against us during the Kilby administration by this precaution." Responding to a Foster question regarding raising out-of-state fees, Denny wrote, "Any increase at all would mark the day when the University's decline will begin. Our fee is already considerably the largest in Alabama." Denny also often sent related newspaper clippings on education, athletics, federal grants, etc., along with his notes.

Foster wrote to Denny in late December of 1939, bringing him up to date on a number of issues and prompting a lengthy January 3, 1940, response from Denny. "I am glad you have had an outing. The legislature and the Southern Association have given you an anxious year," Denny began after saying that both he and Mrs. Denny had been kept indoors by stubborn colds during the holidays. "I am glad you are taking an active hand in the athletic situations. The difference between (Alabama head coach Frank) Thomas on the one hand and (former Alabama coach Wallace) Wade and (Tennessee coach Robert) Neyland on the other hand is in the field of administration. There is no difference in the coaching itself. All are tip-top. Thomas does not, like Neyland and Wade, take control of scouting. He depends on Hank (Crisp), (Red) Drew and Paul (Bryant). He delays; he takes for granted. I hope he doesn't let Don Hutson's brothers get away by delay," Denny said in showing his continued keen interest in football. Hutson's twin brothers Ray and Robert, who were successfully recruited by Bryant, entered the University in the fall of 1940 and were the stars of the freshman football team and outstanding performers in the 1941 A-Day game. With the drums of World War II beating loudly in the summer of 1941, the brothers joined the Army Air Forces a few months before Japanese bombers struck U. S. military installations at Pearl Harbor, Hawaii, on December 7 and both became pilots. Robert was killed in combat in the South Pacific. Ray flew seventy-seven missions "over the Hump" in the China-Burma-India theater and survived the war. Ray did not return to the University after the war as many other football players did, choosing instead to go into business with his brother Don, a former All-America end at Alabama, in Wisconsin. Ray returned to the University campus for the first time in November 2010 when he and several other surviving former University of Alabama football players were honored for their service in World War II.

"I hope the survey now being made by the professors and deans will be thorough and objective," Denny continued in his January 3 letter. "I have found that their personal sympathies frequently obscure their better judgment. I certainly would not promote anyone without personal interviews and thorough investigations. I do hope that with the Southern Association matter out of the way you can again lead a normal life. That will quickly reduce the pressure. I really believe that most busy men in all fields of human endeavor have a certain amount of pressure after age forty-five. May 1940 bring to you and to our great and beloved University every good thing." A few weeks later, on February 26, Denny sent a brief, hurried note to Foster alerting him to "dangerous and vicious bills in Congress backed by the land-grant people." Denny suggested that Foster "urgently" contact senators Lister Hill (Alabama) and Pepper, both University of Alabama graduates, to encourage their opposition to the bills.

Denny attended a special board of trustees meeting on January 23, 1940, in honor of the late Henry B. Foster, who had died suddenly on November 11, 1939, at age seventy-six. Foster, who earned a law degree from the University in 1884, was elected to the board of trustees in 1900 and served on the executive committee from 1904 until his death. Foster was a former mayor of Tuscaloosa (1890-1894), a veteran of the Spanish-American War and had served two terms as a state representative. He served as a circuit court judge from 1916 until his death except for three years when he served on the state appeals court in Montgomery. He was also chairman of the board of deacons at First Baptist Church in Tuscaloosa for twenty-five years. A tribute entered into the minutes of the January 23 trustees meeting called Foster "an extraordinary man" and cited "his exquisite tact, his never-failing courtesy and his constant recognition of the rights of others. He was modest and sensitive, a man of industry, character, honesty, courage, faith, hope, charity and all the rest. He loved his fellow man. To him, duty was a gracious freedom to realize a great purpose. He had three unquenchable public loyalties: community, church and the University, which he loved as if it were his own child," the tribute—likely written by Denny—said.

Denny did not return to Tuscaloosa for the trustee meetings of May 1940, October 1940, May 1941 or October 1941 as his age (seventy) and health issues, including diabetes, became more of a factor. He and Mrs. Denny were mostly confined to Lexington, where his youngest daughter Margaret and her husband, Dr. Hunter McClung, had settled with Denny's only grandchild. Denny's health issues had come to the forefront in early May 1940 when he responded to Foster's invitation to attend the dedication of the new Amelia Gayle Gorgas Library. "Mrs. Denny thinks I am hardly strong enough to go, but I wouldn't miss it for anything," he wrote. "I shall have to be very careful on any trip. I am taking insulin three times a day and I am not strong after five weeks of confinement, chiefly in bed. Won't you send for Stuart Graves (dean of the Medical School) and have him arrange with someone to give me the insulin three times a day just before meals beginning Tuesday evening?" He also mentioned his arrival time and asked Foster to "remind Dr. Lloyd to have one of the boys pick me up at the train station."

Foster's progress report of May 1940 included the welcome news that the legislature had provided a "substantial increase in annual appropriations" beginning in October 1939. The increase allowed the trustees to raise Foster's salary as president to $8,673.32 per year in addition to raising salaries for University faculty and staff. The report also showed that enrollment had reached 5,503 in the spring of 1940 with another 7,216 taking extension courses.

In a summer 1940 letter, Foster asked Denny's opinion on a faculty member's request for sabbatical leave, to which Denny replied, "Sabbatical years have not arrived in this region yet. I wonder where he got the idea." On another personnel matter, Denny wrote, "I don't think I'd turn down the California man merely on account of his youth, provided he is all right on other counts. Perhaps his youth will make him more amenable to your guidance in many matters. You can train him to our Southern problems and ways."

By the fall of 1940, the topic of possible U. S. entry into the war dominated the written conversations between Denny and Foster. Denny offered "a few random thoughts" on September 3 in which he discussed the "general confusion and uneasiness over the war," adding that "even now it may reduce registration of students from distant parts whose parents will in some cases naturally want them nearer home." The military draft, which began on September 16, 1940, with all males ages twenty-one through thirty-six required to register, added greatly to the concerns for future college enrollment. Foster wrote to Denny on September 26, thanking him for his suggestion that he always plan to attend meetings of the Separate State Universities Conference, the Southern Association of Colleges and Secondary Schools and the national Phi Beta Kappa Association. On October 13, Foster wrote Denny to discuss such topics as the upcoming football game with Tennessee, state politics, Denny's health, fall enrollment figures and Southern Association of Colleges and Secondary School standards.

"I am delighted to hear through Jeff (Coleman) that you are making your plans to be with us in Birmingham at the Vanderbilt game," Foster wrote to Denny in early November. "The campus has not seemed natural without you this fall, and in your absence it seems not to possess its full character. All of us have missed you greatly, but we have had even deeper concern over your continued disposition." Foster went on to provide a brief discussion of numerous activities, including the football team and the Southern Association of Colleges and Secondary Schools meeting. Denny responded soon afterward with questions regarding the number of Alabama football players in ROTC as many of the nation's National Guard units were being called to active duty.

Concerned that University of Alabama students would follow the national trend by rushing to join the military in preparation for probable U. S. entry into the war, Denny wrote Foster on April 18, 1941, to suggest that each University professor have a "face-to-face talk with every student on his or her list to remind them of President Roosevelt's appeal to remain in college unless or until he is actually called. I believe it would be really worthwhile to call the faculty together immediately in a formal meeting and impress on the entire group the importance of cooperation. Everyone should be willing to take time to do this job thoroughly. It is a vital job," Denny stressed. "Of course, all the colleges are on the spot," Denny continued. "They know it and are working like a fire brigade. They will leave no stone unturned. If the colleges generally lose students, no one can complain; but if some lose and others do not, there must be an explanation. I feel deeply concerned. The next two or three years are critical years," he added. Denny also urged Foster to send a copy of Roosevelt's nationwide appeal to all students and parents and have it published in the *Crimson White*. Foster responded to Denny on April 26, thanking him for the suggestion and saying, "We have just completed a group of meetings with several faculties at which the request (to meet with each student) was made with gratifying results" and adding that he was sending letters to the students "urging upon them the importance of continuing their work while they can."

The threat of U. S. entry into World War II loomed even greater in May 1941 as Foster reported an enrollment of 5,258 students during the spring, with 7,252 more enrolled in extension courses and 2,635 in summer school the previous year. The extension courses included defense-related classes such as radio technology, foreign languages, welding, flight training and other courses taught at numerous locations around the state, including Huntsville, Birmingham, Tuscaloosa and Mobile as the University became involved in helping the nation prepare for what seemed to be America's inevitable entry into the war.

Denny and Foster corresponded regularly during the spring, summer and fall of 1941, discussing student retention, Denny's health problems, state and federal funding, the government-sponsored campus pilot training program, the governor's race, ROTC and the University's growing involvement with the war effort.

Dr. John McLure, director of summer school, wrote Denny on August 9, 1941, to report on summer school enrollment and inquire about Denny's health. "I do not like to hear of your being flat on your back," McLure wrote. "My picture and thought of you always is in every sense of the word a strong, vigorous standing man—a driving force for a great cause to which you are completely devoted. Please take care of yourself. It would be difficult for me to express my indebtedness to you. You have meant more to me in my educational work than any man I ever came in contact with in any way. I have learned so many things from you," McLure added.

An uneasy, somber mood settled over the nation in the autumn of 1941. Denny seemed quietly resolved to life in Lexington and had become less and less involved with University activities as his health continued to fail. Foster was ably at the Capstone helm and was kept busy by the same demands that were placed on Denny in addition to being involved with increased national defense issues. Little news of the day was good, and it was soon to get much worse.

Denny speaks at a memorial service for Richard Foster in November 1941.

12

Tragedy Brings Recall

"My strength is not what it once was, but such strength as I have I am glad to give to the cause of the thing that I hold most dear."
—Dr. George H. Denny

Unimaginable tragedy stunned the University of Alabama campus and the Tuscaloosa community on Wednesday evening, November 19, 1941, when University president Richard Foster died less than a week after being stricken with what was then commonly called creeping paralysis. The Capstone community had become reconciled to unavoidable war, but it was not prepared for the sudden and devastating loss of its dynamic young president at age forty-six.

"Tolling Chimes Proclaim News to the Capstone," a *Tuscaloosa News* headline read the following day as the story reported that Denny Chimes had pealed for almost thirty minutes immediately following Foster's 8:55 p.m. death in Druid City Hospital, which was then located just two blocks from the President's Mansion. "A hushed campus heard the signal, which had been anticipated for hours following word that Foster's condition had worsened at 11 a.m.," the news report said. The report added that the entire University student body, including 2,200 ROTC cadets who recited the Lord's Prayer in unison, had joined in silent prayer at 12:15 p.m. "Hundreds of faculty members, students, townspeople, relatives and friends from outside the city gathered at Druid City Hospital during the afternoon and night, keeping a constant vigil," the story added.

Foster had become ill on Friday, November 14, less than a week after returning from a business meeting in Chicago. He was unable to attend the Alabama-Georgia Tech football game in Birmingham on Saturday and was admitted to the hospital on Sunday when his condition continued to worsen. He was diagnosed with Landry's disease, or creeping paralysis, which is known today as Guillian-Barre syndrome. The disease, usually brought on by an infection, begins with paralysis in the extremities and spreads over the entire body. An iron lung was brought to Tuscaloosa from Bessemer on Monday to aid in his treatment but it failed to stop the spread of the disease. A Wednesday, November 19, *Tuscaloosa News* headline told of Foster's dire condition, saying, "Dr. Foster's Condition Grave; Little Hope Held," while the accompanying story told of a campaign by Capstone students to raise $1,200 to purchase an iron lung for the hospital in honor of their stricken president.

Denny, notified of his former student and protégé's illness while visiting in New York, rushed to Tuscaloosa and arrived by train on Thursday evening in time to attend the funeral on Friday morning and gather with the trustees in a special meeting later in the day.

"Capstone Mourns Beloved Leader," read the headline in the November 21 edition of the *Crimson White* as it reported Foster's death. "Denny Chimes tolled over a stilled campus a few minutes after President Foster's death and the full realization that the University had lost its great leader saddened the hearts of every member and friend of the Capstone," the story said. A *Tuscaloosa News* report said "a large throng stood in mute tribute" as Foster was buried beside his late wife in Evergreen Cemetery. The newspaper also noted that Foster was the third University of Alabama president to die in office. The others were Burwell Boykin Lewis (1885) and Henry D. Clayton (1889).

A *Crimson White* editorial expressed the mood of the campus and the widespread admiration for Foster. "Dr. Foster is dead," the editorial began simply. "Words are futile at a time like this. None are expressive of the abysmal grief in our hearts. Any eulogy would be meaningless now. Neither can we, with mere words, pay fitting tribute to this great man. His greatness is better reflected in the grandeur of the University he loved, in the loyalty and pride, the respect and admiration of all who knew him. In the loss of President Foster, the University of Alabama, its students and faculty have been dealt a crushing blow. He was the epitome of everything for which this institution stands— culture, education, fellowship. He was a perfect gentleman. This campus will not be the same now that he is gone. His passing leaves a void, an empty space that can never be filled. His simplicity of character, his warm and sincere personality, his pleasant smile and hearty greeting endeared him to every student. His very presence made this a better place. His was the spirit of Alabama. He was our friend and leader. Our heads are bowed."

Foster had become universally acclaimed in the field of education during his short tenure as University president. He was serving his second term as president of the Southeastern Conference, was vice president of the Southern University Conference and had served as president of the National Association of Separated Universities for two years. He had won the support of the students and faculty at the University as well as that of state's newspapers as editorials regarding his death clearly reveal.

Harry Ayers, publisher of *The Anniston Star* and one of Foster's pallbearers, wrote at length of the loss of a personal friend in a Thursday editorial. "There will be no joy of thanksgiving but an ineffable sadness in the hearts of tens of thousands of Alabamians today because Dick Foster is dead," Ayers wrote. "There will be another president of the University and that great institution, in the up-building of which Richard Clarke Foster laid down his life, will go on to an even greater fame and usefulness; but there never will be another leader more greatly beloved than was the man whose sudden passing has cast such a pall of gloom over the entire state today. Dick Foster had a genius for friendship. In every line of his countenance, in the genuineness and warmth of his handclasp, in his unassuming mien, he evoked the spontaneity of friendliness on the part of everyone with whom he came in contact. He gave unreservedly of himself and men gave back in return, and it was because of this that the whole state rallied to his support as soon as he donned the mantle of his great predecessor, George H. Denny. But Dr. Foster was more than a friend; he was a leader. Born of a family of leaders, he topped them all in the few short years of his maturity. As a student in school, as a soldier in France, as a participant in politics on his return, as a lawyer in the practice of his profession, he evinced that faculty. He could have had any political office within the giving of the people of Alabama, but he chose to lead in one of life's greatest endeavors—in the training of the minds of young men and women to the end that they, too, might furnish that intelligent leadership which this state so desperately needs. We dare say that his most enduring satisfaction came in the knowledge that he was privileged to have the love and respect and admiration of the thousands of students to whom he had given so abundantly of himself. And hence maybe there should be no moaning of the bar because Dick Foster has put out to sea. 'But O for the touch of a vanished hand and the sound of a voice that is still,'" Ayers concluded.

The Montgomery Advertiser recalled Foster's selection as president of the University and the early doubts of his choice which he had long since put to rest. "Who was this man who had been suddenly transformed from an attorney to occupy one of the most responsible and exacting posts in Alabama? His friends over the state—friends who had known him as a student in college, who had fought alongside him in the war, who had been associated with him in other ways—knew and applauded. Others reserved judgment. But not for long," the editorial began. "As he began to go about the state, as more and more people came to know him, the first ripple of applause became a wave of respect, of confidence, of affection. Those who saw him for the first time realized instinctively that here was the man, and there was no doubting the wisdom of the board's selection. Both alumni and public became accustomed to constant expressions of the institution's good fortune. People liked the way he smiled. They liked the intense earnestness of him when he talked of education, of the University's job, of its relation to the welfare of the state. And though it worried those who saw him from day to day, they liked the way he labored tirelessly at his job. Hardly a year had gone by before he was being looked upon as a leader in a profession in which he was still a mere freshman. These honors, like every other one that he had achieved, were not sought by him. He was one of those rare men whom recognition seeks...."

"With a suddenness that almost defies realization and understanding, this strong, good man has left us and we, the University of Alabama, the community of Tuscaloosa, the county, this state and the South, are bereaved," a *Tuscaloosa News* editorial said of Foster's death. "Governor Frank M. Dixon's statement issued after Dr. Foster's death Wednesday night must have echoed in the minds and hearts of many who knew this man as a friend. 'He was the finest gentleman I ever knew—capable, courteous, kindly—a prince among men,' said the governor. To many he represented the finest traditions of the old South, typified in the phrase, 'a Southern gentleman.' To all he represented dynamic, purposeful leadership in spiritual as well as physical things. Tuscaloosa recognized him as her foremost citizen, and this community felt great pride in his outstanding success as a University executive. But even yet he was Dick Foster to us."

Two days later the newspaper applauded Denny's return as temporary leader of the University, saying, "Tragic indeed was the loss of President Richard C. Foster, whom we all loved, respected and appreciated. Fortunate indeed is the fact that Dr. Denny, likewise beloved, respected and appreciated, has found it possible to answer the call to an unforeseen duty. The Capstone has an inestimable place in his heart and so does he have such a place in the hearts of all who know and love the University and this man. This veteran of devoted service has earned our devoted following. We can show our devotion by unstinted cooperation, by helping in every conceivable way to make his duties easier upon his shoulders. We can refuse to trouble him with little things and we can share with him the task of meeting the bigger things as they inevitably transpire."

University trustees had held a special meeting on Friday evening following Foster's funeral and persuaded Denny to return as president on a temporary basis, granting him the full power of the office by resolution. The board also asked Denny to prepare a memorial tribute to Foster and he soon delivered a five-page, single-spaced memorial which was later included in the official minutes of the November 21 meeting. Denny briefly recounted Foster's life and heritage, including his years as a student at the University under the close, daily influence of Denny himself as he earned Phi Beta Kappa honors and an A.B. degree in 1914. Foster earned an LL.B. degree from Harvard in 1917 and received honorary degrees from Alabama (LL.D.) in 1936 and the University of the South (DCL.) in 1937. "Such, in barest outline, is a synopsis of the career of President Foster. It would require a volume to tell the whole story," Denny said after introductory remarks in his written memorial. "Standing under the shadow of our great sorrow we shall not attempt to assess the sum total of the contributions he had, within a brief, five-year period, made to the cause of higher education in general, but we do testify to the rich and fruitful service he has rendered to this institution in particular," Denny wrote. "He has beyond all else given to men and women engaged in education in all its phases wherever he has touched their lives, whether in Alabama or in the uttermost parts of the country, a new interpretation and a new significance to the word 'gentleman.' He has illustrated in his life the values that really count. The University of Alabama is vastly richer because of his association with it. It was not merely President Foster's charm and personality that endeared him to trustees, faculty and students. It was not merely his genius for friendship. He did have personal charm and tact in superlative degree. He did have genius for friendship. But he had infinitely more than that to command the respect and affection and confidence of men and women. He had character—the absolutely indispensable quality of a successful college president. The student body was bound to love him. When he walked across the campus, the students spontaneously wished they could be like him. When they were troubled by intimate problems of their own, it was the life of their leader that inspired them instinctively to ask, 'What would the president think about the right and wrong of this?'

"...He took his place naturally and securely in regional and national educational organizations. He was recognized everywhere as a leader. It was not so much the investiture and trappings of high office that made appeal to him, but rather the opportunity to serve his day and time in worthy fashion. To that end he gave his all. President Foster faced death precisely as he faced life—calmly and heroically. In his last hours, when he realized the nature of his illness, he said that he was not afraid to die; that he had rather die than live as a hopeless invalid. And why was that his attitude? Simply because life to him meant service to others. He believed in Him who was the servant of all," Denny added.

Denny delivered a similar tribute to Foster over statewide radio on Sunday, December 14. Denny's memorial tribute—an illustration of his outstanding writing and speaking skills—was part of a larger program that included comments from Alabama governor Dixon, Tulane University president Rufus C. Harris, Vanderbilt chancellor Oliver C. Carmichael and University of Alabama English professor Hudson Strode. The program originated from the University and was broadcast over WAPI radio and its statewide network of affiliated stations. "All Alabama mourns the loss of a great spirit. Dick Foster, as he was affectionately known to all classes and conditions of men, has gone," Denny said as the featured speaker on the broadcast. "Perhaps it is too early to assess accurately Dr. Foster's contribution to higher education, but it is not too early to say that he made one contribution of supreme value to the University, to Alabama, to the South and to the nation. He gave new meaning and new significance to the word 'gentleman.' He possessed in high degree the three qualities most generally associated with distinction—force and charm of personality, balance of mind and integrity of life. He had moral and intellectual courage. He had common sense of the most uncommon kind—a sense of the value and fitness of things. He put first things first. He thought with his mind and not with his emotions. He had pride in his work. No one has ever questioned Dr. Foster's devotion to his work and enthusiasm for it. He had human sympathy. The echoes of our entrancing campus are melodious with the proclamation that his was a friendly hand. He had human modesty. I have known few men to whom notoriety and applause made less appeal. He had a sense of humility never failing and a measure of patience suffering long. Dr. Foster, from every worthy point of view, deserves to rank high on the list of great Alabamians of his day and time. He set a standard of public service that merits the accolade of Alabama's acclaim.

"It is great personalities that make great institutions," Denny continued. "Sooner or later in any fine institution like the University of Alabama the doors close behind one such personality after another, but the fruits of their sacrifice continue to live on and the institution itself inherits their fame. The University is a finer institution because of the life and service of Dr. Foster. He was superlatively devoted to it. If we could read his heart tonight, sealed as it is in death, we would find written there in box-car capitals, 'The torch we have together carried I pass on to you. May God in his infinite mercy give you strength to hold it firm.' I for one, accept the challenge. I shall endeavor with all of my ebbing strength to carry on pending the time when I can pass that torch to someone of Dr. Foster's fiber and purpose who can carry it with clean hands and a stout heart. Such is my passing tribute to a dear friend. I have frequently said that the best in Alabama is as good as the best anywhere in the world. I now say that if Alabama has produced in my day any finer man than Dr. Foster, I have not known him. There are few instances in the history of the University of Alabama where its thousands of friends have been as greatly indebted as they are to Richard Clarke Foster, and we shall cherish his memory," Denny added.

Denny, helping fill the void caused by Foster's death, appeared before a Capstone pep rally crowd on December 10, saying, "I have come back to help bridge this chasm. I love Alabama, but no other spot do I love as I do this campus. All who love it as I do and who want to go forward, all who love it for what it is, rise now and give me your pledge that you will help me in this task." A *Tuscaloosa News* report of the event said, "No sooner than had these remarks been uttered than the entire audience of students that filled the vast auditorium rose as a single person. It was a high mark in University spirit and it will provide a background for much work, much thought and much decision on the part of the student body."

Trustee McCorvey wrote Denny soon after Foster's death, saying, "I just wish to again express to you my appreciation, as well as the appreciation of every citizen of Alabama who is interested in the University, for the great sacrifice which you are making in 'coming home' and holding things together until a worthy successor to you and Dick can be selected. I recall, of course, that it was your brain which conceived the idea that Dick Foster would make a good president, and the splendid success of Dick was just more evidence of your genius. Get busy and pick out another man who will make good in the same way." In response to McCorvey's letter, Denny wrote, "Of course, I would give my life to the University of Alabama, and I simply feel deeply that it is my duty to stand by this dear institution in these tragic hours. I am trying not to overdo matters. "

Benjamin E. Harris, a former University associate professor of vocational education, wrote to Denny on U. S. Office of Education stationery dated November 26, 1941, saying, "Please let me write you what has been in my heart over the past weekend. I must tell someone and I turn to you as I have done in the past. I am heartbroken at Dr. Foster's leaving us. I loved Dick Foster—loved him for what he was—always the kind, gracious and considerate gentleman, fair in all his associations. It was a rare privilege to have known him and worked with him. In my sorrow I find myself thankful that I had the privilege. There are three men who molded the pattern of my life: my father, you and Dr. Hobdy. Dick Foster further enriched it. Truly I have reason to be thankful for these associations. We shall miss him, but we have his ideals of life and service to others and we must carry on as he would have us do."

The 1942 *Corolla* was dedicated to the memory of Foster, "who as president for the cruelly brief span of four years gave without stinting his devotion and his strength to his alma mater." The dedication added, "While some men in positions of importance win only fame, Dr. Foster won the tangible and priceless prize of the love of Capstone students and faculty. This sentiment was compounded of many elements, chief among which was ready acknowledgement of his manliness, deep respect for his executive ability and affectionate regard for his humble Christian approach to the multiple tasks he faced. We strive in vain to make adjectives speak the thoughts of our hearts and verbs the convictions of our souls when we pay tribute to a man of the stature of Dr. Foster. The many and beautiful eulogies that have been spoken in his memory were richly inspired by the compelling example of the life he lived," the *Corolla* added.

In a December 5 response to one of the scores of letters he was receiving, Denny wrote, "I am being overwhelmed with letters from every community in Alabama and many from friends out of state. These letters, of course, make me feel quite at home again. We are moving out of our recent tragedy as fast as it is humanly possible to do. Dick Foster was a popular, able and promising man. All my life I heard of creeping paralysis, but this is the first instance where an actual close friend has been seized and suddenly taken away."

Walter B. Jones of Montgomery was one of those who wrote to Denny. "It is a source of deep satisfaction to the friends of the University and to the people of the state to know that at a time when you are most needed you are there at the helm to pilot the University and direct its affairs," Jones said. "No one ever thinks of the University of Alabama without at the same time thinking of Dr. George H. Denny and all that he has done to make the University one of the great universities of the nation."

Mrs. John R. Thomason, a 1916 University graduate from Leeds, Alabama, wrote to Denny on January 10, 1942, to say, "I am so happy that you are again at the helm of dear old U of A. Things will be okay now that you are where you and none else belong. Our hearts have been hungry for the likes of ye…."

"Your return to the Bama campus has filled my heart with the utmost joy. God bless you," wrote Bob Oshman of New York in a letter to Denny on January 10, 1942. "I have never known my father, and of all the people I've met in my lifetime, you, Dr. Denny, were the one who fitted my ideal of a father. I know you will carry Alabama forward in the great job that lies before her in this war crisis. I feel it so much that just to mention your name gives me courage to do better. The most wonderful days of my life were spent at the University and I will never forget your good influences upon my life…. I left college in 1930 to fight the Depression for the family and now there is a bigger fight on our hands. With leaders like you at the helm, I just know we can't fail."

The Birmingham Age-Herald published a January 10, 1942, letter to the editor from Hopson O. Murfee of Prattville praising Denny's return as University president. "…It has been my privilege to know Dr. George Hutcheson Denny from our University of Virginia days nearly fifty years ago. The University of Virginia, Washington and Lee University and the University of Alabama have been made more illustrious in their fame by the incomparable life and shining achievements of Dr. Denny. It has been my privilege to know also the most eminent of American university presidents, world-famous scientists, illustrious men of letters and the most distinguished American Nobel prize men, scholars, statesmen, scientists and seers. I speak only truth and soberness when I say that George H. Denny, more than any other man of our land and race and age, deserves Shakespeare's supreme praise: 'The foremost man of all this world.' To the youth of Alabama, with rare devotion, he has been an inspiring exemplar of all that makes a man—scholar, gentleman, Christian, patriot, friend. The great University of Alabama is his noble monument. But above all, his supreme praise and fame is in the minds and hearts and lives of a shining host of American youth inspired, strengthened, cheered and ennobled by his presence as exemplar, counselor and friend. Divine Providence has removed from earth the noblest and most beloved of Alabama's native sons, Richard Clarke Foster, who was in truth President Denny's other self in his devotion to Alabama and in the nobleness of his spirit. But Divine Providence has preserved and kept for such a time as this Richard Clarke Foster's master spirit in the teacher, exemplar and friend who breathed into a noble soul the exalted spirit of his high devotion to the University of Alabama and to the commonwealth of his affection and fame. Richard Clarke Foster—a fond farewell! George Hutcheson Denny—all hail!" Murfee was a graduate of the University of Virginia and was president of Marion Institute 1905-1918. He was among the state civic leaders who helped secure a four-year medical school for the state.

Denny responded to many of the letters he received with brief notes of gratitude that always included the mention of his waning health. "I am receiving hundreds of letters from everywhere expressing satisfaction in view of my agreement to help matters along here pending the selection of some young man who can carry on in adequate style," he responded to Mrs. Bill Trueman of Birmingham in January 1941. "Practically everybody wants me to carry on myself, though it must be known that there is a limit to human endurance."

"I want to be a good soldier, yet I realize that I am overtaxing myself and must take things more easily," Denny said as part of his response to James Hendrix of Birmingham. "Of course, I want to do what I can in the hour of distress and uncertainty. Really, I am undertaking more than I ought to undertake, but it is at a period when all of us must face the situation squarely," he wrote to R. H. Wharton of Birmingham. In another response, he wrote, "I have been going at too rapid a gait in my effort to bring the work up to date. That has meant a draft on my reserve strength. I must try to learn a reasonable degree of restraint."

In another he wrote, "Dick's death was a great shock to all of us. He was an outstanding person. I want to do what I can to fill in the gap here. There is no place on earth that I love as I do the University."

Chauncy Sparks of Eufaula, who had just announced his candidacy for governor, wrote Denny to congratulate "first the University and second you on a most happy arrangement." Denny responded, "I realize that I lack physical and nervous strength to carry this heavy burden, yet I want to be a good soldier. I am grateful to have literally thousands of letters, telegrams and telephone calls that have come to me."

To Harry Eddins of Tuscaloosa, Denny responded, "I know that I am daily expending reserve energy, yet I want to be a good soldier. The University is dear to me and I realize that we are now at a crisis." He wrote almost identical responses to scores of other letters, trying to respond to friends and well-wishers while attending to his daily duties as interim president. In a short letter to his sister Otelia, Denny wrote, "I am in the harness again in the sore emergency created by the death of my brilliant young successor, President Foster. I realize that I ought not to be undergoing the tax which I am undergoing, but I simply could not stand aside and fail to step into the breach."

"My devotion to the University of Alabama and to our entire commonwealth could only mean that I must step into the breach at this sad hour. I want to do what I can to help," Denny wrote in one response. In another, he said, "I am again in the saddle trying to carry on. We are all under the shadow of a great sorrow here." He wrote in another response, "Naturally I am working under enormous pressure and emotional strain. I have to take a day or two away to get rested." "I am doing what I can to steady the boat in these troubled times. All of us need to work together now as never before," he said in another.

R. H. Powell of Tuskegee wrote to Denny on December 6, 1941, to wish him a happy seventy-first birthday and added, "We are blessed indeed that you were spared in good health and strength to again take up the burden and march forward in step and time with your past labors." Sheriff Holt McDowell of Jefferson County wrote Denny on December 22, 1941, saying, "Nothing has given me more pleasure than to know that you are again at the head of our University; we all feel that we will enjoy again the good old days."

Having heard Denny's radio tribute to Foster and read the news of Denny's election as president, P. A. McDavid of Clayton, Alabama, wrote to Denny, saying, "Your deep and masterful address during the program dedicated to Dr. Foster was the effort of a great and able man. It was a beautiful tribute to a fine character. Only Dr. Denny could have done it." McDavid added that "University friends everywhere now feel assured of the future destiny of the great institution you built since your genius again steers its course. They know George has the vigor, the vision, the genius and the drive to fully hold for Alabama the place she has attained as a great university." Scores of similar letters poured in to Denny from University alumni and friends, cheering his return as president, if only temporarily.

Foster's death was an emotional blow to Denny and the entire University community, as Denny acknowledged in a letter to his daughter Frances just five days after arriving in Tuscaloosa. "Naturally we have all been working here under stress and strain during the last few days. I am doing all I can to steady the situation and have everything proceed on a normal basis. I have stood up under the strain fairly well, but I realize that after the emotional period is past, I shall need to be more careful than ever. There will then be an inevitable letdown."

There was little time for an emotional letdown, however. The Japanese bombing attack on U. S. ships and other military installations at Pearl Harbor, Hawaii, on December 7, 1941, threw the entire nation into a state of anger, fear and chaos. More than 2,400 U. S. servicemen died in the surprise bombing raid and the nation was suddenly engulfed in World War II. In the aftermath of the Sunday morning attack, Denny found his work as president of the University of Alabama even more difficult.

Denny made an immediate attempt to calm student anxiety on campus. "These are critical times in which we live. We do not know what lies ahead," Denny told *Crimson White* writer Charles McBurney shortly after the U. S. Congress declared war on Japan the following day. Urging University students to resist the immediate emotional urge to rush into military service, Denny said, "There is nothing unpatriotic about remaining in college. On the contrary, it is the highest form of patriotism to prepare oneself to render some really worthwhile service in the time of need. There should be among college students no war hysteria. Young men and women should calmly fortify themselves with courage and with knowledge against the time when they will be called upon to demonstrate in the nation's life their strength of character, of body and of mind. Unless students stick by their academic guns, remain in college, work day by day, continue their education without interruption, they will fall out of line, grow rusty in their studies and find all their life plans dislocated," he added.

The University, in the meantime, committed more resources to the war effort each day. The University adopted the quarter system for 1942-43 to allow students to complete their education in shorter time; the Medical School stepped up its program to prepare more doctors for service; use of electrical power on campus was curtailed in every possible way, and training for ROTC cadets intensified. The University Extension Division was already conducting night classes for defense workers at several centers around the state, and an April 24 *Crimson White* story said that 5,945 workers were enrolled in the classes, which included such essential skills as welding, radio technology and handling of explosives. Campus training for defense involved aircraft mechanics, sheet metal work, airplane design, navigation, engineering, chemistry, foreign languages, telegraph and radio technology, ordnance and map reading among other similar subjects. "Every department and division of the University has been readjusted to fit the needs of national defense," the *Crimson White* story said. "No effort is being spared in the attempt to make the University the service as well as the educational center of the South. The University has pledged itself to serve the nation."

Denny, although away from home only three weeks, revealed his feeling of loneliness in a letter to his daughter Frances on December 9. "I was greatly relieved to hear from you," he said. "I wondered just what on earth was wrong. It is hard to believe, but yet it is a fact that I have heard from neither Mama nor Margaret. I suppose they are so busy with the baby (Margaret's son Hunter, born June 3, 1940) that they have absolutely overlooked the fact that I am away from home. Please get them to drop me a line once in a while. I am trying to take care of myself, but you can understand the pressure that is constantly exerting itself on this office. I believe everyone has steadied down to work again, but I noticed quite a good deal of unrest yesterday when we (the United States) declared war on Japan. I am really hoping that the students will realize that their first duty to the country is to get themselves ready to do something worthwhile when they are actually called into service. Their first great task is here on the campus."

Denny wrote Frances again on December 12, saying, "I get powerful lonesome at times. Much to my comfort and peace of mind, I am glad to report that I had a letter from Mama this morning." A few days later, he wrote friend Stuart Moore in Virginia, saying, "I do not know just when I can get relief from my pressing duties here, but I am certainly putting forth every effort to pass the burden on to younger shoulders at the earliest opportunity. I have been overdoing things. For example, during the past four days I have had to make five addresses. I need rest badly. I hope to get home (to Lexington) next Monday morning for at least a week of quiet and peace and calm." Denny also told Frances that head football coach Frank Thomas was urging him to accompany the football team to the upcoming Cotton Bowl game in Dallas, but that he would only attend if she would go with him. Frances joined her father for the trip as they watched Alabama defeat Texas A&M 29-21 to complete a 9-2 season.

A. C. Montgomery of Birmingham wrote Denny on December 16, 1941, to express his support for his return to the University. "Of course, we were all shocked and heartsick over the loss of Dick Foster and it was a terrible blow to Alabama, but we are happy that the old "war horse" has been spared all these years and is able to take up where he left off. It is a source of great happiness to know that such a man is back in the president's chair. It is with a great deal of pride that I have spoken many, many times of my association, friendship and esteem for George H. Denny, who has done more for Alabama, in his way, than any other man. Twenty years make a generation, and your work is now really beginning to tell, as all of the boys and girls cherish the friendship, love, loyalty, cooperation and encouragement which you gave them. Now you are dealing with the second generation, and it is a great thing to know that we have such a true soldier fighting the greatest war of all—ignorance—and I wish to give you my thanks and praise for what you have done."

University trustees met on January 7 to formally elected Denny president as the search for a new president was launched. Newspaper headlines made major news of Denny's official election as interim president while all but ignoring the mention of possible future successors to Foster. "Denny Re-acclaimed Capstone President," a bold headline in the *Crimson White* said, and newspapers around the state followed suit as they hailed the aging father of the modern Capstone as the returning hero. The accompanying story mentioned several possible candidates for permanent president, including Dr. Raymond Ross Paty, president of Birmingham Southern College; Dr. Carmichael; Dr. Theodore Jack, president of Randolph-Macon College, and Gordon D. Palmer, president of First National Bank of Tuskaloosa and a member of the University board of trustees. Saying at the time that he was "willing to serve to the limit of his strength and ability," Denny dutifully accepted the role of president with mixed emotions despite his age (71 on December 3, 1941) and troubling health issues. At the same time, he made note of the difficulties facing the University because of "war and the past failure of the legislature to provide the state institutions of higher learning with adequate financial support."

"It means much to Alabama to have you back home," wrote Mobile Schools Superintendent W. G. Griggs in January 1942. "When you left us I had the feeling that I had been let down. Now that you are with us again, we all rejoice. I am told that you are about the liveliest man on campus, that you are eclipsing your former self in your daily ministrations, that your health is fine and that you are happily circumstanced. Now here's to you and yours; may you live a thousand years and a day; here's to me and mine less a day, for I would not ask to live when you have passed away." Alumnus Sam Clabaugh wrote, "In the tragedy that has come to the University family, it is comforting to know that the head of the family has returned."

On January 8, 1942, Denny wrote to Mrs. Denny, saying, "I must have my cap and gown and hood at once. Mid-year graduation will be held in the very near future. I think probably you will have to come, certainly for a period, sometime in the not-too-distant future. Otherwise people will think we are about to get a divorce." In a display of his well-known frugality, Denny added as a postscript, "Please use the enclosed mailing label when you send my cap, gown and hood; otherwise they will charge me first-class postage on the package." Denny also noted in his letter that he was living on the ground floor of the President's Mansion and sharing the house with three male students and added that Ida, who had been Foster's cook, was preparing his meals. He wrote Mrs. Denny again on January 26 to assure her that his being named president was only a formality and not a long-lasting arrangement. "I am sure you have expressed the correct sentiment in all that you say regarding my overdoing things," he said. "Do not worry about the action of the board in making me president. That was merely a technicality. Someone has to sign all these government papers and other papers as such. Personally I just wanted to fill in here as chancellor. I still hope to get relief in due time. I am doing my best to locate the right kind of man." He suggested again that she arrange to come to Tuscaloosa, and added, "The most serious part of the situation is that there is inevitably in this war period unrest among young people who are anxious to get into the service before they really ought to go." Denny added that he hoped to return to Lexington soon, saying, "I fully understand that I am drawing on my reserve nervous and physical strength, but I have the consolation of trying to be a good soldier."

Denny wrote to Frances the following day saying that he had recently received "a scorcher" from Mrs. Denny. "She seems entirely out of sorts with me for accepting the presidency. I explained to her that the title means nothing. Perhaps she does not understand that all kinds of government, state and college papers have to be signed by me as president to make them legal, yet she assumes that I am going to stay on here forever," he wrote. "I am drawing on reserve strength all the time and the worry of things is not adding to my happiness in any way. No one realizes more than I do that I ought to be free to rest the balance of my days. I am sure you will talk matters over with Mama and that some of you will decide to visit me soon…."

Responding to a January 15, 1942, letter from his sister Mattie expressing her concerns about the war, Denny wrote, "If I were you I would not worry every time a news dispatch sounds a warning regarding the remote possibility of a bombing in Richmond. There are many other railroad junctions in America."

In answer to a late-January letter from his niece Mary Strickler in Atlanta, Denny wrote, "These are perilous times for the colleges. So many of the boys are going into the war—some of them perhaps never to return. It is all too bad." He added that he was "drawing on his nervous and physical energy, yet I want to be a good soldier. I try to do a little resting every day, but this is an exacting job in these critical times."

Denny devoted much of a February 28 letter to Mrs. Denny to the discussion of his son Buster's (George H. Denny Jr.) upcoming March 4 induction into the Army. "Naturally I should have preferred his having a commission, but I am absolutely certain that it is better for him to go as a private rather than to have him hang around from day to day and month to month and year to year doing nothing," Denny said. "Furthermore, at a time when both married and single men are being taken from important jobs and drafted into the Army, it would seem a family disgrace if Buster, who has nothing to do, should render no service whatever. For that reason, I also think that Buster ought to be happy that he has a chance to do anything at all to join with young people all over the country who are eagerly thronging into the national defense movement." Buster, a University of Alabama law school graduate and age thirty-seven at the time, attained the rank of sergeant during his military service and worked as an attorney for the Veterans Administration after the war.

Writing to his daughter Margaret on April 27, Denny said, "I am back at the office for a few minutes just before noon. For nearly a week I have been at the house and for most of the time in bed fighting a cold. Naturally I feel weak and I suppose that I have already been at the office longer than I should remain at a place where I can be accosted by anybody and everybody…. If I feel strong enough, I want to move on to Lexington on Thursday of this week. I find it more difficult as I grow older to shake off physical troubles."

Denny wrote to his brother Wright Denny in Charles Town, West Virginia, on three occasions in early 1942. In January he wrote, "I am just back at the desk after a week's trip to the Cotton Bowl. We found Texas raw and cold, but we enjoyed the trip as a whole. Everything is very doubtful in these trying times and the only thing any of us can do is to face each day as it comes and goes." On February 17 he wrote, "I got three or four days of rest, but I still need three or four months of rest. I realize that some younger person of greater nervous and physical strength than I now possess ought to be hammering away at the disagreeable job of balancing an unbalanced budget such as we now have due to this war period." In March he wrote, "I am not feeling as well as I ought to feel. I know that I have no business doing what I am trying to do. Yet I want these people to know that I am willing to spend and be spent in their service. In short, I want to be a good soldier."

Denny, however, no longer had the strength to carry on the daily rigors of the office of president, and he, more than anyone, knew it. He mentioned his struggle to carry on in almost every letter to friends and family as he filled the office of president for the next eight months. In rejecting an invitation to speak in early 1942, Denny wrote, "My doctor cautions me not to take on anything for the time being that is not absolutely imperative. He cautions me that I must get far greater relief from pressures of one kind or another than I have been getting."

Addressing the board of trustees at its May 23, 1942, meeting, Denny reported that 4,921 resident students had been enrolled during the spring semester while 13,764 others were receiving instruction through correspondence and extension courses. In addition, 8,050 others were taking courses through the government-sponsored Engineering, Science and Management Defense Training (ESMDT) program at such locations as Anniston, Decatur, Mobile, Birmingham, Huntsville and Montgomery for a total of 21,814 people receiving defense training by the University through various courses of study, including nutrition, flight training and radio programs to boost public morale. In addition to the programs of early 1942, the campus provided special on-campus housing and training for 12,888 active duty soldiers 1942-43, utilizing classrooms and dormitories vacated by male students who had been called to service. Male student enrollment dropped to less than 800 at its lowest point during wartime, with approximately 1,500 female students. "The major problem of all people is the defense of the nation against the strong-arm forces of barbarism and destruction," Denny said. "Every citizen and every institution, educational or otherwise, must find ways of helping to win this war for the preservation of democracy and civilization."

In keeping with an earlier announcement of his intentions to do so, Denny proposed that the new campus auditorium be named Richard Clarke Foster Auditorium in honor of the late University president. The trustees, as expected, heartily approved the proposal. Denny also recommended that the trustees award honorary LL.D. degrees to University graduates Borden Burr and Claude D. Pepper. Burr was a prominent Birmingham attorney and one of the University's most active and loyal alumni while Pepper, also a University alumnus, was a U. S. senator from Florida who had been helpful in securing federal funds for several Capstone building projects, including the Gorgas Library.

"My efforts since resuming the office of president have been devoted largely to balancing the budget," Denny told the trustees, indicating that he had returned to his old habits of keeping close watch on the purse strings. "It has been neither an easy nor a pleasant task to take out of our budget expenditures of approximately $150,000. Yet it had to be done. So far as I can judge, we have currently balanced the budget," he added proudly. "No one can adequately foresee the future, but all of us agree that the spirit of our state budget law must be respected." Although Denny did not make an issue of it in May 1942, state allocations to higher education continued to show a legislative bias against the University of Alabama as it had for decades. State appropriations for 1941-42 included $381.09 per student for Alabama College, $254.21 per student for Auburn and $214.67 per student for the University of Alabama.

Denny also reported that former Marion Military Institute president H. O. Murfee was leading a movement to help develop a four-year medical school and create two medical centers to help meet the present and future health needs of state. "For years thinking people have recognized this need," Denny said. "Such a need ought to appeal not only to the humanitarian impulse of our people, but also to a realization that taking this step will serve the economic and social interests of Alabama. Not only is our own sense of justice involved, but the health of our citizenship is at stake. We must have more doctors and more hospital facilities." Denny urged the trustees to insist that money for the four-year medical school be independent of the operation of the University. "It is high time that Alabama appropriated money on the basis of services rendered," he said.

In asking the trustees to appoint a committee to recommend a new president, an exhausted Dr. Denny said, "I am conscious that I lack the reserve of physical and nervous strength to carry on as I attempted to do as a younger man. It has been a great joy and satisfaction to respond to the call of the trustees at a crisis. This I was willing to do at any sacrifice, for no one could love the University more than I do. Yet there is a limit to all things, and I am asking now that a younger man take up the burden that I have been attempting to carry during recent months." Heeding Denny's plea, the trustees voted to seek a "suitable replacement" for Denny as president, "to be compensated at a salary of not more than $15,000 per year. The search committee appointed included trustees L. L Herzberg, Ferguson, Palmer, Charles S. McDowell Jr. and McCorvey.

The search for a new president was a short one. The trustees met in special session on August 11, 1942, to consider the nomination of Dr. Raymond Paty and immediately and unanimously elected him to succeed Dr. Denny. Paty, president of Birmingham Southern College, had been mentioned among the possible candidates from the start, and Denny had written to him on March 6, 1942, suggesting that they "get together to discuss cooperative efforts of institutions in the area" in what was most likely a thinly disguised pre-interview session. "Dr. Denny heartily approves of Dr. Paty and concurs in the committee's recommendation to the board," committee chairman Herzberg said in nominating Paty as University president beginning September 1. In choosing an experienced college president in 1942, the trustees likely recognized the fact that Denny was no longer able to provide the constant advice and assistance he had provided Foster during his tenure, and archives show that Denny and Paty in fact did not correspond regularly during Paty's tenure. Paty, a native of Bell Buckle, Tennessee, was educated at Emory University, Columbia University and the University of Chicago. He taught high school in Crossville, Tennessee, 1921-29 and served as instructor (1929-1933) and dean of men at Emory (1933-37) before going to Birmingham Southern in 1938.

Herzberg added that the committee "desires to make grateful acknowledgement to Dr. Denny for his tireless efforts for and on behalf of the committee. Time and again he has dangerously exhausted his physical strength traveling throughout the state to attend meetings of the committee and in conference in behalf of the committee in its deliberations. Dr. Denny came to us in time of crisis. He came at great peril to his health, but he came unhesitatingly, and with his rare ability he saw us through a period of grave emergency. He is now entitled to the rest and relaxation he needs and craves. We assume the trustees will permit him to again retire, but will seek to retain the benefit of his matchless faculties by appointing him for the second time the chancellor of this university." The trustees immediately approved the committee's recommendation of Paty as president and Denny as chancellor, citing Denny's "long years of loyal and valuable service to the University and his invaluable knowledge concerning the conduct of the institution."

Weary from a hectic and emotional nine months as University president from November 21, 1941, until September 1, 1942, Denny quietly returned to Lexington without fanfare or ceremony shortly before Paty's arrival on campus on September 5. The *Crimson White* ran a brief statement from Denny in its September 7 issue under the headline "Farewell Message from Dr. Denny," although the message was far from a farewell message. It was instead a typical Denny welcome to incoming students and failed to mention his departure from the Capstone in any way. "The University greets you at the beginning of the new college year. You are welcome to all it has to offer in character, in discipline, in learning and in tradition. There is no finer institution in the world," the message began. "We are in the midst of a world war. This institution has, in one hundred years of service to this commonwealth, to the South and to the nation, survived every war in the nation's history since 1831. We know what war means. We know what sacrifices must be made at a time like this. The federal government from the president down is calling for trained men and women. This war is likely to last for a period of years. Do not become impatient to rush in until you are prepared to render high service. There will be ample opportunity later on to serve the country in high and helpful ways. The one thing each of us must seek now to do is to be certain that we are prepared to render the finest service and in the finest way. That means training and still more training; now is your opportunity.

"We summon you to the high task of answering your country's call to the precise way in which that call ought to be answered," the message continued. "We ask you to keep your feet on the ground and to do your college work in steady and serene fashion. I am sure that we shall not be disappointed. Alabama alumni scattered throughout the world are doing their part. They will continue to do their part. Already a considerable number of them have fallen at the front. They have won the accolades of our undying gratitude. Young women will soon find ample opportunity for participating in the struggle in a way that will reflect high credit on them if they will seize their present opportunity and fit themselves for high office. I am sure our young women will not fail us. We are at your service. We want to help you in every way. Do not fail to call upon us. You have our best wishes for a great college year. Follow the fine leadership of President Paty. George H. Denny, Chancellor."

Denny had been the "good soldier" as head of the University again for more than nine months and was happily back home in Lexington with his family, getting the much-deserved rest he needed, by the time Paty arrived on campus.

Denny spoke on statewide radio after being chosen
Alabama's "First Citizen" in November 1946.

13

A Final Triumph for
the Old Guard

*"I express gratitude once more that I have known and loved the
University and tried to keep its commandments. If I had a thousand
lives, I would gladly give them all in its service."*

—Dr. George H. Denny

The University of Alabama had remained the University of Dr. George H. Denny
during the 1937-1941 presidential tenure of his former student, friend and protégé
Richard C. Foster. Denny's experience and wisdom in a close advisory role as chancellor
and Foster's keen administrative and diplomatic skills proved a perfect combination as
Denny enjoyed a quiet, uneventful semiretirement that allowed frequent, friendly visits
to the Capstone. The same was not true under the administration of Dr. Raymond Paty,
however.

The turmoil of World War II had already brought change to the Capstone, and Paty,
an experienced college president who did not share all of Denny's ideals and principles
of management, brought more when he assumed office on September 1, 1942. Paty's
changes—many no doubt necessitated by an influx of post-war veterans that pushed
enrollment to over 9,000 by 1948—eventually created frustration among veteran
University faculty members, who unhappily complained to Denny and helped create a
rift between Denny and Paty. That rift eventually involved the trustees and might well
have contributed to Paty's 1946 resignation. It also surely added to the burdens Denny
was again called on to bear during his final years.

Denny had returned home to Lexington in August 1942 exhausted and in poor
health. He desperately needed the rest his doctors had repeatedly advised him to get,
but his initial period of rest was short-lived. He was summoned back to the Capstone
two months later because of the sudden death of Dr. James J. Doster, dean of the School
of Education and Denny's closest friend and comrade-in-arms in the fight to improve
education in Alabama throughout Denny's tenure as president. Doster, who joined the
University faculty in 1907 after having taught at Troy Normal School for several years,
died of a heart attack while working at his desk in Graves Hall at 10:15 a.m. on October

21, 1942, at age sixty-eight. Denny was called immediately, and he in turn notified Doster's only son, James F. Doster, who was in graduate school at the University of Chicago.

"Measured by every correct standard and ideal, Dr. Doster has been one of Alabama's really great men," Denny said in a statement at the time. He added that Doster had "served the University and public education in the entire South with outstanding distinction and with the utmost fidelity for a period of thirty-six years. He has contributed immeasurably to the life of the University, to its development and to its spheres of usefulness. Yet his life has been far larger than that. He was one of the most influential factors in the establishment of the high school system of Alabama. In the days to come when men assess in accurate and precise terms really worthwhile contributions made by the leaders of public life in Alabama, Dr. Doster's services will loom larger and larger. All of us on the campus feel a sense of profound gratitude and appreciation of Dr. Doster's outstanding role in the growth and distinction of the University. I can think of no one on the campus who has gone in and out of the highways and byways of Alabama and represented in more distinguished fashion the ideals and the aspirations of this institution than has Dr. Doster," Denny added.

Denny had corresponded regularly with Doster since his retirement as University president on December 31, 1936, and had recently written, "Please take care of yourself. You ought to have many fruitful years ahead of you. You are one of the strong pillars supporting the structure." In another letter, Denny said, "I am awfully sorry to hear that you are under the weather. I do hope you will soon be well again and that you will watch that pressure. You have been, through the years, a great wheelhorse. Certainly, I for one, can never forget your tremendous service to the University and to Alabama. I have often wondered what we could have done without your tireless effort and fearless leadership, both on the campus and in Montgomery." In another letter Denny had written, "When things were going harder than they are going even now with a hostile governor, you were my chief support in Montgomery. The University owes you a great debt of gratitude. Your service to it has been constant and invaluable." Doster served as professor of philosophy and education, dean of the School of Education, director of summer school, state school inspector and as faculty chairman of the athletic committee for many years. He played a major role in the development of the state's high school courses of study and advised the state's normal schools on their courses of study. He was awarded an honorary LL.D degree by the University in 1917. Doster Hall, although dedicated to women's studies such as fine arts and home economics when it was constructed in 1928, was named in his honor.

Denny did not return to Tuscaloosa for the November 7, 1942, homecoming trustees meeting, where a resolution honoring him for his recent nine-month stint as president was adopted. "Among those who love the University and cherish its well-being, the name of George H. Denny will always endure," the resolution began. "Upon his retirement as president of the University several years ago, glowing tributes testified to his magnificent contributions to the life and development of the University. He had given unselfishly of time, talent and health beyond measure. Yet, so great was Dr. Denny's devotion to this institution that without hesitation or regard for self, when called from retirement to active service again by this board at the untimely death of

President Richard C. Foster, he responded. He labored diligently and vigorously at the extraordinary problems confronting the University, which were soon complicated by the necessity for major adjustments of faculty and curricula in order to meet the requirements of the war and to safeguard the financial structure of the institution against the inevitable impact of the war. With characteristic energy and consummate skill, Dr. Denny discharged the trying executive responsibilities until his successor had been procured and assumed office. Disregarding the advice of friends and physicians concerned about his health, Dr. Denny walked the extra mile. In order that so fine an example of devotion to duty may be preserved for future generations and indicative of the deep appreciation of this board for the great service rendered by Dr. Denny in our hour of need, it is hereby resolved that this statement be recorded in the minutes and a copy of it be sent to Dr. Denny by the secretary." The trustees also sent a telegram to Denny, saying, "Each member of the board of trustees wishes to express to you his love, affection and admiration on this homecoming day. Our meeting was not complete without your presence and superb counsel."

At the same meeting, Paty reported to the trustees that only 4,250 students had enrolled for the fall semester compared to 4,921 in the fall of 1941 because many young men had volunteered or had been drafted for service in World War II. He also reported that the University had 740 faculty and staff members involved in various defense training programs. Women students dominated campus enrollment of regular students during wartime, making up 1,367 of the 2,223 students in 1943, 1,794 of the 2,541 students in 1944 and 1,973 of the 3,069 students in 1945. Post-war University enrollment grew to record numbers as thousands of young men and women attended college on the GI Bill. University enrollment figures show 8,626 in 1946, 8,729 in 1947 and 9,105 in 1948 as returning servicemen and women filled the campus to overflowing. The 9,105 students in 1948 included 5,500 veterans.

With Denny's health failing and the University moving at a rapid pace during wartime and immediately afterward, he did not return to Tuscaloosa often during the war. He returned to campus for the November 11, 1943, trustees meeting normally held on homecoming weekend, even though Alabama did not field a football team that year because all but one player from the 1942 football team had entered military service. He attended the May 26 and December 1 meetings in 1945, but did not return again until November 30, 1946, following Paty's announcement in early October that he was resigning effective December 31 to accept the chancellorship of the University of Georgia Educational System. Although Paty assured the trustees on October 24 that "no discord in any department of the University, the board of trustees or state administration had influenced him in his decision" to resign, there is much evidence to the contrary.

A Paty letter to Denny dated October 28, 1946, clearly shows that problems existed between the two for much of Paty's tenure. "I am glad that I had the opportunity of seeing you in Knoxville after receiving your good letter and could there express to you my thanks for the sentiments you expressed. The occasions which have arisen during the past few years when we have not seen eye to eye were viewed by me as indicative of the deep concern held by both of us over the development of a great university. Each of us brought to such occasions different backgrounds of training, experience and age and it was rather natural that differences in opinion should arise," Paty wrote, acknowledging their differences and the fact that Denny had made the first move in any reconciliation efforts. Interestingly, the letter was addressed to "Dr. George H. Denny, Lexington, Virginia," without reference to Denny's well-earned and long-standing title of chancellor. The letter is also one of only two from Paty to Denny found in Denny's files during Paty's four-year tenure as president. That was in sharp contrast to the previous four years, when Foster and Denny corresponded at least once a month during Foster's tenure, discussing all phases of University activities.

A difference in the management styles of Denny and Paty was illustrated at a meeting of the executive committee on August 3, 1945, when Denny, known for his strict accountability, questioned a particular purchase by Paty and expressed concern for the financial management of the medical school in Birmingham, which had operated at a loss since January 1, 1945. Paty acknowledged the medical school deficit and said he expected to see an improvement in coming months. Two years later, a state auditor's report reinforced Denny's concern when it criticized medical school management for "inefficiency" during the year ending September 30, 1947. The audit pointed out several questionable expenditures, "especially in view of the fact that the hospital is not in a sound financial condition and is not in a position to meet current obligations promptly." The audit also criticized the medical school's purchasing department for "using very loose business practices" and said that accounts receivable on discharged patients had been kept "in a most unsatisfactory manner."

Evidence of possible discord between Paty and the trustees appeared in a November 1946 *Alabama School Journal* editorial that criticized the trustees and urged that all state institutions of higher learning be combined under one board. Tuscaloosa trustee Gordon D. Palmer read the following excerpts from the editorial: "As suggested by the Alabama Educational Survey Commission of 1945, the board of trustees of the University is improperly organized. Not only should it be merged with the boards responsible for the administration of higher educational in Alabama, but as a separate board, it is too detached from the tax-paying public. Its members are self-perpetuating; vacancies on the board being nominated by secret ballot and voting being limited to board members. Moreover, the board is largely dominated by a three-member executive committee created from within the group.... One surmises that President Paty felt keenly the limitations under which his office necessarily operated and that his lack of free action was at least one determining factor that sent him to Georgia...." Palmer called the editorial, published by the state board of education, "inaccurate and inimical to good public relations between two important educational departments in the state."

Confidential letters from University faculty members to Denny 1945-46 show a pattern of growing faculty unrest as Paty made changes that disrupted the relative peacefulness of the 30-year Denny-Foster era. Among Paty's first changes was the hiring of Dr. M. C. Huntley, former executive secretary of the Southern Association of Colleges and Secondary Schools, in the newly created position of dean of administration on December 1, 1942. The hiring announcement said Huntley was expected to relieve Paty of many of the routine administrative duties of his office as Paty concentrated on the University's war efforts, although Paty soon hired others to help deal with the war effort. Huntley, like Paty, was educated at Emory, Columbia and the University of Chicago and had previously been on the faculty at Birmingham Southern. Within two years, Denny was deluged with letters from University faculty members complaining of their treatment by the new administration, and Huntley was directly involved in several of the complaints. Additional concerns surfaced in March 1945 with the publication of the findings of the Alabama Educational Survey Commission, which recommended the unification of the state's three four-year colleges under a single board of trustees. Denny had long been openly adamant in his opposition to unification of the colleges for the simple reason that the governor and state legislature, which established the Alabama Educational Survey Commission by law in 1943, was and had long been controlled by political forces openly unfriendly to the University of Alabama.

Governor Chauncey Sparks, who took office January 19, 1943, was strongly in favor of unification of the state's four-year colleges under one board of directors, and he personally appointed the seven members of the Educational Survey Commission, which was granted "full power and authority to summon and examine witnesses, issue subpoenas, administer oaths and require production of such books, papers, documents, records and memoranda as necessary and to utilize the services, information, facilities and personnel of any department or agency in the executive branch of state government" in its study. Not surprisingly, the commission report, published March 1, 1945, concluded that "Alabama should set up a single agency for the control of public education at all levels. The administration and supervision of public education in Alabama should be a single function under a single board." The commission added that a state department of education, made up of a nine-member board appointed by the governor with the consent of the senate, would govern all levels of education. The study recommended that the boards of trustees at the University of Alabama, Auburn and Alabama College "be reconstituted as advisory boards" with control over endowment funds and campus policies.

The report was the main topic of conversation at the May 26, 1945, meeting of the University of Alabama trustees. "The board discussed at length the report of the Alabama Educational Survey Commission and especially the recommendation for the adoption of a constitutional amendment providing for a single or common board for state educational programs," the minutes of the meeting said. "It was recognized that such an amendment would have far-reaching effects on the institutional life of the state, but opinion was divided as to the desirability of such a measure. The ex-officio members of the board favored the recommendation of the commission, but the active members (trustees) who spoke—and Dr. Denny—were opposed to a common board." The ex-officio members of the board were Governor Sparks and State Superintendent of Education Dr. E. B. Norton. Paty reported to the trustees at the meeting that he, as earlier directed by the executive committee, had met with the governor and the presidents of Auburn and Alabama College in an attempt to reach an agreement on some issues raised by the commission that would help avoid legislative unification, but said that no agreement had been reached. Sparks waged his campaign for unification of the state's public educational system under one board for the remainder of his term, but Denny led a determined two-year fight against the plan and finally defeated it.

"This suggestion involves a radical and dangerous departure from the plan of control tested by time and experience," Denny said of the unification proposal. "It is suggested that the plan may curb the alleged spirit of rivalry existing between the institutions of higher education. It is far more likely to throw the institutions into political chaos in a struggle to control the boards, thereby intensifying rivalry and destroying stability of institutional development. Instead of a friendly educational rivalry we shall conceivably have a destructive political rivalry based on a determination to control the board."

Opponents of the unification proposal might well have recalled a similar suggestion made by *Anniston Star* publisher Harry Ayers in 1937 shortly after Denny's retirement. Ayers said placing all state institutions of higher education under a single board would result in greater efficiency and economy by ending duplication of services, thus saving the state money. A *Crimson White* editorial immediately took issue with the Ayers proposal, saying "At first glance this proposal seems to be a very sensible one. But we must bring out certain facts which pertain to the University and then consider whether or not the proposed plan would prove beneficial. Let us suppose that the state government had given freely of funds necessary to cause this school to advance as it has in the past. In such a case, the extra expense of maintaining duplicate schools would unquestionably be unreasonable. But has such been the case? The answer is emphatically 'NO.' The University of Alabama has reached its present position almost in spite of the government of the state of Alabama rather that with its aid. It has grown by using its own funds judicially and by attracting a large number of out-of-state students. If the destinies of this school had been left in the hands of our esteemed lawmakers in Montgomery, it would still be the little two-by-four school that it was twenty-five years ago. Are we going to see the University grow to a place of prominence in the eyes of the nation then turn it over to those who have never displayed any desire to foster its growth, but moreover have actually seemed to resent it? Are we going to become dependent upon the whim of politicians who may seek more votes among the farmers of the state than among the lawyers and doctors and businessmen? Are we going to allow ourselves to be removed from the custody of our board of trustees, which is absolutely free from politics and which has always showed exceptionally good judgment in making its decision? The answer is again 'No.' The people of the state of Alabama have not yet advanced to the point where their selected leaders are as high principled and intelligent as they should be to control a great institution of higher learning. Such a change as is proposed would, we fear, result in such control. The University must be allowed to continue its progress. It is doing a great service to the state and will continue to do so as long as it remains independent under its present leaders."

Huntley, meanwhile, perhaps not fully aware of the importance of football at the University of Alabama, made more than a slight misstep on July 17, 1945, when he sent popular head football coach Frank Thomas a letter making him responsible for intramural sports. "In past years, it has not been clear where the responsibility for direction of this program rested," Huntley said. Thomas, who had been head coach since 1931, did not welcome the assignment and felt threatened by the new administration. He wrote Denny soon afterward to voice his concerns about changes on campus. "I am thinking of asking for a raise and a long-term contract. The way Dean (Agnes Ellen) Harris and several others got pushed around after long, loyal and efficient service makes me wonder what could happen to me," Thomas wrote. "I feel as though now that I have been here fifteen years that I should have some peace of mind and security. Please give me your opinion about this." Following a perfect 10-0 season in 1945, capped by a 34-14 Rose Bowl victory over Southern Cal behind the play of All-America halfback Harry Gilmer, Thomas received a ten-year contract with a $6,000 bonus to be paid at $600 per year. Unfortunately, health issues forced Thomas to retire after the 1946 season and he died May 10, 1954, at age fifty-five. Thomas, who had played quarterback under Knute Rockne at Notre Dame, posted a 115-24-7 record as head coach at Alabama.

Harris, who had served as both dean of women and dean of home economics since 1927, wrote to Denny on September 16, 1945, to express her unhappiness at having been forced to give up her role as dean of women on July 1. "I would be grateful if you will write me you thoughts on this," Harris, affectionately known as "Dean Aggie" on campus, wrote. "I do hope you are planning to come down soon. I, like others, need to see you to hold on to that devotion to the University that you inspired. Your influence is still here—just writing to you inspires me to want to get about the business of working for the University. I think I am past the emotional stage of this situation. I am ready now to work. I need your advice," Harris, the first woman to receive an honorary doctoral degree at the University, added.

Dr. Albert B. Moore, dean of the graduate school and faculty chairman of the athletic committee, wrote Denny regularly during 1945-46, keeping him abreast of news regarding athletics, discussing football games in depth and reporting the latest campus gossip. Based on Denny's personal records, Moore was Denny's primary pipeline to any and all news from Tuscaloosa, although he did receive letters from other faculty members from time to time. Moore wrote to Denny on October 4, 1945, to report on a recent Southeastern Conference athletic rules meeting, but added a complaint about not receiving a pay raise promised by Paty. "I am not going to stand for his shabby treatment of me. If he does not do something, I am going to see if others will insist on his being decent toward me," Moore wrote. "I am not going to carry the heavy load that I am carrying unless he gives me a square deal as to salary." In an October 22 letter to Denny, Moore provided an update on his attempt to secure a pay increase then added ominously, "I have heard through reliable sources about unrest and lack of confidence among alumni and friends of the University that is growing. How soon it will all come to a head I do not know...."

Denny apparently wrote to his allies on the board of trustees to express his concerns with the direction of the University and the unrest among faculty members after receiving Moore's letter. Responding to a Denny letter, trustee McCorvey wrote back on November 12 to say, in part, "I hope that things at the University are getting along much better than you feared from the last letter you wrote me. I am hoping and praying that things will go along all right. All of us realize that the Lord made only one George H. Denny and we all fully realized that whoever tried to fill your boots was going to rattle around in them....There is not a man, woman or child in Alabama who does not fully realize and appreciate the debt of gratitude Alabama owes you and which can never be fully paid." McCorvey followed with a response to another Denny letter on November 21, beginning, "I have received your very confidential letter of the 18th instant, and it is needless to say that I read it with much interest and with deep distress. Frankly, those of us who are not on the ground cannot size up situations affecting the University like those of you who have every detail at your fingertips can. I was somewhat surprised at your comments relative to Hill (Ferguson). I was under the impression that Hill thought that you could make no error of judgment and that he would not, as chairman of the executive committee, be advocating measures which you thought unwise." Denny's letter was apparently critical of a major building program proposed by Paty and already approved by the executive committee which was to be presented at the homecoming meeting of the trustees. "There is one suggestion in your letter which certainly deserves a lot of consideration, and that is your criticism of having a four-million-dollar building program handled at a meeting of the board when we are rushing through to get to see football games, etc." McCorvey wrote. "I don't know that there is any special rush about this matter, and it might be best for us to have a special meeting of the board to consider these matters when we can all be fully advised as to just where we are headed. I am just not in a position to pass judgment on the big matters that you discuss in the absence of more information."

Moore, having heard of the proposed building plan, wrote Denny a lengthy letter on November 23, 1945, to strongly express his objections to the anticipated indebtedness to be incurred by the University. "When our board's transactions are consummated the debt of the University will be more than two million dollars, including the medical school debt of about $1,200,000. Is this not correct? How can those who are stewards of the University sleep? We are indeed in a predicament and there can be little hope of recovery since supposedly intelligent men cannot understand or do not want to understand. We are riding the waves on a mad sea and I do not believe, as you said, that you could do any good in a board meeting to point us to a harbor and a safe landing. One thing I believe you should do if you decide not to come down for the board meeting is to write a letter to each member of the board, or at least a few selected members, and set out your views in full. I would state my views in no uncertain terms and would say that I would not be present because of my physical condition and because my presence would probably cause unpleasantness since I could not sit in silence when a reckless course was being charted for the University," Moore added in urging Denny to protest the proposed building plan.

There was plenty of news at the December 1, 1945, trustees meeting, and much of it was cause for frustration for Denny, who was in attendance. Although Denny had written the trustees to urge further study of Paty's $4.1 million building plan, it was approved without debate. Adding insult to injury, trustee Brewer Dixon of Talladega introduced a resolution to remove both Denny and Paty from the executive committee. Dixon cited the Code of Alabama, which he said limited membership on the committee to members of the board of trustees, and the resolution was approved. Although apparently lawful, Denny, who had been placed on the committee by a trustees' resolution on August 11, 1942, was shocked and offended by the action and it further widened the gap between him and long-time ally Ferguson. Moore, of course, quickly condemned the action. "The deed was utterly ungrateful and contemptible; it should be known among the alumni," Moore wrote to Denny soon afterward. "The other fellow (Paty) thought he played a smart trick but it will be a boomerang when it becomes known."

Denny, still smarting from the board's action three months later, felt unwanted and even unwelcome on campus. He apparently confided to Moore that he had no plans to return. "I know how you feel about coming back to the campus, but your true friends would like to have you," Moore wrote. "You must not let mean and small-gauged souls keep you from visiting the campus that you made and enjoying the friends who love you. We are looking forward to seeing you in Birmingham Saturday (for the April A-Day game to benefit former Crimson Tide football and track star Charley Boswell, who lost his sight in World War II). I believe you will be shown that you are yet appreciated and that you will have a good time." Moore wrote a few days later to again urge Denny to attend the A-Day game, saying, "Borden (Burr), Tommie (Frank Thomas) and I all agree that you should come down for the game. We think it important that you should keep in touch with the alumni and we believe that you will be expected to be present. We also believe that you will find the experience an enjoyable one despite certain things in the picture. So come on down and bless us all again with your presence and with an inspiring talk at the informal dinner following the game. Borden and others plan to have you make a rousing talk of some fifteen minutes. There will be many alumni present—friends who are unshakable in their devotion to you. You will be among true friends and you will have a good time…. Let no pipsqueaks and ingrates stand between you and the great University family that loves you," Moore added.

Tuscaloosa businessman, long-time University booster and Denny friend Hugo Friedman wrote Denny on March 25, 1946, with a similar message of support and an update on ticket sales for the A-Day benefit game. "I sent you another batch of clippings yesterday showing that everything is being done to put over the Boswell game. I feel sure that 20,000 to 25,000 tickets will be sold," Friedman reported before mentioning the recent board action. "I had a chat with Dean Moore and Coach Tommie last night. Both told me to write you stressing the fact that it would be fine if you would come down to the game and the banquet afterwards. I believe that all the alumni would be more than glad and happy to have you on hand. In fact, it would not seem like a complete picture unless you were on hand. You cannot realize how much I regret your feeling as you do about coming back to University affairs, although I fully appreciate that you have just cause to feel as you do. But I am sure that you are wrong in feeling that you will not always be welcomed—more than any other one man in the world—by practically every alumnus. They always will remember and fully realize that you are the man who made this University and they will always give you full credit. As for fellows like Dean Moore, Tommie, Yank (director of alumni affairs Charles Bernier), Borden, myself and hundreds and hundreds of others, you will always come first in our love and affection and we will always want you to come and be with us. If you feel well enough, I do hope you can come down, but if it will tire you too much, I would not do it."

Friedman rushed to Denny's defense on May 30 after hearing a rumor that a resolution to make Denny chancellor emeritus might be introduced at the June board of trustees meeting. Writing to executive committee chairman Ferguson and Alabama alumnus and newly elected trustee Lonnie Noojin, Friedman said placing Denny in emeritus status would, "in effect, eliminate Dr. Denny from any contact with the University and would virtually repudiate our appreciation of the twenty-five years he has labored for the University. Frankly, this may be simply a rumor without foundation, and perhaps it has not even reached your ears, but it might be 'sprung' on you without notice. I feel that it is unnecessary to say to fellows like you that such a resolution would not only mean the absolute elimination of Dr. Denny from the state of Alabama and from the University for which he nearly gave his life, but it would mean that he must resign as a trustee of the Carnegie Foundation, an honor which no other Alabamian has ever received. It would also mean a serious division in the alumni group since thousands of alumni, including the small group which really does things for the University, still holds the impression that Dr. Denny was the greatest college president of our age, and they would seriously resent such action. It would not only be a fatal stab at Dr. Denny, but it would place Dr. Paty under a terrific handicap for the future as he would never be able to pacify many a non-staunch supporter of his administration.

"When Dr. Denny was barred from the executive committee, it hurt him to the quick, but if he were demoted to chancellor emeritus it would be a death blow," Friedman continued. "I stress the fact that from letters I have received from Dr. Denny during the past few months, I can readily see that he will not be a factor in the University's proceedings from now on. I doubt that you will ever again have suggestions from him and I do not think he will show himself at any meetings unless they occur on a day when we have a prominent football game on campus. While I have not heard definitely, I doubt if he will attend the upcoming commencement exercises. I feel there is really little need for me to be writing fellows like you two or Gordon (Palmer). I know that you have an appreciation of and for Dr. Denny's record and you would not wish to do him such a hurt or cause a division in the alumni. I am writing this as one friend to another with the hope that this letter is simply a wasted effort and that no resolution will ever be brought before you," Friedman added.

Friedman's letter hinted that Denny, then seventy-six years old and in poor health, had decided to fully retire and surrender whatever influence he still had to Paty and his supporters. It sounded as if Denny, having been banished from the executive committee for expressing his views, had decided to retreat to the hills of Virginia and live out his life in quiet seclusion. And perhaps he should have; perhaps his time had passed. After all, time, the war years and veterans back from war had brought sudden, dramatic change to the Capstone, pushing aside many of the traditions and ideals of the past. But Denny's friends continued to call him back and he could not refuse them. The Capstone, to which he had devoted much of his life, called him back, too, as it has so many others, and perhaps reminded him of his own words, spoken to an alumni gathering on the eve of his retirement as president a decade earlier: "I love the University. I have given my life to it. I am fatalist and old enough to be resigned to my fate, whatever it may be. But I hope that I shall never so old or so fatalistic that I will not fight in any battle affecting the University. I will not stand on the sidelines, but will enter the thick of the fight and enjoy it." Denny chose not to retreat from what seemed to be a lost cause. He mustered the strength for one last battle and somehow won before finally retiring triumphantly rather than in disgrace.

Burr, a staunch Denny ally, sent Ferguson a more direct letter regarding the rumor of Denny's emeritus status on May 31, writing, "The rumor—and I hope that it is only a rumor—has reached me that a proposal may be made at the meeting of the board of trustees next week to retire Dr. Denny to the status of chancellor emeritus. I hope very much that there is nothing to the rumor and that if there is it will not find your support.

I understand that such an action would necessarily bring about Dr. Denny's retirement from the Carnegie Board, thus leaving Alabama without a distinguished connection with the educational foundations. But beyond this is my distinct aversion to anything happening which would necessarily cause pain and regret to one who has done as much in behalf of Alabama and education in the state and to his friends." Burr wrote Denny the following day to say that he had investigated the rumor and found that "there is nothing to this rumor and I feel absolutely certain that nothing of this kind will be brought up for consideration."

As Friedman predicted, Denny did not attend commencement exercises in June 1946, and his absence was noticed. Dr. Walter B. Jones, state geologist and director of the Alabama Museum of Natural History, wrote Denny on June 5, saying, "Commencement is on but it is not commencement for me. It might as well be happening a million miles away. I had forgotten that the presence of any one man could be so terribly important. I suppose that is an unmistakable sign of old age. The older I get the more importance I attach to friendships. Your friendship has been, is and will always be the dearest of all. I do hope that you are not ill but merely taking it easy. You certainly have that coming to you. For half a century you have been bearing the burdens of others. I know that is the way you wanted it. Still, you must now take care of yourself and add as many days to your span as possible." Bernier also acknowledged Denny's absence from commencement events in a July 1, 1946, letter, writing, "Commencement went off nicely and the campus was green and fresh and beautiful. But with all this beauty and the splendid exercises, we definitely lacked something to round out and complete the picture: Dr. and Mrs. Denny! If I heard one person say this I heard a hundred. These people love you and miss you…."

Moore continued to bombard Denny with gossip and complaints about Paty. In a June 22 letter, he said that an abundance of post-war students and money had provided a boost to the University and a windfall of unearned credit for Paty. "There is lots of money and certain blunders and extravagancies have not been revealed. We are living in flush times and not much ability is required to get along…. In addition to all this, our man talks a good game. He takes credit for all that has been done, talks fluently and plausibly about it and conjures up pictures of a millennium soon to be. His popularity and prestige have not grown on the campus, however. We are still in a muddle and there is much unrest and griping. I have heard a great deal in the last few days about student unrest," Moore added. Moore also delivered the sad news that the body of a newborn baby had recently been discovered in New Hall (women's dormitory). Harris wrote Denny regarding the matter soon afterward, calling the incident a "tragedy of the first order." Harris added that "Friends have said, 'I am so glad you are out of this.' Little do they know the misery of seeing this kind of thing happen to the work to which I gave so many years of my life." Dean of Women Pauline Park Wilson, who had replaced Harris in the position a year earlier, resigned shortly after the incident.

Although Denny felt unwelcome at the University because of his differences with Paty and some members of the board of trustees, he was far from a forgotten man. Thomas, Moore, McCorvey, athletic business manager Jeff Coleman, former Alabama football star Dixie Howell, Senator Harry Byrd of Virginia, Jones and other faculty and friends wrote Denny throughout the summer of 1946 discussing politics, the upcoming football season, Denny's health and other routine matters. Moore, in a September letter, spoke of "growing disgust" with the administration and happily but cautiously reported the rumor that Paty was being considered for the position of chancellor of the University of Georgia system. "I learned recently that Paty told one of his close friends that it had begun to look like he would soon have to make a choice between staying at Alabama or going to Georgia," Moore wrote. "I have serious doubts about this, but I, along with many others, hope that he may have a chance to go and that he will go. It is important that our board members be prepared not to encourage him to stay here if he says he has a chance to go to Georgia. They should advise him to go because of growing opposition to him in Alabama...." In an undated letter, Moore wrote, "We are drifting along. I still hear reports of uncertainty, confusion and disgust among faculty members.... Hope you may be feeling better. We shall expect you for homecoming. Many have asked me if you are coming. Let nothing down here keep you away. Your many friends will be glad to see you. Forget the pipsqueaks." Moore wrote again a few days later to say that the Atlanta newspapers had confirmed that Paty and University of Georgia president Harmon W. Caldwell were in fact being considered for the chancellorship of the Georgia system and that a selection would be made within days. Moore added that John McLure, dean of the School of Education, had said that Paty "knows he is getting into trouble here and will gladly accept the Georgia position. He said Paty is a failure here and would not last five years in the Georgia position. McLure says we are in a bad way with so much dissension and confusion on the campus.... As things now are, there is nothing to tie to, hence the confusion, uncertainty and friction. There is no anchorage, hence the aimless drifting," Moore added.

Thomas, in an October 1 letter to Denny, not only confirmed the rumor of Paty's possible departure but correctly predicted that Paty would take the Georgia position. Thomas wrote that Paty had "paid him a visit" and "he (Paty) says that (Georgia governor-elect Eugene) Talmadge went for him in a big way and wants him to take the job. Paty said Talmadge told several members of the board, 'Don't let Paty get away; he is just the man we want.' I hate to write you this and get you all pepped up for a letdown, but I think luck is going to be with us this time. Worrying over our situation here has helped get me in the fix I'm in," Thomas said in mentioning the blood pressure problems that forced him to resign as head coach after the 1946 season and which eventually led to his death a few years later. "I suggest you write several of the board members a friendly note just to keep in close touch in case something does happen," Thomas continued. "I will keep in close touch with things and will call you if anything develops. If there is any angle to be played, let me know. I did my best to sell him (Paty) on Georgia and tell him of the problems and headaches here. I think I did some good."

News of Paty's acceptance of the Georgia position broke a few days later, prompting a celebration among Denny loyalists, many of whom wrote him to share the moment. Dr. John Gallalee, who was on a leave of absence from the University faculty while serving on the State Building Commission, sent a one-word note dated October 9 that simply said, "Hurrah." Harris wrote on October 14, saying, "No one knows what the news of the week means to me. I have felt like again the University is ours.... I am hoping that Birmingham does not loom so large in the mind of the next president.... I am so grateful that you, Gessner McCorvey and Mr. Carmichael are on the job." Physics professor

Benjamin Wooten wrote on October 11, saying, "At last it has happened! Seriously, he is gone and I haven't seen anybody who cares…. I am a little put out when I think of his successor. I wish on my knees that this time they would consider education and culture and experience and maturity. I haven't worked under a person of whom I was proud since you left, and it's often depressing not to be proud of your boss."

Paty submitted his resignation, to be effective January 1, 1947, on October 9 and University trustees met on October 24 to accept it with "deep regret." With Paty's departure pending, Denny, who had been pushed aside during the Paty reign, was quickly called upon again to help steer the ship. Burr wrote him on October 8 to ask his advice on a possible committee to run the University during the search for a new president. Thomas, Moore, trustees Palmer and Ferguson and several others wrote Denny to seek his opinion on Paty's successor. *Anniston Star* publisher Harry Ayers wrote him to suggest Jacksonville State president Houston Cole as a successor. Tuscaloosa attorney Reuben Wright wrote on October 28 to recommend Dr. Oliver C. Carmichael, president of the Carnegie Foundation for the Advancement of Teaching and former chancellor at Vanderbilt, saying, "He is not a politician, worn-out lawyer or businessman. He is unquestionably the man who ought to be given the place." Wright added that the next president "should be an educator of ripe experience, and I believe Carmichael is the man. No one except you can probably induce him to come." Burr wrote Denny on the same date to suggest Carmichael, but added that Carmichael's brother John had said that O. C. "would not consider the job." Carmichael, who had earned B. A. (1911) and M. A. (1914) degrees from the University, eventually served as University president from September 1, 1953, until January 1, 1957.

Moore, a native of Fayette who earned his B. A. degree at Auburn and served as University of Alabama Graduate School Dean for thirty-five years (1924-58), wrote a desperate letter to Denny in November to report that Governor Chauncy Sparks, who had only two more months to serve, had joined forces with Paty and that they intended to select the next president of the University. "We are drifting into chaos and ruin," Moore began. "The governor is in the saddle and Paty is cooperating with him. Paty went down to Montgomery Tuesday and spent the night with the governor. He remarked when he got back that 'the old guard is out of the picture.' Sparks' plan is to make (dean of the Medical School Roy) Kracke president of the University…. Coach Thomas is discouraged and disgusted. He told me last night that he is ready to bow out of the picture altogether. He said he had worked hard to get a new deal for the University and it looked like his efforts amounted to little or nothing. He says we are about to repeat the mistake we made before…. The Birmingham alumni need a word from you now and you could deliver this word through trusted leaders there. I believe that before the board meets you should write or call McCorvey, Noojin, Carmichael and perhaps Palmer and (Thomas S.) Lawson and appeal to them to save the University and give them your choice for president. The important thing is to foil the other fellow in his efforts to name his successor. Paty and the governor will hear of anything that is done, and they have already done everything possible to forestall you. The issue will probably have to be fought out unless we are prepared to take defeat lying down.

"When the destiny of the University is involved we should not shrink from battle," Moore continued." If we do not take aggressive action and rally the faithful, Sparks and

Paty will pussy foot us into ignominious defeat. I do not believe that conflict can be avoided unless we are prepared to surrender everything to Sparks and Paty, and that means the unification of the colleges and a continuation of policies that are ruinous to us. Sparks announced ten days ago that the institutions must be unified, and if he wants Kracke that means Kracke has promised to support the unification plan. With 2,000 more students than Auburn, we are dividing emergency educational funds for veterans equally with Auburn, and the same goes for building funds. Moreover, as executive officer of a committee appointed to administer the emergency program for the colleges (Ralph) Draughon of Auburn is functioning now as chancellor of the college system of the state, unified for a specific policy or service. This may well be a stepping stone to complete unification, and it will be if we select the wrong man. I repeat my opening sentence: We are drifting into chaos and ruin. Think it over and do whatever you think would be best for the University, and may God bless your efforts," Moore added in urging Denny to take the lead in the fight for political control of the University.

It is uncertain what action Denny took, but it is certain that he acted. There were checkmarks by the names of the trustees Moore suggested that Denny write, and loyal supporters—including Burr—quickly rallied to his side. Denny was honored as Alabama's "First Citizen" at a testimonial dinner hosted by Birmingham alumni on Friday, November 29, in which he made a 30-minute address which was broadcast statewide over WAPI Radio. The address was billed as the first of a planned series of addresses by prominent Alabamians called "Voices of Alabama." Denny's address, a review of the history of the University entitled "Forward Alabama," was reportedly placed in the state department of archives and history. Speaking at the meeting, Denny said, "You ask me how we (the University) have done so much with so little. Let me tell you why. The prime reason is that the University has been served by men and women who over the years have had the courage and faith to take what they found and to make of it something better—something that would take them, with every forward step, closer to a humanly perfect goal. I express gratitude once more that I have known and loved the University and tried to keep its commandments. If I had a thousand lives, I would gladly give them all in its service." The timing of the dinner and honor for Denny was perfect, and it is certain that many of the University alumni and friends attending the event were the same ones he counted on for help in blocking the plans of Governor Sparks and Paty. It is also interesting that Denny's letter file for November 1946 included a hand-written note from Alabama governor-elect James E. "Big Jim" Folsom, who had attended the University briefly during Denny's tenure (1931) and had a class under Moore. Folsom won the Democratic primary in May 1946 and took office in January 1947. Folsom's note thanked Denny for his recent letter and suggested that they visit at the November 30 homecoming game "relative to the great state of Alabama and her future."

The trustees met briefly on November 30 to name a presidential selection committee made up of the executive committee, Dr. John Gallalee and Sparks; elect William E. Key Jr. to the board to replace John Bankhead, who had recently died, and set a special meeting for December 14 in the governor's office in Montgomery for the purpose of electing a new president. With all trustees and Paty present at the December 14 meeting, the stage was set for Sparks to make a grandstand play to nominate Kracke for the position, and he did. After executive committee chairman Ferguson reported that the majority of the committee was not ready to nominate a candidate, Sparks spoke up as the lone dissenter to nominate Kracke as the next president of the University. After some discussion, the trustees voted to delay action on the selection of a president and instead name an interim administrator. McLure, Gallalee and University dean of administration Ralph Adams were all nominated. After several secret ballots, Adams, who had been a member of the University administration for twenty-six years, was elected acting president for the year beginning January 1, 1947.

Following a quiet year during which the University's "stars" evolved into proper alignment again, the trustees met in special session on December 22, 1947, to discuss the hiring of a permanent president. A University faculty committee selected to recommend qualifications for a new president listed "a broad, intensive, formal training; above average education in quantity and quality; a post-graduate degree; able administrator; first-hand knowledge of university teaching; demonstrated constructive ideas on all phases of education, including higher education, and tested qualifications and judgment beyond doubt" as desired traits before the trustees considered nominations. Following a discussion of the suggested qualifications, the selection committee of Ferguson, Palmer and Robert Steiner Jr. nominated Gallalee, dean of the College of Engineering and professor of mechanical engineering at the University since 1912, and he was quickly and unanimously elected as the new president. The board's announcement said Gallalee "knows the problems of the University as well as those of the state and has done much for the betterment of both" and that his selection would "inspire the confidence not only of those on the campus but throughout the state and nation." Gallalee, at age sixty-four, took office on January 1, 1948, at the salary of $12,000 per year. There is no doubt that Denny was directly involved in the selection of the new president. It is likely, in fact, that the decision was placed squarely in his hands. No one knew the University, its faculty, it problems and its needs better than Denny; the trustees still sought and trusted his advice, and the alumni strongly supported him at every turn. Gallalee, like Denny a native of Virginia and University of Virginia graduate, was one of the first faculty members hired by Denny after he took office as University president. Gallalee had also sent Denny the one-word ("Hurrah") note following Paty's announced resignation more than a year earlier. Gallalee served as University president from January 1, 1948, until September 1, 1953, completing more than 40 years of service at the Capstone before reaching mandatory retirement age.

It is worth noting that Key (1921), Palmer (1920) and Lawson (1929) had attended the University during the Denny era. Noojin (former athletic director and baseball coach) and Palmer (former executive secretary) were also among Denny's favorite former associates and had maintained a close friendship with Denny since leaving the University to enter the business world. As an illustration of Denny' influence with at least some—and likely most—of the trustees, one could consider letters from Palmer and Noojin to their friend and former employer. Palmer, responding to Denny's spring 1941 letter congratulating him on being named president of First National Bank of Tuskaloosa, wrote, "As I look back on our years of association together and our additional years of friendship, I realize that I am greatly indebted to you for a substantial portion of any common sense which I may have acquired. I count the three years I was closely associated with you as the best part of my education; furthermore, your friendship is and has been one of my most cherished possessions." Palmer, like Denny in 1925, was honored as Tuscaloosa Citizen of the Year in 1946. Gordon D. Palmer Hall, built in 1967, is named for the former trustee and is home of the departments of mathematics and psychology and the office of information technology on the University campus. Noojin, writing to Denny soon after being elected to the University board of trustees in May 1946, said, "The privilege of my four years of close association with you was the greatest measure of my compensation and one of the high spots of my life. Aside from the personal pleasure which our frequent contacts afforded, as I reflect today, I am confident that whatever measure of success I may have had in later life, your standards of application, your persistent and consistent drive toward the successful culmination of whatever project to which you put your hand, are to a large degree responsible for it. I realize today that I could have worthily coveted the privilege of a continued association with you, sitting in your counsel and appropriating much of your philosophy."

Adams, who had been closely aligned with Paty during his administration as executive secretary, dean of admissions and dean of administration, resigned from the University soon after Gallalee's selection to enter private business. Huntley, hired as Paty's chief aide in 1942, had resigned in December 1945 to return to his previous position with the Southern Association of Colleges and Secondary Schools. As McLure had predicted in October 1946, Paty did not last five years as chancellor of the Georgia system. He served only two years before resigning to become public relations director of Rich's and executive director of the Rich Foundation, a position he held from 1948-1952. He then served as a member of the Tennessee Valley Authority board of directors from 1952 until his death in 1957. Caldwell replaced Paty as chancellor of the Georgia system in 1948 and served in the position until retirement in 1964. Kracke did not fare well after the November 22, 1947, trustees meeting either. A trustee subcommittee conducted a study of the financial problems of the medical school and recommended that the president of the University, Kracke and the medical school hospital administrator "agree on procedures which will result in improvements." Kracke reportedly feuded with Gallalee over the corrective measures during the next two years before his death from a heart attack in June 1950. Sparks ran for governor again in 1950, but was defeated by Gordon Persons. Moore, who came to the University as dean of the graduate school in 1924 and whose letters had urged Denny to lead the fight against Sparks, Paty and Kracke, remained at the University until his retirement in 1958.

With Gallalee installed as president, the Sparks plan for unification of the state's four-year colleges thwarted, old relationships restored and the stormy seas of campus dissent calmed, the University was finally on course again on January 1, 1948, after more than two disruptive years. Denny, having quietly regained his dignity and rightful place in University history, attended the June 7, 1948, trustees meeting with his head held high before quietly fading from the Capstone scene again, triumphant in the knowledge that the "old guard" was back in control. Denny returned to the Capstone on April 2, 1949, when he was honored at an Alumnae Day luncheon for his leadership in the development of education for women at the University, but he returned to the University only twice more—for homecoming weekend on October 28, 1950, and for commencement exercises on June 2, 1952—before his death in April 1955 at age eighty-four.

Denny enjoyed watching the Crimson Tide football team
whether at practice or in the Rose Bowl.

14

The Lust of Victory

"Like all other extracurricular activities, athletics must be kept within bounds. It is of importance in college life—of great importance—but it is a sideshow and not the main performance. College life must not be allowed to swallow up the college curriculum."
—Dr. George H. Denny

For more than a century, former University of Alabama president Dr. George H. Denny has received much of the credit for not only transforming the University from a small college into a modern, nationally known university, but also for his influence in the development of the Crimson Tide's winning tradition in athletics—especially his favorite sport of football—and deservedly so. The improvement of athletic facilities and a higher competitive level figured prominently in Denny's agenda for building a "great university" when he arrived as University president in January 1912.

Denny had a unique appreciation for the game of football, which he played for four years while serving as assistant headmaster at Pantops Academy in Charlottesville, Virginia, and which he coached for one season while a professor at Hampden-Sydney College. He also recognized that football and other athletics could play a significant role in attracting students, building school spirit and in the unification and involvement of alumni in University activities. Most importantly, Denny was fully aware that athletics—specifically too few wins in football—had sparked the dispute that led to the resignation of former University president John Abercrombie in July 1911. Whether it was spelled out or not, Denny was clearly expected to do whatever it took to produce winning football teams, even in the game's early days.

It took time, genius and doubtless a bit of luck, but during the next twenty-five years, Denny not only gave University trustees the campus and student body they wanted but he orchestrated the building of a football program far greater than even the most rabid Crimson Tide fans could have imagined. Denny-era football teams produced four Rose Bowl teams, grabbed newspaper headlines proclaiming the Crimson Tide national champions from coast to coast and, most importantly for many Alabama alumni, finally surpassed cross-state rival Auburn in gridiron glory. The four coaches hired by Denny during his tenure as University president produced a combined record of 222-53-14, including six national championships, eight conference titles and six Rose Bowl appearances as the Crimson Tide claimed a prominent place among the nation's leading football programs.

Denny acknowledged the importance of football and drew the loudest cheers of the evening when he addressed the topic of athletics in his first speech to University alumni in Birmingham on Friday, November 17, 1911, soon after accepting the position of president. "I know a word is expected from me about athletics," *The Tuscaloosa News* quoted Denny as saying after he had addressed what he considered the University's greatest need—increased state funding. "First of all, let me express my views on this question by saying that I sincerely and earnestly hope Alabama will win tomorrow (Alabama defeated Tulane 22-0). I want to share the life of the students, their ideals as well as their sports, and rejoice with them in their enthusiasm over athletics. But the nation is not looking to the colleges for men to conduct its racetracks, sideshows and pleasure resorts. Like all other extracurricular activities, athletics must be kept within bounds. It is of importance in college life—of great importance—but it is a side show and not the main attraction. That gentlemen, is my position on athletics," Denny added "with a finality that defied questioning and an outburst of applause voiced the endorsement of the alumni," the *News* report added.

Although the University of Alabama had been playing football since 1892, the game was still in its infancy in 1912. Coaches were mostly transient, seasonal employees, working only three months a year and never really knowing which, if any, players would return each year. Teams usually had less than twenty players who played both offense and defense. Equipment was primitive at best, with minimal padding and no helmets in the early days. Playing fields were rough and some of the players were, too. An average of twelve high school and college students were killed playing football each year between 1915 and 1920. Until Denny arrived, an unpaid manager hired the coach, scheduled games, handled recruiting and attempted to meet expenses through ticket sales. Ineligible players, known as "ringers" often found their way into games as what few rules were in place were often ignored. Alabama's apparent use of ringers in a 6-6 tie game with Auburn in 1907 led to a bitter break in football competition between the schools that lasted until 1948 and perhaps still fuels the rivalry between the two state schools today.

Statements by Abercrombie at the time of his resignation, in fact, confirmed that Alabama had been guilty of using ringers in the past and that his elimination of the practice in favor of academic integrity had led to discontent among some alumni. "Perhaps that feature of my administration which has occasioned the most dissatisfaction and criticism has been the policy pursued relative to intercollegiate athletics," Abercrombie said in confronting University trustees in a showdown over control of University policies. "…A certain element demands of us winning teams. In order to secure such teams every conceivable pressure is brought to bear upon the authorities (coaches and managers) to induce them to condone, if not to participate actively, in the playing of men who are failing in their studies or who are known to be ineligible under the rules of the Southern Intercollegiate Athletic Association with which the University is affiliated, and with the enforcement of whose regulations the president and faculty are charged. When I realized a few years ago that the authorities were being imposed upon by outside influences, that ineligible men were being paid money to register as students for the purpose of having them represent the institution on traveling athletic teams, and that at least one such man had been matriculated and graduated under an assumed name, I resolved that no such disgraceful imposition should again occur," Abercrombie said. He added that "since that time the rules of scholarship and general eligibility have been firmly and effectively enforced and as a result we have absolutely clean athletics at the University.

"As for myself, I do not consider the mere winning of athletic games to be the chief object of an institution of learning and I am unwilling to subordinate hereto all scholastic standards and ethical principles," Abercrombie continued. "I have no ambition whatever to preside over a corruptly conducted athletic club though it may be called by the dignified name of the University of Alabama." The University president of nine years closed his statements by asking the trustees for a "formal endorsement" of his administration and policies. "In the absence of such action upon your part, please feel free to proceed with the selection of another man," he said. The trustees did not offer an endorsement, choosing instead to accept Abercrombie's resignation effective September 1. University professor Dr. William B. Saffold was elected acting president while the trustees sought a new president. Abercrombie's statewide popularity was affirmed in 1912 when he was elected to the U. S. Congress, where he served until 1916. He later returned to the office of state superintendent of education 1922-1926.

The Montgomery Advertiser was highly critical of circumstances leading to Abercrombie's departure. Under the headline "How Dr. Abercrombie Purified Athletics," a lengthy *Advertiser* story said Abercrombie had been the victim of the spreading worship of athletic heroes. "By this same worship the dignified head of a dignified institution has fallen as a slight sacrifice to the rapacious demands of the American love for the successful athlete," the story said as it documented several instances of Alabama's use of ringers in football games against Auburn. "The lust of victory was upon the (Alabama) alumni. It acted like the lust of wine. One taste doubled the longing for more," the story added in referring to Alabama's 30-0 win over Auburn in 1905. The *Advertiser* also cited a particular star football player who had been barred from play by Abercrombie because of academic deficiencies and added that the player's absence "caused the University to lose the game and Abercrombie to lose his job…. The alumni arose and said Dr. Abercrombie was robbing the University of all its glory…. Alumni and students began to criticize the president…. The storm of discontent reached the trustees and the anti-Abercrombie movement culminated in this decapitation of the president," the story added in casting public shame on the action. Although apparently essentially correct, the *Advertiser* story failed to mention other factors which contributed to Abercrombie's departure, such as the lack of increased enrollment over several years, the suspension of competitive basketball after a brief trial in 1906 and a recent disagreement between Abercrombie and the board of trustees over a planned railroad through the campus.

Denny showed no fear of rabid Crimson Tide football fans in accepting the office of president of the University of Alabama, however. He knew a bit about the game from his days as a player at Pantops Academy and one season as coach at Hampden-Sydney, where his team posted a 2-1 record in 1896, and he had overseen a college football program as president of Washington and Lee University for ten years. He was confident that he could unite the impatient University of Alabama alumni and field winning teams while maintaining academic eligibility standards, and in time he did just that, although not without a minor controversy here and there.

With less than 350 male students on campus in the spring of 1912, Denny knew that recruiting more athletes was a top priority. One of his first actions, taken in February 1912, was to solicit the help of active alumni in recruiting athletes while also making it clear that he would also enforce academic standards and eligibility rules. Soon after his arrival in Tuscaloosa, Denny met with graduate manager of athletics Hugo Friedman, who also functioned as recruiter and business manager of athletics on a volunteer basis, to draft a letter to former players, boosters, active alumni, athletic committee members and others in an effort to unite all parties while at the same time letting them know that Dr. Denny was now fully in charge. Although the letter was signed by Friedman, it clearly included Denny's input. "For the last few years the University and her alumni have been drifting apart. They are now beginning to draw together again," the letter began. "We fortunately have a president who is 'right on the job.' If there is something that you wish to know, educationally, athletically or otherwise, write to Dr. Denny. There is a prompt answer awaiting you, and it is very liable to be in the line with 'what should be.' We are beginning to believe that the very best advertisement our university can have is good, clean, victorious athletics, and we are working toward that end. I am writing this letter to about one hundred of you boys—the ones who we have found do things—and I am earnestly requesting that you look around your neighborhoods and in your high schools to find the boys who are athletically inclined and who are financially and mentally fit to enter the University," the letter continued. "Send me their names together with the names of their parents so that Dr. Denny and I may write them. We do not want ringers but boys who are good, clean athletes. If they can pass in their studies and make our teams, their reward shall be delightful trips and that kind of sport and rivalry that every boy enjoys. We are depending upon you chosen few to respond to this appeal." That letter, coupled with Denny's letters to every high school senior in Alabama and even in some towns in surrounding states, immediately brought in more students and more student-athletes and helped lead to greater athletic success.

Another early action taken by Denny was the reinstatement of intercollegiate basketball at Alabama beginning in January 1913. He also began planning for new athletic facilities for all sports, and within three years the University had a new gymnasium (Little Hall) and new athletic fields for football, baseball, track and tennis just south and east of the President's Mansion. The athletic field was known as University Field until 1920, when it was renamed Denny Field.

D. V. Graves was athletic director and head football coach at Alabama when Denny arrived and he continued as coach through 1914. He offered his resignation in early January 1915, however, citing reports of complaints from disgruntled Birmingham alumni following a 5-4 season. Graves had an overall record of 21-12-3 in four seasons, having posted 5-2-2, 5-3-1 and 6-3 marks 1911-1913. "Through the papers and through (Frank) Moody and Mr. (A. S.) Van de Graaff I learned of a meeting at Birmingham before the holidays which was a protest by the alumni there against Alabama losing so many games of football," Graves said in his letter to Dr. Eugene A. Smith, chairman of the University faculty athletic committee. "Moody and Van de Graaff both informed me that there were two things particularly emphasized at the meeting. One was that a change for the better must be made. Another was that there should be some man here to take charge of the securing of new material, finances and schedules, or to sum it up, have one man for the office part of the work and one for the field part." Graves added that he "heartily" agreed with the proposal and thought the plan should be put into effect immediately. "In accordance with this, I am offering my resignation to the athletic committee. If they think as the alumni in Birmingham and as nearly all with whom I have talked think, we will have two men here next year. If they think that I am competent to fill either place I am anxious to remain and continue in the capacity they designate, either as coach or faculty manager. If on the other hand they think that I am unable to satisfactorily fill either place or for any other reason think that I should be removed, I am offering them this opportunity of saying so by accepting my resignation. I assure you that I do not nor have I ever wished to remain here to the detriment of athletic growth. On the other hand, I realize that a man in a public position like a coach cannot follow explicitly every protest from alumni. I think, though, that it is time for me to get the opinion of the athletic committee. Acceptance or refusal of my resignation is to me the best and surest way. Please let me know their decision as soon as possible after the meeting," Graves concluded.

The faculty athletic committee, made up of Friedman, Smith, University treasurer Shaler Houser and Denny, met in Denny's office a few days later to accept Graves' resignation as football coach, although he remained through the spring to coach the Crimson Tide to a Southern Intercollegiate Athletic Association (SIAA) baseball championship. On February 1, 1915, the committee, acting on the recommendation of Crimson Tide alumnus Champ Pickens, authorized Friedman to employ former University of Chicago player and assistant coach Thomas Kelley as head football coach for one year starting September 1 for a salary of $2,000. Kelley had also been head coach at Muhlenberg College and at the Rollo, Missouri, School of Mines, where his 1914 team had posted a 9-0 record. At the same meeting, Denny offered $1,000 per year to employ Lonnie Noojin as assistant football coach and head baseball coach. The two men made up the University athletic department starting in September. Kelley was named director of athletics and head coach in football, basketball and track. A former Crimson Tide baseball captain, Noojin had been physical activity director and instructor at Howard College for three years prior to returning to the University. He eventually led the baseball team to three straight SIAA titles before resigning in 1919 to enter private business. With the recommendation of Denny, Noojin was elected to the University board of trustees in May 1946.

Alabama opened its 1915 football season with Kelley as its new coach, a new athletic field and its students and alumni hopeful of great change. Kelley, who played and coached for pioneer coach Amos Alonzo Stagg, gained alumni support in his first season as the Crimson Tide posted a 6-2 record, although Noojin had to handle the team alone for its last five games when Kelley was sidelined by typhoid fever during an epidemic that took the lives of at least two University students. The 1915 wins included Alabama's first-ever victory over then-powerful Sewanee behind the outstanding play of

Tuscaloosa native W. T. "Bully" Van de Graaff, who became the Tide's first All-America player after scoring 162 points during four years with the Tide. Kelley's teams went 6-3 and 5-2-1 the next two seasons before World War I interrupted play for 1918 and Kelley left to work for the YMCA in the war effort. Van de Graaff, whose older brothers Adrian and Hargrove also played football for the Crimson Tide, attended West Point after graduating from Alabama and returned to the University in 1923 as a member of the ROTC staff. He also coached the Alabama freshman football team 1923-25, producing three straight unbeaten teams while helping recruit and train members of the Crimson Tide's first national championship teams. Van de Graaff served as head coach and athletic director at Colorado College 1926-42 before returning to military duty during World War II and remaining in the Army until 1954.

Xen Scott, a sports writer who coached football only three months a year, became the Alabama coach in 1919 and gave Crimson Tide fans plenty to cheer about as he produced a four-year record of 29-9-3 with 8-1, 10-1, 5-4-2 and 6-3-1 seasons. Scott's 1919 team, the first in school history to win eight games, won the SIAA championship while allowing only three touchdowns the entire season. The 1920 team, led by halfback E. B. "Mully" Lenoir, who led the nation in scoring with 144 points, became the first Alabama team to win ten games and the first to play in a post-season game with a 40-0 win over Case Western Reserve University. Crimson Tide fortunes took a downward turn in 1921, however, as Scott's team managed only a 5-4-2 record, raising eyebrows and causing some quick-triggered fans to call for another coaching change. Denny was persuaded by Birmingham attorney and former Alabama player Borden Burr to stand by Scott, however, and there was slightly better news for Alabama fans in 1922 as the Crimson Tide posted a 6-3-1 record highlighted by a 9-7 upset victory over Pennsylvania in Philadelphia in what most fans considered the school's biggest win ever. *Crimson White* headlines following the win over Penn boasted "Crimson Tide Swamps Second Strongest Team in The Land; Bama's Greatest Victory is Celebrated by Whole South." The victory helped the Crimson Tide win four of its last five games, attracted the first national attention for Alabama and further incited the rabid Alabama fans. Scott, who battled failing health during the last few games of 1922 and died of cancer 16 months later, did not ask for nor was he offered a contract extension. In fact, a search for his successor had been under way for several weeks.

According to a December 5, 1921, letter from Burr to Denny, Scott had come under fire mainly from Tuscaloosa alumni during the mediocre 1921 season, even after impressive 8-1 and 10-1 records the two previous seasons. Burr, one of Alabama's most supportive alumni and a close advisor to Denny, reported to Denny that in response to the alumni complaints he had held "private, confidential talks" with several of the players in an effort to determine the attitude of the team toward Scott. "It was the unanimous opinion of these boys…that they feel towards both Scott and (assistant coach Hank) Crisp the warmest respect and admiration. In addition to this, they seemed to resent the fact that an effort is being made to lay the blame against Scott for an unsuccessful (5-4-2) season. They said that although they had lost four games, they had not lost confidence in the team to eventually make good. They expressed a determination, if Scott returns (for 1922), to show another result next year. From my conversations with these boys and also because it occurred to me that, admitting for the sake of argument that we had made a bad trade with Scott, we ought to take our medicine, having made it, and not only support him next year but do so loyally and without any disagreeable interference. It is my deliberate judgment that Scott should remain in charge, in accordance with his contract, for another season. If the Tuscaloosa alumni or other alumni are interested in a change, they might busy themselves now in looking out for a full-time coach to take charge at the University following the end of next season. I have written you fully and frankly, knowing that you understand my interest, and I feel that I am entirely right in my conclusion," Burr added. Denny followed Burr's advice and allowed Scott to complete his contract, but started the search for Scott's successor midway through the 1922 season when the Tide stood at 2-2-1 prior to its win over Pennsylvania.

Denny also received a second, thoroughly logical suggestion for a full-time coach from another Alabama alumnus during his search for Scott's successor. In a letter dated December 9, 1922, in which Alabama's football situation was discussed at length in obvious response to a Denny letter, Mason Douglass, a Dayton, Ohio, attorney who had earned B. A. (1914) and law (1917) degrees from the University, said, "May I take this opportunity to say I hope the day is not distant when Alabama will have a football coach who will be a part of the institution and not a transient. It is my belief, from very limited observation, that the successful football teams come from institutions whose football coach is part of the university and whose interests are centered in the university above all else. A salary large enough to compensate real ability and devotion on the part of the student body to the coach and on the part of the coach for the institution ought to make championship teams at Alabama. A system discarded frequently leaves nothing to work with, so I hope that you may find a real coach who will give real service."

Denny took the advice of Burr and Douglass in seeking a full-time employee as Alabama's next head coach, but there was much confusion and controversy in the search as several Crimson Tide boosters offered recommendations and a few of them even attempted to involve themselves in the hiring process. Denny ended up sending a written apology to the president of Centre College after an Alabama representative approached Centre coach Charles Moran without permission. He also bruised the ego of former football manager and loyal booster Champ Pickens when he sent a telegram directing Pickens to cease discussions with Kansas State coach Charles Bachman. In addition, what was thought to be private discussions between University representatives and Vanderbilt head coach Dan McGugin made the Nashville newspapers, creating embarrassment for all parties. McGugin, who practiced law in Nashville in addition to coaching football, showed no interest in Alabama but recommended his assistant, Wallace Wade, who eventually got the job after a month of debate, rumor and confusion.

"It would take Sherlock Holmes and a covey of Ouija boards working on four shifts to clear up the muddle that has grown out of the attempt to select a coach to succeed Xen Scott at the University," a December 10, 1922, newspaper story said. "It would seem that a general misunderstanding has arisen over the selection of a man to guide the destinies of Alabama in a football way, and with some of the 'insiders' at loggerheads, the coach proposition is further up in the air than it has been at any time since Scott resigned." The story added that "some factions at Alabama have a leaning toward the home-bred style of coach and are looking to the South for a Moses to lead Alabama out of the football wilderness while the Tuscaloosa alumni have a leaning toward getting a man out of the West—a coach with a national reputation and a known master of the art of coaching. Tonight, however, everyone confessed that the whole thing was up in the air, with one faction pulling one way and another faction in the opposite direction, all of which has a tendency to create dissension and hamper the selection of a coach that would put Alabama on the football map."

Like many other University alumni, Jelks Cabaniss of Birmingham wrote Denny in late November to offer his advice on the matter. "I am writing to you to give you what I know to be the sentiment of a very large number of the alumni here and elsewhere on the subject of our athletic policy," Jelks wrote. "That sentiment is overwhelming to the effect that nothing should be left undone which would contribute toward the turning out of a successful football team, and the first thing which should be done, in the opinion of these alumni, is to obtain the services of a coach who has already demonstrated by his work elsewhere his unquestioned ability as a coach." Jelks recommended Moran and added that "unless his demands are very extravagant, I would say that they should be met."

Tuscaloosa attorney Edgar Clarkson wrote Denny on December 8 to urge the hiring of Bachman, who had been a teammate of Knute Rockne at Notre Dame 1914-16. "After listening to Champ Pickens' report of his investigation of and interview with Mr. Bachman, I cannot refrain from writing you my views," Clarkson wrote. "Not only am I satisfied that Bachman is a good coach and otherwise desirable but I believe that he fills the bill of the man we are looking for." Clarkson added that he had "talked to many of the leading men of the state who are interested in the University and they have with one accord been outspoken in favor of paying, if necessary, $10,000 or more a year to get a satisfactory man." Tuscaloosa banker Frank Moody also urged the hiring of Bachman. "From the information secured by Champ and some information from other sources, it seems that our Kansas man is certainly the man we are looking for and I feel that we would make a serious mistake should we not secure his services without haggling further as to terms," Moody wrote Denny on December 9.

Burr provided Denny with a lengthy, detailed evaluation of the four leading candidates—Moran, Billy Laval of Furman, Bachman and Wade—on December 12 with the suggestion that the selection of Scott's replacement "be done with the idea of permanence in view." "Georgia Tech, Auburn and Vanderbilt, the three outstanding southern colleges in athletic activities, are outstanding because they have adopted this policy. There has not been a change in the system at either of these three institutions for more than fifteen years while Alabama has sought mentors in the East, West and everywhere with the result that our teams, with a few exceptions, have been more or less a joke," Burr wrote. Burr's letter revealed the feelings of many University of Alabama alumni who were likely more jealous of Auburn's recent football success than disappointed with Alabama's winning but not outstanding record. Auburn, with Mike Donahue as its head coach, had compiled a 91-26-4 overall record with two unbeaten seasons and four SIAA championships 1908-1922 while Alabama went 71-32-7 during the same period.

While many University of Alabama alumni were envious of Auburn's football success, Denny—and no doubt many others—was even more envious of Auburn's larger per-student share of state appropriations to higher education throughout his tenure. Although Alabama College, then an all-girl institution, received by far the highest per-capita funding from the state throughout Denny's tenure, his persistent complaint was that Auburn also received higher per-capita funding than the University of Alabama, even into the 1940s. A 1941-42 funding report showed that Alabama College received state funding of $381.09 per student while Auburn received $254.21 per student and Alabama only $214.67 per student. In addition, as mentioned elsewhere, Auburn received additional funds from federal research grants to the state. While athletic representatives of the schools sparred publically in newspaper stories relating to football and other sports through the years, Denny apparently confined his comments to finances. These factors contributed to the long and often bitter rivalry between the schools even beyond the 1907 split on the football field. There were numerous attempts by governors, legislators and business and civic groups to promote a resumption of an annual Alabama-Auburn football game, but play was not resumed until 1948 following a threat by the state legislature to withhold state funding to the schools.

In response to public calls for resumption of football competition between the two state schools in 1911, University of Alabama graduate manager of athletics Hugo Friedman agreed to resume football competition with Auburn, only to have the offer rejected, according to a December 17, 1911, story in the *Birmingham Ledger*. "Alabama and its authorities are anxious to resume friendly athletic relations with Auburn, but the Auburn authorities have declared that it is better for the game that the two institutions do not meet on the athletic field," the story said. The story printed a statement from C. L. Hare, secretary of the Auburn athletic committee, saying, "In connection with the discussion in your paper in regard to the proposed game between Auburn and Alabama, we beg to inform you that final action has been taken by the athletic authorities at Auburn to the effect that it is best that athletic relations between the two institutions not be resumed in the best interest of true sport." Hare added that the committee has "no criticism of any team, but that it has been found true in every state that certain games produce so great a desire for victory that all sense of true sport that should mark student games is entirely lost sight of, and that for the sake of winning there invariably result questionable practices on all sides with the consequent criminations and recriminations which destroy instead of promote good feeling and fellowship. This undesirable end we wish as far as possible to avoid and we are confident that all true lovers of sport will appreciate our point of view," the statement said.

The feud between the schools jumped from athletics to state funding every four years as they vied for favor during legislative sessions. In response to Auburn president Spright Dowell's public call for special building funds for Auburn in April 1921, Denny wrote to Dowell on April 11 to offer his viewpoint. "Of course, I am sorry to have to differ with you regarding matters," Denny began. "Twenty percent of our work is being done in wooden shacks. Such a situation is critical. You perhaps know that our building fund for the quadrennium (which was initially $10,000 less than yours) had to be largely pledged a year ago, when prices were at the top figure, in adding a wing to the dormitory for women. You will also recall my effort to get special relief last summer when you were granted $65,000. I hardly think that the other institutions will feel that any measure introduced into the legislature that fails to include them will be equitable.... Since all of them are in distress, I feel that it will not be likely to promote harmony unless the whole matter is handled in as large way."

Denny hinted at tensions between the two schools in a letter to Dowell no November 13, 1923, regarding a conference on higher education when he said, "I believe in mutual courtesy, harmony and high-minded brotherhood between our institutions of higher learning. Fundamentally, it is mistaken and uncertain leadership rather than institutional hostility that has hampered the situation. The shadow has too frequently been substituted for the substance, and unwise counsels have too frequently prevailed. I do not think that any plan of procedure ought to succeed that cannot stand the fierce white light of intelligent discussion."

When state officials pushed for the renewal of football between the schools in 1923, Friedman, no longer directly involved in University athletics but still a strong booster, wrote Denny on August 6 to urge him to agree to such a plan. Friedman wrote that "since the University has been forced into the limelight and must give answer—an answer that you may rest assured will be a public document as our alumni will insist on knowing our sentiment—I do sincerely urge that you send the governor a clean and clear-cut reply to the effect that Alabama has always been ready to resume athletic relations with Auburn, that she is now ready, and that in the future, unless something unforeseen arises, we shall be ready. As I and other Alabama officials have said from time to time for the last seventeen years, we are ever ready to resume relations. It is simply a matter for Auburn to acquiesce. As you well know, there is a very remote chance of Auburn accepting. We will not be called upon to play. We do not owe Auburn anything. I have never heard you express any love for that institution. If I understand correctly, Auburn is at this time endeavoring to put through such legislation that will seriously injure the University and greatly enhance her own chances. You have been forced to send your own representative to Montgomery to help defeat this measure. He is relying upon the help of some of the very men who introduced this athletic resolution, so I see no reason on earth for our agreeing jointly with Dowell (as being against the game) in a letter which will repudiate all that we have stood for and bring down on our heads the condemnation of our alumni. You have a great opportunity, right now, to silence any criticism regarding our attitude toward athletic relations with Auburn by coming out flatfooted and aboveboard with the statement that we are ready to resume relations whenever Auburn deems it wise to do so," Friedman added.

University trustee Gessner McCorvey of Mobile said in 1944 that one of the best arguments against a game between Alabama and Auburn was "the excitement and raucous discussion, pro and con, caused by mere discussion of the subject." Pat Moulton of Mobile wrote University president Raymond Paty that year to say that he was "strongly against" the renewal of the Alabama-Auburn football series. Moulton suggested that should the teams meet, "there would be more free and fancy street fighting, bitterness and misunderstandings between our two fine institutions than now prevails. In addition, both schools are blessed with fine coaching staffs; should one of these staffs lose two years hand running, these very same alumni would cry for their scalps. In fact, the very instigators of the resumption of athletics would be the first ones to do the crying."

State newspapers called for a resumption of the Alabama-Auburn series from time to time starting as early as 1922, and joined in almost unanimous support for the game during the 1944-45 discussions. The lone dissenter was the *Alabama Journal* in Montgomery, which spoke out against the game in a January 4, 1945, editorial. Citing the intensity of the Duke-North Carolina series, the *Journal* said the rivalry "has caused the friends of these institutions to lose all sense of proportion and to center major attention on winning football teams." Pointing out that the North Carolina coach was paid more than the president of the school, the editorial added that "we have the spectacle of a great educational institution sidetracking education and putting it in second place with football brawn taking first place. About the worst thing that could happen to football is to have it become so completely commercialized that it outranks scholarship and research and mental development and everything else for which educational institutions were really created." Following a break of forty-one years, Alabama defeated Auburn 55-0 at Birmingham's Legion Field on December 4, 1948, as the storied football series finally resumed. Auburn claimed a 14-13 victory in 1949 before Alabama won four straight under Coach Red Drew. Drew was 5-2 against Auburn, but was replaced after going 4-5-2 in 1954 as University alumni again showed its intolerance for losing football teams. J. B. Whitworth became head coach in 1954 and posted 0-10, 2-7-1 and 2-7-1 records in three seasons, losing to Auburn each year, before being fired. Former Crimson Tide player Paul "Bear" Bryant became head coach in January 1958 and spent twenty-five years as Crimson Tide head coach, going 19-6 against Auburn, including winning nine straight games 1973-81, while going 232-46-9 overall. Ray Perkins followed Bryant and was 2-2 against Auburn in his four seasons as head coach. Bill Curry followed Perkins and was 26-10 in three seasons but failed to record a win over Auburn before departing as consistent dominance of Auburn seemed to become the standard by which University of Alabama coaches are judged, as Moulton had suggested might well occur.

Although Burr offered positive comments about all four of the 1922 Alabama coaching candidates, he clearly favored Wade, the only one who had not served as a head coach at the college level. "He is a native southerner. His entire coaching experience has been in the South. He knows the southern temperament and is better acquainted with southern boys. His personal football experience is as satisfactory as that of any of the others mentioned. For three years he played at Brown, where he was selected as All-America guard on the school's 1916 Rose Bowl team," Burr said. Burr also recounted Wade's record as a prep school coach in Tennessee and as athletic director, assistant football coach and head baseball and basketball coach at Vanderbilt and added that Wade had received "thorough schooling in the tactics and methods" of both the East (at Brown) and the West (under McGugin).

Denny had McGugin's recommendation, however, along with those of trainer Archie Hahn of Michigan, who had been backfield coach at Brown when Wade played there, and W. S. Fitzgerald, who had hired Wade at Fitzgerald and Clarke Military School in Tullahoma, Tennessee, following Wade's service as an artillery captain in World War I. "I know Wade would be a high-class man," Hahn wired Denny on December 11. Fitzgerald responded by telegram on December 11, also, saying, "Splendid coach. Knows game. Excellent in strategy. Leader of men. Commands respect and confidence. Hard worker. Consider most of Vanderbilt's success past two seasons due to Wade. Man of good character and habits. Quiet, unassuming. Essentially a man's man. Recommend him strongly."

Wade, with McGugin along as a friendly gesture, traveled to Tuscaloosa to meet with Denny in mid-December and was offered the job as University of Alabama football coach starting in September 1923 at a salary of $6,500 per year. The salary placed Wade among the highest paid coaches in the South, according to a list of salaries compiled by Denny at the time. By comparison, Denny was making $7,500 per year at the time while salaries for University deans ranged from $3,000 to $3,900 per year. Wade accepted Denny's offer by telegram, saying, "I hereby accept position of head coach at University of Alabama for two years on terms discussed in interview." The University announced Wade's hiring on Saturday, December 16, 1922, in a news release that did not mention Wade's name until the fourth paragraph. Newspapers, however, placed Wade's name in Sunday morning headlines and recounted his athletic background before adding a somewhat lengthy and unexciting account of the official hiring process.

"The Athletic Council of the University...has endeavored in spite of handicaps to proceed with due caution in selecting a football coach," the news release, obviously dictated by Denny, said. "While deploring the various premature and in most instances erroneous speculations that have at times found their way into the public press, we record our appreciation of the solid approval of thinking people that has been forthcoming in view of our effort to act with deliberation, keeping in mind the best ideals and traditions of the University. Naturally we share the desire to turn out winning teams, but we cannot accept the view that in accomplishing that desire it is either necessary or proper to be taking steps, whether financial or academic, that would not be in strict accord with established procedure at our most honored and respected American seats of learning. We feel strongly that in solving the problem committed to us we have not only preserved the high standards of the University in the matter of sound procedure, but have at the same time secured a man whose actual record of achievement will commend him to the mature judgment of all who desire to have our teams coached by men of expert knowledge, successful experience, outstanding personality and, above all else, of tested character." The release added that the council "has, after most careful consideration, decided to appoint William Wallace Wade...as head coach of our athletic teams." Speaking at the annual football banquet a month later, Denny said Wade was "the best man we could get" and the only one of the candidates considered "about whom nothing negative was said by those contacted."

Skeptics might have raised their eyebrows at the time, but over the next eight seasons, Wade led University of Alabama football teams to unprecedented success and national prominence as he compiled a 61-13-3 record with three unbeaten seasons, four Southern Conference titles, two wins and a tie in three Rose Bowl appearances and national championships in 1925, 1926 and 1930. The first two Rose Bowl trips also brought a windfall of $75,000 to the University athletic program, which was used to build the first phase of Denny Stadium. The stadium was inaugurated with a 55-0 win over Mississippi College on September 28, 1929. Wade teams of 1927-1929 did not meet the expectations of demanding Alabama fans, however, going 5-4-1, 6-3 and 6-3. Alumni complaints of too many losses, similar to those following so-so seasons by Graves and Scott and even after two national championships, were widespread.

Wade heard the complaints, of course, and on April 1, 1930, stunned the sports world by announcing his acceptance of the position of athletic director and head football coach at Duke University starting with the 1931 season. Wade said he would honor the final year of his contract with the University of Alabama and little else, but privately vowed to win another national championship on his way out. He did just that, too, as he led the Crimson Tide to its best season in history. Alabama went 10-0, scoring 271 points and allowing only thirteen while shutting out eight of ten opponents. The 1930 season, which again brought conference and national titles, included a 24-0 victory over Washington State in the January 1, 1931, Rose Bowl. Thousands of cheering fans greeted the triumphant Alabama team on its return to Tuscaloosa, and Denny and Wade rode together in a victory parade through the city and campus. Wade quietly left town soon afterward, taking the Rose Bowl trophy with him. In later years, Wade was quoted as saying he left Alabama because he "preferred a private school setting to that of a state university so he could conduct his program as he wanted without pressure from local and state officials." Wade continued his coaching success at Duke, where his teams went 110-36-7 while winning six conference championships and making two Rose Bowl appearances.

Denny did not delay in seeking a replacement for Wade, and in fact asked Wade to recommend a successor in the summer of 1930. Wade suggested Frank Thomas, backfield coach at Georgia, former quarterback at Notre Dame under Knute Rockne and former head coach at Chattanooga, and Denny and Thomas met in Birmingham in July for a brief interview, after which Thomas was immediately hired with a starting date of January 1931. Denny also issued what seemed a word of warning to Thomas, according to Thomas' own words in "Coach Tommy of the Crimson Tide." Denny was quoted as saying, "It is my conviction that material is ninety percent, coaching ten percent. You will be provided with the ninety percent and you will be held to strict accounting for delivering the remaining ten percent." Thomas called Denny's words "the coldest and hardest" he had ever heard.

The 1931 Crimson Tide started the season with three wins but lost 25-0 to Tennessee in the fourth game of the season, prompting Denny to ask for patience from Alabama fans in a somewhat apologetic homecoming message printed in an October issue of the *Crimson White*. "The football situation, which is always of absorbing interest on homecoming day, must be considered in the light of the fact that we are this year installing a new team, a new system of play and a new coach. I am sure the alumni will give the new regime ample time in which to work out the vexing problems that are naturally being encountered. Faith and optimism abound among those of us who are following day by day the process of rebuilding the team after the unprecedented losses sustained through graduation last May." There was little need for worry, however, as Alabama rolled to a 9-1 record in Thomas' first season and followed that with 8-2 and 7-1-1 records before going 10-0 in 1934 to claim conference and national championships highlighted by a 29-13 Rose Bowl victory over Stanford. Alabama returned to the Rose Bowl in 1937 and 1946 and played in Cotton, Orange and Sugar bowl games during Thomas' remaining years as head coach. His teams posted an overall record of 115-24-7 and lost more than two games in a season only three times during his tenure as head coach. Health issues forced Thomas to step down following the 1946 season and he died in 1954 at the early age of 55. Thomas teams contributed greatly to the Alabama football tradition by claiming four Southeastern Conference championships, two national championships, three unbeaten seasons and two wins in three Rose Bowl appearances, pleasing Alabama fans and bringing Denny additional credit for his selection of Thomas.

Thomas left a lasting legacy as a mentor as well as a winning coach as 23 of his former players and assistants became head coaches at the college or professional level. His star coaching pupil, of course, was Paul "Bear" Bryant, a member of the University's unbeaten 1934 national champion Rose Bowl team, who served as an Alabama assistant 1936-39 and returned as head coach of the Crimson Tide 1958-82. The long list of other Thomas pupils who became college coaches includes Harold "Red" Drew (Alabama 1947-54), J. B. Whitworth (Alabama 1955-57), Frank Moseley (Virginia Tech 1951-60) and Don Salls (Jacksonville State 1946-64). Another 62 former Thomas players became high school coaches, mostly in Alabama, and helped provide the University with players trained in Thomas' Notre Dame offensive system for decades.

Denny, with or without frequent nudges from win-thirsty alumni, was the impetus behind Alabama's football fortunes, just as he was every other facet of the University. In addition to having the final say on the hiring of coaches, he attended every football practice, where he stood so close to the action that he was sometimes caught up in the plays. A December 19, 1934, *Tuscaloosa News* story, written as the Crimson Tide practiced for the upcoming Rose Bowl game and headlined "Omen Comes True as Tide Heads for Coast," told how Denny had been "involved in a scrimmage in September before the season opened, although not by his own initiative." The story quoted a September 24, 1934, story regarding a long-standing superstition that claimed Alabama's football fortunes depended on Denny being bowled over during a practice session. "Superstitious football followers who have any luck may just as well start betting their money on Alabama's Crimson Tide to win something this fall, whether it be the Southeastern Conference title or the Rose Bowl game," the September story said. "It's like this: Every time Dr. George 'Mike' Denny, president of the University, takes part in a football scrimmage it is an omen that the Tide will go places that year. And Dr. Denny took part in one Saturday, believe it or not. 'Mike' was standing close to the line when Charlie Stapp, a halfback, came tearing around end. An opposing end rushed in to make the tackle, clasped the runner's flying hips and swung him around like a rock on a string. It so happened that the end made a perfect block of Dr. Denny, who was looking on at close range, sending the president sprawling. Dr. Denny was up and laughing with the boys in a split second, but he had taken part. 'Mike is an ardent backer of the Tide and he spends a while on the sideline every day, a privilege accorded only the college president. This is just one angle, but it seems that every time Dr. Denny takes part in a workout, the Tide fares well that year. Every time he has been knocked down, Alabama has gone forward to win some kind of championship. It happened in 1930 and the Tide defeated Washington 24-0 in the Rose Bowl after annexing the conference title." The story added that halfback Riggs Stephenson had accidently knocked Dr. Denny down in a September 1920 scrimmage before Alabama went on to a 10-1 record and its first bowl game to start the superstition.

Denny enjoyed winning football games as much as anyone, but he never failed to place academics, fair play and sportsmanship first. After a University student was killed attempting to hitch a ride on a freight train to attend an Alabama game in 1922, Denny appealed to students for safety first in a letter published in the October 18, 1923, issue of the *Crimson White*. "Two things I should like to say in connection with the approaching football games: 1. Though the score of the games may be in our favor, we shall be losers if the conduct of individual students shall bring reproach to the student body. Last year, the entire state applauded Alabama for the fine conduct of her boys in Birmingham and in Montgomery. Greater is he that conquereth his own spirit than he that taketh a football game. 2. The greatest tragedy of last season was the passing of Tommie Sikes, whose accidental death in trying to board a freight train for the Georgia Tech game cast a gloom over the campus far greater than the adverse score of the game. Speaking for more than two thousand parents, I want to urge each and every student not merely to maintain our best traditions of good conduct, but to remain at the University rather than attempt questionable or dangerous methods of reaching the games. Not one of you will ever regret it if you will follow these simple and well-intended rules," Denny wrote.

As he did with all University activities, Danny kept close tabs on Alabama football coaches, including offering his opinion on scheduling and overseeing off-season recruiting activities. Denny wrote University president Richard Foster on November 29, 1937, to say that he had heard Alabama's 9-7 victory over Vanderbilt on the radio. The win gave the Crimson Tide a perfect 9-0 record for the regular season, prompting Denny to write, "I wonder what the post-season situation is to be. I shudder to think that we may have to go up against Pittsburgh or Fordham or California. Responding to a Foster letter on December 6, 1937, after Alabama had been invited to play California in the Rose Bowl, Denny wrote, "A Rose Bowl team is not without its liabilities. It brings unreasonable requests. For example, the band; I can recall no Eastern team that has gone that far. It is not only a matter of expense, but also a matter of over-emphasis. It also brings the problem of coaching staff. I have a wire from Coach Thomas asking how soon I expect to reach home. It may be Georgia. It is almost certainly some personal problem of his, though he doesn't intimate anything. I assume that long ago you had him keep his agreement to sign the new contract extending his old one. Drew will do whatever Thomas does, and there are intimations that Mississippi State may want (assistant coach Paul) Burnham. So, I say, the Rose Bowl is not without its liabilities." Denny added that due to the football players having to miss classes for the trip to the Rose Bowl, "the coaches should at once see to it that all these boys get down to work, else they'll regret it at mid-year. If I were you, I'd send for the coaches at once. They should appoint monitors."

Alabama lost to California 13-0 in the January 1, 1938, Rose Bowl with Denny and Foster leading the University delegation in the festivities. The first loss in five Rose Bowl appearances prompted Denny to write to Foster on January 24 to thoroughly discuss the football program. "Until the last two or three years, when poor health reduced my activities, I kept a rather close eye on the activities of the coaching staff from Thanksgiving on. There is a great temptation for coaches to be comparatively inactive when the regular football season ends. I have always felt that with salaries higher than the professors and deans, they ought to give active service beyond the three months of football season. Now that you are providing further salary increases resulting in one of the largest totals paid to a coaching staff in the entire country, I am convinced that every effort should be made to keep these men busy from the top (Thomas) to the bottom (Paul Bryant)," Denny continued. "The present humiliating basketball season illustrates the precise lack of planning that has gone on during the past three years when I have been physically unable to keep behind the situation. Other colleges have been getting better material for athletics in recent years whereas since 1934 our material has progressively been getting poorer until we are now again becoming the Thin Red Line in basketball and track and largely in baseball. If the deterioration continues, we shall complete the recession also in football by 1940 and it will require years and constant changes in the coaching staff to bring things back again.

"If I had kept my health, I would have required, as I did for years, frequent, detailed conferences with the coaches with a view of ascertaining just what they were doing in the off season week by week, what contacts they were working, etc., etc.," Denny continued. "In the absence of this kind of thing there have been slip-shod, unorganized, ineffective procedures which are more and more finding expression in such places as the present breakdown in basketball and track," he added in a clear illustration of his intense interest in athletics. "If changes do not occur there will continue to be chaos and lack of cohesion and leadership, which after a while will inevitably result in the collapse of football also. This will cause alumni uprising and all the rest. Already a few of the alumni are wondering why other Alabama colleges are getting more Alabama athletes than we are getting. I hope you will not think I am overstating matters, but I do hate to think of the day when all that we have achieved athletically in a decade will be liquidated because the highest paid staff in the conference (except perhaps LSU) is inactive for so much of the year."

A note from Hugo Friedman to University president Richard Foster in early 1941 illustrates Denny's own apparent "lust for victory," especially in the University's athletic, academic and political rivalry with Auburn. Following a 35-16 Alabama basketball win over Auburn, Denny apparently wrote Friedman to express his delight with the victory. In forwarding the letter to Foster, Friedman wrote, "I am shocked at my good friend Dr. Mike showing the feeling he evidently still holds against Auburn (our comrades) in their humiliation. He seems to be gleeful concerning the above score. Just think what might have happened if Hank (Alabama basketball coach Hank Crisp) had left the regulars in until the end. It would have been 50-10. Dr. Mike is going to want Hank's resignation when he finds out what he could have done to them and did not."

Denny was correct in his assessment of the liabilities of Rose Bowl teams. In November 1939, Louisiana State University president Paul Hebert wrote Foster to inquire about the availability of Alabama head football coach Frank Thomas. Foster responded to Hebert that "Alabama would expect Thomas to honor his contract at Alabama through December 31, 1943." Foster sent a copy of his response to the LSU president to Denny, who scribbled in the margin of the letter, "Things are bad enough without disrupting the coaching staff!" Thomas, at the time, had a nine-year record of 69-11-5 at Alabama. He continued as Alabama's head coach through 1946, compiling a 115-24-7 record while winning four conference championships and two national championships.

Alabama's Rose Bowl appearances brought greater dividends than liabilities, of course. The first two appearances following the 1925 and 1926 seasons not only brought in the funds to build the first phase Denny Stadium, but the widespread acclaim brought new fans, students and athletes from out of state into the Alabama fold. One of the out-of-state fans was Pine Bluff, Arkansas, pool hall operator Jimmy Harland, who came to Tuscaloosa for Alabama games, met the coaches and helped recruit players to Alabama for years. More than fifty players from the late 1920s until the early 1950s can be traced to Harland's assistance. He remained friends with many former Crimson Tide players throughout his life and his three children attended the University. The list of Arkansas and nearby Mississippi football players recruited to Alabama by Harland included All-America end Don Hutson; future Alabama head coach Paul "Bear" Bryant; brothers Herschel, Russell and Norman Mosley; All-Southeastern Conference guard Charles Marr; 1930 team captain C. B. "Foots" Clements; future Alabama head coach J. B. Whitworth; Alvin "Pig" Davis, whose four sons later played football at Alabama; Tilden "Happy" Campbell, who later served as head baseball coach for the Crimson Tide; 1933 team captain Foy Leach, and 1948 most valuable player and 1949 co-captain Billy Cadenhead. In addition to attending most Alabama home football games for many years, Harland also attended several Rose Bowl games with the Crimson Tide, including the January 1, 1946 game. Although he was never officially associated with Alabama, Harland earned his own special place in Crimson Tide football lore.

Although Denny fully recognized the benefits of winning football teams, he was determined to establish and maintain academic eligibility standards for student athletes. Denny was critical of the minimal and "defective" SIAA rules regarding entrance requirements on his arrival at Alabama in 1912, saying that some member institutions did not have the high academic requirements enforced at the University and that some failed to enforce the rule requiring a year's residency for transfer students. "The very life of the SIAA depends upon such a regulation," Denny said. "In the absence of legislation of this kind it is a matter of time until the standard colleges will be withdrawing and another organization will be effected embracing the higher grade institutions of the South."

Denny wrote to Vanderbilt chancellor J. H. Kirkland in October 1920 asking for a meeting to discuss the problems related to lack of control of amateur athletics in the colleges. He pointed out that some schools were offering "so-called jobs" and holding players for "five, six or seven years to play football—the exact period usually being determined by the date at which any particular student happens to make the football team. It is, I think, a logical deduction that some of these men are receiving money. I regard the so-called jobs as fundamentally undermining our southern athletics," Denny said, adding, "I do not believe the SIAA is going to correct the trouble." Denny suggested that the "better-grade colleges" get out of the SIAA and refuse to schedule teams that do not comply with the fundamental rules of amateur athletics. The SIAA had been formed December 21, 1894, for "the development and purification of college athletics."

The University of Alabama—with Denny as flagbearer—led a mass exodus from the SIAA on February 25, 1921, as fourteen regional teams formed the Southern Conference. The original members of the conference included Alabama, Auburn, Virginia, Clemson, Georgia, Georgia Tech, Kentucky, Mississippi State, North Carolina, Tennessee, Virginia Tech, Maryland, North Carolina State and Washington and Lee.

Florida, Mississippi, South Carolina, LSU, Tulane and Vanderbilt joined the conference a year later and Sewanee, Virginia Military Institute and Duke followed soon afterward. A decade later, and again with Denny and the University of Alabama leading the way, thirteen members of the Southern Conference—those located west and south of the Appalachian Mountains—withdrew from the league in December 1932 to form the Southeastern Conference.

University of Alabama president Richard Foster, following Denny's lead, was among the leaders of a movement to strictly enforce Southeastern Conference athletic rules in 1939 and 1940. *Nashville Banner* sports editor Fred Russell supported the effort when he called on league presidents to clean up the conference by enforcing the rules of eligibility in an August 2, 1940, newspaper column. Russell called the then-current system "vicious" and pointed out that the thirteen conference schools in 1940 had made sixty-six coaching changes in twenty years. Russell said the coaches were often the victims of "evil alumni discontent" and that the only law they obeyed was the law of self-preservation. Foster had placed the University of Alabama in the forefront of the cleanup movement a year earlier when he called on all conference schools to adhere to the same academic entrance and eligibility rules as the University of Alabama.

University Graduate School Dean Albert Moore wrote to Foster on September 27, 1939, to congratulate him on his "progressive and courageous stand." Moore said, "The argument made by some schools that conditions in our conference are no worse than those in other conferences is childish and beside the point. The situation in our conference is in some respects little short of outrageous and demands immediate attention regardless of the conditions which prevail in other conferences. I am delighted that you have put the University in the front ranks of the cleanup brigade. In my judgment, if something is not done to improve conditions in our conference, we shall be held up to national ridicule and it will take a generation of right living to wipe out the stigma. It should mean much to us to assume the role of leadership for decency in our conference. The time has come for the revision of our rules as to scholarships and some other matters and I believe we shall need a commissioner to supervise the administration of the rules. Institutions no longer trust each other and even worse conditions prevail among the coaches and athletic directors," Moore added. Moore was named chairman of the faculty athletic committee in 1941 and served in the role until his retirement from the University in 1958.

With Foster among the leaders, conference presidents responded in 1940 by voting to bring athletic programs fully under their control and hiring former Mississippi governor Martin S. Conner as the first Southeastern Conference commissioner. Foster sought Denny's advice during the discussions of a conference commissioner, as he did in most matters. Prior to 1940, many athletic departments—including the University of Alabama in earlier days—operated almost independently from the universities, with little attention paid to enforcement of rules regarding standardized eligibility requirements and scholarship limits. Denny, however, had exercised strict control over University athletics since his arrival in 1912, just as he had over all other departments.

Denny affixed his distinctive signature (below) to thousands of letters.

Faithfully yours,

President.

15

Letters Offer Hope, Help

"We of the South have been talking excitedly about developing our natural resources, apparently unmindful of the fact that our greatest undeveloped natural resource is the neglected child, and in the balance sheet of a nation, as well as on Heaven's books, men count for more than coal and iron and cotton."

—Dr. George H. Denny

When new University of Alabama President Dr. George H. Denny made his first report to the school's board of trustees in May 1912, he said that only 398 students, including 55 women, had completed the spring semester at the Tuscaloosa campus. The enrollment figures were similar to those of the past ten years, and Denny had taken office on January 1 with the mission of turning the stagnant campus into what some alumni envisioned as "a great University."

Denny had cautioned University alumni soon after he was hired in November 1911 to not expect a miracle, saying that the task would take time, work and money, and those were the resources he asked of the alumni, trustees, state legislature and the citizens of Alabama from the start. He also needed students, and he soon had an extensive and innovative plan for getting them. That plan, much of which had already been in motion for months by May 1912, included a number of recruiting schemes, but it was mainly driven by Denny himself through public speaking appearances and personal letters to high school seniors and teachers in a direct-mail recruiting campaign that produced immediate and long-term results that increased enrollment by 600 percent during his twenty-five-year tenure as president. From Denny's first year to his last, student enrollment was limited only by the lack of dormitory and classroom space as the University achieved his vision of offering the opportunity of a college education to all qualified state applicants. Through his ingenious recruiting methods and his creation of a student self-help program similar to today's work-study programs, he was able to attract and educate thousands of students who might otherwise have never attended college.

Enrollment figures reported by Denny show that a record 533 students completed the spring semester of 1913, and enrollment numbers steadily increased—except briefly during World War I and the Great Depression—each year thereafter. Enrollment topped 1,000 for the first time in September 1918 when 1,165 students enrolled. That number doubled in four years and doubled again within ten years as the young men and women of rural Alabama gladly claimed the opportunity of a college education that Denny had personally offered them. A total of 4,897 students were enrolled during Denny's last semester as president in the fall of 1936, including 1,070 women students. An additional 850 out-of-state applicants were rejected in 1936 due to the lack of dormitory and classroom space, illustrating the overwhelming success of Denny's recruiting efforts. Results of Denny's summer school recruiting campaign were equally dramatic. After summer enrollment figures of 269 in 1910 and 243 in 1911, the number more than doubled to 517 in 1912—Denny's first summer on campus—as his spring recruiting efforts paid immediate dividends. Summer enrollment grew to 735 in 1915, to 1,250 in 1921 and to 2,109 in 1930. A newspaper story reported that 500 of the 735 students enrolled in the summer of 1915 were taking courses for teachers, which had been an early area of emphasis by Denny.

Denny's recruiting letters inviting all qualified high school graduates in the state to attend the University also offered his help "in any way within my power," and a large percentage of prospective students called on him for that help. Denny responded by arranging financial assistance through campus employment, bringing increasing numbers of applicants for similar positions year after year. By May 1913 Denny was citing the need for more dormitory space, especially for women students, and by 1914 students were packed into every nook and cranny on campus, including the lower floor of the President's Mansion. The call for additional classrooms and other facilities followed, forcing Denny to begin what became an annual plea for additional state funding to meet the needs of a rapidly growing University.

There were few ways to reach prospective college students in Alabama when Denny arrived in Alabama in January 1912. There was no radio, television or internet, and newspapers did not reach many of the state's rural areas. There were only approximately 100 high schools in the state in 1912, too, and few of the state's high school teachers were fully qualified. With no state mandatory attendance law and many rural families in need of help on the farms, most young men did not complete high school. With the number of qualified prospects greatly limited, competition between Alabama and Auburn for the state's male students was highly competitive. Few women entered the professional fields of engineering, business and medicine at the time and there was strong competition for women students from the state's two-year teachers' colleges and the four-year Alabama College at Montevallo, all of which offered more subjects for women.

The primary ways of reaching high school seniors in 1912 was by mail, personal contact or through the high schools, and by May of that year Denny was utilizing all three methods fully. He accepted every possible speaking engagement in an effort to spread his vision of universal education and the opportunities offered at the University of Alabama. Within three weeks of his arrival on campus he had already accepted five speaking engagements for May commencement exercises at high schools and two-year colleges. By May he had already sent a personally signed letter to each high school senior in the state inviting them to attend the University and he had spoken at a number of high school graduation exercises to deliver his message in person. He had also called on the alumni and currently enrolled University students to help recruit new students; hired upper classmen to recruit throughout Alabama and Mississippi during the summer; sent letters to high school teachers throughout the state encouraging them to attend summer school; placed recruiting advertisements in the state's largest newspapers, and worked to retain currently enrolled University students through a summer letter campaign that maintained close contact with the students. In effect, Denny left no stone unturned in his efforts to recruit and retain students, and he only added to the recruiting efforts throughout his tenure. Each method produced results, of course, but his letters to high school graduates proved to be an overwhelming success.

Denny's direct-mail recruiting system was surely an innovative approach for the time. After taking office as University president on January 1, 1912, Denny immediately contacted city and county school officials to request the names and addresses of all high school seniors. He not only sent letters inviting the seniors to attend the University, but he invited the teachers, many of who did not have college degrees, to attend summer school. In his letters to the teachers, he wrote, "There is a great demand now for teachers and it looks as though salaries will be much higher in the future. There is also a demand for college trained men who are able to fill positions as principals and superintendents of town, county and city high schools."

In addition to his unprecedented recruiting efforts, Denny was also persistent. If he failed to get a timely response from a high school senior in the spring or a current University student in the summer, he wrote a second letter, and on some documented occasions, even a third, showing a sincere personal interest in each student. Responses to Denny's letters increased each year as the number of high school graduates increased, reaching approximately five hundred a year by 1917 and exceeding a thousand by 1922. The letters to high school seniors—commercially printed with a "Dear Friend" salutation but each bearing Denny's bold and dramatic personal signature—inspired hope for a life beyond the farm for many students who had never dreamed of attending college. For many rural students, it is easy to imagine that Denny's letter might well have been the first they had ever received. Responses, often similar yet still all different, came by the dozens at first, then by the scores, then by the hundreds then by more than a thousand a year by 1920 and thereafter. The letters came from every city and town in Alabama and from remote rural crossroads with names like Omega, Bradleytown, Three Notch, Mertz, Silas, Deer Park, Vinegar Bend, Opp, Veto, Clio, Snow Hill, McFall, Alanda, Miflin, Whistler, Jackson Gap, Samantha, Chandler Springs, Glenwood, Equality, Lapine, Sycamore, Grove Oak, Kelleytown, Brilliant and Mt. Hope —small communities where the receipt of even a form letter from the president of the state university likely became a major topic of conversation.

Denny sent similar but slightly different recruiting letters to high school seniors each year, with separate letters for men and women prospects. No permanent file of sample letters has been located at the University, but a few of the letters were returned to Denny by students who used the back or lower margin of the letters for their responses. The following April 1, 1922, letter was returned to Denny from a high school senior from Meridian, Mississippi, who wrote a note on the lower margin stating his interest in the pre-medical course and requesting a catalog:

"Dear Friend:

"The 1922 catalog will soon be ready for distribution and I shall be glad to send you a copy if you desire me to do so. Please let me know your wishes.

"Are you planning a pre-medical course? The great majority of pre-medical students of this section naturally take their training here.

"Are you interested in engineering? The new courses available in that department will be interesting to you.

"Are you expecting to be a business man? The School of Commerce will give you the training you need. Approximately sixty-five percent of college men ultimately enter business. Ours is the only School of Commerce in this section.

"I am anxious to help you in any way in my power. Do not fail to command me fully.

"Hoping to hear from you very soon. Believe me. Very sincerely yours, George H. Denny, President."

Another example, dated April 1, 1928, was slightly different:

"Dear Friend:

"You will soon have completed your high school course. I congratulate you. Your graduation is an important event to you and to your community.

"You must now reach a decision that will affect your entire future. Are you to content yourself with the basic training that you have received in high school or will you look farther than the immediate future and enter college in the fall, enhancing your opportunities and preparing yourself for happier living, more effective service and greater earning power?

"The University of Alabama offers you the precise opportunities that you need. In arts and sciences, in business administration, in engineering, in education, in medicine and in law you will find here a wide range of courses which will equip you for your proper place in life. Our catalog gives detailed descriptions of the various courses offered.

"You *can* attend college if you *will*. The cost is not great, and certainly it has been reduced to an absolute minimum at the University of Alabama. Moreover, the money which you spend in securing your college education should not be regarded as an expenditure—it is an investment, and one that will return itself to you many times.

"Your environment has much to do with your success in college as in life. Our campus is one of the most beautiful in the lower South. Tuscaloosa, admirably located and easily accessible by three large railroads, is an ideal seat for the University. Progressive culturally and industrially, it fosters a spirit of friendliness and hospitality that readily includes the University students in the civic and social life of the community.

"I am sending you an illustrated folder which describes the University and which will, I hope, give you a good impression of our institution. Our new catalog will come from the press within a few weeks. It contains full and complete descriptions of the courses offered this fall. May I send you a copy?

"I am interested in you and want to see you succeed. If I may help you in any way, do not fail to let me know. Will you not write me your plans?

"Again congratulating you on your approaching graduation and hoping to hear from you soon. Believe me. Faithfully yours, George H. Denny, President."

Denny's offer of help was readily accepted as many of the high school graduates wrote back seeking financial assistance in meeting their college expenses. Denny obliged by somehow providing work to approximately a third of the students who attended the University during his tenure. He created a student self-help bureau to assist the students in finding part-time jobs, and by February 1914 sixty students were employed through the bureau, according to a *Tuscaloosa News* story. A similar story in 1931 said that one third of the 4,104 students enrolled in the spring were employed through the program, illustrating the impact of Denny's version of today's work-study program. Word of the student self-help bureau offering work spread quickly and there were plenty of takers. The new high school graduates, inspired by his offer of assistance and believing him, as he had asked them to, wrote back to ask questions and to claim the prize of a college education that he offered. Denny, in turn, reserved practically all lower-level campus jobs for the students, including clerical, laundry, grounds keeping, power plant firemen, library assistants, stenographers and typists, cafeteria waiters and janitorial staff positions. Pay ranged from a low of $1.50 to a high of $12.50 a week depending on the skill level and number of hours worked. Janitors who worked an hour and a half a day earned $1.50 a week in 1914 and $3 a week in 1924 while power plant firemen who shoveled coal into the furnace earned $5.50 a week, according to information found in various letters.

Denny had brought the concept of "self-help" or work-study with him from Washington and Lee, which had employed a similar program for years. In a 1903 letter urging public support for that school, Denny wrote, "These young men come from every Southern state, and a number of them are from New England and the East. Many of them are poor, and it may not be inappropriate to say that this institution never closes its doors to a worthy applicant because he is unable to pay his fees. For the last forty years fully one third of our students have received assistance in one way or another." One of those students was Rush H. Limbaugh Sr., a native of rural Missouri and the grandfather of talk radio commentator Rush H. Limbaugh III. According to the book, "The Original Rush Limbaugh," the elder Limbaugh wrote to a number of colleges in 1909 about entering law school that fall and was rejected by all but one—Washington and Lee University. Denny wrote back to Limbaugh to explain admission requirements and promised him a job to help fund his education. Limbaugh took the train from Missouri to Lexington, Virginia, and entered school, but became ill with malaria soon afterward and returned home so he could be cared for by his mother. He later attended the University of Missouri and became a prominent attorney, but he never forgot Denny's early efforts to help him achieve his goal of a law degree.

Offering to help the high school seniors placed a greater burden of responsibility on Denny each year as more and more students responded to his call. He enticed them with the promise of opportunity and was often hard pressed to meet the demand. Denny obviously did not get every high school graduate, and not all those who came to the University of Alabama graduated, but Denny's efforts brought the beginning of the cultural change he had envisioned for the state when he left Washington and Lee University to come to Alabama. The students came to the University to learn science, math, medicine and engineering, but they learned much more, some of which came from Denny in his frequent sermon-like speeches on truth, leadership, responsibility and service.

Denny was determined in his recruiting efforts. High school graduates who did not respond in a reasonable amount of time got a second, more insistent letter. A Montgomery senior waited until September 17 to respond to Denny's inquiries in 1917, and his response indicates the tone of Denny's most recent letter. "Your letter of a few days ago received. In reply I am glad to say that I have decided to come to the University and will be there Thursday night. From your letter I inferred that you were under some misapprehension as to my reason for delaying to say definitely whether I was coming to the University this year. It was not, as you seemed to suppose, a lack of nerve but simply that I was uncertain as to whether I could make the necessary financial arrangements for coming. I have succeeded in securing enough money to see me through this year, however, and am coming for this time, though I cannot say what I shall do afterwards."

Denny's letters inspired hope and ambition among the high school seniors. One responded, "Recently I have received quite a bit of literature from the University and it has made me want a college education…." Another wrote, "I am thankful to you for the interest you have shown in me and I am looking forward with enthusiasm for the information I have requested."

John Sparkman of Morgan County was one of the respondents to a Denny letter, but he wrote back only after Denny's second letter. "I received both of your letters of recent date and was only waiting about answering them until I could find out if it would be possible for me to attend college this year," Sparkman wrote on August 26, 1917. Sparkman added that he would be at the University on September 10 "with the expectation of securing some kind of work by which I may partly pay my expenses." Sparkman worked his way through the University shoveling coal in the campus power plant. He also served as president of the Student Government Association and editor of the *Crimson White* while earning a law degree (1923) and master's degree in history (1924) at the University. Sparkman later served 43 years in the U. S. House and Senate.

A student from Albany responded on May 27, 1921, saying, "I have received several communications from you in regard to my future educational intentions. I want to go to college if it is possible. I am willing to work for a college education. I would appreciate any help or advice you could give me in securing a job."

"In regard to the nice and kind letters which I have received from you in the past few weeks, I have decided to write you a few lines for two reasons," a graduate of Piedmont High School wrote in 1923. "First, I wish to thank you for the interest you seem to be taking in me toward my going to college and getting an education. Second, I wish to ask a few questions. What would be the smallest amount of money that would be necessary to go through your college; and would there be any chance for me to work my way through? If so, what sum of money would be necessary and how long would I have to work each day?"

A prospect from Union Grove wrote on September 4, 1917, saying, "Your urgent letter to enroll in your school this coming year at hand and in reply will gladly say I am now making preparations to be with you. I expect to reach the University Saturday afternoon or Sunday morning."

"Your encouraging letter was received, the contents of which were eagerly grasped.

How thankful I am to have as great a man as you are to take an interest in me," a Mobile senior responded to Denny's letter in 1924.

Albert Raines responded to Denny from Pisgah in July 1924, saying, "If there is anything I can do at the University to help defray my expenses I want to do it. I have about $150 and perhaps can have $200 by September. I want to turn that over to you and work the rest of my expenses. I am not afraid of work. Anything that will keep me in school will be delightful to me. Will you let me come?" Raines found work at the University, earned a law degree in 1928 and later served as a state representative 1941-44 and U. S. Representative 1945-1965.

"Your letters reference to my entering the University as a student have all been received," a prospect from Ashville responded. "Until recently, I had been working in Ohio, and so have waited until I came home to reply. I definitely decided some time ago to become a student at the University this year." Another prospective student explained his delayed response by writing that he had been busy on the farm, but would attend school in the fall. "I have a splendid crop of cotton and boll weevils," he jokingly added.

"I have heard time and again that you are immensely interested in helping young men get a college education," wrote a Birmingham student in August 1922. "I am very desirous to study law. I have only enough money to pay for my tuition and books, which I presume will amount to about $125. Is there any opportunity for me to get some kind of work to enable me to pay other expenses? I can use a typewriter and write shorthand at a fairly good speed."

"I am willing to make any personal sacrifice in an effort to get a college education," wrote another student. "I have no desire to get something for nothing and will do anything that may be required of me. All that I ask is an opportunity to study. If you can help me in any way I will appreciate it very much and will try to be worthy of the opportunity."

"It is interesting to me to know that the University maintains a self-help bureau," a young woman from Florence wrote in 1922. "I am prepared to do stenographic work, therefore I shall be glad to know if I can get such work to help me provided that I enroll at the University the coming fall."

"It is one of my highest ambitions to get a college education, but owing to financial conditions my father is unable to send me, so my only hope is to work my own way. I trust that you will do all that is in your power to help me in securing some kind of work that will pay all my expenses because I cannot expect outside help," wrote one high school senior. Another wrote, "Unless I can get something to do to pay my expenses I cannot go any farther. Daddy doesn't feel able to send me to school any longer because there are nine more besides me that he wants to give some education." Still another wrote, "If you can give me a little work I assure you that I shall try hard to make good and that no one will appreciate it more than I will. In regard to work, I can and will do anything."

"I am a poor boy unable to go to college without assistance," a typical response said. "I have an inspiration to go to the top and possess the best obtainable. I will promise to work hard in college and am willing to work at anything to pay for my board and schooling." Room rent and tuition at the University in 1920 was $71 per year. Board was estimated at $22.50 per month. Books and other expenses were additional.

A student from Boaz responded to Denny's letter on March 19, 1923, by writing, "I was enthused and encouraged by your friendly letter of recent date. I suppose that you understand how a fellow feels when someone promises some little hope of some larger meaning. I was thankful for your noticing my letter and taking time to say a few words of encouragement to me. Perhaps there is nothing that will mean more to me than to obtain some position by which I may work my way to the realm of a college graduate. It means much to a fellow with high ideals and enlarged ambitions to be assured of some sympathy or assistance in his course of handicaps. It is beyond the expression of common words to tell you just how much I appreciate your generosity and kindness. I am hoping that I may be allowed to express my gratitude through service, which always tells just what a feller is. I hope that you will very soon be able to let me know what you can do in aiding me."

Claude D. Pepper of Camp Hill wrote Denny in 1917 to request a job through the student self-help bureau. "The kind of work does not matter provided it does not require so much of my time as to defeat the purpose for which I shall be there. If you can see fit, I should like to have a job waiting on tables. If nothing of this kind is open, please inform me of the best that you can offer." Pepper earned a bachelor's degree from the University in 1921 and a law degree from Harvard in 1924. He represented Florida in the U. S. Senate 1936-1951 and in the U. S. House of Representatives from January 1963 until his death in May 1989. Pepper gained national recognition as an advocate for senior citizens and the disadvantaged. He was featured on the cover of "Life" magazine twice, was pictured on a postage stamp and received the Presidential Medal of Freedom from President George H. W. Bush in 1989, just four days before his death.

"No doubt many requests are coming to you daily for work to pay expenses during the next session at Alabama, but I am sending one which I hope will not be unheeded," a high school senior from Fyffe wrote on March 14, 1923. "I am not going to put up a pitiful tale for I am not asking for charity. I don't want anything given me, Dr. Denny. I only want a chance to work my way. I am a young man twenty years of age, finished high school last year at Snead Seminary and have been teaching during the current year. I haven't any money, but have good health and am willing to work. I care not how hard the job. I want something to do to pay my way. Write me, Dr. Denny, saying that you will give me a chance." The same student wrote Denny again on March 31, saying, "For your letter of recent date, I thank you. Nothing could have pleased me better than to have you say that I would be given a chance, and I am very anxious to know what duties will be required of me in the fulfillment of my promise."

A prospect from Hackleburg wrote on March 9, 1924, to inquire about work for himself and his two brothers. "I understand that you furnish employment for about 200 students, which enables them to work their way through college. Two brothers and I are planning on attending the University this coming year if we can arrange to work part or all our way through…." The letter was marked "answered" and "self-help list" in Denny's handwriting, indicating that the brothers were offered work.

A 1924 response from Albertville said, "I received your most encouraging letter and I greatly appreciated it. You told me things that I had never thought of and helped me to see things as I had not seen them before. I am going to school this year if there is any possible chance. I think I now realize what a college education means. I have already filed my application for a position in the student self-help bureau and anything you will do in the way of helping me secure work will be greatly appreciated." The letter was marked "answered," "good man" and "self-help."

"I am appealing to you for work of some kind around the University," wrote a student from Malone. "I prefer a power house job where I can make $17 or $18 a month in helping defray my college expenses. I am not able to come unless I get some work." One University upperclassman wrote to say, "Upon coming home for the summer, I find that financial conditions are such that it will be next to impossible for me to enter school again unless I can get some assistance from the University. I am taking this opportunity to inquire about a job of some kind." A prospective student from Guin wrote Denny to say that he would like to attend the University, but would need some financial assistance. "My father died last summer and my mother has no money to send me to college and that will throw me to have to get some kind of work to pay most of my expenses. I am willing to do any kind of work," he added.

A student from Pleasant Hill wrote in August 1920 with multiple requests of Denny. He first asked for a job waiting tables, then asked to delay his entry into school a few days to finish gathering his crop. Confidently, he added, "I want an education and all I want is a chance. If work and determination will get me through, I can make it." A high school senior from Palos, Alabama, also requested aid. "I am a poor farmer boy struggling against poverty to obtain an education. I am very ambitious and have aims to go higher but financial conditions will not permit me to do so. I wonder, with your help, if I couldn't get some work there that would pay my expenses. I am willing to work at anything," the student wrote.

Responding to a prospective student in February 1918, Denny wrote, "It will be a pleasure to help you in any way possible. I am going to ask you to take up with us some time during the month of May the question of securing a position at the dining hall, at the power plant or on the stoops (janitorial position). I am more than anxious to be of service to you and I want you to know that anything that I can do will be done with the greatest possible satisfaction." A month later Denny wrote to another student that "the opportunities for self-help here are greater than at any institution concerning which I have any knowledge. Most of the positions naturally go to young men who have already been with us for a period, especially the positions in the library. You will have no trouble a little later on in getting the kind of work you want. It may be possible for you to get something to do as a janitor next session."

Denny received a letter from a high school senior from Rogersville requesting work based on the school's growing reputation for student financial assistance. "I understand you are willing and ready to help true American boys through college, or at least part of the way through," the young man wrote. "I have been informed concerning your aid by my excellent teacher and friend for the past three years, Miss Kathryn Perdue."

Students were happy to receive work of any kind. A senior from Haleyville wrote to accept his job, saying, "I received your kind letter offering me the position of janitor in Gorgas Hall this morning. I certainly appreciate this and I am glad to say that I will be with you next year and that I will be delighted to get this job." Another wrote, "I have your letter of the seventh instant offering me a position as janitor for next year and I will say in reply that I gladly accept the position of janitor. You can count on me." A student from North Alabama sent a brief note in June 1920 to accept a job for the fall, saying, "I accept the position as janitor at $3 per week. I shall make the best one I can." Another wrote, "I am in receipt of your letter dated May 7, 1920, in which you offer me the position as stenographer at $12.50 per week. I wish to thank you and shall be pleased to accept same."

"Last year you offered me work as a janitor to help me pay my way through school there," one prospective student wrote. "I was unable to attend school last year and so could not accept your offer. I would like very much to know if I could get the same work to do this year or if there are other places open which I might get. I am very anxious to come to the University this year and any favor will be appreciated."

"I have just received your letter telling me that I have a position as waiter in the mess hall for next year," a Birmingham student wrote in 1920. "I am very thankful to you for granting me the position and will do anything in my power to make the mess hall better."

A 1924 Denny letter to a student seeking work said, "We have found it possible to assign you to one of the sweeping jobs at the University for the coming year. The work will consume about an hour and a half a day and will pay $3 per week."

"Received your letter and was glad to know that I could enter the medical department. It will be after the 18th before I can get away from here but I am coming," Joe Sewell of Titus wrote in September 1920. "I understand that Jones will not be back this year, so his job is open. I would appreciate it if I could get a job something on that order," he added. Sewell became an outstanding football and baseball player at Alabama and had an outstanding professional baseball career with the Cleveland Indians and New York Yankees, posting a lifetime batting average of .312 and setting the major record for fewest strikeouts in a season at four in 1925 and tying the mark in 1929. He also returned to the Capstone as head baseball coach 1964-69 and led the Crimson Tide to a Southeastern Conference championship in 1968. Alabama's baseball stadium, often referred to as "The Joe," is named Sewell-Thomas Field in honor of Sewell and former Crimson Tide football coach Frank Thomas.

Parents often responded for their children or to their own letters from Denny. A father from Ashby responded, "Dear Doctor: My son received your letter and he is anxious to attend the University and I want to send him provided I can arrange to do so. Can he get any work to help pay his expenses? If so, what kind of work? He can milk and do any ordinary work. Any favor you offer me shall be very much appreciated." It is very possible that the young man found familiar work at the University since Mrs. Denny kept a cow, chickens and two horses in a pasture behind the President's Mansion for several years.

A father from Elba, writing for his son in 1922, said, "He seems so anxious for a college education that I have decided to make whatever sacrifice necessary to help him through this year with the fond hope that he may be able to obtain some work which will partly defray his expenses. Please do not allow him to waste any money as it is very hard to obtain and I am borrowing this money to get him started." The father sent a check for $35 and said the son was to bring $18 in cash on his arrival.

A Cuthbert, Georgia, father responded after receiving two letters from Denny, writing, "Acknowledging both your recent letters in reference to the placing of my son at your school for the next year, I wish to thank you especially for the evident interest in the problem confronting me as manifested in your last letter replying in detail and explaining just the things I wanted to know from an unbiased and competent source. I wish to assure you that I have the utmost confidence in your judgment and I am going to do just as you say you would with your son. I have decided to send him to you with the confident assurance that I am adopting the correct course."

Some parents had questions for Denny. "Having never visited your town, please advise me as to the moral conditions and what you expect from your students," one wrote. "What time do they go to bed and what kind of company do they keep? Have you the obscene places—gambling dens, etc.? I feel like it will bring me better luck to keep him at home rather than send him to a place where these things are, that he might go astray."

"After receiving your letter suggesting that he study law, I have canvassed the situation thoroughly with him and in view of the utmost confidence both of us have in your judgment based upon your experience with and life-long study of young men, he has about decided to adopt your suggestion and take up the study of law," a father wrote to Denny in a letter that illustrates the depth of Denny's personal involvement with individual students.

Duff Green of Birmingham wrote Denny on August 15, 1921, to thank him for his interest in his son Benjamin A. Green. "He is already in love with you and I am sure he will be a credit to his alma mater," the father wrote. Ben Green served as sports editor of the *Crimson White* and was elected to Jasons and Omicron Delta Kappa as a student at the University. After graduation, he worked as a reporter, managing editor and editor for *The Tuscaloosa News* for twenty-four years before joining the Keister Advertising Service in 1952. Green was also a prominent civic leader in Tuscaloosa, serving on the Tuscaloosa Charity Board, Black Warrior Scout Council Advisory Board, the War Price and Rationing Board and as a member of the Kiwanis Club, Chamber of Commerce and Tuscaloosa Civil Defense.

"It is our intention now to enroll our son at the Capstone in September and have him join the other loyal boosters of the University and enter all its activities, contributing his mite to the wonderful success that is attending your efforts there," a parent responded in 1923. "Your letter received and in reply will say that I will send my son to the University. He was at the Southern University last session," another wrote. One mother wrote to say that she would reluctantly send her son to the University, but added, "I shall miss him so for he has been such a help and comfort in every way. You will find him just a boy, full of life, fun and mischief."

As one might expect, parents relied heavily on Denny to keep close watch on their children, most of whom were leaving home for the first time. One father, sending two sons to the University of Alabama in 1917, wrote, "The younger of the boys is just a little bit wild, but the principal trouble with them is their tendency to make spend thrifts…. If you can assist me in increasing their earning capacity and decreasing their spending capacity I will be more than grateful, and I assure you that you will meet with no complaint or objection from me in handling them in any way you see proper…." Another father wrote, "…Any influence that you may cause to be exerted over this young man, that he may become a worthy citizen of the state of Alabama, with respect for his fellow man and his god, will be highly appreciated." Another father sending two sons back to school wrote, "On their return to the University, I shall have them call on you and I will thank you if you will take the time to talk to them emphatically as to the great advantages a boy gathers unto himself by concluding a full college degree. And in any way that you may be able to inspire or assist these boys in the making of useful men, our people will greatly appreciate." A parent responding to a Denny letter wrote," I was surprised that you, with all your duties and burdens, should know the students personally, especially the freshmen. It is quite a relief to know that the moral influences of the University are such as they are."

Other parents often wrote to inquire about the status of their children. One father wrote, "How is Jim doing with his grades? Has he gotten down to work? Does he stay with his work in his room? Do you know whether he attends Sunday school and church? We thank you very much to answer by return mail." One parent wrote, "I am writing to you to ask if you, as a special favor, will look up my three boys and see what kind of work they are doing. I know that it is not customary to send out marks except at mid-term, but I am exceedingly anxious to know if they are bringing up their work satisfactorily. As you know, I am making quite a sacrifice to keep them all in college this year."

One concerned father wrote to say that he had not heard from his son in three weeks and asked Denny to determine his status. "His mother is very anxious about him and has been after me to go to the University and make a personal investigation. Please be kind enough to let me hear from you, and I shall certainly appreciate it if you will kindly keep an eye on him." A mother sent a telegram on September 20, 1922, asking about her son. "Please contact him and have him write me at once. Am very uneasy. Have not heard from him in two weeks. Please say no exciting news. Only anxious about him," the telegram said. A father showing his appreciation for Denny's special efforts wrote, "Allow me to say that this is simply another instance of many where your sympathy for and interest in young men is shown. I don't wonder that you are held in such high esteem by the young men who have attended the University and known you personally."

Convincing the high school graduates to attend the University was not difficult. Most welcomed the opportunity for a college education. Convincing their parents, many of whom were often more concerned with matters of the moment like the price of cotton, lack of rain, cattle ticks and boll weevils than a child's dream of a college education, was sometimes quite another matter; therefore Denny often wrote to parents as well, arguing that the University had more to offer than other state colleges. "Your good letter with reference to my son's going to the University came Sunday," one father responded to such a Denny letter. "I read and carefully noted all you said and agree with you that the selection of a college for a boy is a very important thing and one that should be considered in a broad and practical way. He has been somewhat inclined to go to Auburn for no particular reason that I know of. Since reading your letter and having a talk with a student who is there now, I am more inclined for him to go to the University, and shall advise him to that end."

One University student wrote Denny to say that his mother was insistent on his going to a college other than Alabama to continue his education. "I have done almost everything I can to persuade her to let me return to the University, but I'm afraid it will take someone older to change her opinion. Would it be requesting too much if I should ask you to write her a letter urging her to let me return? I would certainly appreciate it if you would." The student wrote Denny two weeks later to say, "I can hardly tell you how very much I appreciate both your letter to me and the one to Mother. I feel certain that they served the purpose and that for the next year at least I will be back at the University."

"I have definitely decided to enter my son in the University under your personal direction and supervision this fall," a Birmingham father wrote in 1922. "He is a good, clean boy morally, physically and mentally, having no bad habits whatever, and I am counting on the University to give him that training so necessary to his future accomplishments. As an alumnus of Auburn, (1889), you must realize my personal appreciation of you and the University by placing my boy in your keeping," the father added.

A father from Athens wrote Denny a similar letter, saying, "I am sending my son to your school because of your association with the institution. I would be glad if you will give the young man some attention and at your convenience advise with him." Another father wrote, "Harry White's most enthusiastic arguments coupled with your very logical ones were too persuasive for us to resist. Charles will be at the University for registration on Monday, September 4."

"I was indeed glad to receive your letter and same came to me as a surprise," one student wrote. "I had not given this matter much thought until your letter came and my father also received his letter. After talking the subject over, he consented to let me come down in September."

Former University of Alabama president Dr. Judy Bonner recalled in early 2016 that her father (Josiah Bonner) and his twin brother James received recruiting letters from Dr. Denny inviting them to attend the University during the 1930s. "They went to Erskine College in South Carolina rather than the University, and when Dr. Denny learned of their decision he wrote their mother—my grandmother—to wish them well. He could have just forgotten about them, but he took time to write and wish them well," Dr. Bonner said. "I saw the letters in my grandmother's papers years ago, and I think we still have them." Josiah Bonner later earned a law degree from Georgetown University and became an attorney in Wilcox County. Dr. Bonner earned B.S. and M.S. degrees from the University of Alabama and a Ph.D. degree from Ohio State University before returning to the University, where she was a member of the faculty for thirty-five years, including serving as president 2012-2015.

A Mobile parent wrote Denny on January 3, 1921, to say, "Please accept thanks for your cordial letter of December 20 urging that Elizabeth return to the University. Replying, I am glad to state that we have arranged for her to return." A later letter from the same parent said, "I want to tell you how much we enjoyed our little visit with you. I feel that Elizabeth is going to be muchly benefitted in every way this year and it is quite a comfort to me to know that she will be directly under your influence and guidance."

Denny made every effort to keep students in school until they graduated, even while serving as interim president 1941-42. When a student dropped out of school to join the Army in January 1942, Denny wrote his father to say, "I was tremendously disappointed that Joseph withdrew from college without talking with me. Personally, I think he made a great mistake. The country needs boys of sound training. We are operating under a selective draft and not an elective draft. This means, of course, that the country wants every man in a position adjusted to his abilities." In urging the father to convince his son to return to school, Denny added, "Ten years hence he will not regret it if he equips himself for high service."

Athletic scholarships during the Denny era were actually working scholarships, and the athletes had to scramble for the same jobs as the other students to pay their expenses. Denny was regularly asked to assist in the recruitment of athletes by writing to them, talking with them or helping find work for them. Mrs. Addie Stephenson of Akron wrote Denny in August 1918 regarding her son Riggs, saying, "We are very anxious for him to return to the University for the next session, but unless he can secure employment at school to help defray expenses I do not see how he can go back. If you can do anything for Riggs, say help him get one of the positions in the dining room or janitor or anything he can do, I assure you we would be deeply grateful for your assistance." Stephenson, an outstanding athlete, got his job and returned to school. He earned All-Southern honors in football and baseball and was captain of the 1921 football team. In awarding Stephenson the University's 1921-1922 all-around athlete award, Denny described him as "the embodiment of cleanliness, manliness and courage." Stephenson played professional baseball 1920-1933 and managed the Birmingham Barons before becoming a successful Tuscaloosa businessman.

Such well-known football players as All-America end Don Hutson and Paul "Bear" Bryant worked on the grounds crew or swept floors in the gymnasium to work their way through college. Bryant, of course, returned to the University as head football coach 1958-82 and led the Crimson Tide to six national championships.

Isaac Morgan "Ike" Boone Jr. of Samantha wrote Denny on August 29, 1917, to thank him for a job that allowed him to join his brother James at the University and play football and baseball for the Crimson Tide. "I sincerely appreciate the faith you have vested in me and I firmly resolve to live up to that trust," Boone wrote. While a student at the University, Morgan served as president of the A-Club, the Pan-Hellenic Council and the Student Government Association and was captain of the 1918 football team. Both Boone brothers went on to play professional baseball. Morgan set minor league records with a .407 average, 55 home runs and 218 runs batted in in 198 games in the Pacific Coast League in 1929. James hit 46 homers the same season in the Piedmont League as the brothers combined for 101 home runs. Morgan's 553 total bases in 1929 also set a professional baseball record. Morgan hit .448 and drove in 98 runs in only 83 games in in the minor leagues in 1930 before being called to the major leagues with the Brooklyn Dodgers. In eight years in the major leagues, Morgan had a lifetime batting average of .321 with 26 home runs and 194 runs batted in in 356 games. As player/manager of the Toronto Maple Leafs in 1934, Morgan hit .372 and was named the league's most valuable player. Overall, Morgan won five batting titles in four different minor leagues, including batting .402 in the Texas League in 1923 as the last man to bat over .400 in the league. He had a .370 batting average and 2,521 hits in his minor league career. James had an 8-13 pitching record in four seasons in the major leagues. He spent six years in the minor leagues, batting .356 and posting a 72-64 pitching record.

Principals and teachers often wrote to Denny to ask for special help for deserving students. One such letter to Denny came from Houston County High School principal L. J. Thompson in August 1921. "This young man says that his father refuses to do anything for him and that he is going to the University anyway. He told me that he is going to leave here within the next week and walk to the University and stay until he can leave with a degree. I believe he means to go, and I am writing to know if you will take him under such circumstances. The distance from here to the University is about 230 miles and if he is so determined to go as to undertake the walk all the way to get the privilege of a university education, somehow I have faith in his ability to make good. Let me hear from you at once, please, if you encourage this boy in his desperate undertaking to start to college without a penny of money with the purpose of working his way through school." Denny apparently advised the young man against his plan since his name does not appear in University records.

Birmingham Superintendent of Education C. B. Glenn wrote Denny on June 6, 1922, to recommend Ethelred Sykes for a scholarship or other assistance. Glenn said Sykes was "one of the finest boys we have had," and added that his "fitness for college is beyond question." Glenn added that Sykes' father was an invalid and that the young man would have to have financial assistance to go to college. Sykes soon received an Alabama Power Company scholarship and became an outstanding student at the University, serving as editor of the *Crimson White* 1925-26 and as a member of the Glee Club, Blackfriars, Gate Club and *Corolla* Board and being elected to Jasons and Omicron Delta Kappa. He also played piano in a jazz ensemble called the Capstone Five and won the University's Pan-Hellenic Cup for overall achievement in academic, athletic and student affairs as a senior in 1926. Sykes, perhaps mercifully nicknamed "Lundy," wrote the "Yea, Alabama" fight song in 1926. The song was selected as the winner of a $50 prize in a *Rammer Jammer* contest to select a permanent Alabama fight song after the school had used the Washington and Lee fight song for several years. Sykes earned an Army Reserve commission through ROTC and transferred to the Air National Guard in 1934 while working for Sparrow Advertising in Birmingham. He was called to active military duty in November 1940 and eventually served in the 20th Air Force in the Pacific during World War II. He remained in the Air Force after the war and later retired as a brigadier general.

The president of the State Normal School at Florence wrote Denny on August 22, 1922, to recommend a student transferring to the University. "I commend him to you. He will never give you any trouble unless you become exasperated because of the ease with which he meets his scholastic duties. Let us hope that he will one day emulate to a degree the high standards, the ambition and the attainments of his distinguished father," the letter said. The student was Archibald H. Carmichael Jr., whose father was an 1886 University of Alabama law school graduate who served in the Alabama House and Senate, on the state board of education, in the U. S. Congress 1933-37 and on the University board of trustees 1924-47.

Montgomery educator and school board member Mary Burke wrote to Denny in January 1921 seeking financial aid for a deserving student. "I hope he will be able to attend the University instead of Auburn," she wrote. "In the first place, I believe the University can do more for him, and next, I am eager for the University to secure students who will reflect credit on our state's greatest institution." Denny later hired Burke as University registrar and a campus dormitory is named for her.

"Can't you manage to let a deserving boy have a room in the gymnasium and give him a job rolling ashes or unloading coal?" a coach from Sidney Lanier High School in Montgomery wrote Denny in May 1923. "He is a graduate from Lanier this spring and has been a leader in many phases of school life." Dothan Schools Superintendent C. C. Moseley wrote Denny in 1932 to suggest that freshman football player Young Boozer be given work to pay his room and board, saying that Boozer's mother was concerned about being able to send both Boozer and his sister to school. Boozer, a member of the Crimson Tide football team, graduated from the University in 1936 and became a prominent business and civic leader in the state.

C. D. Wallace, superintendent of schools in Shuqualak, Mississippi, wrote Denny in August 1920 to recommend two students, saying, "The boys are contemplating going to college and if you will write each of them in regard to the matter it will be greatly appreciated. One is a barber and wishes to know if there would be a chance of getting some work of this kind to help him financially. He is also a good football man and plays basketball and baseball. He has an offer from Mississippi College but I am using the argument that the University of Alabama being on the "A" grade list makes it a college of higher standing than the institutions of this state."

Principal Robert Powell of Jackson Agricultural School wrote Denny in May 1922 to recommend Ralph Adams for a clerical position at the University in the fall, saying that Adams was "an all-round dependable young man from every standpoint" and had earned the highest grades in his class for the last four years. "He is one of the best all-round students I have ever known," Powell added as he pointed out the numerous activities in which Adams had participated. Adams also wrote Denny, saying, "My college education depends on my getting work to get me through." Adams worked his way through the University in clerical positions and remained on the University staff for 26 years, serving in several administrative positions, including executive secretary and dean of administration and as acting president in 1947 between University presidents Raymond Paty and John Gallalee. When Adams resigned from the University on June 1, 1948, to join Coosa River Newsprint Corporation, a *Tuscaloosa News* editorial said, "His leaving brings a tug at the hearts of University of Alabama students, faculty and alumni. He was beloved at the University and was a living symbol of the 'greater University.'"

University alumni were enlisted as recruiters, too, and often recommended students or sent lists of prospective students from their areas for Denny to write. Attorney W. Emmett Perry of Birmingham wrote Denny in 1922 regarding a student from Lawrence County, saying, "Like the rest of us poor devils from Moulton, he must have a job if he attends college. Couldn't he by some means be given a job in the mess hall to pay his board?" Long-time Crimson Tide athletic booster Champ Pickens wrote Denny from St. Louis in 1917 to announce that Talty O'Connor would leave the next day on his way to the University. "He seems determined to make good. He has promised me to study and I trust that he will deliver. He is nothing but a boy and I would appreciate it if you would jolly him as bit until he gets over his homesickness." O'Connor played football at Alabama while earning a degree in engineering.

William Gray of Dadeville wrote Denny and University athletic officials in

December 1921 to suggest that they contact Dadeville senior Hoyt Winslett, an outstanding athlete who was also being recruited by Auburn. Denny wrote to Winslett, who visited the Capstone in the spring of 1922. Winslett family members said that after a brief, friendly visit, Denny gave the young man two options, saying, "If you want to become a farmer, you should go to Auburn. If you want to enjoy the finer things in life, you should come to Alabama." Winslett chose Alabama and played football on the 1923-26 teams, earning first-team All-America honors as a senior in 1926 and helping the Crimson Tide claim conference and national championships in 1925 and 1926. Nicknamed "Wu" because he resembled a movie character named Mr. Wu, Winslett became a prominent Tuscaloosa insurance executive and civic leader following his football career. His was active in many civic activities, included serving as state president of the Exchange Club, chairman of the Tuscaloosa Chapter of the American Red Cross and as a director of the Tuscaloosa Chamber of Commerce. Winslett was inducted into the Alabama Sports Hall of Fame in 1973 and was presented the Paul W. Bryant Alumni-Athlete Award in 1992 in recognition of his community service following his football career. In 1995, Winslett established the Wu and Louise Winslett Endowed Scholarship Fund at the University of Alabama for freshmen entering the University from Dadeville.

U. S. Representative Lister Hill, a 1914 University law school graduate, wrote Denny in June 1924 to request financial aid for a student from his Congressional district. "He is a magnificent boy who has worked in the afternoons all the time that he has attended high school, of fine ability, splendid character and untiring energy. I cannot conceive of a more worthy boy for a scholarship. Can you help us?" Hill wrote.

W. G. Little of Livingston, who introduced football at Alabama in 1892 as a transfer student, wrote Denny in October 1917 to say, "I have found a man who has a reputation as a good catcher and looks like a football player. He is anxious to come to the University but hasn't the money. He is willing to work at anything. Can you get him there?"

Attorney Joe Starnes of Guntersville sent Denny a long list of prospective students from Marshall County in 1922 with a note saying, "I am ready to serve in any capacity that I am able and to the utmost when the (Million Dollar) campaign is launched this fall. I never let an opportunity pass to say something for my alma mater. I know that I will never be able to repay the debt I owe her." Starnes, a World War I veteran and 1921 University law school graduate, served as a U. S. Congressman 1935-1945. As a major in the Alabama National Guard in 1931, Starnes commanded the National Guard troops who protected the African-American "Scottsboro Boys" from angry crowds at the Jackson County Courthouse during a trial that drew widespread attention.

Jasper Attorney Leo H. Pou wrote Denny in May 1922 to recommend a graduate of Walker County High School, calling the young man "a regular John Sparkman type of boy" and adding that "Alabama needs boys of his kind more than any other and I do not want her to lose him." Pou asked Denny to write to the young man's father in an effort to convince him to send him to the University.

In addition to appealing to enrolled University students at an assembly prior to summer break for many years, Denny wrote to the students once or twice during the summer, urging them to return to the University in the fall and to bring new students with them. In an August 1917 response to a Denny mid-summer letter, one student wrote, "I want to apologize for not answering your letter sooner. I am certainly ashamed of the way I did last year and if I do go back at all I am going there with the intention of succeeding. I think a man is a great deal of a coward that fails then gives up completely, so I certainly don't intend to give up. I am going to try again, and when I do come back there I am going to make good. I appreciate the friendly interest you have taken in me and I wish to thank you for it. I shall certainly never forget it. I would be glad if you would write me, Dr. Denny, and advise me what you think is best."

H. H. Vines of Dora, responding to Denny's letter urging him to return to school in the fall, wrote, "I know that what you say about the likelihood of not going to school again after once being interrupted is true. Because my 'rat' days are already past and I am no longer new down there, I consider the hardest portion to be over. Tell me, can I get a place (job) in the library? I think I could come if I could make some expenses."

Fox H. Harmon of Troy responded to Denny's second letter of the summer on August 8, 1924, reporting that "a good many boys from last year's senior class at Troy High School are going to the University next month. I have done my best to get all of them to go to college and as many of them as I could to the University. I know you will be glad to have all of them. Dr. Denny, in your last letter you stressed the point of how valuable it would be to me to return to school and that I really could not afford to quit school at this time. I grant your point and have long realized the true value of a good education, but that fact of itself will not keep me there. As I said in my other letter, I *must* have a job to help defray part of my expenses while attending the University.... If the tone of this letter seems wrong, kindly excuse it, but this is a very urgent matter to me. I am doing all I can to get you more students for the coming year and I will appreciate your help in return. Hoping to hear from you with favorable news." Notations on Harmon's letter included "Please tell me about Harmon" and "SH," meaning he was approved for a self-help position. Harmon got his job, completed his education at the University and enjoyed a career in banking and insurance. His younger brother Theo attended the University a few years later until he was fatally injured in an automobile accident near Reform as he and a fellow University student were driving to Starkville, Mississippi, to attend an Alabama-Mississippi State football game.

Denny did not give up on his students once they arrived on campus. One student who had dropped out of school after only one semester wrote to Denny on March 3, 1922, saying, "To date I have received two very encouraging letters from you and appreciate both. If I am able to save enough money I will be back at Alabama next September if you will give me a job there in order that I may be able to meet my expenses."

"I thank you very much for assuring me of my job next fall, and I assure you I am doing my best to get new students for the University this fall," wrote John Sparkman in response to his mid-summer letter in 1918. "I think I shall be able to bring several new ones back with me. At any rate, I shall try to do so."

"I received your letter a few days ago with reference to my coming back to school," a Mobile student wrote. "I expect to return if I can find work or can get my mess hall job back that I had last year. I have talked to several boys in regard to coming to the University this fall and think we will get some."

"If I return this fall I must have work," wrote an upperclassman from Troy. "Quite a few boys get room rent by staying in the power house, medical buildings and other places. Can I get one of those places next fall and a job in the power plant, picking up paper or sweeping?"

One student responded enthusiastically to Denny's inquiry about her return to school, writing, "Of course, I am coming back this fall. You could not keep me away! Am expecting to bring two new students with me. Hoping we go over the top in student enrollment in the fall."

"As you know, every student promised to return and to bring a new student, therefore I am doing my utmost to get as many as possible and I am sure every other student is doing the same," a student from Baltimore responded to his mid-summer letter.

"When you said you were deeply interested in me it made me feel so good," one student responded to a summer letter from Denny. "I am quite sure I will be back next year for I mean to show you and Dr. Barnwell what is in me…." Another wrote, "I am going to do my very best to return to the University next year. It is impossible for me to express to you my appreciation for the time you encouraged me to continue my studies when I was blue and despondent over one or two studies…. I see now the great folly I would have displayed had I pulled up and left school at that time."

A student from Starkville, Mississippi, answered Denny in 1920, writing, "Another letter came to me from you asking about prospective students for next year and I wish to give you the following names." The student sent the names and addresses of four prospects and confirmed that he would also be returning in the fall.

"I guess I should have written you before now to let you know that I am still planning to be back in school this fall. I realize as you said in your letter that my whole future is at stake now, and I want to make the best of the next few years," wrote another student.

One upperclassman responded from Malette, South Dakota, in 1920, writing, "Please pardon me for not writing you before now. I have been busy working in the wheat fields this summer. Your kind letter was forwarded to me from home about two weeks ago. Yes, it is my intention to be back at the University this fall; however it seems that it will be almost impossible unless I get some work to do down there. Please write me what the chances are of getting a job in the mess hall or sweeping in the dormitory."

In addition to hiring upperclassmen to recruit during the summer, Denny wrote to a number of other selected students to ask their assistance in recruiting efforts also. One such letter, dated May 28, 1920, stated: "Dear Friend: I am sending to a selected group of our student body this request for information concerning prospective students. I am counting on a prompt response to each request. I shall be greatly disappointed if this selected group fails to report, practically to a man. Please give the full name and address of each prospective student, indicating the exact intention expressed by each concerning his or her plans for next session. Please also sign your name at the end of the list of names." Denny took similar action during Christmas break as he gave upperclassmen lists of first-year students to contact to be sure they would return to school in January.

Few women attended college in 1912, but with the growth of public high schools at the time, Denny saw the opportunity and need to recruit and train more women, especially for teaching positions. The University of Alabama had fifty-five women students in 1905, thirty-eight in 1909 and fifty-five in 1912, but that number increased to eighty in 1915 after a women's dormitory (Tutwiler Hall) for fifty women opened in 1914. The number of women students jumped to 214 in 1920 after a fifty-room annex was added to Tutwiler Hall and increased to more than a thousand a decade later.

Denny had made it clear that the University was seeking women students on July 4, 1913, when he spoke to an Independence Day assembly of summer school students, almost all of whom were teachers in a position to help recruit students to the University. A *Tuscaloosa News* report on the Morgan Hall program said, "Dr. Denny took the occasion to state clearly and emphatically the position of the University, the capstone of the state's educational system, on the question of co-education. He said that here and there over the state the question is frequently raised as to whether the University wants young women students. In answer to the question, he said that most emphatically the University wants them. 'We have done everything that human ingenuity can do to let the young women of this commonwealth know that we welcome them to the University,' Denny declared. 'Over my own signature I have stated that fact a thousand times. There is not a young woman graduate of a regular, four-year high school in the state of Alabama during the years of 1912 and 1913 who has not received an invitation to attend the University of Alabama. Moreover, the trustees have set aside still another University building to be used as a dormitory for women. The acts of the University officials show that the institution welcomes young women students, and I declare to you five hundred teachers here assembled that the University's doors are wide open to them.'"

A University of Alabama photograph from Denny's early days shows him at work behind a cluttered desk in the cramped office he shared with the student assistants who typed the many letters he dictated each day. A September 13, 1912, *Tuscaloosa News* column on Denny talked about the unique signature found "at the end of the thousand letters that he writes every day. It looks like the ticket Loo June gives you for your laundry every Monday morning. Fortunately we do not have to read Dr. Denny's handwriting except in his signature and we can guess at that. Every time the bank gets a check they can't read, they charge it to Dr. Denny's account. Dr. Denny writes poorly partly because he is a genius and partly because he is always in a hurry.... Dr. Denny goes at his signature just as he goes at everything else—his fist clinched, his teeth set and his back up."

The estimate of a thousand letters a day was an exaggeration, of course, but perhaps only slightly. Even incomplete files show that Denny received as many as 600 letters from students and prospective students alone each month during May, June, July and August each year by the 1920s. Each letter presented a unique problem for Denny to solve and thus a response to dictate and another letter to sign, and that number related only to the recruitment and retention of students. The available files also include scores of letters each month related to other subjects, all of which saddled him with a heavy load of correspondence each day. The letters, typed on manual typewriters by student assistants who often made carbon copies for the files, were the most modern means of communication 1912-1937, however, and Denny spent much of his time writing, reading and answering mail.

One especially unusual letter dated January 27, 1921, came from a young woman in Birmingham who did not attend the University. After attending a University dance with a Young Women's Christian Association (YWCA) group from Birmingham, the girl wrote Denny a two-page letter providing details of her visit, the good time she had and that she had always "longed to go to the University." She then mentioned a certain boy and wrote, "Doctor, would you mind telling me, in reality, what kind of a boy he is and just what you think about him in general. I surely would appreciate it, and anything you might be kind enough to tell me would be treated strictly confidential...." The letter was not marked "answered," likely meaning that Denny elected not to play Cupid in the matter.

One letter, dated June 3, 1936, surely provided a feeling of great satisfaction to Denny. "Commencement is over for this year, but it is not complete for me until I thank you for your kindly care and consideration of me during my years at the University," the letter said. "Daddy told me from the beginning, 'You listen to Dr. Denny and you won't go wrong,' and I have learned that he was right."

A single day's mail for Denny might include a letter from the Tuscaloosa County Health Officer regarding the improvement of campus drainage to help eliminate mosquitos to aid in the fight against typhoid fever; a note from a faculty member regarding a leaky roof on his house; a letter from Denny to a parent regarding a student's poor academic standing; a stack of mid-term grades to review; a lengthy letter from a former student seeking advice or a recommendation for a job; a bid for a new building to review; scores of letters from prospective students seeking financial assistance; congratulatory letters to recently elected public figures at the state or national level; requests for speaking engagements; requests from professors for more space, heat or lighting in classrooms, and a hundred other subjects. Denny often scribbled in the margins of incoming mail as he contemplated a response, and even "graded" some of the letters by instinctively correcting spelling or grammar mistakes. A request for financial aid from one student included the underlined sentence, "The hard times have kinder got the hold on me." It was those hard times that Denny had resolved to help eliminate by helping to educate the youth of Alabama.

Denny (right) presents an honorary doctor of law degree to Florida senator and University alumnus Claude D. Pepper in May 1942.

16

Heeding the Call to Serve

"If it is the supreme function of the American college to equip young men to seize the immense possibilities that lie before them, the supreme test by which it will be measured will be its success or failure in fulfilling this function. What kind of man will it produce? That is the vital question."

—Dr. George H. Denny

Denny's primary goal as president of the University of Alabama was to educate the youth of the state in the short term and improve the lives of all citizens of the state in the long term. His test for gauging the success of the University in that process was by the kind of men and women it produced, and the results of that test, viewed today, show that Denny and the University of Alabama achieved his goals even beyond his vast imagination.

"The foremost task of the true college is not the training it gives in science and in letters but the emphasis that it puts upon character and upon service," Denny said as he defined the duties of college graduates beyond their chosen professions as "arousing public sentiment to the importance of education, energizing every conceivable movement designed to reduce crime and suffering and to make men better and happier and more prosperous and breaking down every barrier that would impede the onward march of men toward the substantial and the abiding in human progress."

Thousands of University graduates from Denny's quarter of a century as president 1912-1936 achieved outstanding success in their chosen fields of endeavor. Many of those graduates, empowered by knowledge and inspired to meet Denny's challenge to lead and serve, earned national acclaim in the fields of business, law, government, science, medicine, education, athletics and military service. Several, despite persecution from various groups, were recognized for their stands on civil rights, and one of them—Juliette Hampton Morgan—became one of the first casualties of the civil rights movement in 1957 in her home town of Montgomery.

Four former Denny students—three of whom probably would not have attended college without that first recruiting letter from Denny—had a dramatic and lasting impact not only on educational and cultural change in the state of Alabama but the entire nation. Inspired by Denny's charge of service, University of Alabama graduates Lister Hill, Carl Elliott, John Sparkman and Claude Pepper sponsored national legislation that has had and continues to have an impact on the lives of millions upon millions of Americans. These men alone would prove Denny's theories of education and illustrate the success of his work at the University of Alabama, but there are countless other examples.

Denny said in 1936 that 30,000 students had passed through the University of Alabama during his tenure as president of the institution. As a stickler for truth, Denny had probably actually counted them. There is no doubt that Denny left a lasting impression on each of those 30,000 students with his sermon-like speeches and fatherly relationships with most of them. Starting with his recruiting letters to high school seniors in 1912 and continuing with on-campus friendships and personal letters to each student during summer breaks, Denny maintained close contact with his students throughout their years at the Capstone. His inspirational speeches at student assemblies—often on subjects they probably had never before considered—at the start of each semester and on numerous other occasions, along with his visible and energetic presence at campus athletic events, further endeared him to his students. His letters offered hope and encouragement; the jobs he reserved for students helped pay their expenses; his wise counsel pointed them toward meaningful lives.

The students not only heard but heeded Denny's speeches on such subjects as truth, the essentials of success and the responsibilities of leadership and service in civic and governmental affairs beyond their professional fields. Denny often spoke of sending out men and women prepared to take their place as leaders in society and the world. A man of courage and confidence and a sense of duty and high purpose, Denny was the example of all that he envisioned for his students.

In one particular speech, given to various student gatherings and entitled "Certain Practical Duties of Educated Citizens," Denny listed one duty as that of "establishing and promoting a pure and enlightened public sentiment." Urging the education of the masses, including that of the African-American race, Denny said "an uneducated, unguided and debased public sentiment is the greatest curse that can afflict a nation.... Ignorance, so far from standing for the majesty of law and order, is the great fomenter of anarchy; it is the guarantee of nothing more than slavery. As long as the diseased condition characterizes public sentiment, law will continue to yield to lawlessness and mob violence will continue to exist. We are being constantly reminded in these latter days that in our own country an astonishingly large proportion of the population, tightly bound in the shackles of ignorance and prejudice, has already fallen to an appallingly low level, and that at some unexpected hour this slumbering mob is destined to rise, show its bloodthirsty hand and strike a fatal blow.... Men are beginning to recognize, as never before, the necessity for the education of all the people.... Liberal-hearted men of all sections are uniting to bring to pass a better era in our beloved section. The masses need to be educated and all good men should give of their sympathy and their substance to promote and stimulate this great movement."

Many of the students who attended the University of Alabama during Denny's tenure were surely destined for success wherever they might have gone. Many, however, would not have attended the University of Alabama or any other college without that initial letter from Denny inviting them to come and offering his personal assistance in securing a college education. Many of the students who accepted his invitation would not have remained in school without the jobs as janitors, waiters, groundskeepers, secretaries, coal rollers or firemen that Denny made possible for them. Some might not have remained in school without Denny's personal letters each summer encouraging them to return in the fall. Others might not have succeeded without his often fatherly and sometimes stern advice. All were surely inspired by Denny's impassioned words urging them to achieve, to lead and to serve.

Hill, one of the approximately 400 students at the University when Denny became president in January 1912, was among the first to heed Denny's words, and the two remained close friends until Denny's death in 1955. A 1915 University of Alabama law school graduate and organizer and first president of the University's Student Government Association, Hill served as a U. S. Representative and Senator for forty-five years and sponsored legislation to support many of the ideals and changes called for by Denny, including rural health care, rural libraries and universal educational opportunities. An *Encyclopedia of Alabama* biography of Hill calls him "Alabama's premier lawmaker of the twentieth century," saying he sponsored eighty pieces of legislation during almost half a century as a U. S. Representative and Senator 1923-1969.

Hill is widely known for his sponsorship of healthcare legislation, including the 1946 Hill-Burton Act, which provided federal financing for construction of non-profit hospitals and health facilities, and the 1963 Hill-Harris Act, which provided federal funds for the construction of facilities for the mentally retarded and mentally ill. Hill and Elliott also sponsored the Library Services and Construction Act of 1956, which provided federal funds for libraries and rural bookmobiles, and the National Defense Education Act of 1958, which offered low-interest loans for college students. These two acts alone greatly advanced Denny's educational ideals. Hill also sponsored the House version of the bill that created the Tennessee Valley Authority, the Rural Telephone Act, Rural Housing Act, the GI Bill of Rights and the Vocational Education Act. He supported many important public works projects that helped his home state, including deepening the Mobile ship channel, the building of the Gainesville Lock and Dam in Sumter County and the Tennessee-Tombigbee Waterway. Hill also supported President Franklin Roosevelt's New Deal programs and the Fair Labor Standards Act of 1938, which established the 40-hour work-week, raised the minimum wage from twenty-five cents an hour to forty cents an hour and restricted the use of child labor.

At the time of his death, a *New York Times* story said Hill had sponsored "some of the most important health and education legislation in the years after World War II. His slow, persistent efforts in behalf of social legislation made Hill, as much as any legislator of his generation, a key figure in bringing modern medical care and adequate educational facilities to every region of the United States." Calling him "a father of the National Institutes of Health," the story added that Hill "helped bring hospitals to poor and rural areas and contribute funds to build more than 9,000 medical facilities around the country. As a result, the number of people in the United States without access to a hospital declined from fifteen million in 1945 to fewer than two million in 1966." The story added that Hill had "done more for the health of Americans in modern times than any man outside the medical profession." Hill's work for health care could well have been inspired by Denny, who urged University trustees in 1942 to support change from a two-year medical school to a four-year program. "Such a need ought to appeal not only to the humanitarian impulse of our people, but also to the realization that taking this step will serve the economic and social interests of Alabama. The health of our citizenship is at stake. We must have more doctors and more hospital facilities," Denny said.

The son of a prominent Montgomery, Alabama, physician, Hill also studied at Columbia after earning a law degree at Alabama and was admitted to the Alabama Bar in 1916. He practiced law in Montgomery and served on the city's Board of Education 1917-1922 before being elected a U. S. Representative in 1923. He was appointed to the Senate in January 1938 and elected to the position three months later. Hill was reelected to four additional terms prior to his retirement in 1969 at age 74. His important Senate positions included serving as Majority Whip 1941-47 and chairman of the Senate Labor and Public Welfare Committee. Hill was awarded the Public Welfare Medal from the National Academy of Sciences in 1969 and received honorary degrees from thirteen colleges and universities, including the University of Alabama and Auburn University. He died in 1984 at age ninety.

A Hill letter to Denny in the 1920s—possibly at the time of Hill's election to Congress in 1923—spoke of Hill's high esteem for Denny. "As for you, my dear doctor, my heart was never more full of love and affection for you than it is this day, and I still claim you as my best and biggest friend. Your friendship for me in the past has been a boon to me and ever an inspiration to higher and nobler endeavor. I feel that if I have attained any success so far in life that you have played a big part in it. I feel a deep sense of obligation to you. Whenever I can serve you, I hope that you will not hesitate to command me," Hill wrote. The first page of the letter is missing from the incomplete Denny files available.

Elliott, Sparkman and Pepper also rose to national prominence in Congress, and, like Hill, sponsored and supported legislation that helped bring dramatic social and economic change not only to Alabama but to the entire nation. Significantly, it is entirely possibly that neither of them would have attended or completed college without Denny's personal influence and assistance, starting with his letters to them as seniors in high school. All three grew up in rural Alabama farm communities and had little or no means of paying for college. As he promised in his initial letters, however, Denny arranged campus jobs for each of them, as he did for a third of the students during his tenure, to help pay their college expenses. The achievements of these three men alone illustrate the high purpose and far-reaching success of Denny's work as president of the University of Alabama.

Elliott, the oldest of nine children from a Franklin County tenant farm family, was described by a former friend and classmate as one of the poorest students ever to attend the University of Alabama. "He had zero money when he came here in 1930," said Dr. James F. Doster of Tuscaloosa at age 101 in 2013. "He worked every job he could to stay in school and wore his ROTC uniform every day because it was warm and he didn't have any other clothes." Doster added that Elliott "had a brilliant career as a Congressman and was the father of the National Defense Education Act." Doster, who later followed in his father's footsteps and taught at the University for more than fifty years, said the two men remained friends until Elliott's death in 1999.

Writing in his autobiography, *The Cost of Courage: The Journey of an American Congressman*, Elliott said he was all but thrown out of Denny's office when he arrived at the University. "Go home; I don't have time for your troubles," Elliott quoted Denny as saying when he arrived on campus with only $2.38 in cash and a $25 check from a family friend in his home town of Vina. "But I wanted to go the University, so my friend Oscar Nix and I spent a rainy night under a truck and went to registration the next day anyway." Elliott said he bluffed his way through registration by saying he had made arrangements with Denny. With no money for dorm rent, Elliott said he and Nix "squatted" in the old Observatory with "two other students, rats and chinch bugs." Elliott, who had been valedictorian of his senior class at Vina High School, soon secured a job through Denny's self-help program and a year later became the "houseboy" at the President's Mansion, where he "cleaned floors, dusted, fetched groceries and helped Mrs. Denny with the flowerbeds," according to his autobiography. He wrote that he also worked as a waiter in the campus cafeteria and on the grounds crew, earning enough money to pay his way through college and even send some money home to help his family during the Depression. Elliott earned his undergraduate degree in 1933 and his law degree in 1936.

In preparation for his future political career, Elliott was elected president of the Student Government Association as an independent in 1935. He wrote that he approached his job as SGA president the same way he approached his job as a U. S. Congressman years later. "It was basically the less-privileged students who put me in office and they were my top priority," he said, adding that his first act was to build and place fifty "courting benches" on campus. Even with a heavy workload, Elliott made the honor roll each year as a student at the University and was elected to the Omicron Delta Kappa honorary fraternity. He also served on the staff of both the *Crimson White* and *Rammer Jammer*, in the YMCA cabinet, as an officer in the Philomathic Literary Society and the Alabama Spirit Committee. As SGA president in 1936, Elliott represented southern colleges before a joint House and Senate committee in Washington, D. C., where he urged approval of legislation to increase pay from $15 to $25 per month for college students employed in work-study programs under the New Deal's National Youth Administration.

After leaving the University, Elliott practiced law in Russellville briefly before moving to Jasper, where he served two terms as a local judge before defeating incumbent Carter Manasco, a 1929 University of Alabama law school graduate, in the 1948 race for Alabama's Seventh District seat in the U. S. House of Representatives. Elliott held the office from January 3, 1949, until January 3, 1965, serving on the House Veterans Committee, the Education and Labor Committee and the Rules Committee and chairing the Select Committee for Government Research. Remembering his plight as a penniless freshman in college, Elliott joined forces with Hill to co-author and sponsored the National Defense Education Act of 1958, which placed national emphasis on science and technology education and which has since provided low-interest loans for millions of college students. Elliott and Hill also co-authored the Library Services and Construction Act of 1956, which provided library services, including rural bookmobiles, to more than 300 U. S. counties, including twenty-two in Alabama.

Writing of his motivation for drafting the National Defense Education Act, Elliott said, "It was mainly through a program of college and university scholarships and loans for deserving students that I could see us making a life-changing breakthrough, not just for the tens of thousands of young men and women who couldn't afford to attend college at this time, but for millions more just like them in generations to come. The statement I made to open our subcommittee hearings on August 12, 1957, pretty much summed up my feelings then and now about the essential need of making this nation's seats of higher learning available to any deserving young man or woman, regardless of their resources. The words I said then, I believe, are every bit as true today: America's future success at home and abroad, in peace or war, depends on the education of her citizens. Democracy is based on that foundation. Whatever happens in America's classrooms during the next fifty years will eventually happen to America." In echoing the words of Denny from decades earlier, Elliott added, "For decades we in this land have exerted every possible pressure to guarantee the preservation and proper utilization of our natural resources. Yet our need for better prepared personnel has received relatively scant attention. We read about the need in newspapers and magazines. We hear it over the airways. From businesses and professions and from research agencies come constant appeals for educated men and women. Our shortage of engineers, physicists, chemists, teachers, statisticians, doctors, librarians, nurses, executives and other skilled workers has long been described as acute and sometimes desperate. These shortages are not shortages of inborn ability. America is rich in native intelligence; we need only to shape our talents, to educate with discernment, to develop to the utmost the latent endowments everywhere among us, to train each boy and girl to the highest attainable degree, consistent with his or her ambition."

Political maneuvering by Alabama's segregationist governor George Wallace and attacks from right-wing groups like the Ku Klux Klan cost Elliott his seat in Congress in 1965, and with Wallace ineligible to succeed himself in 1966, Elliott chose to run for governor. Wallace outmaneuvered Elliott, Alabama Attorney General Richmond Flowers and former governors John Patterson and James Folsom in the Democratic Primary, however, by running his wife, Lurleen Burns Wallace. Mrs. Wallace won the nomination then defeated Republican James D. Martin in the general election to return Wallace to power. Elliott, a liberal by 1966 standards when he spoke out against the Ku Klux Klan and called for racial tolerance and federal assistance for the needy of all races, finished third in the primary and was left with a large campaign debt. Elliott served briefly on the president's Library Commission and in the U. S. Department of Commerce in the late 1960s before returning to Jasper to practice law during his final years. He also wrote his biography, a history of Red Bay, seven volumes of histories of area coal miners and five volumes of area history called "Annals of Northwest Alabama," but he did not return to politics.

Elliott received national recognition for his efforts in improving educational opportunities for America's youth and for opposing racism when he became the first recipient of the John F. Kennedy Profile in Courage Award in 1990. The award, given by the John F. Kennedy Library Foundation, was presented by late Senator Edward M. Kennedy in Boston. Elliott's Profile in Courage Award was presented to the University of Alabama Libraries in 2015 and is on display in the Gorgas Library foyer alongside Denny's portrait. Elliott was inducted into the Alabama Academy of Honor in 1977 and was featured in the one-hour television documentary "Conscience of a Congressman: The Life and Times of Carl Elliott," produced as an episode of *The Alabama Experience* series by the University of Alabama Center for Public Television and Radio. He died in 1999 at age eighty-five. The Carl Elliott Federal Building and the Carl Elliott Regional Library in Jasper are named in his honor and his former home in Jasper is open to the public as a museum of his life and career.

"I became aware early in my life that brains and ability knew no economic, racial or other distinctions," Elliott wrote in his autobiography. "When the Good Lord distributed intellectual ability, I am sure he did so without regard to the color or station in life of the recipient. In my case, I dedicated my public life to ensuring in every way possible that the sons and daughters of the working men and women of the nation would have the opportunity to achieve the highest level of education commensurate with their ability, unfettered by economic, racial or other artificial barriers. I am proud of the accomplishments that have been made to that end, but our work is not yet finished. As long as we have overcrowded classrooms, underpaid teachers, schools with inadequate libraries and young men and women who are denied an education because they do not have the resources, our work is not yet finished. The thing I cherish today more than any award or honor is the National Defense Education Act. It is still putting equipment into schools, still training teachers and still giving good students an opportunity to go to college. More than twenty million students have taken that opportunity, and I consider them my family in a way, sort of like my own children. There were those who said I was ahead of my time, but they were wrong. I believe I was always behind the times that ought to be," Elliott added.

Sparkman, the seventh of eleven children, needed only an opportunity to achieve great success in life, and Denny, through his persistence, provided that opportunity. The son of a tenant farmer and deputy sheriff, Sparkman attended a one-room elementary school then walked four miles a day to Morgan County High School in Hartselle. When he graduated in 1917, like every other high school graduate in the state, Sparkman received a personally signed letter of congratulations from Denny urging him to consider attending the University of Alabama and to write back regarding his future plans. When Denny received no response from his initial letter, he sent a second letter, again offering his personal assistance, a possible part-time job and urging Sparkman to write back. Finally, on August 26, 1917, Sparkman responded. "Dear sir: I received both of your letters of recent date and was only waiting about answering them until I could find out whether or not it would be possible for me to attend college this year," Sparkman began. "I appreciate very much the help and information you have so kindly given me, and I am glad to say that if nothing comes in my way to hinder, I shall be at the University on the tenth of next month with the expectation of securing some kind of work later on by which I may partly pay for my expenses. Thanking you for all past favors and hoping that by your help I may quickly obtain work, I remain very truly yours, John Sparkman."

Sparkman was given a job as a fireman in the power house, which meant he shoveled coal in the boiler room, and he kept it most of his six-plus years at the

University, along with several other jobs. In response to Denny's usual letter to all students in the summer of 1918, Sparkman provided the names of five prospective students from his home area and said that he indeed planned to return to the University in the fall. "If I do, I shall need some assistance in getting through," Sparkman wrote. "Last year I was, as perhaps you know, a fireman in the power house. If possible, I should like to have this position again this year." The letter, which was addressed to Dr. James J. Doster while Denny was serving with the Food Administration in Washington during World War I, had a hand-written "Job Held" notation showing that Sparkman returned to his old job. In a similar response to a Denny letter in July 1922, Sparkman wrote from Blue Ridge, North Carolina, where he had a summer job, "In reply to the letter I received from you yesterday, I wish to say that I appreciate very much the place in the power house for this coming year and most gladly accept it. I will be there when school opens in September unless unavoidably prevented."

Sparkman excelled at the University, making the honor roll 1918, 1919 and 1920; serving as president of Quadrangle; president of the Student Government Association (1921-22); editor of the *Crimson White* (1920-21); earning membership in Jasons, Omicron Delta Kappa and Phi Beta Kappa and being named outstanding senior in 1921. While still working his way through school as secretary of the YMCA and part-time instructor, Sparkman earned a law degree in 1923 and a master's degree in history in 1924 before returning to north Alabama to teach and practice law in Huntsville 1924-35. He was also active in civic and religious organizations in Huntsville, serving as president of the Huntsville Chamber of Commerce, district governor of Kiwanis and a Sunday school teacher.

When U. S. Representative Archibald H. Carmichael (UA Law, 1886) chose not to seek reelection in 1936, Sparkman ran for the Eighth District seat against four other opponents and was elected in a runoff to start a forty-three-year career in Congress. He served in the House until 1946, when he was elected to the Senate, where he served until retirement on January 3, 1979. As a member of the House, Sparkman supported much of President Roosevelt's New Deal programs, including the Tennessee Valley Authority, which greatly benefited his district. As a member of the House Military Affairs Committee, he also supported increased military spending in preparation for World War II and was instrumental in locating Redstone Arsenal in Huntsville.

According to the *Encyclopedia of Alabama*, Sparkman formed a close relationship with Hill in the U. S. Senate that "led many observers to contend that Alabama's two senators were the most able and effective in Congress" during their twenty years together in the Senate. Sparkman and Hill "collaborated to pour hundreds of millions of federal dollars into Alabama," the *Encyclopedia* said. After being named chairman of the Banking and Currency's subcommittee on housing in 1949, Sparkman sponsored legislation that helped middle-class Americans buy homes and supported additional legislation to provide housing for low-income families. "Sparkman shrewdly used his growing clout in Congress to help both the poor and needy and the business interests that could help him," the *Encyclopedia* said, adding that he was also instrumental in the development of the Marshall Space Flight and Rocket Center in Huntsville.

Democrats chose Sparkman as presidential candidate Adlai Stevenson's vice presidential running mate in 1952 but the team was defeated by the Republican ticket of Dwight D. Eisenhower and Richard M. Nixon. Sparkman became chairman of the Committee on Banking and Currency in 1967 but gave up that position in 1975 to become chairman of the Committee on Foreign Relations, which he held until his retirement in January 1979. He died of a heart attack on November 16, 1985, at age eighty-five.

Although he was the son of a poverty-stricken sharecropper family from east Alabama, Pepper managed to graduate from high school in Camp Hill in 1917, but he could not afford to attend the University of Alabama even with Denny's promise of a job to help pay his expenses. Denny wrote Pepper at least three letters, and even wrote directly to Pepper's father in his efforts to recruit Pepper. After writing to Denny on August 31 that he would attend school in the fall of 1917, he wrote again a week later to say that his plans had changed. "It is indeed with shame and regret that I tell you of my inability to come to the University this term after positively telling you that I would come," Pepper wrote on September 9. "As you know, Dr. Denny, in my letters to you I told you of my financial condition and asked you to secure employment for me. This you did. But there still remained a considerable amount of money that I would need. The only way that I could have secured this money at present would have been for me or my father to have borrowed it. Then I would have been forced to work next year to return the borrowed money. On account of my age, I determined to work this coming year then be able to enter the University next year without embarrassment either to myself or to my parents. I have tried to follow the wisest course in the matter. Please don't think that I am little enough to have been blinded by the offer of a little job. I will be at the University next September and will be there for a diploma. I appreciate what you have done for me and I count you as a friend while I boost the University."

Pepper taught school in Dothan and worked in a Bessemer steel mill before entering the University in September 1918 with some savings and a job as a waiter in the student-operated cafeteria. He soon rose to a management position in the cafeteria and often sought advice from Denny in its operation. In a written response to a Pepper request for advice, Denny wrote, "I cannot give the time necessary to look after every minute detail. I can say, however, with the utmost frankness, that the mess hall will be a colossal failure unless there is sound financial administration." Pepper pushed himself through the University of Alabama in three years while participating in several extracurricular activities, including serving on the *Crimson White* staff, *Corolla* board, varsity debate team, YMCA cabinet, Forensic Council, cross country track team, president of the Philomathic Literary Society and secretary-treasurer of the Students' Boarding Association. He was elected to membership in Phi Beta Kappa, Jasons and Omicron Delta Kappa honor societies. Pepper graduated from the University in 1921 and earned a law degree from Harvard in 1924.

After teaching law at the University of Arkansas for a short time, Pepper moved to Perry, Florida, where he opened a law practice. He was elected to the Florida House of Representatives in 1929, but lost in a bid for reelection and moved to Tallahassee. He was defeated in a race for the U. S. Senate in 1934, but won a 1936 special election to fill the seat of Senator Duncan Fletcher, who had died. He served as a senator from November 4, 1936, until January 3, 1951, having been defeated by Representative George Smathers in 1950. Pepper was not easily deterred, however; as he had written to Denny while in law school at Harvard, "I have never heard that failure was sufficient excuse to entitle one to quit trying." And Pepper did not quit trying. He was elected to the U. S. House of Representatives in 1962, took office on January 3, 1963, and served his state and nation in Washington until his death on May 30, 1989.

Pepper, like Hill, Elliott and Sparkman, was known as a liberal in Washington from the start, when he supported President Roosevelt's New Deal programs. "He was unusually articulate and intellectual, and, collaborating with labor unions, he was often the leader of the liberal-left forces in the Senate," his 2013 *Wikipedia* biography claimed. The biography added that his reelection in 1938 "solidified his reputation as the most prominent liberal in Congress." He supported the Fair Labor Standards Act of 1938 and sponsored the 1941 Lend-Lease Act, which provided military aid to foreign allies such as Great Britain, China and Russia during World War II. Pepper's support for universal health care and other liberal ideas reportedly led to his defeat by Smathers, who had the support of President Harry Truman.

Pepper was elected from a newly created district in the Miami area in 1962 and over the next twenty-six years became known as the "grand old man of Florida politics" as he held a number of important positions. He chaired the Joint House-Senate Committee on Crime in the early 1970s, became chairman of the House Select Committee on Aging in 1977 and was elected chairman of the House Rules Committee in 1983. As chairman of the Committee on Aging, Pepper gained national recognition as the nation's leading advocate for senior citizens. His accomplishments included strengthening Medicare, reforming the Social Security system and helping secure passage of a law abolishing most mandatory retirement ages. He was featured on the cover of *Time* Magazine in 1938 and 1983, received the annual Jefferson Award for Greatest Public Service Benefitting the Disadvantaged in 1982 and was featured on a thirty-three-cent Distinguished Americans series postage stamp in 2000. He died in his sleep on May 26, 1989, just four days after being presented the Presidential Medal of Freedom by President George H. W. Bush. Pepper has been honored in Florida by having a number of landmarks named in his honor. These include the Claude Pepper Federal Building in Miami, the Claude Pepper Memorial Highway, the Claude Pepper Center at Florida State University and several public schools. The National Institutes of Health in Bethesda, Maryland, also has a building named for him. Pepper's many honors included an honorary LL.D degree from the University of Alabama in 1942 while Denny was serving as interim president following the death of Dr. Richard C. Foster. Pepper also received the 1984 University of Alabama Hugo Black Award in recognition of his distinguished service to Alabama and the nation.

Denny spoke often of the need for greater access to higher education, the importance of libraries, adequate health care for rural communities, leadership and service by educated men and "more civilized" living conditions for the poor. Hill, Elliott, Sparkman and Pepper heard his call to arms and carried his flag to Washington, where, during a combined 144 years in Congress, they passed legislation fulfilling many of Denny's visions and raised living standards for millions of Americans. Denny asked his students to be more than what they studied to be. Hill, Sparkman, Elliott and Pepper studied law, but they became much more as they carried the Denny torch forward. Denny died on April 2, 1955, only months before Elliott and Hill wrote, sponsored and helped pass the 1956 Library Services and Construction and the 1958 National Defense Education acts. One can only imagine Denny's pride had he lived until then.

With Denny's urging, former University of Alabama students had a major impact on state government also, and Denny maintained close contact with those alumni throughout his tenure as president and chancellor of the University. In 1935, University alumni had claimed the last three Alabama governorships while sixteen state senators and thirty members of the state house of representatives were also University alumni. In addition, the state's two U. S. senators and seven U. S. congressmen were University alumni. In a May 1938 memo to University president Richard Foster following the state Democratic Primary elections, Denny sent a "scorecard" of the election results showing that University of Alabama alumni had apparently gained a majority in the senate. "This is the best showing in many years. It is a fine group. I congratulate them and you," Denny wrote with the added note that Law School dean Albert Farrah should write "his boys." Denny, and Foster after him, made a practice of sending congratulatory letters to all elected officials. The list of University of Alabama alumni claiming state primary wins in May 1938 included lieutenant governor Albert A. Carmichael (1915) and sixteen senators, twelve of whom attended the University during Denny's tenure as president.

Denny was honored at a special dinner hosted by the Alabama Congressional delegation in Washington in 1948. Attendees included area University alumni and friends along with the Alabama Congressional delegation of Senators Hill and Sparkman and Representatives Sam Hobbs (UA, 1908), Albert M. Raines (UA, 1928), Pete Jarman (UA, 1913), Manasco (UA, 1929), Robert E. Jones Jr. (UA, 1937), Laurie C. Battle (UA, 1946), George W. Andrews (UA, 1928), George M. Grant (UA, 1922) and Frank Boykin (no college) and Florida Senator Claude Pepper (UA, 1921). University of Alabama alumni held all but one of the state's Congressional seats at the time and only Hobbs, Battle and Boykin did not attend the University during Denny's tenure as president.

Denny's speech on the duties of educated citizens also included the quotation that "nothing is politically right which is morally wrong," and several of his students seem to have recalled that message as they courageously defended the civil rights of African-Americans even as they faced personal persecution during the 1950s and 1960s. Juliette Hampton Morgan, Hazel Brannon Smith, Gould Beech, Nina Miglionico and Clifford Judkins Durr are among several University of Alabama graduates who not only joined the civil rights movement but played leadership roles.

Morgan, a 1934 Phi Beta Kappa graduate, was an outspoken critic of the mistreatment of African-Americans by Montgomery bus drivers long before the arrest of Rosa Parks and Reverend Martin Luther King's involvement in the Montgomery bus boycott of the late 1950s. Morgan earned a master's degree at the University in 1935 and remained at the University to teach English for three years before returning to her home town of Montgomery, where she spent the remaining eighteen years of her life as a teacher and librarian. Because of an anxiety disorder that prevented her from driving, Morgan rode segregated city buses to and from work each day and often saw African-American riders abused by white bus drivers. In addition to often immediately objecting to racial abuse on the buses, she began writing letters to the editor of the *Montgomery Advertiser* to protest the abuse and other social injustices as early as 1939, according to various published biographies.

According to a biography produced by the Southern Poverty Law Center, a Morgan letter published in the Advertiser in 1952 said in part, "Are people really naïve enough to believe that Negroes are happy, grateful to be pushed around and told they are inferior and ordered to 'move on back'? They may take it for a long time, but not forever." African-American passenger Rosa Parks was arrested on December 1, 1955, for refusing to give up her bus seat to a white passenger, prompting a boycott of city buses by African-Americans. A Morgan letter published in the December 12 Advertiser said, "The Negroes of Montgomery seem to have taken a lesson from Gandhi. Their task is greater than Gandhi's, however, for they have greater prejudice to overcome. It is hard to imagine a soul so dead, a heart so hard, a vision so blinded and provincial as not to be moved with admiration at the quiet dignity, discipline and dedication with which the Negroes have conducted their boycott." The Southern Poverty Law Center biography added that Morgan received threatening letters and telephone calls and that the mayor of Montgomery demanded that she be fired from her job at the city library because of her public stand. The library director refused to fire Morgan, but did ask her stop writing letters to the editor.

Morgan wrote Tuscaloosa News publisher Buford Boone in January 1957 to support his call for patience, tolerance and obedience to the law at a January 5 White Citizens' Council gathering in Tuscaloosa. "I believe that if we really stand for liberty and justice, it must be for all," Boone told the group. Morgan's letter to Boone congratulated him for his "wise and courageous" speech, saying "There are many Southerners from various walks of life that know that you are right. They know the (Supreme) Court is right; they know that what they call 'our Southern way of life' must inevitably change, but they are afraid to express themselves. Everyone who speaks as you do, who has the faith to do what he believes right in scorn of the consequences, does great good in preparing the way for a happier and more equitable future for all Americans. I had begun to wonder if there were any men in the state—any white men—with any sane evaluation of our situation here in the middle of the twentieth century, with any good will, and most especially any moral courage to express it. It is now time to get on with a job that we have put off far too long—full citizenship, equal rights and respect for all people. If the University has any lesson in its hall of learning more important than that, I am unaware of it," she added. Morgan's letter to Boone was not meant for publication, but Boone convinced her to allow him to print it, and it was published in the January 14, 1957, edition of the News. Sheryl Spradling Summe, writing in "Stepping Out of the Shadows: Alabama Women 1819-1990," said Morgan's letter to Boone was also reprinted in the March issue of the States' Rights Advocate, a monthly publication of the Montgomery White Citizens' Council, resulting in Morgan receiving additional threats and criticism from friends and co-workers. She took a leave of absence from work for treatment of her anxiety problems in early summer, but soon after returning to work and facing additional harassment, including having the windows in the home she shared with her mother shattered and a cross burned in her yard, she resigned from her job and committed suicide, leaving a note that said. "I am not going to cause any more trouble to anybody," according to a Wikipedia biography.

Morgan, only forty-three years old at the time of her death, was inducted into the Alabama Women's Hall of Fame on March 3, 2005, and on November 1, 2005, the Montgomery City Council voted to name the city's main public library the Juliette Hampton Morgan Memorial Library in her honor.

Hazel Brannon Smith, a native of Gadsden and a 1935 University graduate, became the first woman to win a Pulitzer Prize for editorial writing in 1964 when her editorials in the Lexington *Advertiser* supported the civil rights movement in Holmes County, Mississippi. In honoring Smith, the Pulitzer panel praised her for "steadfast adherence to her editorial duty in the face of great pressure and opposition," recognizing the fact that one of her four newspapers was bombed and others boycotted by advertisers because of her public stand on civil rights. A biography of Smith by Joanne Sloane in "Women Who Made a Difference in Alabama" said Smith modestly accepted the Pulitzer Prize by saying, "All we have done is try to meet honestly the issues as they arose. We did not ask for nor run from this fight with the White Citizens' Council. But we have given it all we have, nearly ten years of our lives, loss of financial security and a big mortgage. We would do the same thing over again. My interest has been to print the truth and protect and defend the freedom of all Mississippians. It will continue."

Smith, a former women's editor and assistant managing editor of the *Crimson White* while a student at the University, used a $3,000 loan to purchase her first weekly newspaper (the Durant *News)* in 1936 and bought the *Advertiser* four years later. She added the Flora *Banner County Outlook* and the Jackson *Northside Reporter* to her group in 1956 in a successful start to a career as owner, publisher and editor that spanned almost fifty years. According to a March 2008 article by Mark Newman in *Mississippi History Now*, Smith's editorials and columns under the heading "Through Hazel's Eyes" often focused on gambling, bootlegging, political corruption, social injustices and civil rights issues. In 1954, she condemned the shooting of a young black man by the local sheriff, saying the shooting "violated every concept of justice, decency and right." The editorials drew the ire of the Holmes County White Citizens' Council, which started a rival newspaper in 1958 and pressured advertisers to boycott the *Advertiser*. The group also pressured the local hospital to fire Smith's husband from his administrative job. Smith maintained her editorial stance, however, condemning the lynching of an African-American man by a white mob in 1959 and calling for an end to violence against civil rights activists. Newman wrote that a 1964 Smith editorial welcomed civil rights workers to Holmes County to begin a voter registration drive by saying, "These young people wouldn't be here if we had not largely ignored our responsibilities to our Negro citizens." Newman added that Smith also entertained civil rights leader Martin Luther King Jr. as a house guest in the summer of 1964. Her *Northside Reporter* newspaper office was bombed during the same summer.

Despite Smith's long and courageous support of the civil rights movement, Newman's article said African-Americans "broke with her when she began criticizing their leadership for a black boycott of Lexington's white merchants in 1973 and accusing them of intimidating other African-Americans." Even then, she remained unreconciled with whites, according to Newman. Smith sold two of her newspapers in the 1970s in an attempt to continue to publish the *Advertiser*. Smith's husband died in 1983 and she filed for bankruptcy two years later, citing indebtedness of more than $250,000, according to Newman's article. Smith spent her final years in a nursing home in Cleveland,

Tennessee. She died May 14, 1994, shortly after viewing "A Passion for Justice: The Hazel Brannon Smith Story," a television movie about her life starring Jane Seymour in the title role.

In addition to the Pulitzer Prize, Smith received recognition from the National Federation of Press Women in 1946 and 1955; the National Headliner Award from Theta Sigma Phi in 1952; the Herrick Award for Editorial Writing in 1956; a 1957 Mississippi Press Association award; the Elijah Lovejoy Award for Courage in Journalism in 1960; the Golden Quill Editorial Award from the International Conference of Weekly Newspaper Editors in 1963; the Woman of Achievement award from the Mississippi Press Women in 1971; the Fannie Lou Hamner Award for community service in 1993, and was named Woman of Conscience by the National Council of Women in 1964. She served as president of the Mississippi Press Women 1956-58 and as president of the International Society of Weekly Newspaper Editors 1981-82. She was also honored by the National Federation of Press Women as its Woman of Achievement in 1972 and inducted into the Mississippi Press Association Hall of Fame in 1987.

Gould Beech, a 1934 University graduate and former *Crimson White* editor, became a well-known journalist and liberal political activist. Beech, who had worked for *The Anniston Star*, *Montgomery Advertiser* and *Southern Farmer*, helped run James E. "Big Jim" Folsom's victorious populist gubernatorial campaign in 1946, incurring the wrath of powerful business and agricultural interests in the process. Beech moved to Houston, Texas, in 1950, where he was involved in several political campaigns, including helping Barbara Jordan—later a U. S. Congresswoman—become the first black woman elected to the Texas state senate. Beech's editorials as a journalist in Alabama included voicing opposition to the state's poll tax, which disenfranchised many blacks and poor whites, and other political and social injustices. The editorials brought criticism and harassment from opposing groups and prompted Beech's move to Texas. A native of Florence, Beech was inducted into the University of Alabama College of Communications and Information Sciences Hall of Fame in 2002.

Judkins Durr, a 1919 Capstone graduate and Rhodes Scholar who studied at Oxford, earned a law degree and eventually became a noted civil rights activist, is another former Denny student who helped bring social and cultural change to his state and nation. Durr practiced law in Birmingham until 1933, when he went to Washington to accept a legal position with the Reconstruction Finance Corporation, a New Deal agency in the Roosevelt Administration. Durr was recommended for the position by Alabama Senator and future Supreme Court Justice Hugo Black, whose wife was the sister of Durr's wife. Durr spent seven years with the RFC before being appointed to the Federal Communications Commission (FCC), where he focused on protecting the public interest and became an advocate for public access channels for community participation. He resigned from the FCC in 1948 in protest of President Harry Truman's Loyalty Oath order, which he felt violated his individual rights, and established a private law practice that focused almost exclusively on civil liberties cases, according to the *Encyclopedia of Alabama*. Durr drew the close interest of the Federal Bureau of Investigation (FBI) when he became president of the liberal National Lawyers Guild in 1949, and in 1951 he moved back to Alabama and set up a law practice in Montgomery. Many of Durr's cases in Montgomery involved civil rights issues and included his participation in the defense of Rosa Parks, a black woman whose arrest for refusing to give up her seat on a city bus to a white person in December 1955 focused national attention on civil rights issues in Alabama. According to the *Encyclopedia of Alabama*, Durr was praised by eulogists following his death in 1975 as "an honest and principled lawyer and public servant and a devout man who worked tirelessly to support the Bill of Rights, his country and family." Durr's wife, Virginia Foster Durr, was also a prominent civil rights advocate.

Nina Miglionico, the daughter of Italian immigrants who earned a law degree from the University of Alabama in 1936, was a leading political activist in her home town of Birmingham before, during and after the city's often-violent civil rights struggles of the 1960s. Miglionico, who practiced law for seventy-three years before her death at age ninety-five in 2009, was the first woman elected to the Birmingham City Council and fought for gender and racial equality through numerous organizations for decades. Like many other civil rights activists of the era, Miglionico received telephone threats and hate mail for her liberal stance on racial issues. She also had a bomb, which was disarmed by her father, placed on her front porch in 1965 during her first term on the Birmingham City Council and a cross was burned in her yard in 1974. She was elected to the city council in 1963 and served until her retirement in 1985, including serving as council president 1978-81. She was also the first woman in Alabama nominated to a Congressional seat by a major party (Democrats) in 1974, but lost to incumbent Republican John Buchanan.

Miglionico, who graduated first in her class at Howard College (now Samford University) in 1933 before attending law school at the University of Alabama, was an early advocate for the elimination of poll taxes; allowing women to serve on juries; improving prison conditions; revising the probate laws of descent and distribution to grant women the same rights as men, and improving child labor conditions. She served as president of the Alabama Merit System League, the Alabama Federation of Business and Professional Women's Clubs and the National and Alabama Association of Women Lawyers and was one of the original board members of the Alabama Women's Hall of Fame. She also served in leadership roles in the American Association of University Women and the Zonta Club. She served nationally on the Citizens Advisory Committee to the Commissioner of Internal Revenue and on the 1961 President's Commission on the Status of Women that recommended passage of the Equal Pay Act of 1964 and other actions to reduce gender bias in the workplace. Always a groundbreaker, Miglionico was the first woman elected president of the Alabama League of Municipalities and the only woman among two-hundred-fifty attendees at the 1959 American Bar Association House of Delegates. She was named Birmingham's Woman of the Year in 1963, received the Margaret Brent Award from the American Bar Association as one of the five outstanding women lawyers in the United States in 1996 and inducted into the Birmingham Gallery of Distinguished Citizens in 2008, the Alabama Lawyer's Hall of Fame in 2011 and the Alabama Women's Hall of Fame in 2012.

The educational philosophy of the University of Alabama during Denny's tenure—rooted in the ideals of Jefferson, Franklin and Lee and refined by Denny to meet the needs of the state—produced a number of home-grown faculty and staff members during the Denny era to keep his philosophy alive for decades. Richard C.

Foster, the prominent Tuscaloosa attorney who succeeded Denny as University of Alabama president on January 1, 1937, was one of those. Foster served impressively as president—with Denny in an active advisory role as chancellor—until his untimely death on November 19, 1941. A 1914 University law school graduate, Foster earned the admiration of his community as a civic leader and served in the state legislature before being chosen as Denny's successor at age 41. As president of the University, Foster quickly gained regional and national recognition for his leadership and administrative skills as well as his professional demeanor.

Other home-grown faculty and staff members who remained on campus or later returned to the Capstone included Hudson Strode (1913), professor of English and creative writing 1916-1963; Clarence Cason (1917), professor of journalism 1928-35; Brooks Forehand (1921, 1924), long-time professor of English and head of the English department; Dr. Eric Rodgers (1931, 1932), professor of physics and dean of the graduate school during a thirty-eight-year career ending in 1971; Dr. James F. Doster (1932), professor of history for fifty-two years; Dr. Charles Summersell (1929, 1930), professor of history for forty-three years; William F. Adams (1924, 1928), math professor, assistant dean of the School of Arts and Sciences and dean of admissions for more than three decades; Fred Maxwell (1912), professor of engineering and consulting engineer 1920-1956; Dr. Walter B. Jones (1918, 1920), state geologist and director of the Alabama Museum of Natural History 1927-61; Paul "Bear" Bryant (1937), who posted a 232-46-9 record as Alabama's head football coach 1958-83 after hearing "Mama" call him home; Jeff Coleman (1928), business manager of athletics, manager of the University Supply Store and director of alumni affairs for twenty-seven years during a fifty-four-year career at the University, and William E. Pickens (1928), who served as secretary to Denny as a student and later returned to the University to serve in the positions of bursar, comptroller and treasurer from 1935-1975. A careful analysis of any of these men—most of whom came from modest backgrounds—will quickly show that they shared many of Denny's ideals of service, dedication to duty and the uplifting of others.

Bryant not only serves as a highly visible example of the success of Denny's efforts in the area of athletics but as an example of the far-reaching residual effects of that success. Bryant, an All-State football player from rural Arkansas, was drawn to the University of Alabama because of the Crimson Tide's Rose Bowl teams of 1925, 1926 and 1930. He played on Alabama's January 1, 1935, national championship Rose Bowl team and remained with the Crimson Tide as an assistant coach 1936-1939. After serving in the Navy during World War II, Bryant earned a national reputation as head coach at Maryland, Kentucky and Texas A&M 1946-1957 before returning to the Capstone after the school's worst three-year record (4-24-2) in history under former Tide player J. B. Whitworth. In accepting the position of head coach at the University of Alabama in December 1957, Bryant requested a salary equal only to that of the highest paid professor at the time. That professor was noted author and English and creative writing professor Hudson Strode, whose salary was $17,500 per year. Bryant quickly revived the Alabama program and Crimson Tide football teams averaged 9.3 wins per season over his twenty-five-year tenure as head coach, winning six national championships, thirteen conference titles and going to twenty-two consecutive bowl games. Bryant had a career record of 323 wins, 85 losses and 17 ties in thirty-eight years as a head coach and retired with more wins, more national championships, more conference championships and more bowl appearances that any college coach in history. Another Bryant record includes the number of former players and assistants (fifty-four) who later became head coaches at the college or professional level, with most of those getting their start with a personal boost from Bryant. Two of Bryant's former players— Mike Riley at Nebraska and Joey Jones at the University of South Alabama—were still serving as head coaches in 2015 and a former Bryant assistant, Bruce Arians, was head coach of the Phoenix Cardinals of the National Football League.

Bryant's unprecedented success brought widespread publicity to the University, of course, attracting more students and rallying alumni support that brought increased financial contributions to the school, just as the football success during the Denny era had done. Denny had recognized the value of successful athletic programs decades earlier, and it was his emphasis on winning teams that brought the University its first national football acclaim, along with such out-of-state students as Bryant. In an unprecedented gesture prior to his death in January 1983, Bryant established a scholarship fund at the University to assist children of his Crimson Tide players in attending college. Records indicate that more than six hundred children of former Alabama football players have attended the University with financial assistance from the Bryant Scholarship, further extending not only Bryant's reach but the reach of the University of Alabama and Denny in his goal of bringing social, economic and cultural change to the state of Alabama and beyond.

Paul W. Bryant Jr., a 1966 University graduate, could well be counted as a second-generation Denny product. Because of his parents' intimate ties and devotion to the University, Bryant Jr. also felt an obligation to the Capstone and served as a member of the University board of trustees for fifteen years before his retirement in September 2015. The younger Bryant, a successful businessman with diverse holdings, has also served as chairman of the Crimson Tide Foundation and is regarded as one of the University's largest financial benefactors.

Thousands of others heeded Denny's call to leadership and service roles in professional, civic, government and religious life. Many of those entered the growing field of education, sharing Denny's messages with generations of youth as they answered his call for universal education. Others chose business, medicine, military or myriad other careers. Most did more than simply live their lives; they did as Denny had encouraged them to do and contributed to the lives of others through leadership and service.

James Sidney Tarwater accepted Denny's invitation to attend the University of Alabama after graduating from Fayette County High School in 1916 and later answered Denny's call to a life of service. He entered the University in the fall and worked his way through school, earning a medical degree in 1922. Dr. Tarwater served as a staff physician at Bryce Hospital in Tuscaloosa 1924-1945, as assistant superintendent 1945-1950 and superintendent 1950-1970. He was named Alabama's first Mental Health Commissioner in 1970 and died June 5, 1974, after devoting his entire adult life to providing healthcare for Alabama's mentally ill. Tarwater's sisters Lucy and Marguerite followed their older brother to the University and Marguerite (Mrs. A. K. "Temo"

Callahan) eventually earned a bachelor's degree and became a teacher after working her way through school. Tarwater family records show that Denny wrote personal notes on each student's grade report and sent personal letters to each student during the summer. One such letter, written to Marguerite on July 9, 1930, serves as an example. "What are you doing this summer? I wish you could be with us. Drop us a line and let us know how you are enjoying your vacation. We look forward with pleasure to welcoming you back to the campus this fall. Please let me hear from you," Denny wrote. He then added a hand-written note, saying, "You have done wonderfully well. You now stand under the shadow of the great goal! I congratulate you."

In 1925, Ruth Robertson of Clayton, Alabama, became only the second woman to graduate from the University's two-year medical school in an era when few women entered professional fields other than education. She earned her M. D. degree from Tulane University two years later and married Dr. Ivan Berrey, who she had met at the University of Alabama. The Berreys moved to Birmingham in 1929 and both soon became prominent professional and civic leaders. Ruth Berrey practiced pediatrics; served as medical supervisor with the National Youth Administration during the Depression; was a consultant to the Jefferson County Board of Health; served as assistant professor at Howard College (now Samford University), and was an associate professor at the University of Alabama Medical School. Following her husband's death in 1957, Ruth Berry followed Dr. Denny's call to service and began regular medical missionary tours in West Africa, where she saw as many as two hundred children per day five days a week, and the United States, where she became widely known for her achievements in the areas of children's diseases and nutrition. Following a heart attack that curtailed her missionary work, Dr. Berry served as county health officer in Barbour, Macon and Bullock counties until her death in 1973.

Dr. Berrey also served as president of Children's Hospital in Birmingham, president of the Alabama Pediatric Society, a diplomat of the American Board of Pediatrics and a fellow member of the American Academy of Pediatrics. She was listed in *Who's Who of American Women* and *Who's Who in Alabama* and received the Outstanding Alumnae Award from Judson College, which she attended for a year before entering the University of Alabama. Dr. Berrey was inducted into the Alabama Women's Hall of Fame in 1976.

Doris Marie Bender of Mobile, who earned a B. S. degree from the University of Alabama in 1933, devoted her professional life of forty-three years to the welfare of others as a social worker in her home state. Bender, who also took graduate courses in social work at Tulane University and the University of Chicago, began her career in public service in 1933 with the Mobile County Relief Administration. She served as director of Public Welfare (now the Department of Human Resources) in Shelby, Macon and Montgomery counties and worked in the state department before being appointed director in Mobile County, where she served from 1943 until her retirement in 1976. She was the first woman elected to the Spring Hill College board of trustees, the first woman elected to the board of directors of First Southern Federal Savings and Loan Association and the first woman outside the University of South Alabama staff to serve on the Admissions Committee of the USA School of Medicine.

Bender established the first organized volunteer division in a county Department of Pensions and Security and was on the committee which developed the Alabama Office of Volunteerism and served on its board of directors. She initiated an adult foster care program for the elderly and disabled and an adult homemaker services program designed to delay nursing home admission for people who could no longer provide all their own care in Mobile County. These programs served as models for the Alabama Department of Pensions and Security's statewide program for adult foster care, which was authorized in 1972, and the statewide homemaker services program, which began in 1973. She also appointed the first black social worker in a county department in 1946 and "was an advocate for fairness and opportunity for all, regardless of race and other differences," according to a biography published by the Alabama Women's Hall of Fame, into which she was inducted in 1994. The biography added that Bender's "competence, integrity and wisdom, along with the manifold accomplishments that marked her career, serve as an example to all." She died in 1991.

Dr. George Vernon Irons Sr. was one of the many Denny students who chose education as a profession. A Tuscaloosa native, Irons earned fame on the athletic field and a Phi Beta Kappa key in the classroom. As a student at the University of Alabama 1920-1924, Irons set records in four distance events in track and won national Amateur Athletic Union distance championships 1921-1923. He earned a bachelor's degree and was selected as the state Rhodes Scholar nominee in 1924 before earning a master's degree in 1925. After earning a doctorate at Duke University, he joined the faculty at Howard College (now Samford University), where he earned national acclaim as a distinguished professor of history and political science for more than four decades, passing on Denny's philosophy and wisdom to a record seventeen students who became college presidents. Known as a brilliant lecturer and speaker, Irons received the Freedom Foundation George Washington Medal in 1962, and with Irons as director of its program, Samford won a record eighteen consecutive Freedom Foundation awards. Irons was a founding member of the Alabama Historical Society and a member of the Alabama Academy of Sciences and was listed in *Who's Who in America*, *Who's Who in American Education* and the *Directory of American Scholars*. A veteran of World War II, Irons was inducted into the Alabama Sports Hall of Fame in 1978. He was honored as a national leader in education and a distinguished American by the U. S. Senate in 1976 and recognized in the Alabama Senate in 1999 as a respected leader in numerous civic, social, church, professional and honorary organizations.

"Dr. Denny took Dad under his wing at Alabama," said William G. "Billy" Bean Jr. of Lexington, Virginia, in 2013 as he recalled the close, fifty-year relationship between Denny and his father. "Dad lost his father when he was young and Dr. Denny became a father figure for him at the University of Alabama. For some reason, Dr. Denny liked my dad. He was Dad's mentor; they were very close. He helped Dad get into Harvard after he graduated from Alabama in 1914 and was instrumental in getting Dad a job as a history professor at Washington and Lee in 1922," Billy Bean added. Dr. William G. Bean Sr., a native of Heflin who served in World War I, shared ground-floor living quarters in the President's Mansion with three other students due to a lack of campus housing while attending the University, according to Billy Bean. After earning a doctorate from Harvard, the elder Bean taught at Washington and Lee for four decades and served as professor emeritus until his death in 1974 ended a fifty-two-year affiliation with the school. Dr. Bean also taught summer school at the University of Alabama for approximately fifteen years.

"Dr. Denny was after Dad for years to write a book about the Liberty Hall Volunteers, and Dad finally wrote it after he retired," Billy Bean said. "After Dr. Denny retired and moved back to Lexington, they would talk for hours and hours about it every Sunday afternoon." The book was important to Denny because it was an account of the Washington College (later Washington and Lee University) students who left school in the spring of 1861 to form a military company to serve with Lexington native and Confederate general Thomas J. "Stonewall' Jackson's forces during the Civil War. According to Bean's book, "The Liberty Hall Volunteers," only eight members of original seventy-six students who formed the company remained on duty to surrender at Appomattox in 1865. Thirteen of the students were killed in battle, nine died of disease and the others were wounded or taken prisoner. Reverend Givens B. Strickler, rector of the Washington and Lee Board of Trustees 1899-1913 and Denny's father-in-law, rose from the rank of corporal to captain while serving with the Liberty Hall Volunteers. He was wounded at First Manassas and Second Manassas, captured at Gettysburg and imprisoned at Fort Johnson, Ohio, until the end of the war. Strickler returned to Washington College to complete his studies after the war during Robert E. Lee's tenure as president of the school. Denny married Strickler's daughter Jane in 1899.

Elton B. Stephens, who earned a law degree from the University of Alabama in 1936, was an example of all that Denny urged his students to become. A native of Clio, Stephens worked his way through law school at the University by selling magazines door to door after doing the same while earning a bachelor's degree from Birmingham-Southern College. At the University, Stephens served on the honors committee and the appeals committee. At Birmingham-Southern, he was elected to Omicron Delta Kappa, a national leadership honor society. Stephens founded what became EBSCO industries in 1944 and grew it into one of Alabama's largest private companies. The Birmingham-based company is recognized today as a major international conglomerate with thirty-five different companies and nearly 6,000 employees in twenty-three countries. Stephens helped the family owned company amass assets valued at more than a billion dollars before his death in 2005 at age ninety-three.

Stephens and his wife, Alys Robinson Stephens, who died in 1996, also became known as two of the state's leading philanthropists as they donated millions of dollars to charity, educational institutions, the arts and various civic causes, including the Alabama Symphony Orchestra, the University of Alabama's 1995 capital campaign and the United Way of Central Alabama. Many of their major contributions earned recognition, including the Alys Stephens Performing Arts Center at the University of Alabama in Birmingham and the Elton B. Stephens Science Center at Birmingham-Southern College. Stephens received the Jonnie Dee Little Lifetime Achievement Award from the Alabama State Council on the Arts in 1999 in recognition of his financial support of the arts. Stephens founded the Metropolitan Arts Council of Birmingham in 1986, served as chairman of the Alabama Symphonic Association and was a major contributor to the Birmingham Museum of Art. The city of Birmingham and the state honored Stephens for his support of civic projects in 1975 by naming the Red Mountain Expressway the Elton B. Stephens Expressway. The Stephens children—sons J. T. and

Elton B. Jr. and daughters Jane Comer and Dell Brooke—continue the philanthropic work of their parents in many areas.

Woodrow Wilson "Foots" Clements, the youngest of nine children from Windham Springs in northern Tuscaloosa County, was one of the many University of Alabama football players from the 1920s and 1930s who attended college on a "working scholarship." Clements, a 1937 University graduate, once said he "dug ditches, swept floors and worked as a butcher" while at the University. A 1932 graduate of Tuscaloosa County High School, where he played football and basketball and was president of the student body, Clements joined Dr. Pepper Bottling Company as a truck route salesman as a senior in college and worked his way up through the ranks to become president of the company in 1969. He retired in 1986 after fifty years with the company and died in 2002 at age eighty-eight. "I always thought of salesmanship as the gentle act of letting other people have your way," Clements once said. As a member of the Horatio Alger Association for Distinguished Americans, Clements was the recipient of the 1999 Norman Vincent Peale Award, which honors members who have made exceptional humanitarian contributions to society and who have continued to exhibit courage and integrity in the face of great challenges. The W. W. Clements Free Enterprise Institute, which opened at the Dr. Pepper Museum in Waco, Texas, in 1997, is dedicated to helping people discover and understand the importance of morals in their personal and business lives. Clements served on the University of Alabama President's Council and on the board of the Southern Methodist University Foundation for Business Administration.

Birmingham native Morris "Munny" Sokol earned a business degree from the University in 1933 and for more than fifty years exemplified all the traits Denny often spoke about when describing the responsibilities of educated men and women. After working to establish a furniture business in Tuscaloosa and serving in the Army during World War II, Sokol soon became one of Tuscaloosa's best-known and respected leaders in business, civic, religious and charitable matters in addition to supporting the University of Alabama in many ways. Sokol served as president of numerous organizations, including the Chamber of Commerce, Tuscaloosa Credit Bureau, Tuscaloosa Federated Jewish Charities and B'nai B'rith Lodge, and served on the boards of what is now DCH Regional Medical Center, the Tuscaloosa County Park and Recreation Authority, First National Bank, Federated Life Insurance Company, Cotton States Life Insurance Company, the United Way of Tuscaloosa County, the Salvation Army, American Red Cross and the Council of Boy Scouts. In 1972, he founded the annual golf tournament to benefit the Sheriffs' Boys and Girls Ranches. Sokol was a member of the University of Alabama Commerce and Business Administration Board of Visitors, a member of the University President's Cabinet and co-chairman of the University of Alabama Development Program. He was named national chairman of the Commerce Executives Society of the College of Commerce and Business Administration in 1982 and in 1984 received the University's first Dr. Lee Bidgood Award for Distinguished Service by the Alabama Finance Association.

Roderick Beddow admired Denny enough to follow him from Washington and Lee University to the University of Alabama, where he earned a law degree in 1913. Beddow was born in Whiteside, Tennessee, in 1889, but his family soon moved to Birmingham, where his father practiced law from 1895 to 1924. Beddow graduated from high school in Birmingham and attended Washington and Lee, where he earned a bachelor's degree in 1911. He started law school there in the fall of 1911, but when Denny became president of the University of Alabama on January 1, 1912, Beddow transferred to Alabama to complete his law studies under Denny. Beddow earned wide acclaim as a criminal defense attorney and was known as the "Perry Mason" of Birmingham because of his honesty, tenacity and success, according to his Alabama Lawyers Hall of Fame biography. "Mr. Beddow was recognized by his peers for his high ethical standards and for his leadership," the biography added. Beddow served as president of the Birmingham Bar Association and the Alabama State Bar. Following Denny's admonishment to serve others, Beddow was active in several civic organizations and served as president of Lions International in 1933, representing the organization throughout the United States and in several foreign countries. His biography said Beddow was "a successful attorney, a mentor to several generations of lawyers and a respected civic leader who took a keen interest in the life of his community."

Five former Denny students from the University of Alabama served in the rank of general during World War II and at least five others reached the rank soon after the war. Those serving as generals during the war included Brigadier General Charles H. Barnwell Jr. (1915), Inspector General on the staff of General Douglas MacArthur in the Pacific Theater; Brigadier General Harwood C. Bowman (1916), commander of the Kwangsi Command in China; Brigadier General Aubrey T. Hornsby (1916), commander of Gunter Field in Montgomery; Major General Thomas Wade Herren (1917), assistant commanding general of the 76th Infantry Division in the European Theater, and Brigadier General Edwin Jones (1918), commander of the Army post at Nome Alaska. Denny-era students who attained the equivalent rank of general after World War II included Air Force Major General James Baird Tipton (1938); Air Force Brigadier General Ethelred "Lundy" Sykes (1926); Army Major General George F. Hamner (1939); Navy Rear Admiral W. C. Baty (1924), and Air Force Major General James C. McGehee (1931).

Hamner, like thousands of other students, worked his way through the University at a variety of jobs provided by Denny's self-help program. Hamner, recalling Denny in 2014 at age ninety-seven, said, "He made me feel like I was somebody special. If he ever met you, he knew you. He had a powerful memory. He was quite a character." A native of Northport, Hamner said he heard Denny speak on several occasions as a student at the University 1935-39 and heard him speak on the radio once. "We had two special people at the University when I was there and I knew them both," Hamner said, naming Denny and Paul "Bear" Bryant as the two. Hamner was commissioned into the Army through ROTC in 1939 and said he stopped to visit Denny at his home in Lexington, Virginia, on his way to engineering school at Fort Belvoir in 1940. "We had a nice conversation," Hamner said. "He was a real gentleman. We talked for about thirty minutes." Hamner served in Africa, France and the Pacific during World War II and in several positions on active duty and in the Army Reserve after the war, retiring at the rank of major general in 1977. During World War II, Hamner met President Franklin Roosevelt, King George VI of England, famous aviator Charles Lindbergh and Army generals Omar Bradley and Mark Clark. Hamner was active in numerous civic and community organizations in Tuscaloosa, including serving as president of the Rotary Club, chairman of the Tuscaloosa Symphony Orchestra, vice president of the Black Warrior Council of Boy Scouts, secretary-treasurer of the American Red Cross and president of the Tuscaloosa County Preservation Society. He and his wife Elizabeth received the Patron of the Arts Award from the University of Alabama College of Arts and Sciences Society of Fine Arts in 2000. Hamner was honored by the University College of Engineering in 1991 when he was named a Distinguished Engineering Fellow and presented the Department of Industrial Engineering's Outstanding Fellow Award. He was also honored as Alabama's outstanding citizen soldier in 1980 and the Tuscaloosa County Citizen of the Year in 1990.

Ehney Addison Camp Jr. is another former Denny student who achieved high honors in college, professional and civic endeavors. The Columbiana, Alabama, native earned Phi Beta Kappa honors at the University and was named the outstanding male scholar in the class of 1928. While a student at the University, Camp served as president of Omicron Delta Kappa leadership fraternity and Sigma Eta and was a member of Jasons, Beta Gamma Sigma, Rho Alpha Tau and Sigma Nu fraternity. He was the recipient of the Algernon Sidney Sullivan Award, the Ward Sterne & Company Prize, the Alpha Kappa Psi Cup and the Scholarship Key of Delta Sigma Pi.

Camp worked in banking in Birmingham for four years before joining Liberty National Life Insurance Company, where he rose through the ranks to become executive vice president and treasurer in 1960. He also served on the company's board of directors and as a member of the executive committee before retiring in 1973 after forty-one years with the company. Camp, who was inducted into the Alabama Academy of Honor in 1976, earned national recognition in his profession from the American Life Convention, the Life Insurance Association of America and the Mortgage Bankers Association of America. He also served on numerous government agencies, panels and boards, including the Voluntary Credit Restraint Committee convened by the Federal Reserve Board in 1951, the advisory committees to three federal housing commissions, President Eisenhower's Special Advisory Committee on Government Housing Policies and Programs and the Alabama Governor's Committee to Fight Inflation.

Camp served on the University of Alabama board of trustees 1959-1979 and was a former president of the University's National Alumni Association. He was honored as the outstanding alumnus by the Jefferson County Chapter and received the National Alumni Association Distinguished Alumnus Award in 1985. He also served as president of the Jefferson County Anti-Tuberculosis Society and as a member of the boards of directors of the Jefferson County Tuberculosis Sanitarium; president of the Birmingham Kiwanis Club and a member of its scholarship committee; a member of the board of the Birmingham Boys Club; a co-director of the Jefferson County Community Chest campaign, and a member of the Birmingham Committee of 100. Donations from Camp, who died in 1993, and his wife, Mildred Fletcher Tillman Camp, in 1998 established the Ehney A. Camp Jr. Endowed Chair in Finance and Investment in the Culverhouse College of Commerce and Business Administration at the University.

Sarah Hamner Faucett of Northport was one of the thousands of high school teachers who earned degrees at the University of Alabama before returning to their home communities to teach, inspire and lead others to similar opportunities. Mrs.

Faucett earned a bachelor's degree in education from the University in 1935 and a master's degree in 1955 as she taught in Tuscaloosa County schools for more than thirty years. Her influence extended beyond the segregated schools in which she taught, however. In 1957, Mrs. Faucett hired Susie Washington Miller, an African-American teenager, as a domestic worker in her home and quickly took more than a passing interest in the high school sophomore from nearby all-black Riverside High School. "Mrs. Faucett soon began to question me about my plans for higher education," Mrs. Miller said. "She monitored my assignments, course selections and progress just like she did her own three children. She and her children all supported me and were always so respectful. They treated me in a way that if I wanted to move forward, I had no excuse. Mrs. Faucett's mind was set on my going to college, and when I finished high school she put me in her car and drove me to Stillman College and introduced me to people and helped me get enrolled. She made me promise to try just one semester, but after I got there I saw a whole new world and I didn't want to leave," Mrs. Miller added proudly.

Mrs. Miller worked for Mrs. Faucett through high school and college and graduated from Stillman in 1964 before beginning her own thirty-five-year teaching career. "Mrs. Faucett could have just worked me as a domestic, but she made sure I grew as a person, too, and we remained friends for life. She sat beside my mother at my wedding and I was at her side when she died in 2005 at age ninety-four," Mrs. Miller said. Mrs. Miller was one of the first two black teachers hired at Northport Junior High when schools were integrated there in 1967 and she remained there until retirement in 1999. Mrs. Miller also earned a master's degree from the University of Alabama in 1977 and followed Mrs. Faucett's example by helping her younger sister and two nieces attend college and become teachers. "Mrs. Faucett was a friend of education and humanity. She taught me love, kindness, tolerance, compassion, encouragement and perseverance, and I tried to teach the same lessons to my students," Mrs. Miller said.

These and others like them were the men and women Denny came to Alabama to find, educate and inspire to leadership roles in helping bring positive change to the state. They were, like Denny himself, intelligent, idealistic, courageous and compassionate. For twenty-five years, persuasive letters from Denny brought young men and women to the University of Alabama from all corners of the state. What they learned from Denny and his hand-picked, like-minded Capstone faculty carried them far beyond the borders they had known before, and they in turn helped bring the social, cultural and economic changes to the state—and even the nation—that Denny had envisioned when he accepted the presidency of the University of Alabama in 1911.

No single person or incident brought the changes Denny envisioned, of course, and the changes were greatly influenced by such factors as industrialization, World War I, the Great Depression, Roosevelt's New Deal programs, World War II and the GI Bill. But the roots of many of the changes can be traced directly to the words and deeds of Dr. George H. Denny and to those who heard his call to duty and continued his work. As he told a record University of Alabama graduating class in May 1936, "A group of five hundred young men and women going out into this immense world would seem, in comparison, a relatively small group. Yet history furnishes many instances of groups smaller than this group which, moved by great faith and great desire, have wrought far-reaching changes—material, social and spiritual. It is not a matter of mere numbers or of mere chance or of mere circumstance. It is a matter of purpose. It is a matter of spirit. It is a matter of power."

Denny was widely known for his impassioned speeches.

17

Brilliant Writer, Passionate Orator

"No great movement, whether social, political or religious, has ever been successfully launched without appealing to the power of speech, earnest and eloquent, to convince the reason, to persuade the will, to inspire the imagination and to carry conviction to the soul of men."

—Dr. George H. Denny

Denny was a brilliant writer with a scholarly, masterful command of language and history and he drew wide praise as a persuasive, inspiring and passionate orator as he spoke with unchallenged authority on his chosen subjects. No matter the audience, he never lost sight of his life-long mission, which was a crusade for the progress of mankind and society through universal education. He pursued that mission by informing and influencing his many widespread and diverse audiences almost completely through person-to-person contact, which was the primary means of communication for most of the thirty-five years he served as a college president.

Denny drew many to his side in a call to duty that he professed throughout his career as he campaigned for educational opportunities and a better quality of life for all citizens. He did that the only way possible at the time—by repeating his messages in person countless times through the years. And he did it under difficult travel conditions and without the aid of a public relations staff, large arenas, the internet, television or even radio except for a few rare occasions. His was a long, arduous, one-man campaign for education of the masses in an agrarian age when few others saw the need for more than minimal formal education. And though he tired, he never shied from the challenge.

Denny's speeches were often reported in local newspapers and he drew editorial support from the press from time to time, especially in Tuscaloosa. He did not rely on the press to promote his cause, however, since newspaper circulation was limited. When printed, his orations calling for local taxation to support education regularly competed for newspaper headlines with somewhat more pressing or sensational issues such as the boll weevil, moonshiners, hookworm, the arrival of electricity, cattle ticks, train robbers, lynchings, typhoid, Mexican bandit Poncho Villa, rabid dogs, World War I, prohibition, stunt pilots, mine disasters, Chicago gangsters, women's suffrage and, of course, University of Alabama football.

Denny delivered his first public address as a graduating senior at Hampden-Sydney College in the spring of 1891, and he recalled the occasion on June 5, 1939, when he returned to his old school to address the Hampden-Sydney alumni. "Forty-eight years ago—and it seems but as yesterday now that it is past and as a watch in the night—I delivered in the old College Church what was then called the Philosophical Oration. It was not much of a speech, but it was a proud day in my young life, touched then as it has been to this day with a sense of loyalty and pride and faith in this dear old college in her unquenchable ideals. That was a long time ago. The college then was inconceivably poor in material resources but fabulously rich in imponderable and spiritual values. Yet, even though she was forced to exclaim, 'Silver and gold have I none,' there was never an hour when she could not and did not say to her struggling sons, 'Rise up and walk.'"

Denny praised his mentors and other long-time Hampden-Sydney faculty members in the 1939 speech, saying, "Who can say that they did not choose the better part when they subordinated the limelight to quiet service, when they dedicated themselves to leading youth not merely to the tree of knowledge but also to the tree of life. Certainly members of this faculty, as I have known them, have seen life broadly and seen it whole. They never fancied they were treading the stage alone. Around them was never wrapped the Napoleonic cloak of egotism. Such teachers are the cornerstone of the temple; they are the real architects and builders of men. And I believe that all of them, living and dead, if they could speak to us today, would gladly testify that here, under these great oaks, they had a thrilling experience in erecting signposts that have led thousands of flaming youth into the portals of truth." The same, of course, can be said of Denny.

Archives hold only a few Denny speeches and essays between 1892 and 1901, but he obviously grew in knowledge, experience and reputation as an educator during that period. His demand as a speaker grew rapidly after he was named president of Washington and Lee in 1902, however, and he spoke throughout the South on a variety of educational topics tailored to his audiences, including the difficulties of education in the South; technical schools; rural school teachers; college admission of special students; the call for more college men; the dependence of colleges on preparatory schools; what colleges could do for public schools; Robert E. Lee as a college president; various issues and holidays and tributes to individuals in addition to making inspirational orations to the students of each incoming class throughout his career. The welcoming addresses included such titles as "Certain Larger Duties of the College Man," "Two Essentials of Success," "Devotion to Truth," "Certain Responsibilities of the Christian Student," "Certain Practical Duties of Educated Citizens," "Certain Peculiar Duties Imposed by Education" and several similar, untitled speeches. One twenty-seven-page, handwritten and undated speech on "The South's Contribution to Our National Greatness" included Denny's pithy observation that "ignorance arises from a lack of opportunity to learn," and that statement was the fundamental cause to which he devoted his life.

Denny's lengthy inaugural address at his installation as permanent president of Washington and Lee University in 1902 offered his view of the opportunities and obligations of the nation's institutions of higher education. Denny said that "education of the future will be designed to lead and not to drive" as it fits men for life's duties. He also listed standards of scholarship; the keeping of educational opportunities within reach of the common people; the obligation of the colleges to serve the state; the elevation of the moral standard of the nation, and the building of character as some of the responsibilities of the nation's colleges.

While president of Washington and Lee University, Denny delivered a speech entitled "What Our institutions of Higher Learning May Do for the Public Schools," in Norfolk, Virginia, on December 7, 1904, in which he outlined a plan for a statewide educational system at all levels, from rural grade schools to the universities, and called for the state legislature to support it. It was evident then that he held a far greater goal as an educator than merely that of serving as a college president. His plan then was the same plan he supported and helped to implement in Alabama over the next thirty years. Although he is most often remembered for his work as president of the University of Alabama, he should not be forgotten as the primary force behind the building of a complete state educational system, atop which he conceived the University as its capstone.

Denny first won admirers among University of Alabama trustees, alumni and students on May 29, 1907, when he delivered the baccalaureate address at University graduation exercises. "Although of shorter length than such addresses usually are, it was yet one that was teeming with the high purposes and high ideals for which all thorough education stands," the *Tuscaloosa Times-Gazette* said of the speech. "The oration was delivered with grace and force and was filled throughout with happy illustrations and recurrent bits of wit and humor. Prolonged applause greeted the speaker when he had finished," the report added. Denny spoke on "The Insistent Demand and Need of College-Bred Men," saying "the greatest field of his (the college-bred man) usefulness perhaps lies in the molding of good and correct public sentiment." Denny pointed out that legislative enactments, laws and economic conditions are directly the result of the prevailing public sentiment. Saying that "a state or government becomes, in nature and quality, the facsimile of the men who make it," Denny added that college educated men were also needed to dispel the "prevailing misconceived ideas of geographical patriotism, to raise the ethical standards which obtain in our states and elsewhere" and "to combat the idea that material and commercial advancement was the highest aim of a man or a country." No doubt the positive and lasting impression Denny made among University loyalists in 1907 contributed to his becoming president of the University less than five years later.

Denny immediately won over University alumni and the local press in a triumphal return to the state on Friday, November 17, 1911. It was his first appearance in the state after being named president of the University, and he spoke at a banquet in his honor shortly after arriving by train the same day. "Dr. Denny's Address Direct and Vigorous" read the headline in the *Crimson White* the following day, with a subhead saying, "Future President of Alabama Stirs His Audience at Banquet in Birmingham." The accompanying article said that when Denny arose to speak for the first time "the gathering went wild" and that he was cheered for several minutes before delivering "a striking, virile statement of ideas and purposes." Sam Clabaugh, writing for *The Tuscaloosa News* on November 19, said Denny's speech "thrilled every alumnus present. It was a masterly analysis of the situation at the University of Alabama and a clear and unmistakable statement of his policies. He spoke plainly but eloquently, positively but tactfully. He has the true ring. He is sincere. He is fearless. He is ready to do a man's work." The *Birmingham Age-Herald* offered a physical description of the new University president, saying that "Dr. Denny is perhaps five feet ten inches high and is as erect as an Indian."

The *Tuscaloosa Times-Gazette* of November 21, 1911, went farther in its analysis of Denny, saying, "Everybody liked Dr. Denny. It is seldom any man makes so good an impression and if first impressions count for anything the new president is going to be one of the most popular men that has ever come to the state. He gave people who talked with him and who heard him speak the notion that he had ideals which he hoped to reach in the conduct of the University of Alabama but he was mighty strong and clear on the point that quality was far and away to be desired above quantity. Dr. Denny said he was coming prepared to do a man's work. We all do know that it is a man's job that he is tackling and all who have met him feel that he is the right man for the job. He is a man all right. He has courteous, even courtly, manners. He has a suave and delightful way of speaking to people and his manner in making an address is extremely happy. But he is not all manners by any means. He is a good-looking man, but there is a sense of power and strength about his face that is more impressive than his pleasant expression. He has a clear gray eye and it can look keenly at a person. It is likely that he is a man pretty hard to deceive. He speaks decisively and he evidenced in his talk in Birmingham that he is a man of marked firmness. He has a remarkable memory. He remembered people on Saturday that he met casually on Friday night and he recalled some old members of the University Glee Club that he had seen at Marion several years ago. He is a thinking man and his use of the English language was a great pleasure to hear. He knows the words to use and he knows how to use them fitly and expressively. He has ideas on education and he does not mind expressing them. He on all sides impressed people pleasantly and while he was making friends for himself personally he was winning admiration for the intellect and the calm, serene, force of the man. Dr. Denny is going to be a success if he gets half cooperation in the presidency of the University and the feeling shown at Birmingham was to the effect that the whole state was ready to act for him and with him in the uplifting of the great institution over which he is so soon to preside. He seems to have come into the kingdom for such a time as this."

A highlight of Denny's initial speech to University alumni was his discussion of expectations the alumni might have of him. "I know that something is expected of me in regard to the hopes and plans for the University of Alabama," the *Crimson White* quoted him as saying. "I know something of the storms and struggles that have marked its history and the prospects that loom large in its bright future. First of all, let me say that the University of Alabama needs money. The income is shamefully deficient. While it is true that its revenue has grown in terms of thousands, it is also true that its expenses have grown in terms of hundreds of thousands. The state should be doing five times as much for the University as it is, not as doling out charity but as increasing its greatest investment. I have no idea of setting the woods afire. I shall merely try to do what I can with the tools at my disposal. In coming here, I can only say that I pledge my best efforts to do a man's work without fear or favor. The alumni must waken the public mind to realize what the state must do. Much has been said concerning a greater University.

Frankly, I do not believe we are ready for that term. Let's build first a great college," Denny added. "Someone has said something of a thousand students in the next four years. Get that idea out of your minds right now. There are not one thousand prepared college students in all the colleges of Alabama combined at the present time. We should not be swept off our feet by false numerical standards. Forced to choose between a student body of four hundred trained and prepared students and one thousand men sent to college to gratify personal vanity, I should not hesitate to choose the former. We do not want numbers brought merely by winning teams, over-zealous solicitors or low standards." In addressing athletics during the speech, Denny added, "Athletics, like all other extracurricular activities, must be kept within bounds. It is of importance in college life—of great importance—but it is a sideshow and not the main performance. College life must not be allowed to swallow up the college curriculum."

Denny was in great demand as a speaker throughout his thirty-five years as a college president, and there is no doubt that Denny impressed his audiences. The *Crimson White* reported on a Denny speech to the Alabama Education Association on October 15, 1914, saying, "He is sincere and he is thoroughly acquainted with the topics with which he deals." University alumnus Floyd Tillery of Birmingham heard Denny speak at an alumni gathering on May 24, 1920, and was moved to write to Denny the following day to share his impression of Denny's speech. "There was that something in your words and in your voice that grafted you into our hearts," Tillery said.

Denny surely drew on the sermons of his father as he often inserted Biblical passages, but he did not overlook his experience and classical education, including training in public speaking, as he addressed the subjects dear to his heart, including truth; discipline; frugality; Christianity; the need for taxation to educate the masses; service to mankind and, of course, education in general. Denny also spoke with authority when he stepped outside his area of expertise briefly to support women's suffrage and local prohibition during those emotional public debates.

A portfolio of Denny speeches in the Washington and Lee University Library archives contains dozens of formal speeches dating from 1892 to 1939. Many had been revised or updated in the margins in Denny's cryptic handwriting and a few are entirely hand written. That number does not include the numerous speeches he made throughout the South while serving with the U. S. Food Administration during World War I or the many non-scripted appearances at high school graduations, YMCA meeting and civic club luncheons.

Denny spoke early, often, at length and pleadingly for the education of the masses of both races in the rural South and for local, self-imposed taxation to support the cause at a time when neither ideal was accepted or practiced in the region. In a speech entitled "Education in the South: Its Difficulties and Its Needs," Denny called education the "supreme question of civilization, whether viewed from the standpoint of the individual, the community, the state or the nation. How are we to convince all our people, or even the great majority of them, that every human life without a single exception is a plan of God and has its place in the divine economy? How are we to convince all our people, or even the great majority of them, that it is a social and a moral wrong to make education a thing apart from the condition and participation of the great mass of men? How are we to make them understand that universal education is from every rational consideration the fundamental need of our civilization and the bulwark of our liberty?"

After outlining the many difficulties facing the region, Denny said, "It is an easy matter to talk of difficulties. Remedies are harder to devise. We need an educational campaign conducted by specialists who have devoted their lives to the problems and who can speak words of wisdom and authority. Our great need is wise, tactful, aggressive agitation by trained specialists who know the truth and are not afraid to speak it. The teacher as well as the statesman must point the way to this great Southern people, a nobly patriotic and self-sacrificing people willing to pay taxes without limit for the freedom and happiness of their fellow men if the path of duty is made plain to them. Let us as educators devote our lives, if need be, to this issue. Let us teach our people the fundamental truth that no man is free who cannot read and write; that no tyranny is so great or so dangerous as the tyranny of ignorance, inefficiency and poverty. And when the people know the facts, we shall have their sympathy. When they know their duty they will do it without fear and faltering, though it means sacrifice and even death." The speech clearly defined Denny's objectives and he worked toward those objectives throughout his life.

Denny's early speeches were often long, to say the least, as he poured his vast knowledge onto page after page for delivery to audiences throughout the South and beyond. It could easily be said that he never used one word when ten would do, and some of his addresses ran twenty five or more typewritten pages in a day when lengthy orations were commonplace. When a speaker addressed a large gathering in the days before radio and television, he, by necessity, took full advantage of the opportunity to present his message.

In addition to speaking to student assemblies each semester and to annual alumni gatherings, Denny was in great demand as a speaker and rarely declined the opportunity to educate and influence an audience. He delivered the president's annual address at the Association of Colleges and Preparatory Schools of the Southern States November 2-4, 1904; spoke at the inauguration of William L. Poteat as president of Wake Forest College in 1905; addressed the Birmingham Chamber of Commerce on April 10, 1913; gave the commencement address at East Alabama College in Lineville in May 1914; delivered the Founder's Day address at the University of South Carolina and spoke at the inauguration of Bishop Knight as chancellor of the University of the South, both in June 1914; addressed the Virginia Education Association in Richmond on November 27, 1916; spoke to a special assembly of the Marion Military Institute Corps of Cadets on November 2, 1917, regarding America's participation in World War I; discussed "The Next Step in Our Educational Program" before the Alabama Educational Association convention in Mobile in 1919; delivered the baccalaureate address at Tuskegee Institute, where Robert Russa Moton, like Denny a native of Amelia County, Virginia, was principal, in May 1919, and addressed the New York Southern Society, of which he was an elected member, on October 27, 1934, in a few examples of his many appearances.

Speaking before a gathering of approximately 300 engineers in Birmingham in December 1920, Denny called on the group to support the education of men who could help develop the state's natural resources. Pointing out that in 1861 the South held forty-five percent of the nation's wealth compared to only ten percent in 1920, Denny said the state was not developing its coal, iron, cotton, lumber and water resources as it should be. "The people of Alabama will not achieve until they realize that education is an investment, not an expense, and that nothing is so costly as ignorance," Denny said, adding that "the state's institutions of education must receive the equipment necessary if they are to fit the young men of Alabama to make the state what it should be."

Denny was heard by perhaps his largest audience on October 27, 1933, when he gave a nationwide radio address over a network of National Broadcasting Company (NBC) stations. The broadcast originated in New York and Denny's topic of discussion was "Education in the South in the Recovery Period."

Denny addressed the graduating class at Opelika High School in May of 1915 in what a local newspaper account called "a rare treat." "Those who failed to be present and hear Dr. Denny missed one of the ablest and most scholarly messages of the character that it has been the good fortune of an Opelika audience to hear," the article said. "Dr. Denny had not visited this city before and was therefore in a manner a stranger to us all, but he is a man of wonderful personality and from the first word uttered he had the large audience spellbound, and when he had finished his forty-minute address he had practically a personal friend in every person within the sound of his voice," the story added.

On one unusual occasion, Denny delivered the commencement address at Dallas County High School in Plantersville on May 20, 1913, despite being injured in an accident on his way to the event. Denny took the train from Tuscaloosa to Maplesville, where he was changing trains for the trip to Plantersville when the accident occurred. He was riding in a horse-drawn carriage between train stations when the carriage tongue broke and the horses ran away. Denny jumped from the runaway and fell on his right shoulder. Denny made it to Plantersville in time to deliver his speech, but a newspaper story (*Tuscaloosa News*, May 22, 1913) said he was in pain and "even further handicapped on account of the fact that the injury was to his right arm, seriously interfering with his gestures, which are so characteristic of his forceful remarks." The story added that Denny was forced to cancel speaking engagements in Mobile later in the week due to the injuries.

As its most prominent and widely known citizen, Denny became an official spokesman for the city of Tuscaloosa shortly after his arrival in town, welcoming conventions like the Alabama Bar Association and greeting visiting dignitaries, and he even welcomed conventions to Birmingham on occasion. He was also a frequent speaker at the Tuscaloosa Rotary Club, where he was a member for a while, and at the YMCA's weekly religious service. As perhaps the state's most educated, liberal and worldly wise citizen, Denny frequently spoke on current events, including state politics.

Speaking at the opening session of the Alabama Sociological Conference in Birmingham March 12, 1917, Denny discussed a number of the state's fiscal, educational, economic and social problems. "I think now is the time for the voters of Alabama to concentrate themselves on fiscal, financial and economic reform," Dr. Denny was quoted as saying in a *Tuscaloosa News* report of the speech carried on its editorial page. "We should rally and inaugurate an era of fiscal and financial reform. That is the issue in Alabama. The people should call upon a great man to take the governor's chair and give him a legislature that will help to give us an administration without a deficit. We must inaugurate business reform and have a business administration with a business-like legislature. Send to the legislature men who will permit this state to take her proper place among the sisterhood of commonwealths," the report added of Denny's speech. "Every thinking man in Alabama will endorse these utterances—it matters not what his ideas may be on liquor, local option or prohibition. They are the words of a man who appeals to intelligence instead of passion. Plain, quick and well poised, he speaks convincingly. Dr. Denny is one of nature's noblemen. He sounded the clarion call to higher things," the editorial said of the University president. "Safe business methods, greater development and elimination of politics all make for a higher and nobler citizenship," *The News* added in support of Denny's statements.

Appearing before University alumni in Mobile on April 6, 1922, in observance of the hundredth anniversary of the first meeting of the University board of trustees, Denny addressed three major issues facing the state, including the development of the Muscle Shoals area and the port of Mobile. "The grand battle of the future is fighting the markets of the world and the only way that Alabama can do this is to develop the port of Mobile. This is the only salvation," he said. "The third thing that must be done is to hang together and educate the people or else hang separately." Saying that "a great many people are asking for lower taxes," Denny remarked that "You can't appropriate money from an empty treasury."

The *Times-Gazette* reported that "spacious Morgan Auditorium was filled to the doors" with students, faculty and interested visitors as Denny spoke on campus for the first time at noon on January 9, 1912. "Dr. Denny stirred up considerable enthusiasm when he said that he was a friend to college athletics, from tennis to football," the *Times-Gazette* account said. Denny added, however, that "the law of leisure is that leisure shall follow and not precede labor," clearly placing athletics second to academic work. He further urged the students to abstain from "shiftlessness, self-indulgence and disorder" as he set a fatherly tone that endured throughout his twenty-five-year administration at the University of Alabama.

In addition to regularly welcoming incoming classes with an address, Denny wrote brief greetings for publication in the *Crimson White*, offering sage advice and direction for the year ahead at the beginning of each semester. The following such welcome, printed in the September 27, 1925, *Crimson White*, is a classic example of his thorough, fatherly greetings:

"The University of Alabama welcomes its fine student body to the campus with high hopes and great anticipation. Let us make this the best year in all the long life of our honored and historic institution. Thousands of homes are looking to you and counting on you. Fashion your life in accordance with the best traditions of the homes from which you come. Put manhood and womanhood first. Use your opportunities in the right way. Do your full duty. At first, the work may seem difficult. Do not get discouraged. If you do your part, your work will get easier all the time. Pluck, energy and consistent effort will win. Thousands of others have year by year overcome the difficulties of these early, difficult days. So can you. Do not shun difficult or even disagreeable duties. They are the counterpart of life's duties. Some day you will value the discipline that comes from doing difficult things. Try to include in your program of studies for the year at least one study that you do not like. The training will be good for you. 'How many hours shall I work a day?' In answering that question, do not listen to the indifferent student but to the outstanding student. Your education, according to modern estimates, ought to be worth $76,000 to you. In any task other than your college task, you would be willing to put in a good many hours of work daily for four years to earn that sum. Why not show the same spirit in college? A farm hand or a janitor or a clerk works eight or ten hours a day, and for very small consideration. Why should not the college man, with great rewards held out to him, do as well? Do not forget that your whole future is at stake. Now is your opportunity.

"Homesickness is no discredit to you unless you yield to it unduly. It will pass away all the more quickly if you keep busy. Do not worry. Keep steadily at your task and all will be well. Remember that hundreds of thousands are today thronging the colleges and equipping themselves for high service. You can do what so many others are doing. Be economical. You are making the best investment in the world in spending money on your education, or even in borrowing money to spend in this way. But unnecessary or uneconomical expenditures cannot be justified. You will need to learn economy if you want to succeed in life. Besides, I know that most of you cannot afford to spend money unwisely. You will need it later on in order to complete your education. Give your parents a square deal. Go to church and to Sunday school. Support the YMCA and the YWCA. You will not regret it ten or twenty or thirty years hence. Your parents want you to cultivate the spiritual as well as the intellectual life. Really, the spiritual is the most important phase of all life. You have my confidence and my best wishes and my benediction, now and always. George H. Denny, President."

A rare tone of sadness was evident in Denny's February 24, 1936, farewell address to University alumni gathered in his honor in Montgomery as he recounted the years spent beneath the oaks of his beloved Capstone. "There are no words, formal or informal, that are adequate to express the emotions that spring up in my heart as I face this great gathering," he said. "I feel utterly unworthy of the honor that is being done me today. I would have this day signify for each and every one of us something more than a testimonial of personal friendship for a single individual. I would have it signify an unforgettable renewal of vows of loyalty to the great institution which has made possible such a scene as this. On January 1, 1912, I came to Alabama over the unanimous protests of my best friends of my younger days and with a single objective. To that objective I have subsequently devoted every conscious hour. 'This one thing I do' has been the daily text and the daily guide of all these years…. As I look back over the years I wonder how it all has happened. For my own part, I wonder if I could again summon either the courage or the energy to attempt what has been attempted. And here let me add that it has been by no means a triumphal procession. There have been defeats as well as victories, and, I am convinced, more defeats than victories. Yet I have found and still find comfort in the fact that, after all, it is not so much what we actually accomplish but rather what we attempt together that makes us brothers and friends."

Three months later, at age sixty-five, Denny delivered his last, and perhaps shortest, commencement address as president of the University of Alabama. In typical fashion, he focused completely on the accomplishments and hopes of the students without reference to himself in any way. "And now, my dear friends," Denny began, "you have reached the end of another chapter in the book of life. This is a significant day for all of you. It is a day of memories. It is a day of hope. It is a day of anticipation. We acclaim you as you face the great and uncertain future. We have faith in you. We count on you. These diplomas which we hand you today are not merely certificates of sound training and of high purpose; they are pledges of good faith. They summon you to the first-line trenches where life's real battles are fought and won. They are designed to clothe you with power to do your part in the work-a-day world. We bid you carry your share of the load…. A group of five hundred young men and women going out into this immense world would seem, in comparison, a relatively small group. Yet history furnishes many instances of groups smaller than this group which, moved by great faith and great desire, have wrought far-reaching changes, material and social and spiritual. It is not a matter of mere numbers or of mere chance or of mere circumstance. It is a matter of purpose. It is a matter of spirit. It is a matter of power," he told the graduates in his usual powerful and inspiring fashion.

Many of Denny's speeches, especially to student assemblies, were much like sermons as they touched on matters of character, service to mankind and moral and Christian principles. Denny delivered such addresses to incoming classes at both Washington and Lee and the University of Alabama throughout his career, utilizing the same speeches time after time.

When Denny spoke of Robert E. Lee, he could just as easily have been speaking of himself because he had patterned his life as closely to that of Lee as humanly possible. He, like all Virginians of his era, had admired Lee as a boy. As president of Washington and Lee, Denny studied closely the work of Lee as president there 1865-1870 and followed closely the words and habits of Lee. As Denny often said, "Show me the man you honor. I know by that symptom better than by any other what kind of man you yourself are." For Denny, that man was Robert E. Lee, a man considered by most historians as having been a man of principle and honor and one of America's most revered leaders of men.

No student of history of the University of Alabama, of education in the state of Alabama or in the South can fully understand their subject without reading the impassioned words of Dr. George H. Denny from his earliest writings to his last. They are, in effect, a record of a decades-long crusade to bring about universal education in the region, written on the battlefield by one of the nation's most prominent educators of his time. His words revealed his heart; he never attempted in any way to conceal his true thoughts and emotions or deceive his audience on any issue. His words revealed his intelligence and classical and practical education. They revealed his character and ideals. They defined his objectives and he never faltered in his pursuit of them. They revealed his compassion for the children of impoverished, rural tenant farmers and their lack of opportunity for education. They revealed the depth of his vision, the thoroughness of his thought and his foresight in defining the requirements of a truly independent, democratic society. They revealed his sincere affection for Washington and Lee University and the University of Alabama and the students who attended those schools.

One who reads the words of Dr. George H. Denny will surely come to know and appreciate the higher calling that inspired him to dedicate his life to one of service to the thousands of students, the states of Virginia and Alabama, the South and the millions who have benefited directly and indirectly from his efforts through the many thousands who heeded his call to a greater service beyond that of leadership in their chosen professions. One who follows his path through more than half a century as professor, college president and chancellor will surely discover the flags of victory he planted from rural schools to statehouses, state and regional educational conventions, the White House and a national radio broadcast as he waged his campaign for a better world. Sons and daughters of rural Alabama farmers were quickly drawn to Denny and the University of Alabama by his letters promising hope for the future through education. Their parents, swayed by the same letters and same hope, confidently entrusted their children's futures to him. His hardest battles were fought in Montgomery, where Denny faced the greatest resistance to his persistent calls for increased educational funding for public schools and colleges—especially the University of Alabama—from legislatures and governors elected and controlled by farm interests. That wall proved hardest of all to scale for Denny, and though he made significant inroads, he never achieved the complete victory he sought.

Denny's ability to sway public opinion was so powerful that few dared question his reasoning or facts, allowing him to convince citizens of a poor, agrarian state and region to approve self-imposed taxes to establish a statewide system of public schools for the education of its youth. At the same time, working under extreme financial constraints, he transformed the University of Alabama from a small, aristocratic school with little or no national or even regional significance into a university of national recognition.

He was a liberal in a state of independent, suspicious, rural conservatives, yet he faced them unafraid. His scholarly demeanor and Christian lifestyle and attitude commanded respect. He knew his subject and spoke the truth without fear of rebuttal. His well-researched facts and sound logic defied debate and inspired trust, allowing him to sway audience by audience in his favor. He won converts to his cause against great odds with the only tools at his disposal—his missionary zeal, well-chosen words and his confident and caring personality. Those rare traits, coupled with his superior education and national reputation as a college president, set him apart as a leader in his field. He was nationally acclaimed as an educator and administrator and widely sought as a speaker, and he used each address to inform, inspire and educate his audiences on the issues at hand.

Denny's words tell us what he knew, what he believed, what he taught and what he thought the civilized world should become. They told us who he was, and who and what the students he taught should and could be. They inspired those who heard and heeded them, and they remain as true and inspiring today as they were when he spoke them a century ago.

Dr. Denny's portrait, presented to the University in 1944, continues to greet visitors to the second-floor lobby of the Amelia Gayle Gorgas Library on the University of Alabama campus.

18

Denny Spirit Still Present

"It is impossible to think of the University of Alabama without thinking of him, for after all is said and done, an institution is but the lengthening shadow of a great and victorious personality."

—Dean Albert B. Moore

Newspaper headlines of Sunday morning, April 3, 1955, announced the news of the death of Dr. George H. Denny, who had died from heart failure on Saturday following surgery to amputate his left leg a week earlier. "Dr. Denny To Be Buried Monday In Lexington, Va.," *The Tuscaloosa News* headline said. A subhead read, "Man Who Built Modern UA Dies At Age 84," and an accompanying photograph caption identified him as the "father of the modern Capstone." "The nickname 'Mike' stuck with Dr. Denny during and after his service to the University, and a familiar campus sight during his administration was him walking with a coat thrown around his shoulders and a pipe in his mouth," *The Tuscaloosa News* story added in recalling Denny's tenure as president and chancellor of the University. "He was noted for his keen memory and is said to have never forgotten a name," the story added.

"In the passing of Dr. Denny, we have lost one of the great leaders in American education," University of Alabama president Oliver C. Carmichael was quoted as saying. "His loss will be keenly felt throughout the nation by all who knew him, but especially by more than 40,000 alumni of the University of Alabama. Dr. Denny's unparalleled devotion should serve to stimulate in all of us who are left behind a new sense of dedication to that institution which he served so long and so well," Carmichael added. Carmichael was joined by Dean Albert B. Moore, Dr. Brooks Forehand, Dr. John Gallalee, Dr. Walter Jones, Dean James H. Newman and athletic director Henry G. "Hank" Crisp in the delegation to Denny's funeral in Lexington, Virginia, on Monday, April 4.

"Chimes Toll Last Tribute To Dr. Denny," a Monday *Tuscaloosa News* headline said. The accompanying story reported that Denny Chimes on the University of Alabama campus had "tolled Chopin's Funeral March as the man they were constructed to honor was buried in Lexington, Virginia. The Chimes, erected by students and alumni as a tribute to the man who built the Capstone into an internationally famous institution, began the funeral dirge this morning at 10 o'clock, the time of the graveside services in Stonewall Jackson Cemetery in Lexington. The Chimes followed the Funeral March with the hymns Nearer My God To Thee and Abide With Me," the story added. The story also announced that a special radio program entitled "Portrait of Dr. Denny" would be presented that evening on WUOA-FM Radio and on WAPI Radio in Birmingham. The thirty-minute program consisted mainly of recorded excerpts from speeches given by Dr. Denny during his tenure as president of the University, the story said.

An April 5, 1955, *Crimson White* editorial noted Denny's passing under the headline, "Dr. Mike—builder of the Capstone." "We didn't know Dr. George Denny," the editorial began. "Those who knew the white-haired man with the penetrating steel-blue eyes had nothing but good things to say of him. A favorite story is how when he would meet them on the sidewalk, with a coat draped over his shoulders and a pipe between his teeth, he would greet students by name. We did not know him but we can witness Dr. Denny's wonderful spirit—his efforts to make the University the "capstone" of Alabama education. May that spirit always be prevalent here. While Dr. Mike's friendliness and sincerity won him a spot in the heart of his adopted home state, his greatest monument will be the University and her sons and daughters."

"When Dr. Denny took office as president in 1912 the campus consisted of four classroom buildings, three dormitories, a fraternity house and 400 students, including 55 women. Twenty-five years later, when he retired in 1937, the University enrollment totaled nearly 5,000 and the campus included sixteen major buildings, twenty-two fraternity houses, thirteen sorority houses, a football stadium and many other buildings," a *Crimson White* story recounting Denny's contributions to the University said. "One of Dr. Denny's proudest boasts was that the building program had been accomplished largely with funds derived from other than public sources. The entire building program, he often said, had cost Alabama taxpayers only $365,000." The story added that Denny had referred to the University as "the Capstone of Alabama's educational system," thus giving the school its nickname, and had also been the impetus behind the University of Alabama's rise to prominence in athletics and that the football stadium had been named in his honor.

A *Tuscaloosa News* editorial called Denny's loyalty and service "unsurpassed" as it praised his decades of devotion to the University. "For a man who was not a native Alabamian nor an alumnus of the University, there never has been a more loyal and hard-fighting friend of the institution both while he was serving it and in the years later when he was chancellor. There are many things that could be said of him and for him, but nothing that embraces his service to the University and the state more than, as he put it in his own words, 'that I did the very best I could to give the people of Alabama the kind of institution which they have coveted.' And the unselfish devotion to the University which Dr. Denny demonstrated throughout his long years of association with the institution certainly should serve as an outstanding challenge to all those who love and respect this great University to seek, in some measure, to emulate his record," the editorial said.

"Dr. Denny had notable assets for his post," said an April 5 *Birmingham News* editorial. "He was an able administrator and executive. He could tie together the many strands of a university without interfering with the academic freedom without which no university can remain great. He knew how to pick good men and turn them loose on their jobs."

"It may be doubted if any single educator ever wielded the power in Alabama affairs that Dr. Denny did," a *Montgomery Advertiser* editorial said, "Certainly no single educator possesses such power today. Where other school leaders have been inclined to rely upon the mass impact of men and women working for a great cause, Dr. Denny was a leader who got things done in Napoleonic fashion, thorough his own individual drive and powers of persuasion. Dr. Denny was often pictured as 'dictatorial' and the allegation seems to have been well made. The point was that he could dictate in such a way as to inspire respect and downright affection in a great many of those to whom he dictated."

The Anniston Star said, "It well might be said of Dr. Denny that he was a mental prodigy. For while he had been schooled in the classic tradition, when he was elected president of the University of Alabama he became one of the best businessmen this state has known. He could make a dollar go twice as far as the ordinary citizen…. Dr. Denny will probably be remembered most by his students because of his fantastic memory. He seemed never to forget a student, each of whom he could call by name years hence."

The 1956 *Corolla*, like those of 1913 and 1936, was dedicated to Denny with these words: "The memorable years of the University of Alabama will never be recalled without fond and nostalgic recollection of the years Dr. George H. Denny served as president. The fruitful term of Dr. Denny was one of remolding an already outstanding university into a fountainhead of learning. Now he is passed. But the footsteps taken by University of Alabama students in the past, in the present and in the years to come will be directed to landmarks honoring this man. In humble addition to Denny Chimes and Denny Stadium, the students of this University dedicate their 1956 Corolla to Dr. George H. Denny." The 1931 *Corolla* had also beautifully lauded Denny at the height of his career. A Denny photograph caption read: "Dr. George H. Denny, president of the University of Alabama, through whose guiding hand, spirit and heart the University has grown to magnificent proportions. Loved, honored and revered throughout the state and Southland by myriads of friends and faithful admirers, our beloved 'Mike,' through his infallible wisdom and sterling personality, continues to direct the Capstone to yet greater heights and fields of conquest. The University, the commonwealth and the nation owe to him a debt of gratitude that cannot be recompensed with human hands but can only come from a bountiful Father." A 1949 *Corolla* photo caption of Dr. Denny said "The history of the Capstone during the past thirty-seven years is almost a biography of Dr. George H. Denny. No man has done more toward the development of the University."

University trustees paid a final tribute to Denny with a resolution at its annual spring meeting on May 28, 1955. The resolution, written by Dean Albert B. Moore and read by trustee and Denny friend Gordon Palmer, said:

"WHEREAS, on April 4, 1955, Denny Chimes tolled a mournful funeral dirge and flags were at half-staff on the University campus to mark one of the saddest occasions in the University's long and colorful history in the death on April 2, 1955, of its beloved chancellor and president from 1912 to 1937, George Hutcheson Denny, whose passing was quiet after an extended illness in Lexington, Virginia, at the age of eighty-four, and

"WHEREAS, the more than 30,000 alumni who loved and served under this great leader will, at his passing, pause to relive in their minds and hearts their association with him and feel again the inspiration which he imbued; and"WHEREAS, the legislature of Alabama in whose halls were fought his greatest battles for higher education and the public schools in the state in special session paid last homage to this great American in a joint resolution expressing its deep sadness and sympathy; and

"WHEREAS, the members of this board who knew and loved him and have followed the course of his service to the Capstone that he loved so well now affectionately recall the forty-one-year-old Washington and Lee president and Virginian who brought energy, enthusiasm, a sense of humor and courage to a little–known college boasting four classroom buildings clustered about a quadrangle with 400 students; and

"WHEREAS, they recall the warmness of his personality, his unswerving devotion and loyalty to the University, his remarkable memory which prompted many affectionate stories from his students and his financial acumen which was responsible for building a large endowment to give strength and life blood to the institution while not sacrificing the building program or academic standards and his strong faith in God and leadership in the affairs of the Presbyterian Church; and

"WHEREAS, they also recall the clarity of his vision, his ability to make wise decisions and to follow his chartered course with force and vigor, his power of persuasion and his magnificent oratorical ability, his love for sports and devotion to his beloved Crimson Tide, and the firm manner in which he painstakingly built during his presidency a strong university of national significance of more than 5,000 resident students and 10,000 Extension Center students with twenty major campus buildings, thirty-five fraternity and sorority houses and twelve separate schools or colleges with a range of instruction as broad as the needs of the people; and

"WHEREAS, the members of this board have warmly endorsed the many honors and tributes which have been made to Dr. Denny, including Denny Chimes, Denny Stadium, his portrait which hangs in the Gorgas Memorial Library, a bronze bust in the rotunda of the Union Building, his election by popular vote in 1925 as 'the most distinguished professional leader in Alabama' and his selection in 1946 as 'First Citizen of Alabama;' and

"WHEREAS, this board in former years by many resolutions and other official actions which are of record in the minutes of this body have paid tribute to Dr. Denny, again recognizes the unsurpassed contributions he made to the University and his unflagging loyalty best exhibited in his own words, 'I have known and loved the University and tried to keep its commandments. If I had a thousand lives I would gladly give them all in its service. I did the very best I could to give the people of Alabama the kind of institution they have coveted;'

"NOW, THEREFORE, BE IT RESOLVED by the board of trustees of the University of Alabama that this body expresses its feeling of irreparable loss and profound sorrow in the passing of its friend, leader and benefactor, George Hutcheson Denny, and that its sympathy be extended to his family."

Denny not only left his mark on Washington and Lee University and the University of Alabama, but on the entire public educational systems of both states and even the nation during an active career of more than half a century as an educator and administrator. His leadership extended far beyond the college campus, and his achievements were rewarded with many honors. The following list offers a glimpse of many of Denny's honors and achievements:

-Received Union Literary Society Medal at Hampden-Sydney College, 1891.
-Graduated first in his class with A.B. degree from Hampden-Sydney College, 1891.
-Earned master's degree from Hampden-Sydney College, 1892.
-Assistant master at Pantops Academy in Charlottesville, VA, 1892-1896.
-Received Ph.D. degree from the University of Virginia, June 1896.
-Professor of Latin and German, Hampden-Sydney College, 1896-1899.
-Professor of Latin, Washington and Lee University, 1899-1901.
-Elected acting president, Washington and Lee University, September 1901.
-Elected president, Washington and Lee University, June 1902.
-Received honorary doctor of law degree from Furman University, 1902.
-President of the Southern Association of Colleges and Preparatory Schools, 1905.
-Received honorary doctor of law degree from Tulane University, 1905.
-Trustee of the Carnegie Foundation for the Advancement of Teaching, 1905-1947.
-Chairman of the Virginia State Board of Charities and Corrections, 1908-1911.
-Elected president of the University of Alabama, October 1911.
-Chairman of the Alabama Rhodes Scholarship Committee, 1912-1947.
-President of the Alabama State Board of Arbitration, 1912-1916.
-Member of the reception committee at the inauguration of President Wilson, 1913.
-Received honorary doctor of law degree from Washington and Lee, 1913.
-Elected president of the State Society of Sanitary and Moral Prophylaxis, 1913.
-Received honorary doctor of civil law degree from University of the South, 1914.
-Named to World War I Military Training Camps Committee, February 1916.
-Chairman of the National Association of State Universities, 1918.
-Head of Cotton Seed Division of U. S. Food Administration, 1918.
-Elected to honorary membership in University of Alabama "A" Club, 1918.
-Chairman of Educational Committee of the Alabama Sunday School Association, 1919.
-Member of the committee to build a Tuscaloosa hospital, 1919.
-Tuscaloosa chairman of a state World War I memorial drive, 1919.
-Appointed chairman of the Alabama Coal Commission, 1920.
-Chosen Most Distinguished Professional Leader in Alabama, 1925.
-Named to Advisory Commission to the Sesquicentennial Exhibition Association, 1925.
-Elected president of the Association of ROTC Colleges in the U. S., April 1927.
-Named to the National Advisory Commission on Education, 1929.
-Elected president of the Association of Separated State Universities, November 1930.
-Delegate to the White House Conference on Child Health and Protection, 1930.
-Elected to the national Phi Beta Kappa senate, 1930.

-Spoke on "Education in the South" on NBC Radio in New York, October 27, 1933.
-Honored by the New York Southern Society in New York, October 27, 1933.
-First recipient of the Tuscaloosa Civitan Club Citizen of the Year Award, 1934.
-Selected to the Advisory Board of the American Youth Congress, February 1935.
-Chairman of the Virginia Educational Study Commission, 1944-1945.
-Member of Phi Beta Kappa, Omicron Delta Kappa and Newcomen Society.
-Named First Citizen of Alabama at a dinner in Birmingham, November 1946.
-Elected to the Tuscaloosa Civic Hall of Fame, 2007.

Denny might well have added governor of Alabama to his resume had he elected to offer himself for such service. Friends and admirers suggested Denny for governor in 1922 and 1934, and Denny gave serious consideration to the latter date amid much public discussion of his possible nomination. Denny acknowledged his consideration of a possible try for the governorship in a story in the October 2, 1933, issue of *The Tuscaloosa News*, saying, "I regret that I have unduly delayed acknowledgment of the many individual and joint communications urging me to offer for the gubernatorial nomination in the forthcoming primaries. I value highly the generous outpouring of confidence and good will thus elicited. Alabama has been through the years more than good to me. I am keenly conscious of the debt I owe to the people of the state. If my own personal comfort were consulted, I should without question remain where I am. On the other hand, I do not feel at liberty, under all of the circumstances, to refuse to give serious consideration to the judgment of the large groups of representative citizens from practically every county in Alabama who have been pointing to an avenue of service that greatly concerns the entire commonwealth, and this I am doing," he added.

A *University of Alabama Alumni News* editorial during the same month heartily endorsed Denny's possible candidacy. "Pressure has been placed upon Dr. Denny for some time for him to enter the race for governor," the editorial said. "There seems to be a general opinion that putting all politics aside, Dr. Denny would prove a godsend in the gubernatorial chair. If he were placed at the helm of state matters his remarkable executive ability, his economical ideas, his breadth of culture, his knowledge of men and principles of government would make Alabama a state to be known throughout the nation for progress and safe and sane management of affairs."

Dr. John Abercrombie, who preceded Dr. Denny as president of the University, wrote a letter to the editor of the *Montgomery Advertiser* endorsing Denny for the governorship. "…There never was a time when the people needed a rock-ribbed states' rights Democrat for governor more than now; a man who will be governor for all the people, free from the dominating influences of the professional politician and the corporations, a man friendly to the poor and to the rich, treating all alike; a man who believes in the fundamental principles of democracy—equal rights to all, special privileges to none," Abercrombie wrote in part. "The man for governor, in my mind, is Dr. George H. Denny, president of the University of Alabama. I believe that he will make one of the best governors the state has ever had, and will balance the budget by cutting useless expenses rather than by raising taxes," Abercrombie added.

An October 6, 1933, *Crimson White* editorial reluctantly endorsed Denny, saying, "It is with keen interest and a little apprehension that University students learn of the proposed nomination of President Denny for governor of the state. We are interested because we are fully aware that Dr. Denny richly deserves the highest honor Alabama can bestow upon a citizen. We are apprehensive because we are a little afraid of being without the guiding hand of our beloved leader. Our distinguished president has achieved an enviable record both as an administrator and as an educator. He has developed the most efficient educational system in the state and one of the most efficient in the entire nation. Through his efforts, the cost of a higher education has been lowered so that finances are no longer a serious hindrance to the earnest student. We could easily devote an entire column to a list of the multitude of achievements of our eminent and benevolent president. There is no question as to his being by far the most thoroughly capable person the people could choose as their leader in these troubled times.

"We feel perfectly safe in saying that no other man in the state has given himself so unselfishly and so unreservedly to public service as Dr. George H. Denny. Although as he said in a recent statement to the press, he would be happier to remain in his present position, but if the public considered that he could be of more value to Alabama in the capitol than at the University, he would gladly sacrifice his personal preference. The students of the University would indeed be reluctant to give up their cherished leader and most outstanding personality. His withdrawal would be a serious handicap to the institution. His character has become a tradition of the campus and a symbol of respect and honor. No chief executive could ask more loyalty or more whole-hearted support than that eagerly given Dr. Denny by the entire student body. We are totally at a loss to imagine what we would do without his understanding direction; but if the people of Alabama feel that our 'Mike' is more needed in Montgomery than at the University, then we, too—following the splendid example of our chief—are also willing to make a personal sacrifice for the common good," the editorial concluded. Denny, at age sixty-three in 1934, eventually chose not to enter the political arena, citing continued health issues.

Denny's spiritual presence at the University of Alabama has endured for generations after his death. The children, grandchildren and great-grandchildren of students who attended the Capstone during his tenure as president still retell stories of Denny's special assistance or acknowledgement of their ancestors. Untold thousands have benefitted from his work; others have been inspired by his words. Many more have benefitted from the work of his former students, including that of Carl Elliott, who as a U. S. Representative drafted and helped pass the National Defense Education Act, which has provided low-cost loans for millions of college students. It has been clearly established that Denny, as he set out to do, raised the standards of education and expanded the opportunities for education and better living conditions for generations of Alabamians.

Even his death did not mark the end of Denny's material contributions to the University of Alabama. It has been estimated that Denny earned $250,000 as president and chancellor of the University of Alabama from 1912 until his death in 1955. Monetary gifts from his last two surviving daughters, Frances Denny and Margaret Denny McClung, upon their deaths, provided $1.2 million to establish the Dr. George H. and Jane Strickler Denny Memorial Scholarship, which provides scholarships to full-time students in need of financial assistance at the University. Similar scholarships honoring Denny were established by Margaret McClung at Hampden-Sydney College and Washington and Lee University. There is also a Dr. George H. and Jane Denny Nursing Scholarship at the University.

The University of Alabama further honored Dr. Denny in 1998 when it created the Denny Society, a University program of giving through estate planning. The Denny Society, which currently has an enrollment of approximately 900 members, is open to anyone who wishes to include the University in his or her will.

Ironically, Denny's personal life was marked as much by tragedy as his public life was by achievement. His health began to fail in 1920, when he first considered retirement; his daughter Charlotte died in an accident just two years after graduating from the University; his only son, George H. Denny Jr., died of a stroke in April 1954 at age forty-nine, and his only grandchild was born with severe birth defects and died at age fifteen.

Denny and his wife Jane had three children—Frances, eleven; Charlotte, nine; and George Jr., six—when they arrived in Tuscaloosa in January 1912. Their fourth child, Margaret, was born in Tuscaloosa on June 28, 1914. All four of the children earned degrees from the University.

Frances, a 1920 University of Alabama graduate, taught school in Tuscaloosa, Birmingham and Roanoke, Virginia, before moving to Lexington to help care for her parents in their later years. She never married and died November 7, 1988.

Charlotte received additional training in Chicago after graduating from the University in 1923 and was in her second year as supervisor of music in the public schools of Jackson, Mississippi, when she was seriously burned on Friday evening, January 14, 1927, when her clothing caught fire as she stood before an open fireplace to warm herself as temperatures hovered in the teens, according to news reports. Mrs. Denny rushed to her daughter's side immediately and Dr. Denny followed soon afterward. Early reports indicated that Charlotte was expected to make a full recovery, but she died on January 26. A *Tuscaloosa News* report said her death "was all the more distressing" because her chances for recovery had been favorable. She was first buried in Evergreen Cemetery across the street from Denny Stadium and later moved to Tuscaloosa Memorial Park. Dr. Denny had Charlotte's remains moved to a family plot in the Stonewall Jackson Cemetery in Lexington, Virginia, in September 1954 after her brother was buried there in April 1954.

George H. "Buster" Denny Jr. earned a law degree from the University in 1929 and practiced law in Washington, D. C., until he enlisted in the Army Air Forces in March 1942. He served with the Flight Control Command in Winston-Salem, North Carolina. He remained in Winston-Salem after the war, working as an adjudicator with the Veterans Administration until his sudden death from a stroke on April 24, 1954. George Jr. married Evelyn Olson in July 1943, but they did not have children. Evelyn Olson Denny died May 20, 1986, and is buried beside her husband.

Margaret, a 1936 University graduate, married Dr. Oscar Hunter McClung Jr. of Lexington, Virginia, on April 14, 1939, and remained in Lexington until her death at age seventy-nine on September 25, 1993. At the time of her death, she was the last surviving member of her immediate family. Her husband had died at age seventy-eight in May 1992 from injuries suffered in a bicycle accident. Mrs. McClung once served as editor of the *Rockbridge County News*. Margaret's only child and Dr. Denny's only grandchild, Oscar Hunter McClung III, was born June 3, 1940, with severe birth defects and died in November 1955.

Mrs. Denny, a native of Virginia who was educated at Agnes Scott College in Atlanta, died May 24, 1957. The Denny family plot in Stonewall Jackson Cemetery is only steps from the grave and monument to Lexington native Thomas "Stonewall" Jackson. The cemetery is located only a few blocks from Washington and Lee University, where Denny taught and served as president from 1899-1911. Denny's name marks two streets (Denny Circle and Denny Lane) in Lexington in addition to Denny Chimes and Bryant-Denny Stadium in Tuscaloosa.

Dr. Denny's nearest known living relative in early 2015 was ninety-eight-year-old Mildred Denny Routt, the daughter of Dr. Denny's younger half-brother Robert Denny, who was a prominent attorney in Nicholasville, Kentucky. "I remember him very well," Mrs. Routt said of Dr. Denny. "He took us to some Alabama football games against Kentucky in Lexington, and the thing I remember most is that he smoked cigars that about got us," she said. Denny was known to smoke strong Virginia cheroots from time to time in addition to his trademark pipe. Robert Denny earned a law degree at Washington and Lee University in 1910 while Dr. Denny was president there. A biography of Robert Denny described him as "one of the first citizens of Jessamine County, known throughout central Kentucky, a moving spirit in civic affairs and looked to for leadership in every endeavor for civic and social betterment. With a personality and a professional and business record that inspires confidence, he is a notable figure in leadership."

Another Denny brother, Wright, was one of the earliest school principals in Charles Town, West Virginia, and Wright Denny Intermediate School there is named in his honor. Denny's other siblings included brothers Richard and Barnes and sisters Mattie and Otelia.

Denny received universal praise for his development of the University of Alabama and his contributions to education in the South, but he was also known for his management style, which featured a strict, hands-on approach and tight purse strings. "My father (Fred Maxwell, a University faculty and staff member for thirty-six years) used to say that Dr. Denny would squeeze a nickel until the buffalo hollered," Camille Maxwell Elebash said.

Denny's budget constraints applied to every University department, including athletics, of course. Rumors persisted for decades that head football coach Wallace Wade resigned in 1930 after winning three national championships in eight seasons because of management and/or financial differences with Denny. A 1930 expense report turned in by assistant football coach Hank Crisp following an August 1930 recruiting trip to nine cities in Arkansas and another in Louisiana listed only $51.87 spent over several days, with the notation that he had traveled by automobile with other coaches during much of the trip, avoiding additional expenses. It is worth noting that the 1930 Arkansas recruiting trip was responsible for the recruitment of future All-America end Don Hutson of Pine Bluff and that Crisp made a similar recruiting trip to Arkansas in 1931—likely at similar expense—in which he returned home with Paul "Bear" Bryant of Fordyce.

University football booster and promoter Champ Pickens wrote Denny in October 1923 to question Denny's refusal to approve the expenditure of athletic funds to advertise an upcoming football game in Birmingham, saying, "How are we going to get any money (gate receipts) without advertising? I must be allowed to spend at least $100, for which you will be given receipted bills." Pickens, a pre-1900 football manager, had previously been directed by Denny to discontinue his unauthorized involvement in the search for a new football coach in December 1922, which prompted a response of compliance addressed to "George H. Denny, Sole Owner, University, Tuscaloosa, Alabama."

"Dr. Denny conceived his job to be the education of young men and women, not only in academics but in the personal character required for carrying out life's responsibilities," said Dr. James F. Doster, a 1932 University graduate and long-time Capstone history professor. "He (Dr. Denny) was a harsh and demanding taskmaster, but when a student got into trouble, there was no better friend. He was dedicated to the accomplishment of his objectives despite the severe weakness of the financial resources with which he had to work. He was always desperate for money and did what it took to get the job done. The University was run on half a shoestring, and Dr. Denny had no objection to faculty members taking outside work to sustain themselves. My father (University professor of education Dr. James J. Doster) took the train to Livingston each Saturday to teach classes at what is now the University of West Alabama and engineering professor John Gallalee did work for Bryce Hospital and was rewarded by having his white suits cleaned by the hospital's residents," Doster added.

Although Denny has no remaining direct descendants, many of his thousands of former students at Washington and Lee and the University of Alabama—whom he counted as his own—have passed along his ideals to other generations, keeping his legacy intact for generations yet to come. He personally invited—even sometimes dared—thousands of boys and girls who might never have attended college to come to the University of Alabama, and once they arrived he arranged jobs to keep them there to teach, befriend, guide and inspire to do the same for others. His legacy includes such recognizable names as Lister Hill, Carl Elliott, John Sparkman, Claude Pepper, Paul "Bear" Bryant—men whose work touched millions, but it also includes tens of thousands of others, including the thousands of grade school and college teachers who returned to their home communities to teach, befriend, guide and inspire others to similar success. It took time, dedication to a high purpose and the work of many disciples, but Denny clearly succeeded in helping to break the cycle of poverty and bring social and cultural change to the poor, rural state of Alabama and beyond through the University of Alabama.

The 1939 *Corolla* offered an appropriate, lasting but not final tribute to Denny, saying, "Almost any afternoon during football season or on a bright day in spring, a familiar figure can be seen sauntering across the green Capstone campus. He is distinguished in appearance, gray-haired, and if the breeze is brisk, a topcoat will likely be draped over his slightly stooped shoulders. 'Mike,' as he is affectionately termed by young and old alike, can rest on his laurels. In his twenty-five-year tenure as Alabama's president, he brought the University from a lowly place to a pinnacle of eminence. That is honor enough for any man, for as a recent speaker asserted in recounting the magnificent accomplishments of Denny: 'We recall the young man who took his place and cast his lot among his own people, who knew it was better to give than to receive, became the servant of all of us and built here this great university, so strong and so great that it is recognized and acclaimed among men, and students come to it from the four corners of the nation.' It is well for all Alabama students to contemplate the inspiring example of the character, the service and the life of George H. Denny."

Denny attends an Alabama football game, circa 1945.

Appendix A

Excerpts from several speeches by Dr. George H. Denny. An extensive archive of Denny's speeches is on file at the James Graham Leyburn Library at Washington and Lee University, Lexington, Virginia.

Inaugural Address, Washington and Lee University

"…It will hardly be questioned that the tendency in recent years, in this country at least, has been to emphasize the opportunities of our literary foundations and to say comparatively little of the service they should render in the pursuit of their ideals. Indeed, it would seem that there is a growing tendency to overlook the fact that every opportunity that comes to these institutions must of necessity carry with it a corresponding responsibility; that the greater the opportunity so much the greater the responsibility it involves; and that just in proportion as these responsibilities are faithfully met and discharged are these institutions worthy of the great opportunities which this strenuous age has laid at their doors. Service is everywhere the measure of human worth and excellence…. Service must likewise be the measure of the worth of academic attainment. It is deemed appropriate to this occasion, therefore, to inquire as to the nature, character and importance of several of the more striking and fundamental responsibilities that belong in common to all of our institutions of higher learning….

"I name first as an obligation on the part of our institutions of higher learning a well-defined catholicity in their attitude towards all realms of knowledge. It is recognized, at last, that…there is an education of the learned professions, states craft, science and philosophy, and that there is an education of the industrial and mechanical arts. The time has passed when our institutions of higher learning can ever again recur to the narrow curriculum of a half century ago. The old-fashioned course has served its day. The education of the future will be designed to lead and not to drive. Human reason, unfettered by tradition or the dicta of authority, is subordinating the sense of study as an obligation to the sense of study as an opportunity. It is everywhere proving all things and holding fast only that which is good. Many of the ancient theories of education which were supposed to involve a finality of wisdom have been exploded by the facts of experience and observation. It is no longer seriously contended that a narrow group of subjects can, by any chance, possess exclusive qualities for mental training. It is true that the study of mathematics develops the logical reason, that language trains the power of interpretation and science that of accurate observation. But these are not to be considered exclusive rights. It must be admitted that other subjects of equal intrinsic value may be used as instruments to develop precisely the same power…. It has been demonstrated that the elective system, under definite and proper restrictions, furnishes room for both the old and the new. Our institutions of higher learning may, under the influence of such a system, become indeed temples of learning, dispensing a broad and catholic culture and giving to the world not only great teachers, statesmen and clergymen such as the old system produced, but leaving room also for the introduction and dissemination of industrial and technical knowledge, which is the foundation of wealth and comfort and upon which this section of our country is expectantly and impatiently waiting.

"…I shall mention as a fourth obligation resting upon our institutions of higher learning the duty and responsibility of keeping the educational advantages they offer within the reach of the common people. In order to accomplish this, these institutions must themselves be brought nearer the common people and the common people must be brought nearer the institutions…. Our institutions must sooner or later face the practical question of furnishing an adequate system of education that will come within reach of the masses who constitute their natural constituency. To accomplish this, adequate invested endowments are needed. It is perfectly clear that if the scale of expense is such as to exclude young men of moderate means we shall not be able to secure their patronage. We must then return to the training of a privileged class. Our system will in that case become, so far as the masses are concerned, the instrument of oppression instead of the instrument of freedom, for the uneducated masses will become practically the slaves of an educated oligarchy. But instead of an educated class, our great need is an educated community. The problem, then, is to offer educational advantages under such conditions as are adapted to the resources of the masses of the people; to make our institutions of learning living fountains to water every portion and not isolated spots of our social garden. It is a social wrong to make education a thing apart from the condition and the participation of the great mass of men…. Our Southern people need to be aroused to their duty in the matter of giving to their institutions of learning. They need to recognize more clearly the obligation resting upon them to strengthen their own institutions…. It is infinitely better to prevent pauperism by educating the masses than to relieve it by public and private charities. It is literally true that the best political economy is the care and culture of men.

"If we are to bring the common people within the reach of our institutions of higher learning, public sentiment needs to be aroused as to the importance of education. It may be true that we cannot control the public appetite for knowledge and the public willingness to acquire it; but a vastly larger number of men can be made to learn more distinctly that education, not merely of a privileged class but of the masses, is essential if our section is not to be practically excluded from the counsels of state and to become a dependent province instead of a coordinate portion of the nation…. It is no longer a disputed fact that the material progress of a people is in direct proportion to their education. It devolves, therefore, upon our institutions of higher learning to impress these facts upon the minds of the common people. It is vitally important that our institutions of higher learning, as the exponent of our higher ideals, should recognize their obligation to bring the masses of the people within their reach and salutary influence.

"I should name as a fifth obligation resting on our institutions of higher learning an intelligent recognition of their relation and duty to the state. These institutions are not merely laboratories for the investigation of chemical or physical properties. They have a higher mission and are expected to perform a more important function than that. They are training schools, not merely for the making of scholars whose supreme thought is of a mathematical formula or a rule of syntax but also for the development of patriotic men who will lend a helping hand in the solution of the great problems of city, state and nation at this stirring period in the history of our country. These institutions must therefore teach the interdependence of learning and of life…. They must emphasize the fact that an intelligent citizen ought to be a great public blessing, and that every man owes a duty to his neighbor, to the community in which he lives and to the commonwealth of which he is a member. They must recognize the fact that a democratic government founded upon an electorate without intelligence is as a house whose foundation is sand; that democracy is still on trial and has yet to establish its right to exist as the ultimate form of government; that education alone is able to save the masses from becoming the dupes of designing men and to give them the means of detecting a wrong and applying a remedy. Education, therefore, in a democracy where the people are sovereign, is not merely a question of philanthropy and expediency; it is also a question of life and death. The sovereign people must be educated or we must live under an ignorant sovereign.

"In our own country, for instance, great and fundamental questions concerning finance and trade, questions involving political expediency and moral right are decided by the people as the court of final appeal. These questions are daily becoming more complicated and serious…. To whom has the nation a right to look for help and leadership in these matters? To whom has the nation always looked? Is it not true that the founders of states have likewise been the founders of colleges? Have we not ample testimony to support the view expressed by John Adams to the effect that 'our republic is indebted to her seminaries of learning for her liberty, independence, glory and prosperity?' Did not Washington, Jefferson and Franklin recognize this when they founded institutions to train young men for citizenship and the public services? We need not expect that the national life of the country will be stronger or nobler than its institutions of learning. It is evident, therefore, that these institutions are under obligation to exercise a proper influence upon the life of the state…. The growth of crime, the defiance of law and the presence of mob rule all confirm the suspicion that there is danger ahead. How is this danger to be averted? Whose duty is it to meet it? Where does the solution of the problem lie if not at the door of our institutions of higher learning?

"…I would mention as a seventh obligation resting on our institutions of higher learning the elevation of the moral standard of the country. This means that these institutions must stand for character…. It is important to exercise the reason, the memory and the imagination; it is more important that the conscience should be awake and active. We need knowledge chiefly to enable us to perform service. We need right theories of life chiefly to persuade us to right living. It therefore becomes the duty of our institutions of higher learning to establish and propagate a high standard of moral integrity, to teach men that might does not and cannot make right…. We need physical wealth; we need inventive genius; we need literary and scientific achievement; but our greatest need is for the highest type of man; the type of man indeed who 'sweareth to his own hurt and changeth not.' Washington's idea that a university is a place which should train not only the intellect but also the character is the correct one. Our country is rich in things material. It is now calling for men—not merely those trained in social and political science, but more especially those who possess such an instinct of rectitude as would 'shrink from the false and the base as from the contamination of the plague.' Upon this rock should be based the training of the American college. Such training alone will enable the college graduate to demonstrate to the world he must fashion and mold that it is not heredity nor manifest destiny nor force of circumstances but character and conscience that constitutes the governing force of national and personal life. If it is true that the moral life and the moral instinct will not last longer than the moral conviction, nor the moral conviction longer than the salutary influence of our institutions of higher learning, then must it not also be true that these institutions hold in their hands the key to national destiny so far as morality is concerned? **(Delivered to students, faculty, trustees and guests at Denny's June 17, 1902, inauguration as permanent president of Washington and Lee University, Lexington, Virginia, following a year in which he served as acting president.)**

Devotion to Truth

"It is my purpose this morning to elaborate briefly on two of the most important ideals that may be expected to determine the ambition of every student, whether in the lowliest rural schoolhouse or in the stateliest university pile.... The two ideals to which I refer, and upon which I shall dwell at this time, may be briefly summarized as (1) an ardent desire to find the truth and (2) an unfailing courage to follow it, after its discovery, wherever it leads. On these two ideals 'hang all the laws and the prophets' so far as academic and professional training is concerned. In the first place, then, we remark that the most cherished word in the vocabulary of education is 'truth.' Our institutions of higher learning rightly pronounce this to be the very goal of their aspiration. The motto of Harvard, for instance, is *veritas*, truth; the motto of Yale, *lux et veritas,* light and truth. The motto of every institution of learning of a right ought to be 'Ye shall know the truth and the truth shall set you free.'

"To seek the truth; to find the truth; to know the truth; to guard the truth; to desire the truth; to proclaim the truth—this is the prime condition of intellectual life and progress. To seek the truth for truth's own sake; to make this search for truth a vital principle; to allow it to animate and govern the operations of the mind and heart; and to remember that 'he who intentionally cheats himself will not scruple to mislead another.' This should constitute the foundation principle of scholastic endeavor. Education will have missed the mark and we shall have fed only on its husks if it fails to affect the philosophy of life and aspiration; if it fails to strengthen the moral purpose which sways our destiny or to lead us to a clearer conception of truth and duty.... Indeed, it may be said that the attainment of all human happiness and utility worthy of the name is to be attributed in its last analysis to the reign of truth and obedience of its laws.

"The world has a right to expect of the educated man impartial and patient investigation. The world has a right to expect that he will reason on data and not from emotion; that it will be his effort to try all things and to hold fast only that which is good; that it will be his effort to substitute reason for fanaticism, fact for unsupported dogma, logical truth for argumentative casuistry; that nothing short of the whole truth will satisfy him—not the half-truth, not the perverted truth, not the partisan truth, not the sectional truth, not the sectarian truth, but the truth, the whole truth and nothing but the truth....To walk in the path of truth with a reasonable hope of finding it, several qualities are essential; chief among them moral earnestness of purpose, intellectual clearness of vision and freedom from passion and prejudice…. Men will continue to differ in their view of the truth, but the man who seeks it with a calm and open mind will find it while the bigot and the blockhead will continue to grope in the outer darkness…. The man of trained mind, quickened conscience and tolerant judgment need not be afraid to seek the truth wherever it may be found and whatever may be the result to established systems.

"The second ideal that should dominate the purpose of aspiring young men involves a sincere purpose to follow the truth wherever it leads. It is important to seek and find the truth; it is equally as important to possess the courage of one's convictions to follow it, after its discovery, wherever it leads. This will often require the exercise of all that is heroic in us. We shall often be found in an insignificant minority. We shall often run counter to public opinion. It may be that we shall be called to stand alone. Such action may not pave the way to a vote of thanks or a nomination to Congress, but it is the sole guarantee of a healthy self-respect and peace of conscience, which is far better. It will not call forth the plaudits of designing men. It may even escape their observation, but it will receive the divine recognition and approval, which should be man's chief concern. Thus it is that we should be encouraged to seek and find and follow the truth with courage and faith, looking only to conscience and recognizing our responsibility only to the Supreme power who ruleth all things well, exercising less concern for what the eye and voice and conscience of the world may see or say or sanction…. In seeking these higher ideals, our literary institutions should play the leading part. Such ideals, young gentlemen, we are endeavoring to cherish and to place before you here…. It will be our endeavor not to drive you in any direction but merely to lead you in the ways of truth with the simple faith that it will make you free. *(**Delivered to incoming classes at Washington and Lee and the University of Alabama on various occasions.**)*

Two Essentials of Success

"A great occasion, it is often claimed, makes great men; but there is a false philosophy in this assumption. A great occasion merely serves to give a great man the opportunity to manifest the essentials of greatness he has all along possessed. Indeed, it is purpose and efficiency that in most instances make the opportunity which is the occasion for the manifestation of greatness. Nothing is more important to a successful career than a definite purpose or aim. It is not sufficient, however, that there shall be a definite purpose. This definite purpose must also be a worthy purpose; it is the character of the purpose, or motive, or ideal, whichever you choose to call it, that determines the character of the man, and therefore the character of the success he will achieve…. There are sound reasons that explain why it is that a definite, high purpose plays such an important part in determining the success of a man. The first reason is that such purpose of itself incites a man to train his faculties and thus make them effective…. This is true with regard to matters physical, mental and moral. The man possessed of a high and definite purpose will turn possibilities into powers.

"The second requisite of success is efficiency. This involves three elements: ability, or capacity, industry and preparation. Ability added to industry, if rightly directed, means preparation. Aim without efficiency falls as far short of success as does efficiency without aim; the one is the support of the other. Mental capacity is, of course, the fundamental basis of efficiency. Industry is the second element of efficiency. It is unquestionably easier not to develop than to develop; it is unquestionably pleasanter to let the moss grow on our backs; but efficiency requires industry. Whatever the profession, whether engineering, law, medicine or whatnot, there is need of industry in order to attain proficiency…. The third element of efficiency is preparation. There is no doubt that the lack of preparation explains its full quota of failure. Success depends upon equipment and training for service. This explains the existence of institutions of higher learning. The laws that underlie success must be learned if success is to be achieved. It is capacity, preparation and industry guided by purpose that enables a man to succeed." *(Delivered to various student assembly audiences at Washington and Lee University and the University of Alabama.)*

Certain Peculiar Duties Imposed by Education

"It has been suggested in some quarters that the acquisition of learning imposes no special, peculiar duties whatsoever; that education is merely a boon whereby one is enabled to pass a life of retirement and ease in the sphere of speculative reasoning, in the contemplation of the abstract and in the companionship of books. It will be apparent upon reflection that such a scheme of life, so far from being correct, is most ungenerous and unworthy. The acquisition of learning not only brings its substantial rewards but no less certainly imposes special and peculiar duties of the highest moment…. First of all, we would mention the duty of educating and giving tone to public opinion. Whatever other duty is imposed by education, it cannot be denied that there exists, and ought to exist, a demand upon the time and service of the educated masses in establishing a healthy and proper public sentiment…. The voice of public justice demands it, and the divine rights of humanity invest this demand with a solemn significance. A healthy public sentiment is the great moral and moving power among civilized nations. It is, indeed, the vital breath of republican institutions. The democratic government under which we live is, as yet, merely an experiment; it stands on trial before the gaze of the world. Under such a government an uneducated and debased public sentiment is the greatest curse that can afflict a nation.

"The flag of freedom will not continue to wave long over a nation of blockheads. Ignorance and vicious knowledge, so far from standing for the majesty of law and order, are the great fomenters of anarchy and so far from establishing freedom, they are the surest guarantee of intellectual and moral bondage…. The supreme question, therefore, is this: how may we contribute to the proper education of public sentiment? I answer in a most direct and concrete form that we can contribute to this end by giving our cordial support throughout life to our literary institutions, whether universities, colleges, secondary or primary schools…. Men are beginning to recognize, as never before, the necessity for the education of all the people; that this is the foremost task of our statesmanship and the most worthy object of our philanthropy; that it is better to spend money to save children than it is to sacrifice children to save money. There is a deep-seated conviction that the masses need to be educated; that it is a social and moral wrong to make education a thing apart from the condition and participation of the great mass of men.

"If we would exalt public sentiment; if we would be clad in new robes of civic usefulness and civic self-respect, the educated masses are not to separate themselves in Olympic isolation, but must rally around the schoolhouse as the temple of our liberty and the palladium of our hope. They must convince the rich man that it is far more blessed to give than to receive in such a cause; that he should find in his wealth not a treasure to be hoarded but a mighty lever to lift need to the level of self-help. They must convince the illiterate poor man, bound to a life of poverty and toil, that life will be brighter for his boy and girl than it had been for him if he will deny himself for their sake…. We can contribute to the proper education of public sentiment by seeking to inspire in those whom we may be enabled to influence a spirit of self-reliance, of independence and individuality of character. Great is the difference between the trained and untrained mind. On one hand is to be found a calm, steadfast spirit of independence; on the other a vacillating irresolution, born of a mind that is to be swayed by appeals, however irrational, or that may be swept away by the tempest of its own passions. The untrained mind, therefore, needs to be taught by the trained mind that individuality of thought and action is alone able to guarantee freedom; that a man can never be free until he thinks for himself, acts for himself, and learns to make answer to his own conscience for his conduct; that such independence and individuality of character alone fit a man for the duties of life and their proper performance…. Is there not a crying obligation upon us to use all rightful means to stem the tide of ignorance and evil and place truth and righteousness on the throne? There can be but one answer to this question and upon this answer hangs the destiny of popular sentiment in our section. If we would escape the mournful duty of having to behold with mingled awe and humiliation the caprice with which hosannas are turned into execrations at the bidding of the demagogue; if we would save the masses from becoming the dupes of designing men and from yielding their convictions and their consciences to be trampled in the dust by the buffaloes of the herd as they snuff the air and scour the plain, the intelligence and integrity of the country must do its duty, and do it bravely.

"…A second great duty imposed by the discipline of learning is the obligation to foster a spirit of genuine patriotism and to establish a right standard of political integrity…. The great political need of this day is to teach men what real patriotism is; to convince them that it is not merely an outward performance of certain duties, but that it is also a precious and sacred sentiment of the heart; that it is or ought to be a principle that strikes its roots deep down into the individual conscience; that it should mold into the very stamina of those who possess it such a spirit of unselfish loyalty to correct principles of government as will not suffer them to be surrendered or bartered away to any unholy ambition for personal advancement or to any fear of personal consequences…. Only that patriotism which can refine itself into martyrdom if need be; which can suffer as well as act; which is intelligent and strong in the consciousness of rectitude is worthy of the name; and only such a patriotism can and will survive the storm and stress of attack and adversity and assist at the coronation of a brighter destiny for our country.

"America's best heritage and her highest glory will rest, ultimately and eternally, upon the character and sacrifice of those of her sons who are moved by a passion to respect the rights of others rather than selfishly and dishonestly promote their own; who are possessed with a burning zeal to do what is right rather than merely to seem right in the eyes of somebody else; who are inspired with an ambition to deserve rather than to reap the fruits of reward…. The world needs to be convinced that life is not to be regarded as a mere feast of the senses where waist deep in the icy waters of avarice men dig up ounces of gold, but as the scene of a more earnest and a wider-reaching work where duties ever surround us, the performance of which constitutes a solemn obligation. It is your mission, if you are true to the vows of learning, to carry this conviction to the hearts of men. If we as a nation expect successfully to storm the heights of twentieth century opportunity, first of all comes, as already indicated, the great practical duty and necessity of establishing and educating public sentiment, of inspiring and cultivating a feeling of genuine patriotism among the masses clinging to the principle that nothing is politically right which is morally wrong; and finally, of elevating the moral standard of the nation. Our appeal to you, therefore, is to unite in this struggle for the higher and better destiny that is soon to come if the educated masses resolve to face their duty fairly and squarely." *(**Delivered to incoming students at Washington and Lee University and the University of Alabama on various occasions.**)*

Certain Responsibilities of the Christian Student

"There is an impression in many minds that the acquisition of learning need not impose any special duties and responsibilities. It is argued that the educated man is at liberty, if he so chooses, to pass his life in the sphere of speculative reasoning, in the contemplation of the abstract, and in the companionship of books; that he may, with perfect propriety, withdraw himself from the world, its struggles and cares, and lead a life of retirement and ease. I do not hesitate to express the conviction that the acquisition of learning, whether classical, scientific or professional, not only brings its substantial rewards, but no less certainly imposes practical duties and responsibilities of the highest moment; that it develops just those faculties which enable a man to deal most mightily with his fellow men; that it places in his hands the very instruments by means of which the status of society is mainly fashioned and controlled. And I am equally as clear that upon the Christian student rests the solemn duty of sounding the bugle call in this age of darkness and doubt to the higher life of Christian morality, faith and fortitude; that upon the educated, Christian citizen rests the duty of summoning men to the life of heroic struggle and civic virtue. We are beginning to realize as never before that education in a democracy is not merely a question of philanthropy and expediency but of life and death; and realizing this, we cannot escape the conviction that the highest, noblest and best product of education—the Christian student—must stand as the surest preserver of our liberties and the ablest defender of our peace. Perhaps there is no country in the world where popular ignorance, and even education with moral degeneracy, is attended with more disastrous consequences than in our own.

"Great and fundamental questions concerning taxation, commerce, finance and morals—questions lying at the very root of our social and political life—are decided by the people as the court of ultimate appeal. It is true also that these questions are becoming more complicated and numerous every year. To whom has the country a right to look for help and leadership in these matters? To whom has she always looked? Who is competent to meet and solve them with patience, with intelligence, with sympathy and with righteousness? Who are the men that are able and willing to assume these fearful responsibilities? Upon whom, more than upon the educated, Christian citizen, rests the duty of the hour? The highest glory of our country will not ultimately rest upon her fertile fields and extended plains, her populous cities and expanding commerce, her wealth of forest, field and mine; but more specifically upon the character and sacrifice of her sons. This nation is rich in things material. It is now calling for men not merely trained in language, philosophy and science but men possessing that instinct of rectitude which 'shrinks from the false and the base as from the contamination of the plague,' men who know their duty and have the courage of their convictions to do it. It is not heredity, therefore, not manifest destiny nor force of circumstances but character and conscience that constitute the governing powers of national and personal life. The highest type of manhood consists not in science and letters but in the strenuous life of faith and devotion to duty. Finally, let me say that in meeting the great responsibilities to which we have directed your attention tonight—the duty to the state of which you may become citizens, the duty of resisting the material and commercial craze of this stirring age, the duty of establishing a high moral standard and the duty of promoting the Christian faith—the Christian student will hasten the coming of that day of universal wisdom and righteousness." *(Delivered to student assemblies at Washington and Lee University and the University of Alabama at various times.)*

Education in the South: Its Difficulties and Its Needs

"To say that education is the supreme question of civilization, whether viewed from the standpoint of the individual, the community, the state or the nation is only to express the conviction of a great multitude of men whose keen foresight, sober patriotism and sympathetic service have most contributed to the growth and prosperity of our common country. It is true that the conviction of many of our leading men has at last found utterance in the declaration that the education of all the people is the foremost task of our statesmanship and the most worthy object of our philanthropy. It is also true that these men have expressed the conviction that this ought to be the primary policy, as it is now the immediate duty, of our Southern section. But, unhappily, this is not enough. It remains to make this conviction the common and universal expression of our civic patriotism and civic aspiration.

"How are we to convince all our people, or even the great majority of them, that every human life without a single exception is 'a plan of God' and has its place in the divine economy? How are we to convince all our people, or even the great majority of them, that it is a social and moral wrong to make education a thing apart from the condition and participation of the great mass of men? How are we to make them understand that universal education is from every rational consideration the fundamental need of our civilization and the bulwark of our liberty? Any rational attempt to answer these questions intelligently brings sharply to our attention the general problem of education in the South, its difficulties and its needs.

"We should mention first in the catalogue of difficulties that confront the advocates of universal education in this section the ancient barrier of social tradition and social prejudice. It seems all too clear to us at this time that the social organization which obtained in the Southern states prior to the Civil War was from the very nature of the case prejudicial to the education of all classes and conditions of men. The ideal then cherished was distinctly an aristocratic ideal, born of the conception that the need of a country is an educated class rather than an educated community. This conception produced a galaxy of stars in the learned professions but it utterly failed to recognize the two cardinal principles in any sound philosophy of education—universality and diversity. It failed to recognize the fundamental fact that all forms of human service are equally honorable, and that education, whether of the heart, the head or the hand, is demanded in every vocation of life; that there can be no aristocracy in skill and learning; that the great need of society is such training as will develop what is best in each individual and fit him for the environment in which he is to move....

"A second difficulty in the way of universal education in the South, quite as embarrassing as the traditional social prejudices to which we have referred, is the comparative, and in many sections the absolute, poverty of the Southern people. This is to be traced largely to the financial and political results of the Civil War and the period of reconstruction. A third difficulty becomes apparent from a consideration of the fact that we have a scattered and heterogeneous population. The former condition is due to the fact that the South is essentially an agricultural section; the latter due chiefly to the introduction of African slavery. The great mass of our people live and work in the country and hence must be educated in the rural school. A fourth difficulty is the spirit of ultra-individualism that prevails in our section. Individualism has gone too far in the South, certainly in educational matters. We emphasize the idea of individual liberty. If rightly understood, that is a good thing. We emphasize the idea of individual initiative. If rightly understood, that is a good thing. But when we carry the idea of individualism to the point of dooming hundreds of thousands of Southern children to the tyranny of ignorance and weakness and poverty on the pretext that the individual as an individual rather than society as a society is responsible for the crime, we abuse the meaning of the term and perpetuate a grievous wrong upon civilization. This is the kind of individualism that proclaims the doctrine that it is robbery to tax Brown's property to educate Smith's children. This is the kind of individualism that denies the right of the state to tax the property of both Smith and Brown to educate the children of both for intelligent citizenship and service.

"What does this kind of individualism have to say as to the cooperative idea in establishing prisons for criminals and asylums for the insane? Carried to its logical and legitimate conclusion, such a theory would wreck society. Local taxation for local needs is a fundamental doctrine in democratic government; and local taxation for education, the greatest of all needs, is a fundamental duty in democratic society.... It is the boldest inconsistency to be vaunting our devotion to individual liberty and individual initiative to the extent of spending precious human lives and millions of dollars in freeing Cuba and the islands of a distant sea and at the same time neglecting to give freedom to our own children resting under the shadow and pall of ignorance and poverty.... Away, then, with the false and ill-conceived idea of an individualism that would deny to the great masses of the people freedom and light.

"One other difficulty in the way of universal education in the South arises out of a prejudice on the part of some as to the wisdom of including the Negro race in any scheme proposed. It is still maintained by some that the education of the Negro means that he will get ahead of the white man. This is simply absurd. It is a stern fact that no race can rise indefinitely above a lower race living on the same soil. The higher will inevitably be dragged down by ignorance and vice on the part of the lower. For this reason, if no other, it is our duty to help the Negro. The proper kind of education can injure no man. Every rational being will concede that it pays to train dogs or horses or mules. Then why in the name of common sense would we make the Negro the only exception in the animal kingdom? It is surely better for the whites to have among them ten million thrifty, enlightened, law-abiding Negroes than this great black mass of his numbers, his ignorance, his idleness and his lethargy. Happily the day has come when this great problem is receiving a calmer and more faithful consideration. The minds of men are being swept clean of passion and resentment; and the great heart of the people is anxiously waiting to welcome the day when every child of the nation, high or low, bond or free, shall be ushered out of the dark and forbidding valleys of ignorance into the threshold of humanity and light.

"It is an easy matter to talk of difficulties. Remedies are harder to devise. Perhaps the fundamental need at this juncture is an intelligent appreciation of the facts of the situation on the part of our people. Such an appreciation of the facts will inspire a persistent and determined discharge of the duties growing out of it. Our Southern people must be made to recognize the necessity for it. This will require an active propaganda on the part of the able and eloquent men. In other words, we need an educational campaign conducted by specialists who have devoted their lives to the problems and who can speak words of wisdom and authority. Our great need, then, is wise, tactful, aggressive agitation by trained specialists who know the truth and are not afraid to speak it. The teacher as well as the statesman must point the way to this great Southern people, a nobly patriotic and self-sacrificing people willing to pay taxes without limit for the freedom and happiness of their fellow men if the path of duty is made plain to them. Let us as educators devote our lives, if need be, to this issue. Let us teach our people the fundamental truth that no man is free who cannot read and write; that no tyranny is so great or so dangerous as the tyranny of ignorance, inefficiency and poverty. And when the people know the facts, we shall have their sympathy. When they know their duty, they will do it without fear and without faltering, though it means sacrifice and even death.

"This remedy is, in brief, a self-imposed local taxation for the support of the public schools. There is no solution of the problem except in raising the money necessary to secure longer school terms, more competent teachers with a permanent tenure, more comfortable schoolhouses with adequate equipment and appliances, more efficient superintendents and trustees. Our people need to know the value of education, even on the farm. They need to learn that it is no longer a disputed fact that the material progress of a people, to say nothing of their political and social prestige, is in direct proportion to the quantity and quality of its education. Teach this lesson and we shall hear less of our poverty and incompetency. We shall no longer be saying that we are too poor to educate our youth. The fact is, we are too poor to neglect it. The poorer and more ignorant the community, the more need for education, for sacrifice, for taxation. Education is the only permanent cure for the disease of poverty." *(Delivered to various educational conventions throughout the South.)*

The Rural School Teacher: An Appreciation

"The importance of the education of all the people has received a new emphasis in recent years. It has come to be the supreme question of our civilization and faith. It has been very justly characterized as the foremost task of our statesmanship and the most worthy object of our philanthropy. It should be made the primary policy as it is beyond question the immediate duty of our Southern people. Under a democratic form of government where the people are sovereign, it is not merely a question of expediency but a question of destiny. The sovereign people must be educated or we must live under an ignorant sovereign. If we were asked to name the ideal citizen of the present and of the coming years, he would be the man eager to make cause with the larger conscience of the nation; the man willing to contribute something towards creating a greater average intelligence among the masses, a greater exactitude of thinking among the leaders, a soberer discipline, a quieter tone in the life of the people; the man of patience and of sympathy with the good of men; the man who cares less for the honors of high station, which are at best soon turned to ashes, than for the immaterial and spiritual heritage of an abundant life; the man who believes that honor is to be measured by service; and that he best serves the nation who enters humbly into the task of serving his fellow man.

"It may be true that this desire for helpfulness brings at times the burden of isolation, yet it is also true that it is sweetened by the consciousness of dignity and high purpose. There is no higher type of the ideal citizenship concerning which we have made mention than the rural school teacher whose life is all too often one of unappreciated sacrifice and toil and whose patience, fidelity and resolute courage are all too often forgotten in the frequent lament that the rural school has fallen upon evil days.… Can we expect to find it a simple task to improve these conditions when we consider that twenty-seven percent of the people of our section can neither read nor write; when we consider that the average length of the school term is only 107 days; when we consider that the population is rural and hence scattered; when we consider that the people are poor; when we consider that there are two races living side by side demanding separate schools; when we consider that one of these races, though approximately equal to the other in numerical strength, pays only an insignificant part of the public taxes though it shares equally in the appropriations for school purposes in proportion to school population. Such a task will bring a searching test to the character of our people. Such a task will bring a searching test to their wisdom, their courage and their heroism. To meet this task we shall need money, and perhaps more of it than we may hope to command for many years. But more than money, we need the sympathy and devotion of the men and women who cherish the conviction that it is better to spend money to make men than to sacrifice children to save money. Most of all, we believe that the nation stands in need of the service and sacrifice of those who are willing to devote their lives to this supreme task. And in the final analysis, it will be found that the rural school teacher is the vital factor in the struggle.

"…The poorer and more ignorant the community the more need for education, for sacrifice, for taxation. We have been forty years in the wilderness of poverty, struggling along, asking no man to forgive us for what our fathers have done. But we must now face the fact that a new era is upon us; that our children need education to fit them for the strenuous life of this age; that it is cheaper to support our schools and colleges than to enlarge our prisons and asylums…. Let us pledge all the property of the commonwealth, if need be, to the education of the youth, that they may be fitted for the right performance of their duties, social and political. I close with a simple and yet fervent appeal to this audience to do its patriotic duty, however trying the situation may be. Give support and honor to the rural school teacher. He is the uncrowned king of our democracy. If he is not what he ought to be and criticism has failed to make him better, may not our sympathy and support serve a higher purpose than our criticism has done? With the opportunities and resources at his command, he has made a record of surpassing splendor, and I am here to praise what he has accomplished rather than to censure his failures…. We shall meet criticism and opposition such as are always encountered in every good work. But we shall prevail if we do our duty with faith and courage…." *(Delivered at the Fourth Congressional District Teachers Meeting in Petersburg, VA, May 25, 1903.)*

A Plea for Training in the Art of Public Speaking

"…It is perhaps true that there is no function of college work more vitally connected with this active and strenuous life of the world than the art of public speaking; and yet we are confronted with the fact that in recent years this art has in large measure fallen into desuetude in our institutions of higher learning. There is at the present time unmistakable evidence that the exacting demands of the classroom, the exciting distractions of the athletic field and the merry round of social pleasures have in large measure discounted the work of the literary society…. We are told that the world has lost its interest in public speaking; that the rostrum has surrendered its place to the modern newspaper and magazine; that the masses are too busily engaged in the pursuit of commercial and industrial gain to spare the time necessary for discussion and oratory; that men are more concerned with the acquisition of knowledge and the discovery of truth than with the ability to communicate knowledge and truth with force and grace and power to the minds of others; that it is more important to think with accuracy than to speak with precision; as if it were possible to become an effective speaker without the discipline of knowledge and thought.

"…The enforced contact of the mind with the best in literature is a course in character building. The notable historical instances of the abasement of the bad, the exaltation of the good, the retribution of the guilty and the reward of the faithful with which the public speaker is called to deal develop in him personal strength, courage, manliness and nobility of character since the mind must grow by that upon which it feeds. The mental and moral horizon is broadened when we come in contact with the thought and life of the world. The sense of responsibility to be accurate, direct and sincere is cultivated; for the public speaker soon realizes that he must know what he undertakes to communicate to others; that he must be direct; that above all else, he must be sincere.… The trained public speaker must be convinced that what he says is true; that it is worth saying; that it is worthy to command attention; and under a moral conviction that he is speaking the truth, he must speak it with directness and with power.… The gift of persuasive public speech distinguishes a man from the mass of his fellow men. It makes him sought in public assemblies. It opens avenues to preferment. It constitutes him a natural leader of men. The power of speech, convincing the minds of men and inciting them to action, has won triumphs as great in magnitude and as permanent in result as the combined results of diplomacy and of the sword. Who are the men who have most mightily moved the multitudes of mankind to great deeds and heroic sacrifices when law has proven powerless and patriotism seemed dead? Who are the men who have wrought the deepest impress upon the history of nations? Are they the men who made use of physical force or men who made appeal to the moral sense of their fellow men?

"No great movement, whether social, political or religious, has ever been successfully launched without appealing to the power of speech, earnest and eloquent, to convince the reason, to persuade the will, to inspire the imagination and to carry conviction to the soul of men.… The very fact that eloquence works so mightily upon the public mind makes it the patriot's highest trust, a talent lent for the public good, a divine seed, as has been said, implanted within you to be reared for the fruitful harvest of truth and justice, and not for the perishable food of personal ambition. Our Southern country once shone with resplendent glory in the councils of the nation through the exhibition of a rare patriotism and eloquence. The fire of patriotism is still burning. The fire of eloquence has almost turned to ashes. Will not the coming generation kindle it afresh and behold our section rise again from desolation and darkness, clad in new robes of civic usefulness and civic self-respect and with the light of the morning on her face and immortal hope in her heart enter upon a new era of prosperity and happiness?" *(Delivered to incoming classes at both Washington and Lee University and the University of Alabama on various occasions throughout his career.)*

Washington and Lee Welcome Address to Students

"There is but one regret that I feel at this hour, and this regret springs from the fact that there are empty seats in this auditorium which ought to be occupied by young men whose college careers have terminated before they fairly began. This fact suggests the brief remarks that I now desire to make; and in order that no one shall misunderstand my meaning, I am going to preface what I shall have to say with the statement that in my sincere judgment there could hardly exist in the institutions of the world a higher and more exacting moral tone than that which has proverbially marked the life and history of Washington and Lee. I could have nothing but praise and commendation for the delicate and courtly bearing, the high and chivalrous sense of personal and private honor, which I believe, with singular power, move and sway the great mass of young men who come to this place. But the fact remains that these empty seats, to which I have referred, where we might have hoped to find some of our associates of last session present a forceful reminder that there are at least some temptations, even in this favored place, against which we must guard.

"…There are, in my candid judgment, two forces especially active in recent years, which are aggressively hostile to the best interests of college men. I refer, in the first place, to a growing tendency on the part of young men to exercise less care in the matter of contracting debt; and in the second place, to an increasing disposition on their part to undervalue the saving of time. Whether they intend it or not, both classes are seeking something for nothing. The one is seeking personal pleasure and gratification; the other mental improvement and progress, yet neither class has anything to offer in return. I beg you, therefore, as you value your future and your good name, which is to be chosen rather than great riches, to begin, to continue and to end this session with the resolve that so far as you can you will 'owe no man anything save to love one another.' 'The gods for labor give us all good things.' Such was the philosophy of the ancient Greeks, and this philosophy the ages have tested and approved. I do not reckon material wealth as chief among the good things to which I now refer. Poverty is in itself not an evil thing. Many a man is poor because he has intellectually refused to pay the price of wealth…. Whatever you seek, you may be certain that it will cost you labor. The gods have so ordained. You will, of course, someday be entitled to a fair amount of leisure if you wisely provide for it in advance. This is the due of every normal human life; but the law of leisure is that it must follow, and not precede the labor which the gods enjoin…. Chose, then, if you please, a leisure which you have not earned; put yourself under the most exacting creditors; and you will pay the price of failure, of discontent, and perhaps of shame.

"Your time is your capital; its use is your income. Let it be understood, however, that power is only a relative term; it depends upon the factor of time. Time is the great multiplier; and if this multiplier is made sufficiently effective, it matters little what the other factor is. If, therefore, it is true that 'every lost day takes a cubit from our stature,' it follows that our careers will be largely determined by the use we make of time. You will need to understand at the beginning that education is expensive; that it costs time, energy, money and consecration. You will need to understand, too, that ignorance is still more expensive; that it costs idleness, sloth, the surrender of civic aspiration, and oftentimes carries with it the penalty of moral ruin. What are you going to do with these opportunities that are now within your reach? That is a question which silence cannot dissipate nor indifference answer. You are today joining a democracy where merit wins. Whatever may be your lineage, you will now learn that there is no aristocracy in the republic of skill and learning.

"…Do not be led away into the perilous paths of physical ease and financial uncertainty. Do not be fed upon the husks of a flattering and senseless optimism. Such a course will someday 'turn again and rend you.' There is a universal law that 'whatever a man soweth, that shall he also reap.' Will you make this opportunity for training an investment or a wasteful expenditure? That is a serious and vital question. If you are industrious and economical, you may now enter into your rightful heritage and enjoy the glory and honor of an abundant life." *(Welcome address to Washington and Lee University student assembly September 10, 1903.)*

Welcome Address to Incoming W&L Students

"We welcome you, young gentlemen, to splendid opportunities in this atmosphere so long and so densely charged with the finest and most splendid traditions of sound learning, of simple dignity, of settled sobriety and of gracious conduct. But I should be quite unfaithful to my duty if I failed to say that we welcome you at the same time to the most real and most intense responsibilities involving, at many points, a vital test of your moral purpose and of your essential manhood. No institution of learning, rightly considered, is an end in itself. It is an agency of human society. It prepares for human service. This college exists for you and for the vast and ever-growing host of American youth who are to come after you. Your contribution to its reputation and to its power must consist in your devotion to its ideal of scholarly efficiency, of moral rectitude and of spiritual steadfastness. This means, of course, a constant and insistent abstinence from shiftlessness, self-indulgency and disorder.

"Let me give you as a maxim for this session some fine lines which a distinguished American artist recently quoted as describing, more completely and more concisely than any language he could command, the beautiful life which General Lee lived, not only throughout his brilliant public career, but also in his last years here on this campus. The lines are these: 'Straight is the line of duty; curved is the line of beauty; follow the first and thou shalt see the last will ever follow thee.'

"The first days of a college session are days of enthusiasm for some and of depression for others. Let me urge you to preserve your equanimity of temper and a calm judgment of men and of things. Do not be driven into anything. Take your time to consider and to act. I said that this is a time of depression. The remedy for this is a little time with a judicious admixture of old-fashioned hard work. I also said that this is a time of enthusiasm. I do not mean to strike the heart out of the man who is enthusiastic in the right way. I do not mean to say that we do not need the right kind of enthusiasm and fervor. The simple fact is that we do. Have enthusiasm, but see that it finds expression in the right channels. The faculty, for instance, will sustain me when I advise you to express your enthusiasm, from the very beginning, in the preparation for your lectures.

"…Another thing I will dare to say. Everything depends upon your getting the right kind of start. The choice of friends, the attitude you take at the very beginning upon questions involving the use of your time and your father's money, of making bills at the stores in town, which is a violation of a Virginia statute, of attending church as you are accustomed to do at home—in short, your attitude with reference to questions of conduct involving duty and morality and religion, the standard of honesty in your personal dealings, the standard of thoroughness set for yourself in the classroom, which will, sooner or later, be discovered by your teachers. All of these are crucial points in these early days…. I ask you to remember that the main thing never to be lost sight of is the establishment of moral persistence, of intellectual sturdiness, of unbending rectitude of conduct and of a steadfast reliance upon the ancient virtues that exalt human character and upon the God who implants these virtues in the human soul. That is the path, and the only path, that leads to the permanent regard and good will of your fellow students. This is the only path that will lead you to high station in the great world of action for which you are preparing…." *(Delivered to a student assembly at Washington and Lee University September 17, 1908.)*

Inauguration of Washington and Lee president Henry Louis Smith

"…It is a gracious privilege to come back to the shadow of these beautiful hills and to greet again those with whom I was permitted to make those long forced marches in the wilderness through which a gracious and kindly hand has led us into the land of promise. Not one of us would forget the past even in the blaze of a more brilliant present. The exhilarating atmosphere of the altitude which has now been reached will not, I am sure, cause us to despise even an insignificant round of the ladder by which we have climbed.

"…More than a decade has passed, President Smith, since I took the oath of office that you have taken today. It seems but as yesterday, now that it is gone, and as a watch in the night. It is true that a decade is but an atom of time in institutional life. Yet it is not an inconsiderable period in the brief span of human life. To those of us who wrought here in that period there are grateful memories of friendships cemented, of service rendered and of progress made. Do you ask me whether it was worthwhile? Ask me rather, 'Is it worthwhile to live?' Ask me rather, 'Is it worthwhile to die?' But this is neither the time nor the place to review the events of those years that are now a completed chapter in the life of this institution. We are today turning our eyes to the future. We are here to salute a new leader. We are here to bid him welcome to his great new task and to pledge to him our loyalty.

"…I congratulate you, President Smith, that you are to do your day's work in an atmosphere where sound learning, simple dignity and gracious conduct perpetually abide. I doubt if any living man has had more frequent occasion than I to express in a public way unquestioning faith in the sincerity of the training for which this institution stands and in the integrity of the ideals that dominate its life. I dare to assert that its worth is absolutely genuine and its ideals absolutely correct. If its ideals were anything else than genuine it would be strangely untrue to the fathers who founded it, to the colossal character (George Washington) who gave to it its first permanent endowment, and to that myriad-minded and myriad-hearted man (Robert E. Lee) who came to it from a soldier's tent in that hour of distress when its light had been blown out by the angry gusts of war; who contributed to its history that splendid closing chapter of his own career; and whose sacrificial life, glorified and strengthened by high purpose to the very end, pronounced upon it a benediction that will never cease to be its largest asset, its richest tradition and its noblest memory.

"I congratulate you, President Smith; you are to serve an institution in which a high sense of honor is a required and not an elective study; in which the standard of simple and sincere living is as potential today as it was when the great figure of Robert E. Lee trod this campus. Here, I verily believe, is at least one spot where manhood comes first and the almighty dollar second. No man who believes as I do in the sincerity of the training here given and in the integrity of the ideals here maintained could fail to have faith in the future mission of Washington and Lee, even if its promised millions were still a mere illusory dream. It has known the discipline of poverty and of hope deferred. There have been days when nothing was left but grim courage. Yet it has weathered each historic danger that has hitherto marked its progress forward until today, after all its trials, it stands supreme and confident upon the mount of faith and opportunity.

"…Not many men have left this campus and gone out into the busy world to conduct the race tracks, the sideshows or the pleasure resorts of the nation. They have been too busily engaged in making its laws, in interpreting its statutes and in fashioning its life. Do you ask me why Washington and Lee men, out of all proportion to their numerical strength, have risen to high station? It is in large measure because they have here fed on something more than the mere husks of formal discipline; and that something, I believe, has rarely failed to vitalize the moral purpose that sways a man's destiny or to give to him a clearer conception of truth and duty.

"…I congratulate Washington and Lee upon the leadership of a strong, broad-minded, able scholar whose executive skill has been amply tested in another college presidency and whose ideal of service is worthy of one who is to sit in the seat once filled by the greatest man who has ever adorned the presidency of an institution of learning, not merely within Virginia, not merely within the South, but, I dare to say, within the limits of the American republic…." *(Delivered at the inauguration of Dr. Henry Louis Smith as president of Washington and Lee University in Lexington, VA, on May 7, 1912.)*

Memorial Day Address, May 26, 1912

"I greatly value the opportunity of participating in the celebration of this hour. Such an occasion, with its hight memories, its patriotic impulses and the fine sincerities, may, with entire restraint, be characterized as perhaps the most unselfish and the most grateful ceremony in which we as an enlightened community can engage. It is a fine and helpful thing to pause once in a while in our restless modern life in order to review the past, to note the distance we have travelled in a generation and to ask ourselves whether, in the rapid material progress we are making, we are still holding fast to the best traditions that have come to us out of a gracious and unique civilization. Such is my own feeling as a Southern man born and reared amid the red hills of old Virginia. I am profoundly grateful for the privilege of birth in that commonwealth, on whose watercourses our civilization began and in whose mountain valleys our democracy was cradled; a commonwealth whose ancient authority stirred the colonies to revolution and led victoriously the legions of way; a commonwealth that built the framework of the national constitution and adapted its spirit to the philosophy of democratic life; a commonwealth that gave to the nation its supreme national hero and to humanity the highest type of manhood. I am grateful, too, for the privilege of residence in Alabama and for the opportunity of doing my day's work among a people of kindred stock, of kindred hopes, of kindred memories and of kindred sympathies. It has been a gracious task to learn to love Alabama and to taste the quality of its life. I crave no higher honor than to spend my strength in the service of this commonwealth, the fabric of whose life is woven out of the same kind of stuff that gave to Virginia its ancient distinction and authority.

"The men and women of the South owe to themselves no duty more sacred than the duty to render perpetual tribute to the genius and heroism of the Confederate soldier. Out of the clouds and darkness he is at last emerging victorious. It is true that human issues are ever shifting. It is true that the human motives are ever changing. But spiritual values endure. Men may someday forget the exact issues of the War Between the States. They may continue to debate the exact causes that brought to pass that war. Some may assert that it was the mere operation of economic forces. Others may explain it as the mere clashing of irresistible historical tendencies. Others may ascribe it to a mere impact of conflicting ideas concerning the nature of the federal union. Others may declare that it was a mere matter of African slavery. Indeed, the time may never come when men will agree as to the issues of that day; and even if they should thus agree, is it not a fact that these issues are destined to be superseded, and indeed have already in a large degree been superseded by other issues?

"One thing, however, is certain; the spiritual values of that stormy period, when men were willing to sacrifice themselves for a conception of public duty, are destined to live long after every issue involved has been forever settled. And after all is said, are not spiritual values greater than issues? Picture in your mind the visitor, standing on the Heights of Abraham above Quebec and looking at the names upon the monument there. Does he pause to consider what were the issues involved? What cares he who was victor or who was defeated on that ground made sacred by the blood of Wolfe and Montcalm, whose heroism is the common heritage of mankind?

"…I have no fear that the South will never forget the men whose lives in our great national crisis taught us the lesson that no man has fully learned to live until he has found principles for which he is willing to die; the men who bequeathed to us and to our children the ideal of right, of duty, of heroism and of sacrifice. So far from forgetting them, let us thank God for the privilege of remembering them and of remaining steadfast and loyal to the best and the highest and the truest things that have come to us out of their examples and their lives. In showing honor to the men who have stood in the forefront of our lives in great moral crises, we honor ourselves and show that we have a care for the ideals of the generations that are to come after us. Happy is the land that can claim for its leaders such men as Lee and Jackson and Stuart and Johnston and scores of other Southern captains who will live in history. 'Show me the man you honor. I know by that symptom better than by any other what kind of man you yourself are, for you show me then what your own ideal of manhood is, what kind of man you yourself long to be and would thank the gods with your whole soul for being if you could. The virtues of superior men are like the wind; the virtues of common men are like the grass. The grass, when the wind passes over it, bends.'

"Let there be no place in our economy for the pessimist or for the man whose memory is no longer charged with loyalty to the days and to the scenes out of which has come our surest claim to recognition as a people whose god is neither silver nor gold, but who love righteousness and freedom and who fear no human power. Let us face the future with a calm and serene confidence, remembering how, in a single generation, our section has risen from dust and ashes, from desolation and darkness, and how with uplifted face she has come radiant from the graves of her dead and the ruins of her hearthstones to move swiftly onward to prosperity and happiness." *(Delivered at a student assembly May 26, 1912, and printed in The Tuscaloosa News.)*

Argument in Favor of Continued Prohibition

"My credentials for my appearance tonight are my loyalty to a great trust and my duty to young manhood of Alabama. As a matter of fact, I should be, in plain language, a moral coward if I declined to say what I ought to say at this hour of our peril. When I came to Alabama at the beginning of this year, my heart was deeply touched in view of the overwhelming assurances that came to me from the citizens of Tuscaloosa that I might count on their cooperation and support in the great task of building here an institution of learning that should deserve and command the respect of every man, woman and child of this commonwealth. I come to you tonight and ask you to redeem that pledge. I come to you and ask you to refuse to legalize in this community the conscienceless traffic of whiskey. I am not asking any extraordinary action at your hands. So far as I know, there is not a single state university in the South that has not already asked of the community in which it is located precisely the same action, and in not a single instance has that request been denied.

"…This is not a community of and by itself. Alabama has made it trustee of this most solemn and far-reaching task—the task of fashioning manhood. It is not a question as to what any individual man living in Tuscaloosa may think regarding the moral influence of a dry regime on the one hand or the open saloon on the other hand. Considered from the viewpoint of the welfare and prosperity of the University of Alabama, it is solely a question as to what the men and women scattered throughout the state of Alabama think about it; and no man will dare to deny the fact that there are thousands of good men and good women in Alabama who are unwilling to send their sons and daughters to an institution of learning located in a wet town. Whatever may be your opinion or my opinion concerning the effect of the open saloon or of community prohibition upon the moral status of this community, thousands of the best people in this state, who alone have the decision in this matter, have made up their minds never to send their sons into any community where they will not be protected from the temptations and pitfalls of the open saloon. This community, acting as trustee of the commonwealth of Alabama, owes to itself no duty more sacred than the duty to consider this question from the viewpoint of the entire people of this commonwealth; otherwise we cannot complain if the entire people of this commonwealth shall someday refuse to view certain matters from our standpoint.

"Let no man say that I am bringing the University of Alabama into this fight. The University of Alabama has brought me into it; and the advocates of the saloon have brought the University of Alabama into it…. There is no voice, living or dead, that humanity may safely heed that is not at this solemn hour summoning us to do our duty. Shall we heed these voices? Above all, shall we heed that still small voice that is calling to us above the din of the multitude, beckoning us onward and forward in this great struggle? May God in His infinite wisdom guide us and clothe our right arm with majesty and power." *(Delivered at a public gathering at the Tuscaloosa County Courthouse Monday, June 10, 1912.)*

Some Criticisms of Public Education

"The very fact that a system of schools is public in the sense of being tax supported must always mean that the public will feel free to criticize it. Indeed, fair criticism should never be discouraged. On the contrary, it is greatly to be desired. Private institutions are largely immune from such criticisms, but wherever men are taxed to support its institutions of learning, it is their right to know what is going on. It is my earnest wish that the entire people of this commonwealth shall know in detail every single thing connected with the administration of the University of Alabama. That I conceive to be the wise and sound policy in the conduct of the state's chief institution of learning.

"There is no man however high and no cause however sacred that does not at some time become the target of human criticism, if not of human calumny. Public education is no exception. It has from the beginning been the target of criticism and will continue to be criticized now for one reason and again for another…. I have the utmost faith that those who are charged with the great duty of directing the destiny of public education in Alabama will pilot the ship safely through the shoals. I believe that at bottom public sentiment is overwhelmingly friendly. No one has larger faith than I in the essential rectitude of the cause and in its ultimate triumph. I am an optimist in all these matters. The public school system has weathered each historic danger that has hitherto marked its progress forward, until today, after all its trials and all its discipline, it stands serene upon its mount of faith and opportunity. It will live so long as democracy and civilization shall live, a fountain of life to all who thirst for the lofty faith, the unquenchable hope and the super-abounding energy of the disciplined life." *(Delivered before city and county school superintendents at an Alabama Education Association convention in Birmingham in October 1912.)*

An Address to Southern People

"In the short time since the very form of our society was subverted by the ruthless hand of war, the South has, along all lines of development, set the example of the world. Our people have shown a self-reliance and courage seldom equaled in any land; and in the short time since bayonets were removed from polling places and legislative halls, wonderful results are indicated in our commercial and industrial growth that has few equals. During the past thirty years, capital invested in the South increased 724.9 percent. During the same period, the capital of national banks in the South increased 284.8 percent; individual deposits in national banks increased 996.9 percent, and deposits in state banks and loan and trust companies increased 749.9 percent.

"The real revival has just begun. We have made great progress under adverse conditions, but we are in our infancy. We have scarcely crossed the threshold of the entrance upon a greater career that inevitably awaits the Southland. Cheap land, a good climate and other favorable conditions make certain the day, just now dawning, when the sunlight of prosperity will flood every part of our land that has suffered, struggled and prospered. The great and lamented Honorable William T. Harris, United States Commissioner on Education, said, 'They are building a new South, and its cornerstone is a school.' We have made tremendous progress along educational lines during the past two years, and we are striving to build in practically every community in the South a school building that will be an expression of parental love and whose modern conveniences will make it a factory for American manhood and womanhood. And the day is not far distant when we will have every healthy child in school for at least eight months in the year. We will have the crushing penalty of the law fall upon the wretched father who counts cash above character and who would block the pathway from his home to the schoolhouse.

"Many of our leaders in educational thought are coming into a clearer vision of an ideal industrial supremacy. We are awakening to the marvelous possibilities that lie in the soil, the rich deposits of coal and iron, in the great forests and in the wonderful water power. And many realize now that schools must be linked more closely to life and must prepare their students for efficient service in the life into which they are sent. The wonderful achievements in agriculture, engineering, manufacturing and commerce are forcing many of our people to regard these occupations as in every sense as necessary and as highly honorable as the so-called earned professions. And many of our schools are coming to recognize more and more that studies which prepare children for successful experience in these occupations have as legitimate a place in the school curriculum as Latin, Greek, geometry, music and painting." *(**Delivered before the Birmingham Chamber of Commerce meeting April 10, 1913.**)*

Certain Larger Duties of College Men

"I do not underestimate the value of this opportunity of speaking to this fine group of South Carolina college men upon whom, in common with tens of thousands of young men gathered in other great American colleges, will rest the duty of fashioning the destiny of the nation in the next generation. There is national appreciation of the fact that though less than two percent of the young men of this country go through colleges, and out of this two percent the nation draws four fifths of its leaders in all walks of life. There is national satisfaction that college men, reflecting the changing attitude of the colleges, are constantly lending themselves in a larger and finer way to the service of their fellow men. There has never been an age in which there was a larger opportunity or a more insistent demand for such service. There has never been an age in which there was a more powerful incentive to render such service.

"The untrained mind needs to be taught by the trained mind that individuality of thought and action is alone able to guarantee freedom; that a man can never be free until he thinks for himself, acts for himself and learns to make answers to his own conscience for his conduct; that such independence and individuality of character alone fit a man for the duties of life and their proper performance. The country is tired of the kind of leadership that leads only into the blind alleys of selfish interest and organized greed. It is calling for the man who is ready to concern himself in the common welfare; who will strive to lift the public impulse, quicken the public conscience and who is willing to follow blindly no mere 'wind of opinion;' who knows how to resist gregarious habit of conscience, and who is ready to devote every energy of the body, every power of the mind and every virtue of the heart to the solution of the problems that vex us.

"Are our colleges breeding such men? Does our college metal run into such molds? Are we giving to young men that kind of purpose, that kind of vision, that kind of power? I have faith in the college man and in his ideals of service, even though he may be forced to exclaim, 'Silver and gold have I none.' Yet I think of him as going forth into life with the power and the heart to say to struggling humanity, 'Rise up and walk.' I think of him as having fed on something more than the mere husks of formal discipline. I think of him as energizing every conceivable movement designed to reduce crime and suffering and to make men better and happier and more prosperous. I think of him as breaking down every barrier that would impede the onward march of men toward the substantial and the abiding in human progress. I think of him as the foremost exponent of the kind of self-remuneration that is enjoined in these words: 'If any man would be great among you, let him be your servant.'

"...Do not understand me to say that education can do it all. My sole contention is that the foremost task of the true college is not the training that it gives in science and in letters but the emphasis that it puts upon character and upon service…. Do we really seek a higher ethical standard in business, in government and in society? Then let us have the type of college man to whom education means something more than a mere wage-earning device and something more than a mere intellectual refinement." *(Delivered at the University of South Carolina Founders Day celebration on January 15, 1914.)*

A New Spirit of Optimism

"...If there is in this company of men a faint-hearted soul that needs a bath of optimism in our American life, I commend to him the spirit that has within a quarter of a century shown itself in the rapid transformation of this community from a land of depression to a land of achievement. Let me remind you that in the single state of Alabama we have not only a great supply of iron and lumber and cotton, the three raw materials necessary to industrial prosperity, but also a great supply of coal and waterpower, the two things necessary to convert the raw materials into the finished product. Is there any other American community which offers such a fruitful opportunity to industry and to capital? …There is only one thing needed in this section. That thing is the more complete education of our people. I do not hesitate to say that the industrial supremacy of this section awaits merely the more adequate training of our youth, and I am glad to report that progress in this direction is constant.

"For years we have been talking excitedly about developing our natural resources. We have, however, apparently been overlooking the fact that our greatest undeveloped natural resource is the neglected child. Yet it is a fact that we are at last beginning to understand that on the balance sheet of a nation as well as on Heaven's books men count for more than coal and iron and cotton. There has been a time when this Southern section, from the point of view of actually accumulated wealth, took high rank. To restore that rank is our aim and purpose. And it is through education that the great end will be attained. The paramount question in Alabama today is local taxation to reconstruct the public schools. That issue will be fought out on the ideas of November, and no man who has faith in the civilization of this commonwealth will for a moment dare to question the result. *(Delivered to a gathering of 500 persons at a hardware convention in Birmingham April 29, 1916.)*

Tuscaloosa Centennial Address, 1916

"An institution of learning is in a very vital way affected by its location and its environment. There can be no question that the fathers made a wise choice when they selected a site for the chief institution of learning of this commonwealth. It has meant much to the University of Alabama that has done its work in a community of refinement and culture where spiritual values are not forgotten. On the other hand, I may be permitted to say that the University of Alabama has contributed largely to the life of this community. Of course, it has helped in a material way. Yet that has not been its chief contribution. It has played a conspicuous part in every movement for civic and social progress…. If it is true that the entire commonwealth is profoundly concerned in the expanding influence of the University of Alabama, surely this community must in a special sense feel an interest in its growth and prosperity. The past of the University is secure. Its history is written in a large and fine way in the minds and hearts of all our people. It has rendered great and enduring service to this commonwealth. That service has affected every phase of its life. Throughout its long career it has furnished its due share of the leaders in both public and private life.

"…The people of Alabama owe a peculiar debt of gratitude to their foremost seat of learning in view of many other achievements. This debt they should repay, not merely by expressions of sentimental pride in its fine history, but more especially by giving to the institution the kind of support that its service to the commonwealth entitles it to receive. They should support the acknowledged head and crown of their school system, not as if they were doling out charity but as if they were increasing the noblest investment. The University of Alabama is conscientiously meeting the demand for a sound type of educational leadership, which is universally conceded to be the primary function of a modern state university. It is not only enriching the content of its curriculum but it is also studying the wiser application of that curriculum to the needs of human society. It is concerning itself with every phase of the educational process, considered as one great whole existing to serve the needs of the state. It recognizes that it is the servant of all the people.

"…The University of Alabama does not hesitate to stand on a platform that looks to an era of helpful cooperation with the individual citizen in this everyday task. It believes that knowledge should become more widely diffused and that the whole commonwealth should profit in a large and helpful way from the service it can render. The importance of a policy demanding a systematic dissemination of knowledge in forms accessible to the people cannot be overestimated. When this policy has been carried out in a logical and definite way, the people of Alabama will be getting that kind of help from their university which will most surely be appreciated, and in return for which they will desire to give a more liberal and adequate support. They will look to it, ever more and more, for their ideals of life and action." *(Printed in the May 29, 1916, centennial edition of The Tuscaloosa News.)*

Commonwealth Building in the South

"Fifteen years ago when I succeeded to the presidency of Washington and Lee, the great educational renaissance in the South was just beginning…. Five years ago when

I went to the lower South I was inspired by the single purpose of helping forward this great movement. I so stated at the time. There is no institution of learning in the country that a Virginian would desire to serve in preference to Washington and Lee. There is no institution that excels it in high purpose or in human interest. Yet there is one institution in each and every American commonwealth that is of greater importance than any single seat of learning. That institution is the public school system. I have never for a moment regretted the fact that I accepted the opportunity to attach my energy to the larger task, for it is along this path that lies the strategic opportunity in commonwealth building.

"I doubt whether any Southern legislature in fifty years has done so much for education as did the Alabama legislature of 1915, and it is a remarkable achievement. That legislation made provision for the creation of an illiteracy commission; a constitutional amendment permitting an adequate local tax; a special state appropriation to those counties that levy an additional local tax; the establishment of county boards of education; a compulsory attendance law; the voting of a special fund for the erection, repair and equipment of rural schoolhouses, and the authorization of the election of women to serve on boards of education. Few, if any, American commonwealths can now claim a more progressive system of school laws than the Alabama system. The most significant and far-reaching event in the history of Alabama within a half-century was the passage three weeks ago of the constitutional amendment providing for the levying of an additional six-mill tax for the support of the public schools.

"We of the South have been talking excitedly about developing our natural resources, apparently unmindful of the fact that our greatest undeveloped natural resource is the neglected child, and that in the balance sheet of a nation, as well as on Heaven's books, men count for more than coal and iron and cotton. Universal education permeating every phase of our industrial life is the first great step in the remaking of our Southern country. And we are acting under that conviction, for these Southern states are now expending annually the huge sum of one hundred million dollars on schools. We hear much concerning preparedness. The kind of preparedness that is most needed in the South is intellectual discipline that will fit our youth for industrial leadership and for intelligent farming. I have already referred to the need of training for industry. The time has already come when our so-called 'virgin soil' is no longer virgin. The time has come when it is no longer available for unintelligent exploitation. Our greatest asset, therefore, in commonwealth building is the schoolhouse.

"...The school is the great agency which democracy has set up to train men for productive and efficient citizenship. Property has no value of itself; it is merely the creature of education. It is, therefore, the teacher who constitutes the strategic factor in modern commonwealth building. God alone gives genius and faculty. He has been lavish in bestowing these gifts on our Southern stock. We have no right to complain that he has entrusted to human agencies the solemn task of training the human mind. Therein lies the whole purpose of public education. We are indeed co-workers together with Him in the supreme task of fashioning our civilization. I confess that I am not greatly concerned regarding the future status of education in the cities and towns. Wherever men congregate they will take care to provide for the training of their children. Daily contact will stimulate pride and community rivalry will guarantee a sound school system. It is in the country where wealth is wanting, where a certain lack of contact and isolation exists, that challenges our loyalty as efficient toilers in the great field of commonwealth building.

"We cannot evade the issue by saying that we are expending for education more than we once spent. That is true, but it is also true that we have more than we once had. The trouble is that what we spend is not keeping pace with what we get. The simple fact is that the public school system is the most powerful ally of every force that is working in this country for the coming of that day of universal wisdom and righteousness, foreseen by seers and divinely promised, toward which it is the glory of our age to be marching with strenuous celerity." *(**Delivered before the Educational Association of Virginia November 29, 1917.**)*

University of Alabama Centennial Message

"To all who love the University of Alabama and are striving to keep her commandments, this centennial day is a day of memories. It is a day of prophecy. It is a day of renewing our vows. No one can look back over these hundred years without a sense of gratitude in view of the high ideals of service and the uncompromising standards of achievement that have from the beginning marked every step of the way. Founded in the cradle period of the state's history, the University has through the intervening years sought, without shadow of turning, to clothe the youth of this commonwealth with correct standards of service. It has led successive generations not only to the tree of knowledge, but also to the tree of life. Few, if any, communities of this region have been denied the beneficent leadership of University men and women who have gone out from the shadow of these great oaks to fashion the social, economic, industrial, professional and spiritual life of Alabama.

"When we consider the financial background of the University throughout the nineteenth century and the early years of the twentieth, it is easy to understand that its procedures had to be both traditional and restricted. Yet it never sacrificed its high character. If its faculty was small, there were on its roster some of the finest names in the educational history of the country. Though left in ashes by the War Between the States and hampered by the inconceivable poverty attending reconstruction, its spirits survived. Though forced to exclaim, 'Silver and gold have I none,' it still had the power to cry aloud to its struggling sons, 'Rise up and walk.' Loyal men stood at its side. Able and devoted teachers never failed it. It is a tremendous tribute to the character and the loyalty of the stricken people of this state who rallied to the institution for a third of a century following the sixties that they refused to desert it in the presence of disaster; that they continued to proclaim it their greatest single asset. Glorious memories cast a halo about it. It had become and remained not merely the Mecca of sacred traditions for Alabamians, illustrating their best aspirations, but for four years it was the chief training ground of the Confederacy in the lower South.

"During the last quarter of a century a new University has been developed out of the old. While clinging to the ancient ideals, it has cherished a new hope. It has adopted a new philosophy of education. It has related itself to the public school system of the state. It has taken its place at the head of that system. It has cherished the words of Benjamin H. Hill, 'Education is like water; to fructify it must descend.' As a result of this new hope and new philosophy, intelligent people now recognize that as the University goes, so go the public schools; that it is no mere accident that the strongest school systems are found in those states in which higher education is best developed; that in a sound educational body no member can say to any other member, 'I have no need of thee.' Such has been the rich fruitage of modern University effort and leadership.

"The University of Alabama has within a decade achieved the ideal of a university in a democracy. It has done this not merely by broadening the range of instruction and by opening its doors to all who are qualified to enter; it has done it by going out into the highways and making the entire state its campus through correspondence and extension courses. It has done it by the development of research and graduate work in the interest of the people of the state. It has taken its place as a university of the people, by the people and for the people, which is the proper role of a university in a democratic society. The recent growth of the University, relatively speaking, is perhaps unparalleled in American education. Twenty years ago it served Alabama alone. Ten years ago it served a section. Today it serves the nation. Its enrollment in the regular winter session has increased from four hundred students to more than four thousand within two decades. It is no overstatement of the matter to say that its name is known across the seas and around the world.

"The University enters upon its second centenary with serene faith and super-abounding hope. Radiant with the transfiguring beauty of age, it still wears the fresh glory of a vigorous prime. It is securely established in the affection of a constituency that has sprung from the finest racial stock in the world. It is strategically located in the most rapidly developing section of the country. It is in the keeping of people who still believe in and subscribe to the fundamental verities of life. Its traditions are sound. Its ideals are correct.

"In conclusion, a personal word: For twenty years—one fifth of the life of the University—it has been my privilege to serve it with such strength as I have been able to summon. I have studied the laws of its growth. I have learned to love it. I express, here and now, my gratitude. On this centennial day I ask the opportunity to express this sentiment to the people of Alabama: The University is your university. Its single ambition is to serve. Give to it your loyalty, your support and your benediction. Give it a chance to serve with ever-increasing energy and power. Alabama will inevitably be judged in the eyes of mankind by its University rather than by its factories and furnaces. From this historic spot will radiate, ever more and more, the impulse and the inspiration that will distinguish us as a people who live not by bread alone, but as a people who reckon the things of the mind and the things of the spirit as of first importance in the balance sheet of a nation." *(**Delivered as part of the University of Alabama centennial celebration, 1931.**)*

The Present Crisis of the Schools

"The University of Alabama is resourced in the public schools and the public schools are resourced in the University. They stand or fall together. We are all members of one body. No part of the public school system can say to any other part, 'I have no need of thee.' What we need at this hour of uncertainty and anxiety and depression is not a debating society committed to narrow views, but a unified force attacking with singleness of purpose entrenched ignorance, mediocrity and inefficiency. It is my opinion that the real battle centers around the problem of maintaining existing appropriations pending the dawn of better times. On that point we have taken the unmistakable position that we, each and every one of us, will stand or fall together. The talk of cuts is in the air. Powerful influences are behind this talk. There is widespread opposition to new taxes. There is insistent demand for curtailment in government expenditures. If Alabama resorts to a cut, where shall the burden of the cut rest? If there is a cut, shall it be uniform and universal? Shall health and education and social welfare be given preferred consideration as in other states or shall they carry a disproportionate share of the cut?

"These are questions of serious and vital import which we must be ready to answer, perhaps sooner than we realize. Are we ready? Now is the time to consider soberly the problem in all of its phases. The teacher has always been and is now being underpaid. He has never had a comparable salary. He did not share proportionately in the prosperity of recent years when outside salary scales were moving upward faster than his own. He has never shared proportionately. Surely, then, he deserves decent consideration rather than added punishment in times of depression. We realize that we must work out our own financial destiny. No one else will help us. We must lift ourselves by our own bootstraps. There is but one way out of such a dilemma. That way is the way of struggle and sacrifice. We had just as well recognize that fact and frankly face a tax burden relatively greater than in most prosperous states if we are ever to bring to Alabama greater earning power and wealth. There is no other way to break the vicious circle. There are two types of philosophy governing men in their attitude toward public education: One type views education as an expenditure; the other type views it as an investment. What is to be Alabama's educational philosophy as reflected in the legislation to be enacted in 1932?

"It is true that we are living in a period of contagious pessimism. But no great problem was ever solved in terms of pessimism. What we need is more confidence and more courage—confidence in our mission and courage to proclaim it. There are three classes of men according to Nicholas Murray Butler: One class, comparatively small in number, makes things happen. Another class, considerably larger, merely watches things happen. And a third class, embracing the overwhelming majority of people, has no notion of what does happen. To which class do we belong? Measuring my words, I want to say to you that the chief duty of our present leadership is to insist that the schools shall not be made one of the first objects of any super economic program that may lie ahead of us. We should be ready with our defense mechanism. For myself, I have nothing to ask. I have had my reward. I am old enough and perhaps enough of a fatalist to be reconciled to my own future, whatever it may be. But I am willing to fight for the rights of childhood and, God being my witness, I intend to fight." *(Delivered before the joint meeting of city and county superintendents of schools at the meeting of the Alabama Education Association in Birmingham March 16, 1932.)*

Higher Education in Alabama

"No informed citizen can fail to feel a sense of grave concern regarding the support of higher education in Alabama. It is not merely a matter of the Depression. There are other factors involved. One of these factors is a certain lack of conviction regarding the importance of our colleges. Perhaps there is need of reinterpreting the objectives of college training—not merely the more obvious and immediate objectives, but more especially those remote and little-understood objectives by means of which it is molding the future of our commonwealth. In the course of great business depressions, we test our intelligence and inventory our convictions.

"…Nothing is so costly as ignorance. Men pay for the things they do not have far more dearly than for the things they do have. An undisciplined nation possesses few of the blessings and comforts of life. On the other hand, nations which have courageous and forward-looking leaders who dare in crises to foster education, including especially education for leadership, are the nations destined to make history and are in fact making history. Alabama is on trial. Our people have yet to decide once and for all that they really regard higher education as an asset rather than a liability. We have had during recent years evidence of an unsympathetic attitude toward higher education in Alabama from unexpected sources. Naturally such an attitude finds, here as elsewhere, more frequent expression in periods of economic distress. Nothing has caused me greater concern than to find in this group of critics some of our own graduates—men who in their youth enjoyed the intellectual offerings of this University and who apparently now fail to interpret correctly its social importance and its spiritual significance. It is difficult to grasp the meaning of such a situation. Are we neglecting these alumni? Do we fail to keep them informed? They follow the football team. Can they not be persuaded to follow the more important functions of the institution?

"Two years ago I recited two or three outcroppings of this unhappy and discouraging phase of contemporary criticism of higher education as it has found expression in Alabama. (1) The serious effort made in 1932 to establish priorities in appropriations to public education in Alabama and to do it in such fashion that higher education would be denied any reasonable or equitable part, if indeed any part at all, of the public revenues devoted to education.… No one questions the fact that the public elementary school and the public high school will always have a prior claim to public support; but that does not mean that public higher education is not an essential part in the life of a modern commonwealth. (2) The persistent misinterpretation of the significance of the out-of-state student, both as an economic and as an educational factor in the life of the University. Here again the unsympathetic attitude in evidence is to be traced in large degree to a mistaken conception. Five years ago it was being rather confidently asserted here and there by individuals who neither knew the facts nor sought to ascertain them that Alabama was educating "foreigners." Then followed an exhaustive, scientific and detailed study of the entire problem by an able faculty committee. And what was the result? It was clearly demonstrated that instead of educating "foreigners" at the Alabama's expense, these "foreigners" were in fact substantially helping to educate Alabama students. The simple and indisputable fact is that without the help derived from this source the University could hardly have stemmed the tide of the Depression. Still another important fact was that the out-of-state student has helped to raise the scholastic standards of the institution. (3) The effort made to minimize or to obscure the plain facts concerning the drastic reductions already made in appropriations to higher education, and especially the ominous silence regarding the alarmingly low per capita costs at the University.

"…Higher education needs to survey and to evaluate itself with an eye single to the welfare of the state. It needs to repudiate everything that smacks of an atomistic conception of institutional functions. It needs to substitute for such a conception a program that gives greater emphasis to the obviously essential requirements of the commonwealth. More than two decades ago, shortly after my arrival in Alabama, I expressed substantially these views in a number of public addresses. Promptly there was dissent from various sources. Motives were challenged then in even greater degree than at the present time. Now, after the lapse of more than twenty-three years, I am again giving voice to the views expressed in 1912. These views were subsequently stressed in 1919 and again in 1927 in public documents. Perhaps I may now be permitted, in the absence of any possible motive of self-interest at this stage of my career and in the light of the present financial situation, to repeat what has so frequently been stressed by me through the years, and to do it without subjecting myself to misunderstanding again. For I do feel strongly that the responsible educational leadership in charge of higher education should not shrink from the duty of facing the problem firmly, intelligently and sympathetically. On the contrary, this leadership should rise to the occasion and present to the people of Alabama a chart that will guarantee a program which, in all its details, will have regard to maximum efficiency at minimum cost. This duty we owe not only to the state but also to the cause we represent.

"…Undoubtedly there are in Alabama some people who fail to understand the need for a modern state university. They concede that other states may wisely develop the field but they are not convinced that our state should follow their lead. There are among the older generation of our own alumni still a few men here and there who would not only be willing to see the University revert to the status of their own period, but who actually think it would be better if that procedure were adopted. They have little sympathy with or conception of the function of a state university. The real issue that we need to settle just now is imperative. It relates itself to this fundamental question: Shall we have a modern state university? The answer to that question cannot be longer evaded. The friends of the University ought not to deceive themselves in this situation. The real solution to our particular problem can come only by intelligent and resolute action. There is but one test, and that is a simple test. It is the per capita test. Two important and scientific tests of that precise kind give the plain facts and give them in such dramatic fashion that no one can fail to understand them.

"For more than a third of a century, first at Washington and Lee and now at Alabama, I have been wrestling with the ever-increasing strain of executive work. That is a long term of service for a college president. Only one or two presidents of American state universities have served for so long a period. For several years it has been clear to me that I should seek to lighten my load. From time to time I have discussed the situation with friends intimately related to the entire problem. I now feel that in justice to myself and to the University I should without further delay request the trustees to relieve me of my official responsibilities as soon as my successor can be installed. My single regret is that I have not been able to do more than I have done to accomplish the great objectives that governed my purpose when I agreed, in the fullness of my physical strength, to give the best years of my life to this work in which, in spite of all the cares and anxieties and handicaps, I have found so many compensating satisfactions." *(Delivered in annual report to University of Alabama trustees May 27, 1935.)*

Farewell Address to University Alumni, 1936

"I shall not attempt to put into formal words my gratitude to and appreciation of those who made possible the events of this, to me, deeply moving hour. Indeed, there are no words, formal or informal, that are adequate to express the emotions that spring up in my heart as I face this great gathering. I feel utterly unworthy of the honor that is being done me today. I would have this day signify for each and every one of us something more than a testimonial of personal friendship for a single individual. I would have it signify an unforgettable renewal of vows of loyalty to the great institution which has made possible such a scene as this.

"Nearly a quarter of a century has elapsed since I began my work at the University. It seems but as yesterday now that it has passed and as a watch in the night. The intervening years have measured in fact the major part of my native life. On January 1, 1912, I came to Alabama over the unanimous protests of the best friends of my younger days and with a single objective. To that objective, I have subsequently devoted every conscious hour. 'This one thing I do,' has been the daily text and the daily guide of all these years. I would have you believe that the University has meant to me not something to profit by, but something to love and to serve. As the state's first-born spiritual child dedicated by the founders to every high and helpful end, I have conceived its mission in terms of service. This child of destiny is, I am persuaded, Alabama's supreme asset and supreme hope in the struggle forward to a happier and better-ordered life. I have conceived my own mission as president of the University in terms of stewardship to the people of this commonwealth. That conception I have sought to clothe with majesty and power. And now as the shadows lengthen, I ask the privilege of saying in the presence of this great company of friends, to whom I acknowledge myself debtor, that I have without any shadow of turning attempted, under every circumstance however trying, to keep the faith.

"And there have been, in truth, trying circumstances all along the way. Curiously enough, the most trying circumstance of all has habitually traced its parentage to the fact that—in spite of the really serious efforts which have, for more than two decades, been made at the University to establish new standards of thrift, industry and economy in the administration of higher education in Alabama—there have been few periods during my entire term of office, from the very beginning of it, when I could honestly say that old-fashioned notions regarding those ancient virtues have not been subject to penalty rather than reward. On the contrary, year after year my experience has brought me face to face with the astonishing paradox of a later-day doctrine that challenges the wisdom of 'keeping one's house in order in anticipation of the storm.'

"Perhaps these things viewed in retrospect may now be taken as matters of course. Yet Heaven alone will reveal the handicaps that have, in true perspective, lurked in the background of every forward step. The saving factor in the record is that there has been in the foreground, everywhere and all the time, on the part of the trustees, of faculty, of alumni and of successive student bodies the unquestionable spirit of service and of sacrifice. Largely because of that spirit, the University of today has emerged with the light of the morning on her face and immortal hope in her heart. May that spirit of the past live on as the spirit of the future! For it is out of that kind of stuff that great institutions of learning are made. It is out of that kind of stuff that the great capitals of the mind and of the spirit are built.

"As I look back over the years I wonder how it all has happened. For my own part, I wonder if I could again summon either the courage or the energy to attempt what has been attempted. And here let me add that it has been by no means a triumphal procession. There have been defeats as well as victories, and really, I am convinced, more defeats than victories. Yet I have found, and still find, comfort in the fact that, after all, it is not so much what we actually accomplish in this world but rather what we attempt together that makes us brothers and friends. I am aware that many of you think that I have attempted to travel faster than my physical strength has justified. Perhaps that is true. Perhaps I have gone too far on the theory that it is better to waste health like a spendthrift than hoard it like a miser when so much needed to be done. Perhaps I have taken things too seriously. Perhaps I have undertaken too much. Perhaps I should have lightened the burden, even when it refused to be lightened. The simple truth is that no one can do the kind of work he ought to do if he does it merely with his mind. He must put his whole soul and his whole self into it, particularly when he is dealing day by day with the issues of human destiny.

"And so I made my choice. As a result of that choice I can testify that after frankly reckoning all the liabilities resulting therefrom, the fact remains that the greatest satisfaction and the greatest reward of these years have come not from the investiture and the trappings of high office which are sure to vanish like a shadow, but from daily association with vital and picturesque youth, all the way from their scholarly enthusiasms in the classroom to their victorious shouting on the field of sports. I am superlatively happy to say that it is in that association with a vast army of young men and women numbering some thirty thousand human souls and scattered throughout the world that I have found and now find all the compensation that I covet. 'Life's truest romance lies in one's devotion to a worthy job.' Thus spoke one of the great spirits of all time. Frequently I have wondered whether any man has ever loved his work more than I have loved mine. While the results of that work have been frankly disappointing to me, the integrity of it, with all its imperfections, I am willing to subject to the scrutiny of Him whose eyes are in every place. I am conscious that when I lay it down I shall miss it far more than it will miss me. From a full heart I would add that I love those who have been and are now associated with me in every phase of it even more than the work itself. That is my confession to the dear friends who are gathered here today.

"During recent months I have been attempting to review in my own mind the events of the past quarter of a century, to take stock of the present and to forecast the future. I shall not, here and now, venture to elaborate on the conclusions I have reached. These conclusions may, after all, be faulty. For as someone has said, 'a man's conclusions simply mark the place where he got tired thinking.' But this I do say: That is an unresponsive soul which, with full knowledge of the facts, reacts with no sense of pride and satisfaction in view of the past achievements of the University, whether in peace or in war. That is an unresponsive soul which, with full knowledge of the facts, reacts with no sense of gratitude in view of its present eminence at home and abroad. To quote an authority of high standing: "The University of Alabama is today known and respected not merely from ocean to ocean, but across the seas and around the world."

"And as for the future, I am profoundly convinced that we have every reason, in spite of difficulties and disappointments that periodically harass all human undertakings, to look to the coming years with super-abounding faith. And why not? Surely in this new age in which we live, emphasis on superiority and excellence as illustrated and exemplified in the great and glorious history of the University will continue, ever more and more, to be the supreme demand and the supreme test of our comparatively young and developing civilization. Nothing relating to the future is more certain than that from this time forward social and economic blueprints in the drafting of which our colleges, if they are to survive must have a large part, will in essence constitute the real and true map of a modern commonwealth.

"In conclusion, I want to say simply this: God being my witness, I shall never forget those who have wrought with me in the stirring events of the quarter century now drawing to a close. Happy days to all of you who love the University and are striving to keep her commandments! Happy days to all of you who give unstinted credit to a faithful foster mother for nurturing, in your youth, those ideals of manhood which now in your prime have flowered into your richest and most enduring possession! I pledge you, one and all, that in whatever fashion memory shall bring back in future years this day to my mind, it will say to me, '*That* was a good moment!'" *(Delivered to a gathering of University of Alabama Alumni celebrating Denny's silver anniversary as University president in Montgomery on February 22, 1936.)*

General Robert E. Lee as College President

"It is perhaps safe to say that every phase of the character and career of General (Robert E.) Lee has been thoroughly discussed with the single exception of his work as college president. It has more than once been suggested that the closing years of General Lee's life were years of stolid stoicism and of passive futility. But no one who has read the story of his career, from the memorable day when the curtain fell on the great drama at Appomattox to the closing scene of his life, can truthfully charge that he frittered away an hour in vain lament or erected a single monument to past achievement or to former greatness. If there remained a single scar of the conflict that had vanished, a single pang of hope deferred or a single wave of despair that washed his great purpose, authentic history does not record it. General Lee's life after the war was not lived in the past tenses of the subjunctive mood, nor was he accustomed to express himself in the language of the unreal wish or of unfulfilled duties. He lived an active, an aggressive and a constructive life characterized by conspicuous determination and tireless energy consecrated to a great ideal.

"...General Lee was a man of wonderful executive ability. I do not offer in support of this statement his marvelous record in planning and executing military campaigns.

He demonstrated this ability quite as signally in his notable service as head of the United States Military Academy at West Point. He demonstrated it with equal if not greater force as president of Washington College (now Washington and Lee University). He came to Lexington as the executive head of this institution at a time when it had been literally blasted by the thunderbolts and charred by the fires of war. The college had reached the lowest point of depression it had ever known. It lay prostrate and bleeding. Its light had been dimmed and was only faintly burning. It was the great executive who gave anew to the institution organization, unity and an assured career. No college executive has ever given himself more completely or more methodically to his work than did General Lee. His clear, penetrating foresight made him aware of the magnitude of his undertaking and its colossal difficulties, but his courage never failed him. He was in constant and vital touch with everybody, no matter how humble, and with everything, no matter how minute. Nothing seemed ever to escape his notice. He had that genius which Goethe defines as 'the infinite capacity for taking pains.'

"But General Lee was a great college president not merely on account of his rare executive capacity. He exhibited far higher claims to pre-eminence in this position than constructive executive genius. Prominent among these higher claims may be mentioned his rare influence with men, young and full-grown. He engaged the friendship of leading citizens of every section of the country. He knew each student personally. He did not use the club of sarcasm or the rapier of ridicule in dealing with them. He recognized the sacredness of individuality and was never a dictator to tyrannize over the thoughts, the words or the acts of others. He did, however, lay emphasis on the essential facts of conduct and did demand respect for and compliance with the basic principles of living. He would never have allowed professional athletics to masquerade under an amateur banner. He would never have permitted hazing to exist in order to uphold a false standard of tradition or a false code of honor. He never for a moment allowed a shadow to rest on the clearly marked lines of candor and truth. He was never a man to indulge in flattery, but he was always generous in expressing honest recognition and appreciation of what a young man had accomplished and in manifesting genuine sympathy with what he was striving to do. The devotion of the students to their great leader was, therefore, the logical outcome of his marvelous personal influence over them, his interest in them, his sympathy with them, his affection for them.

"He was distinguished also on account of the great and overpowering purpose that he brought with him to his work, or perhaps I should say, that brought him to his work. We speak of consecration. Consecration, however, was not to him a penal servitude. It was freedom to realize a great purpose, an unselfish ideal. Nor was consecration, in his view, a waste heap for the sacrifice of physical, mental or moral energy. It was freedom to devote himself to essentials, to look at life with clear and steady eyes and to do a great, majestic work for the republic. When General Lee accepted the presidency of Washington College, it was not for fame or reward, not for place or rank. He was neither lured by ambition nor goaded by necessity; he acted in simple obedience to duty as he understood it. Other avenues of service offered larger returns and more flattering financial inducements. General Lee, however, refused to take counsel of his personal ease and ambition, preferring to follow the path of duty, though it might also prove to be the path of sacrifice.

"He refused to hearken to the siren voice that has diverted so many men from the course of manly honor and consecrated purpose. But when there came to him a call to service as companion and guide of young men he answered the summons and gave to the holy cause, whose advocate he had decided to become, a never-failing stream of devotion and of loyalty until his hair had whitened in the service and his fading life, glorified and strengthened to the end, pronounced upon it a benediction which can never cease to be a stimulus and an inspiration. He said, 'I have led the young men of the South to battle. I have seen many of them die on the field. I shall devote my remaining energy to training young men to do their duty in life.' And with this high purpose was blended the note of consecration which made him add: 'I pray that I may be spared to accomplish something for the benefit of mankind and for the honor of God.' And how well he did teach these young men the value of character, the simplicity and the nobility of life and the highest duties of citizenship!

"…In all the essentials, in all the real and abiding qualities, he stands forth as a great college president, great in executive gifts, great in the power to influence men, great in consecration of purpose, great in his own character and example before young men. His life and service is the largest asset, the richest tradition, the noblest memory of the institution he resurrected. If one is tempted at times to grow impatient over the progress and growth of the college which he loved, such impatience must vanish in the reflection that General Lee believed in the institution and gave it service. If one is tempted to anxiously wonder what the future, with its rapid and uncertain changes, has in reserve for this foundation, he can cherish the feeling that somewhere, somehow, the great spirit of General Lee is looking down in benediction upon this child of his declining years, and then he may have faith in the final rectitude of the cause and a splendid ultimate victory.

"And now, Virginians, a word with you in closing: 'Show me the man you honor; I know by that symptom better than by any other what kind of man you yourself are. For you show me then what your ideal of manhood is; what kind of man you long possibly to be, and would thank the Gods, with your whole soul, for being if you could.' Whom shall we consecrate and set apart as one of our sacred men? Sacred that all men may see him, be reminded of him, and by new example added to old perpetual precept be taught what is real worth in man. Whom do you wish to resemble? Him you set on a high column that all men looking at it may be continually apprised of the duty you expect from them." *(Delivered to various student assemblies at Washington and Lee and the University of Alabama and to other audiences on numerous occasions throughout Denny's career.)*

1936 University of Alabama Commencement Address

"And now, my dear friends, you have reached the end of another chapter in the book of life. This is a significant day for all of you. It is a day of memories. It is a day of hope. It is a day of anticipation. We acclaim you as you face the great and uncertain future. We have faith in you. We count on you.

"The Dean of the Harvard Graduate School in the last issue of the *Saturday Evening Post* said to college graduates of 1936, 'Jobs this year will go to men who have something real to offer. It is still a buyer's market. The young college graduate looking for a position today will find success in getting a job furthered, or failure to get one assured, by his personality and attitude. He must sell in a buyer's market.' No baccalaureate sermon could be more complete, constructive or inspiring that this article written especially for this year's college graduates.

"These diplomas which we hand you today are not merely certificates of sound training and of high purpose; they are pledges of good faith. They summon you to the first-line trenches where life's real battles are fought and won. They are designed to clothe you with power to do your part in a work-a-day world. We bid you carry your share of the load. The University expects you to do your part; to keep up with the great procession or ahead of it. Some of you will lead in that procession. The rest of you will surely strive to keep step according to the talents committed to you. It would be little less than a tragedy to take away from this spot, whose great traditions and great ideals are in your keeping, any impression that you have yet attained. The summation of achievement lies ahead of you.

"This is for each and every one of you commencement day in the highest and best sense. Let its chief lesson be the lesson that greatness is wisdom multiplied by power. If that lesson has been learned, you will continue to seek wisdom and power. Your education now happily begun will go on and on. That is the first article of the confession of faith to which your college opportunity has invoked your subscription. We expect great things of the great class of 1936. We expect you, with simple faith and devotion, to make living a great adventure. For it is in this way that you will make life significant and happy. The path leading to the ultimate goal is not an easy path. The only sure way to that goal is through service and, if need be, through sacrifice.

"A group of five hundred young men and women going out into this immense world would seem, in comparison, a relatively small group. Yet history furnishes many instances of groups smaller than this group which, moved by great faith and great desire, have wrought far-reaching changes, material and social and spiritual. It is not a matter of mere numbers or of mere chance or of mere circumstance. It is a matter of purpose. It is a matter of power.

"We base our hopes for the future—and we pledge you that these hopes are unquenchable—not merely on the super-abounding energy of the disciplined life we have urged you and now expect you to lead, but also on our supreme faith that, through great desire disciplined by the training you have acquired here and will acquire hereafter and through great commitment to fine purpose, this class will constitute a potent force for the remaking of human society, wherever its influence is felt. And may God, in His infinite wisdom, keep you and guide you, now and forevermore." (***Delivered to the 1936 University of Alabama graduating seniors on May 26, 1936.***)

Appendix B

University of Alabama Presidents 1831-2016

Alva Woods 1831-1837
Basil Manley 1837-1855
Landon Cabell Garland 1855-1865
(Reconstruction) 1865-1870
William Russell Smith 1870-1871
Matthew F. Maury 1871
Nathaniel Thomas Lupton 1871-1874
Carlos Green Smith 1874-1878
Josiah Gorgas 1878-1879
William S. Wyman (acting) 1879-1880
Burwell Boykin Lewis 1880-1885
Henry DeLamar Clayton 1886-1889
William S. Wyman (acting) 1889-1890
Richard Channing Jones 1890-1897
James Knox Powers 1897-1901
John William Abercrombie 1902-1911
George H. Denny 1912-1936
Richard Clarke Foster 1937-1941
George H. Denny 1941-42
Raymond R. Paty, 1942-46
Ralph E. Adams (acting) 1947
John M. Gallalee 1948-1953
Lee Bidgood (acting) 1953
Oliver C. Carmichael 1953-1957
James H. Newman (acting) 1957-1958
Frank A. Rose 1958-1969
*F. David Mathews 1969-1975
Richard A. Thigpen (acting) 1975-1977
*F. David Mathews 1977-1980
Howard B. Gundy (acting) 1980-1981
Joab L. Thomas 1981-1988
E. Roger Sayers 1988-1996
Andrew A. Sorensen 1996-2002
J. Barry Mason (acting) 2002-2003
Robert E. Witt 2003-2012
Guy H. Bailey 2012
Judith L. Bonner 2012-2015
Stuart R. Bell 2015-Present
*Secretary of Health, Education and Welfare August 1975-January 1977.

Washington and Lee University Presidents

Robert Alexander (Augusta Academy) 1749-1762
John Brown (Augusta Academy) 1762-1766
William Graham (Liberty Hall Academy) 1782-1796
Samuel L. Campbell (Liberty Hall Academy) 1797-1798
Samuel L. Campbell (Washington Academy) 1798-1799
Rev. George Baxter (Washington Academy) 1799-1813
Rev. George A. Baxter (Washington College) 1813-1829
Rev. Henry Ruffner (acting) 1829-1830, 1834
Louis Marshall 1830-1834
Henry Vethake 1834-1836
Rev. Henry Ruffner 1836-1848
Rev. George Junkin 1848-1861
Robert Edward Lee 1865-1870
George Washington Custis Lee 1871-1897
William Lyne Wilson 1897-1900
Henry St. George Tucker III (acting) 1900-1901
George H. Denny 1901-1911
Henry D. Campbell and John L. Campbell (acting) 1911-1912
Henry Louis Smith 1912-1929
Francis Pendleton Gaines 1930-1959
Fred C. Cole 1959-1967
William Webb Pusey III (acting) 1967-1968
Robert E. R. Huntley 1968-1983
John Delane Wilson 1983-1995
John William Elrod 1995-2001
H. Laurent Boetsch Jr. (acting) 2001-2002
Thomas Gerard Burish 2002-2005
Harlan Ray Beckley (acting) 2005-2006
Kenneth Patrick Ruscio 2006-present

Postscript

A simple search for knowledge led to the start of this long overdue biography of former University of Alabama president Dr. George H. Denny. I wanted to know more about the man of whom so many of my former teachers had reverently spoken. I wondered why Denny Chimes was dedicated to him. I wondered why he called the University of Alabama the "Capstone." While sorting through more than two dozen boxes of Denny letters at the University of Alabama and Washington and Lee University, reading newspapers covering fifty years and sifting through scores of other related archives for the answers, I was consciously moved by Denny's admonition to seek and follow the truth wherever it leads. I was truly amazed by his dedication to the University of Alabama and to providing the opportunity of a college education to the young men and women of Alabama.

My work quickly became more a duty, to borrow a phrase from Denny himself, than just another writing assignment. I realized that the story of his life of service should be fully told both as a lesson in the history of the University of Alabama and as an inspiration to others. His life offers a lesson in the power of a dedicated and determined individual and his influence has reached millions through those who learned his lessons and followed his path. After reading all of Dr. Denny's preserved words and all that I could find that was written about him over half a century, I feel close enough to him to proudly call him "Mike," as thousands of his students did.

This book contains more details about Denny's years at the University of Alabama than at Washington and Lee, but not by design. The simple reasons are that Denny spent more years at the University of Alabama and that more records of his actual work were available in University of Alabama archives than at Washington and Lee. As a native Virginian who drew strongly on the educational principles of Thomas Jefferson and the character and leadership traits of Robert E. Lee, Dr. Denny remains an important figure in the growth and traditions of both Washington and Lee University and the University of Alabama.

—**Delbert Reed**

Other books by
Delbert Reed

*All of Us Fought the War: The University of Alabama
and Its Men and Women in World War II*

When Winning Was Everything: Alabama Football Players in World War II

Paul 'Bear' Bryant: What Made Him a Winner

Order additional copies of *Mike Denny: The Shadow of a Single Man*
and the above books by contacting the Paul W. Bryant Museum
Toll-free 1-866-772-BEAR (2327) or (205) 348-4668 or
visit www.BryantMuseum.com